# A Taste of

# Puerto Rico, Too!

## COOKBOOK

# A Taste of
# Puerto Rico, Too!
# COOKBOOK

BY BEST-SELLING CARIBBEAN COOKBOOK AUTHOR

*Angela Spenceley*

Coconut Press, LLC
P.O.Box 309540
St. Thomas, VI 00803

# CONTENTS

Also by *Angela Spenceley*

Home of the Caribbean Cookbook Series

- **A Taste of the Virgin Islands**

- **A Taste of Puerto Rico**

- **A Taste of the Caribbean**

- **Just Add Rum! Cookbook**

- **Don't Drink the Water! Caribbean Bartending Guide**

- **How To Have Your Own Caribbean Luau**

To order any of the Caribbean cookbook series books, call
787-248-3774 or email: vicards@islands.vi

# Praise for *Angela Spenceley*'s CARIBBEAN COOKBOOK SERIES

## "FANTASTIC!

"…I can trust Angela Spenceley to give me a recipe that works with a manageable amount of ingredients. The rum desserts in this cookbook are just to die for. I made the Fallen Chocolage Rum Cake for my sister's rehearsal dinner. The guests couldn't stop raving about it."

**—Lucinda, Miami, FL**

"I loved this cookbook! It really does include everything you need to know about Puerto Rican cooking—history, cooking utensils, techniques and a warm sense of humour." **—Elena, Warner, NH**

"Angela has the most brilliant knack for making the most uncomplicated, simple ingredients into simply elegant, spectacular dishes that taste and look like you slaved in the kitchen all day. Unlike other regional or ethnic cookbooks, I could find all the ingredients in my local grocery store."

**—Roger, Dallas, TX**

"My daughter-in-law gave me this cookbook for Christmas and I adore it! I have a large collection of cookbooks from all over the world and this is one of the best. This book is well-written, organized, with easy-to-find ingredients and the recipes are deliciously authentic."

**—Louise, New Orleans, LA**

"I have never been very good at cooking and have been discouraged when using other cookbooks—the recipes never come out. I have bought three other of Angela's cookbooks. My family and friends cannot believe the meals I have been making. My only suggestion is to watch the size of your portions—her recipes are delicious." **—Tina, Boston, MA**

"This is probably the most complete Puerto Rican cookbook on the market. Every facet of Puerto Rican cuisine is covered. I especially liked the cooking tips and the extensive dessert chapters." **—Tim, Nantucket, MA**

# Forward and Acknowledgments
## by Angela Spenceley

Soon after I began work on *A Taste of Puerto Rico, Too!* I quickly realized I would need help. Despite the fact this would be my ninth Caribbean cookbook, the tools, cooking methods and ingredients were unique to Puerto Rico and had but little similarity with other Caribbean cooking styles.

Finding this help was easier said than done. Since I typed my notes at night, I needed someone who had their days free to cook and experiment with me.

My friend Livia Torres, a local artist who creates brilliantly colored ceremonial masks, recommended her cousin Anna Gonzales Lopez, a home economics teacher from Canòvanas, a small town about 20 minutes from San Juan. *Perfect*. But, there was a small catch.

Anna had taken a year long leave of absence from teaching to stay home with her first child. Unfortunately her husband, a lineman with the local power company, subsequently suffered an accident and broke his leg. Their income reduced, the young economics teacher faced a tough decision. If she went back to work, she'd have to leave her six month-old baby in day care as her husband was unable to care for the child. If she didn't return to work, they would have to give up their newly built home and move in with her in-laws until they got back on their feet.

Livia asked me if Anna could bring the baby to my house while we experimented with the recipes?

Hmm, a baby, I thought. Not four weeks ago, I had tearfully bundled my daughter Roxanne off to her first year at college, U-Mass Amherst. Chin up, I had told myself. This was my big chance to burn the midnight oil and get some work done for a change. I had grandiose plans for two cookbooks a year, a couple hard-cover coffee table books on the islands, a new line of local postcards. Roxanne's cat, Tasuki (pronounced Tawski), also had big plans. With no one around to tease him, he intended on getting some uninterrupted sleep for once.

Instead, both of us went into deep mourning.

Tasuki would find a leftover piece of clothing from Roxanne, roll until it wrapped itself about his head. Each time the door opened, he would run to see if Roxanne had returned. I stared at pictures of a blue-eyed strawberry blonde toddler clutching a toy owl in her chubby hands, an eight-year-old in a hot pink swimsuit building sandcastles at Magens Bay St. Thomas, a gorgeous young woman in a sophisticated red prom dress.

Yes! I told Livia. Anna could bring her baby. The following week, a knock sounded on my door. Tasuki raced under my legs, nearly tripping me. He knew I was going to open the door, and lately he had been desperate to escape to the outside world. I inched the door open, holding Tasuki back with my foot. Despite my best efforts,

Tasuki squeezed out the door and made a mad dash for the second floor of my condo building. A high-pitched squeal drew him up short.

"Si, gato, Natalie," Anna said. Another shriek caused Tasuki's ears to flatten against his orange and white skull. Without a peep, he did an about face and dashed back into the apartment.

Anna and I were a bit worried about Tasuki becoming a little to curious about the baby, but since he was nowhere to be found, I held Natalie, while Anna set up a playpen in a corner of the living room. The baby was gorgeous, ivory-skinned, shiny brown hair, with huge chestnut-colored eyes that seemed to take in everything all at once. One of Tasuki's toys fascinated her—a scratching post with a feather and a rubber ball dangling from the top. It was brand new and both the feather and the ball were secured by a wire spring, so we put the toy in the playpen with her.

While the baby cooed over Tasuki's toy, Anna and I hit it off over a cup of strong Puerto Rican coffee, and my latest attempt at flan. The chapter with flan would later take the most time, as we experimented with nearly a dozen cooking methods.

We settled into a routine. Each morning Anna would arrive at 8:30, we would cook or bake until 1:00 p.m., then have that morning's recipe for our lunch. Some days lunch consisted of fritters, soup, or a rice dish. Other days, we would have Tres Leches cake or Mango ice cream for lunch. In the afternoon, we spent another four hours in the kitchen. This would become our dinner. Anna would take most of the dish home, and the next day come back with comments and suggestions from her husband, in-laws and grandmother.

As I researched, I kept finding more recipes I wanted to incorporate into the book. It became evident at six months, that we needed help. We were less than halfway through and I had a deadline. Anna's aunt, Doritza Romano, recently retired from the post office, graciously offered to help us. I was glad for the extra set of hands and wealth of cooking experience Doritza brought.

Secretly, I was thrilled there would be an extra person on hand to taste the recipes. I had begun to put on weight. In fact, by the time we finished cooking, each of us put on between five and ten pounds.

Hence the LOW-CARB recipes were born. I have to say it was quite a challenge, given the amount of rice and starchy root vegetables indigenous to Puerto Rican cuisine. After much adding and subtracting of flavorful herbs, spices and the occasional generous splash of Puerto Rican rum, we were able to add mouth-watering LOW-CARB recipes to nearly each chapter.

Now, I'm sure you all have been wondering what happened with Tasuki and the baby. Go to the recipe for *Basic Alcupurria Dough* and find out!

Happy cooking!

*Angela Spenceley*

# Just where is Puerto Rico, anyway???

When I tell someone I live in Puerto Rico, I often get a blank look. It's as if I had asked them a game show question for which they had not been prepared. Then their faces brighten as clarity sets in.

"Hey, that's really cool living in a foreign country. Puerto Rico's in South America, right?" they crow triumphantly.

No.

Puerto Rico is not a foreign county, having been established in 1952 as a self-governing commonwealth of the United States. This means the island has control over its internal affairs. Executive power is exercised by the governor, who is reelected every four years. The governor, with the approval of the local legislature (27 senators, 53 representatives), appoints 15 cabinet heads. Together with a sophisticated judicial system, they run the island, in accordance with U.S. laws.

The United States government controls: foreign relations and commerce; customs administration; control of air, land and sea; immigration and citizenship; currency; military and its bases; agriculture; mining; highways; postal system and other areas generally controlled by the federal government.

It would seem like a marriage made in heaven, local and federal government, but since 1952 the status debate never ends.

Nonetheless, despite minor political turmoil, Puerto Rico offers a good bit of paradise for everyone. The island, three times the size of Rhode Island (36 by 111 miles), is located between the Caribbean Sea and the North Atlantic Ocean, east of the Dominican Republic, and 1000 miles southeast of Miami (2 ½ hours jet time).

Warm and sunny most of the year, the temperature averages 80°F, dipping to 68° or lower in the mountains at night.

Most of the terrain (60%), is mountainous (up to 4400 feet at its highest point). The remainder of the island offers an astonishing variety of topography: rain forest, beaches, desert, caves, ocean and rivers.

Puerto Rico has three main physiographic areas: the mountainous interior, the coastland plains, and the karst area.

The mountainous interior consists of one central mountain chain known as the "Cordillera Central." The chain divides the island from east to west. The coastal lowlands, extend 8 to 12 miles inward from the north coast, and

2 to 8 miles inward from the south. The karst region in the north was formed from volcanic rock dissolved by water through the geological ages. This limestone region is interesting, noted for its haystack hills, sinkholes, caves and cliffs. Some of the most important caves in the western hemisphere are found here. Rio Camuy is the third largest underground river in the world.

Three hundred miles of coastline encircle Puerto Rico, along with a handful of charming offshore islands. Palm-rimmed beaches give way to the Caribbean National Forest, known as El Yunque to the locals. Under an hour's drive from San Juan, these 28,000 acres are all that remain of the rainforest that covered most of the island. Foot trails meander past tree ferns, hot pink impatiens, coqui frogs and misty waterfalls.

Several thousand varieties of tropical plants grow in Puerto Rico, including the kapok tree, the poinciana (it grows to 12 feet here!), orchids, hibiscus, breadfruit, citrus and root vegetables. Coffee and bananas grow in the mountains, sugarcane and pineapple along the coast.

The island has no large wild mammals. Lizards are everywhere, as well as iguanas, and bats are multi-present. Roosters seem to have a special affinity for multiplying. They're everywhere, even in the city their deafening crows can be heard at 5:00 a.m.

A few native creatures are indigenous to Puerto Rico. The famous coqui tree frog, which serenades islanders to sleep with it's 'coqui, coqui' song, and the Puerto Rican parrot, a species of Amazon. There are less than 40 Puerto Rican parrots left, habitating in the Caribbean National Forest.

To the south lies picturesque Ponce and Castillo Serralles, about 1 ½ hours from San Juan. Evoking the era of the sugar barons, this impeccably maintained Spanish revival mansion was built in the 1930's for the Serralles family, owners of the Don Q rum distillery. The gardens are some of the best I've ever seen on the island-featured is a gorgeous bromeliad and orchid pavillion.

Past Ponce is the Guanica Forest, a dry tropical forest on the coast, peppered with cactus, other xeroscopic plants and a plethora of bird species. La Parguera is a seacoast resort featuring a Phospherescent Bay where luminescent dinoflagellates light up the sea on moonless nights.

The capitol of San Juan has one of the biggest and best natural harbors in the Caribbean. It is the oldest city under the U.S. Flag, founded in 1521. Ponce de Leon founded what is now known as Old San Juan in 1508.

San Juan is divided into numerous municipalities: Old San Juan; the beach and resort area known as Condado; and Isla Verde (part of Carolina, where I live); Miramar; Puerta de Tierra; Santurce; Ocean Park; and the outlying municipalities of Rio Piedras, Hato Rey, and Bayamon.

**Old San Juan** is a charming 465-year-old neighborhood originally planned as a military fortress. It's seven block area encompasses both commercial and residential areas. Blue cobblestones, brought over as ballast on Spanish trading ships, pave the often steep and winding streets. Pastel shades of pink, sea green and yellow ochre, weathered by time, decorate the over 400 lovingly restored 16th and 17th century Spanish colonial buildings.

The highlight of the old city is El Morro fortress. Begun in 1540 and completed in 1589, San Felipe del Morro was named in honor of King Phillip II. The fort is a maze of dungeons, barracks, and ramps. Small, circular sentry boxes called *garitas* are unique to the forts of Puerto Rico and have become a national symbol. The views from the fortress are fantastic. Declared a National Historic Site in 1949.

The **Condado** district is linked to Old San Juan by a bridge built in 1910 by two brothers (The Behns), early 20th century immigrants from St. Thomas. This beachfront area is wedged between the Atlantic Ocean and several large inland bodies of water, including Los Corozos and Lagunas Condado. With its glittering casinos, high-rises and luxury hotels, Condado is a near-perfect replica of Miami Beach.

**Isla Verde** is the Las Vegas of San Juan, located to the west of the airport and east of the Condado. The area's development began with the San Juan Intercontinental in 1958 and has expanded to become the island's premier resort area.

Whatever your idea of paradise may be, sparkling waterfalls in a lush rainforest, secluded palm-rimmed beaches or glittering nightlife, you will surely find it in Puerto Rico.

# A bit of Puerto Rican culinary history
*The Spanish arrive ...*

Things were pretty mellow on the island until Columbus landed in 1493. Taino Indians, migrated from South America, inhabited the island and called it *Borinquen* which means: 'land of the great lords.' The Tainos lived in small villages led by a *cacique* or chief. They were a simple, peaceful people with limited agricultural knowledge, subsisting on pineapple, cassava, yucca, arrowroot, peanuts, gourds, and peppers.

The women made bread from grated cassava, *casabe*, formed into loaves and baked on clay griddles. The bread kept for a long time in the hot climate. *Casabe* was an important part of the Taino diet.

Tobacco, corn, beans and squash were also cultivated. Living near the sea, diets were supplemented with seafood, turtles and an occasional parrot or iguana. A *pilon* was used to mash ingredients. Often meat or fish were tossed into what would later be known as a pepper pot, along with other liquids and vegetables, and simmered over an open fire for hours. This open air cooking method was called *barbocoa* (barbeque).

On April 17, 1492, Ferdinand and Isabella of Spain signed an agreement to finance Columbus's voyage to the Indies. The document declared that Columbus would become the viceroy and governor of all discovered land as well as 10% of the assets. On August 3, his fleet of three ships: the Niña, the Pinta, and the Santa Anna, discovered land on October 12. They landed at San Salvador in the Bahamas. Mistakingly thinking he had reached the East Indies, Columbus named the natives of the islands 'indians'.

His first voyage was so successful, Columbus had little trouble arranging for the financing of a second. This would not be an exploratory voyage, but rather a massive colonization effort. On September 25, 1493, Columbus left Spain with 17 ships and 1,500 men. Horses, sheep, cattle, pigs, seeds, citrus plants, wheat, barley, and the infamous sugar cane, traveled along. The Moors had taught the Spanish how to raise rice and pigeon peas, hence the favorite dish of 'arroz con gandules' or rice and beans was born in the new world.

On November 19, Columbus discovered Puerto Rico, inhabited by 50,000 Taino and Arawak Indians. The Indians would make the huge mistake of showing the Spaniards gold nuggets. Forced into mining, the Tainos were unable to farm, eventually dying from malnutrition and overwork.

In 1508 Ponce de Leon traveled from Santo Domingo to resume his search for gold. The Indians continued to die out from overwork, suicide, and murder. A number of the Spaniards married Indian women, but less than a 100 years later the Tainos were almost extinct.

Time passed, and the mild and fertile climate encouraged the raising of cattle, sugarcane, ginger, coffee and tobacco. Diets began to change as Spanish cooks incorporated their favorite ingredients, olives, bacalao (dried salt codfish), cilantro, sofrito, garlic, and other spices and herbs, with the local fare. Other foods native to Latin America were brought to the island with Spanish trade, such as cocoa from Mexico and yams from South America.

## African culture

*and sugar cane production..*

When the Spaniards discovered that little gold existed on Puerto Rico, they turned to other revenue-increasing methods in the mid-1500's. Sugar production. Every thing related to sugar production was imported: the technology, equipment, even African slaves.

The Africans brought okra, bananas, plantains, coconuts watermelon, black-eyed peas, tamarind and millet to the island. They taught the islanders basket, pottery making and their favorite way of cooking—frying.

Later, the Dutch, French, Italian and Chinese immigrants further influenced the culture and cooking to form *La Cocina Criolla*.

## Rum industry ...

Around this time, 17th century, an insatiable demand in Europe for sugar led to the establishment of hundreds of sugar cane plantations. Mills crushed the cane and extracted the juice, which was then boiled, causing crystallized chunks of sugar to form. The remaining liquid was melazas (from 'miel', the Spanish word for honey).

Molasses is a sticky syrup that still contains high amounts of sugar. Plantation owners soon noticed that the molasses mixed with water and left out in the sun would ferment. By the 1650's, this former waste product was being distilled into a spirit. Hence, the birth of the Caribbean rum industry.

Locally, rum was used as a panacea for many ills and pains afflicting those that lived in the tropics. Plantation owners also sold it at discounted prices, to naval ships to encourage their presence in local waters and afford protection from pirates. By the 1730's the British navy adopted the quaint custom of a daily ration of a half-pint of 160 proof rum. Later the rum was diluted by half with water and known as grog. This ration remained a staple in the British navy until 1969. And here I thought all this time grog was a version of light beer.

Grog aside, a thriving rum export trade developed, and rum was shipped to Great Britian and the British colonies in North America where it replaced gin. This export of rum to North America, in exchange for lumber and dried cod (still a culinary staple in the Caribbean and Puerto Rico) soon switched to the export of molasses to distilleries in New England. This was to circumvent a law from the British parliament, which protected British distillers by outlawing trade of rum directly between the colonies. Smuggling soon became rampant. Sounds a lot like money-laundering to me.

Shipment of molasses to manufacture rum in New England distilleries became part of the infamous 'slavery triangle.' This went hand in hand with the ever-increasing demand for slaves to run the sugar plantations. A skipper would leave with a cargo of rum to West Africa. There he would trade the rum for slaves and head back to the Caribbean to exchange the slaves for molasses. The molasses was transported back to New England to be distilled into rum.

The disruption of trade caused by the American Revolution and the rise of whiskey production in North America caused the slow decline of rum production. In Europe, the extraction of sugar from sugar beets lessened the demand for Caribbean sugar. Many plantations closed.

With the back scaling of the sugar industry, the population began to unify. Slaves, slave owners and Spaniards began to inter-marry. The Puerto Rican people became creole, bronze in skin tone, and more racially mixed than in other countries where slavery existed.

In the 18th and 19th centuries other agriculture: coffee, ginger, tobacco and cattle, flourished. Puerto Rican coffee was in demand in Europe. Ships from Spain, France, Portugal and England came to trade wine, cast-iron pots and utensils.

In 1865, Don Juan Serralles produced the first few casks of rum at the Hacienda Mercedita sugar plantation, near Ponce. This would later become the famous Don Q rum label. Don Q is the most popular rum in Puerto Rico.

In the 1930's Barcardi opened a distillery in Puerto Rico, now located in Catano, minutes from San Juan. Today, Puerto Rico is known all over the world for its light bodied golden rum, aged a minimum of three years.

# Today ...

Now, back to Puerto Rican cuisine or *comida criolla*. Today unfortunately, you can find a fast food chain restaurant on nearly every corner and these have had influence on island cuisine as well. Interestingly, some of the chains have adapted a pseudo Puerto Rican menu to their fare. It's not unusual to walk into a well-known steak house and see *alcapurrias* offered on the salad bar.

You will also find *come y vetes* (eat and run establishments) and other wonderful open-air eateries serving rice and beans, crab with rice, seafood pasteles. There are also many fine food restaurants, with eclectic menus: Thai-Latin, Mediterranean-Latin; even Chinese-Latin, offering expensive wines and candlelit ambiance. Old San Juan must have at least thirty fabulous restaurants. One could live in Puerto Rico and never dine at the same restaurant twice in one year.

## So, what exactly is Puerto Rican food?

Almost all Caribbean cooking has been influenced by the Spanish, English, Danes, Africans, other Europeans and Orientals. Although Puerto Rican cooking bears a similarity to both Spanish and Mexican cuisine, what makes it different is the seasoning. Think of freshly cracked black pepper, *culantro* (wide coriander leaf), oregano, crushed rock salt, garlic, ginger, lime, sour orange and cinnamon. There is occasional use of hot peppers. However, most Puerto Ricans prefer small sweet peppers called *aji dulce*.

The island has a rich source of foods in its verdant hillsides. Traditional Puerto Rican recipes were born in these rural areas. Modern kitchens have replaced the old cooking methods to a greater extent with exception of a couple utensils such as the mortar and pestle, a cast-iron cooking kettle similar to a Dutch oven.

The base of all Puerto Rican cuisine is *sofrito* and *achiote*. A caldero and a mortar and pestle are the indispensable tools behind it all.

*Sofrito* is made from: garlic; black peppercorns; rock salt; cilantro; *culantro*; parsley; oregano; sweet bell peppers; onions, and olive oil pounded into a fragrant paste, then sautéed with smoked ham, bacon, or chorizo, a Spanish sausage.

*Achiote* or annatto are the seeds of a small, flowering tropical tree in South America. The seeds are used to color and flavor oil.

A mortar and pestle mashes and melds garlic, onions, black peppercorns, rock salt, herbs and other spices into a heavenly seasoning paste.

A *caldero* is indispensibe for cooking rice recipes such as *arroz con pollo*. Made from iron (preferable) or heavy cast-aluminum, with a round bottom and straight sides, this kettle conducts heat evenly-a very important feature for Puerto Rican cooking.

*Plátano*, a.k.a. plantains are a mainstay in all the Caribbean islands. They're eaten ripe (my favorite) or green; served boiled, roasted or fried. The leaves of the plantain plant, as well as banana leaves, are used to wrap *pasteles*.

Soups are popular fare in Puerto Rico, either as a first course, or more often than not as a main meal such as *sopón de pollo con arróz* (chicken soup with rice) or *sopón de pescado* (fish soup). *Asopao* is a type of gumbo, much thicker than a soup, but not a casserole dish either, made with chicken or fish. *Asopao de pollo* is lovely with chicken, garlic, paprika, oregano, salt pork, ham, chili peppers, and tomatoes. *Sancocho* is perfect for the health conscious with its abundance of local vegetables, plantains and fresh meats.

At Christmas and other holidays, roasted pig is very popular. Basted with sour orange juice from *Seville* oranges and *achiote*, the roast is served with *aji-li-mojili*, a garlic sauce made with sweet peppers, vinegar, salt and olive oil.

Other popular types of main dishes include fried beefsteak with onions, rice with chicken, paella, and roasted meats served with a creole-style sauce.

While on a photo shoot in Puerto Rico, I discovered *tostones*, fried green plantain slices, lightly salted and crunchy.

Delicious *bacalaitos*, fried codfish fritters, can be found on every street corner, as well as *alcapurrias* (dumplings made from green bananas and *yautía*, stuffed with shellfish, chicken or fish), *pastelillos* (small flaky turnovers made from a flour dough, stuffed with cheese, meat, chicken, fish or guava paste) *frituras* (fritters made with bananas, vegetables, seafood, and meat) *piononos* (stuffed plantain rolls) *pinchos* (shish-kebabs) *empanadas* (deep-dish meat pot pies) and *surullos* (cornbread and cheese sticks).

Puerto Rican grown pineapple is among the sweetest and most fragrant in the world. Road side stands offer pineapple cut up and ready to eat. You'll also find *coco frio*. These are still green coconuts, chilled, tops cut off with a straw and spoon inserted in center to scoop out the jelly like meat and sweetly refreshing nectar. Papaya, mangoes, lime and tamarind are also grown locally and used to make iced fruit drinks.

*Flan* (custard) and *tembleque* (coconut custard) can be found on any good restaurant menu. The best *flan* I ever had was at the *Hotel El Convento* in Old San Juan, where it was served with a mango sauce. I've seen homemade *Cuadritos de Coco* (coconut squares) offered everywhere, even in gas station convenience stores. *Arroz con dulce* is made from cooked rice, coconut cream, sugar and cinnamon. Candied papaya, cooked in sugar and cinnamon, must be accompanied by *queso blanco* (white cheese).

Puerto Ricans love their coffee. Justifiably so, for centuries its reputation is the best in the world. Rumour had it the late Pope would only drink Puerto Rican coffee, served very, very strong with hot, steamed milk.

Puerto Rican rums are the most popular worldwide. By law, they must be aged for years, hence their smoothness. Don Q rum is considered the best on the island.

So now you have a good idea of the diversity of *cocina criolla*. Puerto Rican cuisine embodies the spirit and the very best of Caribbean cooking.

Let's get started and learn about the unique tools and ingredients of Puerto Rican kitchens.

# Glossary of Ingredients and Terms

**Adobo**:
Adobo is a blend of ingredients rubbed into fish, meat or poultry, excellent as a marinade, and a temporary preservative. I prefer to make a fresh batch when needed instead of using commercially packaged products with their accompanying preservatives.

**Aji Dulce**: (*Capsicum annuum*)
Sweet chili pepper, a dwarf with a mild and distinct flavor. Not to be confused with hot peppers.

**Alcaparras**:
Capers. I prefer Spanish capers, but any variety of caper preserved in vinegar or oil will be fine. Taste them first. If too vinegary, soak in a bowl of cool water for 15 minutes, then rinse.

**Annatto**: (*Achiote*)
The use of *achiote* to flavor and color food has always been an important part of traditional island food. When combined with other herbs and spices, this emulsion gives Puerto Rican cuisine its distinctive aroma and flavor.

Annatto dates back to the Tainos who called it *bixa*. Lard or vegetable oil is heated in a saucepan at *low* heat, together with *achiote* seeds to release a rich, orange-yellow color and mildly pungent flavor.

The seeds are then strained and the emulsion reserved in a jar. Annatto's employ vary from flavoring and coloring rice dishes, adding an orange-brown color to white meats, substituting for tomatoes, and adding complexity to vegetable dishes. The use of this flavoring and coloring agent was the most efficient way to deal with the many staples not found in the kitchens of Spanish colonial Puerto Rico. Known as the poor man's saffron.

**Breadfruit**: (*pana, panapen*)
Large, roundish fruit (some as large as a soccer ball) of a tropical tree. A thick, greenish rind covers the sweet, starch flesh similar in taste to a potato. Do not eat raw. Fried green bread fruit are served as *tostones* to accompany drinks, meats, chicken or fish.

**Cassava**: (*yuca*)
Tuber of a shrub that has large palmate leaves. Can grow up to ten feet in height, native to Brazil and Mexico. Also known as manioc or yuca, not to be confused with yucca. Tuber is conical in shape, brown skinned, and the flesh can be white, yellow or red. Tubers can grow up to three feet in length and weigh 50 pounds or more. There are many varieties of cassava, all of which contain hydrocyanic acid, a poisonous substance eliminated by cooking or dehydration. Used to make tapioca.

**Chayote**: (*Christophene*)
Pear shaped, looks like a pale avocado, grows on a climbing plant extensively in the Caribbean. Similar in flavor to summer sqush.

**Chironja**:
Cross between orange and grapefruit known only in Puerto Rico.

**Chorizo**:
Highly seasoned Spanish pork sausage, sun-dried and hot to palate.

**Cilantro**: Coriander leaves

**Coconut**: (*Coco*)
The use of coconut in Puerto Rican households is divided into two categories: *fresco de agua* (ripe with water) and *seco* (dry). The ripe with water coconuts are used in the making of desserts. The water is drained and used for making rum drinks, or simply as a refreshing, non-alcohilic beverage. The dry coconut is used to make coconut milk and intensely flavored sauces.

**Codfish**: dry and salted (*bacalao*)
Dry, salted codfish has its origins in Europe, in the Scandinavian countries. It made its way with the Spanish explorers to Puerto Rico in the early sixteenth century. Inexpensive and popular in fritters and salads.

**Criolla**:
Creole, a term used to describe Puerto Rican culture and cuisine.

**Culantro**: (*recao*)
Long, serrated leaves of a small herb, wide coriander leaf, which grows wild in the Caribbean.

**Flan**: Custard

**Gandul or gandules**: Green pigeon peas

**Guayaba**: Guava

**Garlic**: (*Ajo*)
Spanish colonists introduced garlic to Puerto Rico.

Recently I had dinner at my friend Griselle's house. I watched her make a to-die-for shrimp and pasta dish. I couldn't believe how much garlic she added. Literally handfuls of the stuff (they sell crushed garlic in quart-size jars in Puerto Rican grocery stores). No wonder Griselle always looked so good, her skin clear, eyes bright. Garlic is an excellent detoxifier. However, later that evening when Griselle and I stopped by the Hotel El San Juan for after dinner drinks, no one came within two feet of us!

**Ginger**: (*Fengibre*)
A spicy root, ginger is the main ingredient in Island Bouquet Garni. Ginger is best when fresh. Purchase only as much as you will immediately need. Puerto Rican gingerroot is smaller and more pungent than the sort available stateside.

**Green Onions**: (*Cebollin*)
Also known as scallions, are used for their subtle flavor enhancement in sauces, salads, meat, fish and poultry. The high water content of scallions is beneficial when sautéing fresh herbs as it will provide some liquid to the drier ingredients. Garlic will cook and burn quickly upon a hot surface, but scallions will slow down the reaction time. Another use is to absorb some of the strong odors given off by lamb or seafood during cooking.

**Ham**: (*Jamon*)
Smoked cured ham is indispensable in the Puerto Rican kitchen. Used as a base for *sofrito*, and for soups, rice, main courses, etc.
Fresh ham is used for pork fillings in *pastels*, *alcapurria* and *empanadas*.

**Lechon**: Cooked pig

**Machengo cheese**: Originally from Spain, made with sheep's milk. A nice cross between white milk cheddar and a parmesan. Crumbly. Lovely piquant flavor, not too strong or too weak.

**Mojo**:
Most popular sauce for seafood, features sweet cherry peppers and *culantro* leaf.

**Olive Oil**: (*Aceite de Oliva*)
Centuries ago, olive oil was highly prized in the New World and Puerto Rico, not just for cooking, but as a lamp oil, and lubricant for machinery. Because of piracy and foul weather, often it would be one or two years before a cargo ship reached the island. Prices on commodities and necessities soared, including olive oil.

**Olives and Capers**: (*Alcaparrado*)
*Alcaparrado* is a delicious combination of olives and capers preserved with vinegar and salt. Wonderful in *rellenos* as a stuffing, *pasteles*, and salads.

**Plantain**: (*Amarillo*)
Fruit of the banana tree, a giant herbaceous plant native to Malaysia, related to the sweet banana. Also known as the 'cooking banana.' Ten to fifteen inches long, its green skin is thicker than that of the banana, its flesh firmer and not as sweet. When fully ripe, the skin turns black. Not to be eaten raw.

**Recaíto**:
Seasoning made with recao, cilantro, onion, garlic and peppers that adds a distinctive flavor to food. Always part of the *sofrito* base.

**Sofrito**:
Base for Puerto Rican cooking made from *recaíto* cooked with ham, tomato sauce and/or *achiote* (annatto)

**Yautía:**
Starcy root (taro) of a tropical, large-leaved plant. Flesh is creamy white or yellow, similar in flavor and texture to Irish or Idaho potato.

**Yuca:** see cassava

# Stocking Your Puerto Rican Pantry

Like every cuisine, Puerto Rican cooking has some basic ingredients. The backbone of this tropical cuisine lies in its seasonings and herbs.

**Spices and herbs in order of importance:**

Black peppercorns (ground)
Garlic
Culantro
Cilantro
Oregano
Parsley
Ají Dulce (sweet chili pepper)
Recao (herb used to impart piquant flavor)
Onion and/or onion powder
Annatto seeds
Thyme
Basil
Bay Leaves
Rosemary
Sage
Ginger
Hot Chili Pepper
Mustard
Curry powder
Cumin
Allspice
Cinnamon
Anise
Tarragon

**Other important ingredients:**

Adobo (see index for recipe)
Alcaparrado (purchase ready-made or see index)
Bacalao (dry, salted codfish)
Calabaza (West Indian pumpkin, substitute acorn or butternut squash)
Coconut (see index for use)

Gandules or Green Pigeon Peas (found dried or canned on mainland)
Guanábana or soursop (find frozen concentrate in grocery)
Habichuelas (beans, canned or dried)
Ham, smoked (essential ingredient for *sofrito* and other dishes)
Lechosa or papaya
Parcha or passionfruit (frozen concentrate fine to use)
Plátano or plantain (use green or ripe according to recipe)
*Recaíto* (see index for recipe)
Salchichas (Vienna sausages, a popular addition to rice dishes)
Sofrito (see index)
Tamarind (find in Latin groceries)
Tocino, dry salt-cured pork (used in *sofrito*)
Tomato sauce
Vinegar.

## Tools and Techniques of *Comida Criolla*

Many of the items listed below are already in use in the modern kitchen. Some, like the *caldero*, a cast iron kettle, and the *pilon y maceta*, mortar and pestle, are new to non-Puerto Rican kitchens. Even so, they play an important part in the success of *comida criolla*.

### Cast Iron Kettle: (*caldero*)
Cast iron kettles are indispensable because of their unique ability to absorb heat slowly and evenly. Made of heavy cast-iron (preferred) or cast-aluminum (now suspect as a link to Alzheimer's) with a round bottom and straight sides. A heavy kettle or Dutch oven may be substituted.

### Cutting Boards:
I prefer wood cutting boards over glass, which dulls a knife, or plastic, which can retain harmful bacteria. To sanitize wood cutting boards: using a fresh paper towel, dampen in warm water and add a ½ teaspoon dish liquid or castile soap. Scrub board thoroughly, rinse and discard paper towel. Next, pour 3% hydrogen peroxide (available in drug stores) over all surfaces of cutting board and allow to sit for 20 minutes. Rinse off with water, pat cutting board dry with fresh paper towels. Then pour white vinegar (I buy the $3.00 a gallon kind) over all surfaces of cutting board. Allow to sit overnight. No need to rinse. The vinegar will deodorize as well.

It's best to purchase four cutting boards: one for vegetables and herbs; one for meats; one for seafood; and another for kneading dough.

### Food processor:
Some people consider a food processor cheating, preferring to use a knife or mortar and pestle. But in this day of hustle and shrinking leisure time, a food processor makes quick work of tedious chores. Buy the best quality one you can afford.

The food processor has all but replaced the mortar and pestle.

**Mortar and Pestle** (*Pilon y Maceta*)
The Tainos used a *pilon* carved from stone to grind their paints, root vegetables, grains and seeds. Early Spanish colonists also used the *pilon*. It was made from glazed clay, used to grind nuts and garlic and make *picada*, a seasoning base of garlic, saffron, paprika, parsley and lemon juice used in paella.

In Puerto Rico, the process of pounding and grinding spices and herbs in the *pilon* is called *machando* or *moliendo*.

Mortar and pestles can be purchased in metal, marble or wood, although I prefer the latter. Look for ones made or cedar, teak or oak. Eight to ten inches tall is a suitable size.

**Curing**: Combine ½ cup hot water with ½ cup white vinegar and pour into bottom of *pilon*. Allow to sit for one hour, then drain and dry with white paper towel. Add six peeled cloves of garlic, one at a time, and pound and grind into a smooth paste. To keep the garlic from flying out of the *pilon*, place one cupped hand over the rim of the mortar. Pound in an up and down fashion.

DO NOT WASH *pilon* AGAIN! Yes, that's right. Garlic is a marvelous disinfectant. Simply wipe out mortar after each use, cover with a brown paper bag, and store in cool, dry place. If you feel the need to clean it, before each use, pour 3% hydrogen peroxide into bottom of mortar, allow soaking for 20 minutes, drain and rinse, the wipe out with clean paper towel soaked in vinegar.

**Uses**: To mince, grind, crack or crush herbs, spices, grains. Excellent for making marinades or pastes.

**Instructions**: Place the largest pieces, i.e. garlic, onion, peppers, into the bottom first. Then the most textured, rock salt, peppercorns. Then, in one hand, take the pestle, place into center of mortar, cup your other hand over rim of mortar, then pound up and down slowly. Add liquid ingredients, olive oil, vinegar, etc. last. When a smooth paste has formed, cover with a clean dish towel and place in a warm spot to allow flavors to mingle. After removing paste, do not wash. You may wipe out with a cloth dampened in vinegar. A cured *pilon* adds a lovely complexity to a dish.

# Basic Seasonings, Sauces, Marinades and Dips

The heart and soul of Puerto Rican cooking lies in its seasonings and marinades. The basic sauces are *recaíto, sofrito, escabeche, ajilimójili, mojito de ajo* and *mojito isleño*. Try the following recipes. They'll take a bit of time, but make extra and freeze in ice cube trays for future use in rice, fish, poultry and meat dishes.

## Adobo

Many Puerto Ricans, pressed for time, purchase dry, powdered adobo from the grocery store. Anna's aunt, Doritza, convinced us to use her recipe for fresh adobo. This versatile seasoning is a blend of dry and wet ingredients rubbed into meat, poultry or seafood. Think of it as Puerto Rican *jerk* (similar to that of Jamaican jerk seasoning). Also may be used to season vegetables, rice, soups, oils, etc.

Quick and easy to make, the flavor difference between fresh and store-bought adobo is well worth the effort.

You will need your mortar and pestle for this seasoning. A food processor may be utilized, but at least grind the spices, especially the peppercorns with the mortar and pestle first.

**8 garlic cloves, peeled**
**1 ½ teaspoons pulverized rock salt**
**1 teaspoon black peppercorns**
**1 teaspoon paprika**
**½ teaspoon ground cumin**
**½ teaspoon cayenne pepper**

**1 ½ teaspoons fresh, chopped oregano**
**1 ½ teaspoon fresh, chopped cilantro**
**1 teaspoon fresh, minced ginger**
**¼ cup olive oil**
**3 tablespoons fresh lime juice or vinegar**

1. Place garlic in bottom of mortar and pestle. Following the instructions in *Tools and Techniques* section, pound garlic into a paste. Add rock salt and peppercorns, pounding and incorporating into garlic paste.

2. Add paprika, cumin and cayenne, grinding into mixture.

3. Add oregano, cilantro and ginger. Pound until smooth.

4. Stir in olive oil and fresh lime juice.

5. Allow to sit for one hour. Use immediately or transfer to sterile glass jar and refrigerate. Use within one week or freeze for up to two months.

**Yield: a little over a ½ cup**

# Recaíto

*Recaíto* is the base of most *sofrito* recipes. It's a little bit simpler and quicker to make than *sofrito*. You can use *recaíto* for all types of foods, and they needn't be Puerto Rican dishes. To make a larger batch and freeze, double or triple the recipe.

For the *culantro* used in these recipes, Anna brought me some seeds, which we grew while we worked on desserts.

½ cup coarsely chopped green bell pepper
½ cup coarsely chopped yellow onion
4 cloves garlic, peeled
2 teaspoons freshly chopped *culantro*, also known as *recao*

1 teaspoon freshly chopped cilantro
1 teaspoon freshly ground peppercorns
½ teaspoon pulverized rock salt

1. Place all ingredients in food processor. Process until mixture resembles oatmeal. Do not over-puree.
2. Place into a sterile jar and refrigerate for up to 3 days. Alternatively freeze for up to 2 months.

**Yield: a little over1 cup**

## Sofrito

The heart of Puerto Rican food lies with the following basic ingredients: garlic (of course!), black peppercorns, rock salt, cilantro, *culantro* (wide leaf coriander), parsley, oregano, sweet bell peppers, onions, tomatoes and olive oil. This heady mixture is then sautéed with smoked ham, bacon or chorizo (Spanish sausage) to produce *sofrito*. Always try and make your own *sofrito*. It's quick and easy and well worth effort. It may be frozen for future use, but fresh is really best.

# Traditional *Sofrito*

Transfer the *sofrito* to a sterile glass jar and refrigerate. Use within three to four days. You can also freeze it in ice-cube trays and later transfer to a plastic freezer bag.

¼ cup diced lean, cured ham

3 tablespoons salt pork

¼ cup, plus 2 tablespoons olive oil
6 garlic cloves, peeled and crushed

½ cup chopped onion

¼ cup chopped green bell pepper

¼ cup chopped sweet chili pepper

1 teaspoon ground black peppercorns

1 tablespoon chopped fresh *culantro* leaves

1 tablespoon fresh chopped parsley

2 teaspoons fresh chopped oregano (or 1 teaspoon dry)

1 teaspoon chopped fresh cilantro leaves

½ teaspoon pulverized rock salt

¼ cup, plus 3 tablespoons dry sherry

1. Brown the cured ham and salt pork in a deep skillet over medium-high heat for 3 to 4 minutes until lightly browned on all sides.

2. Reduce heat to *low*, add olive oil, garlic and onion. Sauté for 3 to 4 minutes until onion is just clear.

3. Add green bell pepper, sweet chili pepper, *culantro*, parsley, oregano, cilantro, salt and ground peppercorn. Sauté over about 10 minutes, stirring occasionally.

4. Reduce heat even further and add sherry. Cover and simmer for ½ hour. Remove from heat.

**Yield: about 1 cup**

## Peppers

Peppercorns are the fruit of the vining pepper plant (up to 33 feet), native to India. It has been in use for thousands of years not only as a condiment, but as a tax and a currency. Today India and Indonesia are the leading producers of pepper.

**Purchasing:** Green peppercorns are very mild, while the black (considered half-ripe) peppercorns are piquant and full of flavor. Buy whole peppercorns and grind yourself for maximum freshness.

**Cooking:** Add ground pepper at the end of cooking, as it tends to lose its flavor and become bitter if cooked more than 30 minutes.

**Storing:** Whole black peppercorns may be kept at room temperature for very long periods of time without losing freshness. Green peppercorns only last a week or so. Ground pepper should not be kept more than a couple of months. Note, freezing foods with black pepper in them intensifies the spiciness of the pepper.

**Nutrition:** Black pepper is rich in potassium.

# Escabeche Sauce

*Salsa de Escabeche*

*Escabeche* sauce is popular throughout the island. Use white vinegar for a traditional recipe, or experiment with balsamic, raspberry and other exotic vinegars. Serve with fried fish, chicken, green bananas, or beans.

1 cup extra-virgin olive oil

2 medium yellow onions, sliced

½ cup white vinegar

1 teaspoon salt

1 teaspoon black peppercorns

2 bay leaves

3 large garlic cloves, peeled and minced

1.  Heat the olive oil in a non-reactive 2-quart saucepan over moderate heat. Add onions and sauté for 5 minutes.

2.  Add all other ingredients, lower heat, and simmer for 15 minutes.

3.  Allow to cool completely.

**Yield: about 2 cups**

## Did You Know?

Just off Mayaguez on Puerto Rico's west coast, **Mona Island**, teems with enormous iguanas, several species of endangered sea turtles and numerous sea birds. Dramatic two-hundred foot limestone cliffs encircle the island. There are no hotels on Mona Island, but you can camp for $4.00 a night. For more information, contact the Puerto Rico Department of Tourism at 787-721-5495.

# Annatto Oil

*Achiote*

Nicely flavors rice dishes. Imparts a lovely pale yellow-red-orange shade. Used both as a coloring and flavoring in the islands.

**4 tablespoons of annatto seeds**          **1 cup olive oil**

1. Heat oil in small saucepan over low heat.
2. Add annatto seeds and cook until oil turns red-orange. Remove from heat at once. Do not overcook or this will lend a bitter flavor to oil.
3. Cool and strain. Discard seeds. Keep in refrigerator for up to 1 week.

**Yield: 1 cup**

# Garlic and Pepper Sauce

*Salsa de Ajilimójili*

Traditionally served with barbequed suckling pig, this mildly pungent sauce goes well with poultry and seafood also. Note: you can prepare this recipe in a blender or food processor.

**8 cloves garlic, peeled**                    **½ cup olive oil**
**1 ¼ cups chopped sweet chili pepper**        **¼ cup white wine vinegar**
**8 peppercorns**                              **¼ cup fresh lime juice**
**1 teaspoon pulverized rock salt**

1. Pound the garlic in a mortar and pestle until smooth. Add chili peppers, peppercorns and rock salt. Pound weel.
2. Stir in olive oil, vinegar and lime juice.
3. Allow to sit one hour. Keeps for up to three days in the refrigerator.

**Yield: a little more than 1 cup**

# Aji-Li-Mojili Sauce on the Spicy Side

If you like garlic and you like fire, this is the condiment for you. Be certain to wear gloves when handling hot chili peppers and keep fingers away from eyes. I serve this with fish or shellfish.

| | |
|---|---|
| 8 cloves garlic, peeled | ½ cup red bell pepper |
| 1 to 2 habanero peppers, seeded and minced or, | 8 peppercorns |
| 3 red hot peppers, seeded and minced | 1 teaspoon pulverized rock salt |
| ¼ cup sweet green cooking pepper | ½ cup fresh lime juice |
| (those banana shaped ones) | ½ cup olive oil |

1. Pound the garlic in a mortar and pestle into a smooth paste. Add hot peppers, sweet green pepper and red bell pepper. Crush with pestle.
2. Add peppercorns and rock salt, grinding until smooth.
3. Stir in lime juice and olive oil.
4. Serve at once or refrigerate overnight.

**Yield: more than 1 cup**

# Traditional Garlic Dipping Sauce
*Mojito de Ajo*

This habit-forming sauce is delicious alongside *tostones*, green bananas or other vegetable dishes. Try it on French Fries. Note: you may use a blender or food processor for this recipe.

| | |
|---|---|
| 8 large garlic cloves, peeled | 1 teaspoon salt |
| 1 cup extra-virgin olive oil | |

1. Pound the garlic cloves in a mortar and pestle. Drizzle in olive oil and salt.
2. Pour into a clean covered container in the refrigerator.

**Yield:  approximately 1 cup**

## Healthy Hint

Research shows that eating ½ to 1 clove of **garlic** a day may reduce blood cholesterol up to 8 percent. Also called Russian penicillin, excellent when a cold is felt coming on.

# Island Sauce
*Mojo Isleño*

This is the island's most popular sauce to serve with fried fish or any other seafood. Featuring mild sweet cherry peppers and *culantro*, this sauce bursts with intense flavor. Keeps for several days in refrigerator.

½ cup extra-virgin olive oil

1 cup minced yellow onion

6 large garlic cloves, peeled and crushed

1 *aji dulce* or Serrano pepper,
  seeded and minced

1/3 cup dry sherry

1 tablespoon fresh lime juice

1 tablespoon vinegar

½ cup canned tomato puree

¼ cup fresh *culantro*

1 teaspoon fresh chopped oregano

1 teaspoon pulverized rock salt

24 pimento-stuffed olives,
  chopped

2 tablespoons capers

1. Heat olive oil in a skillet over medium heat. Add onion, garlic and peppers, sautéing until onions are clear. Deglaze pan with sherry.

2. Stir in olives, capers and tomato puree. Lower heat, add tomato puree and simmer for 5 minutes.

3. Fold in *culantro*, oregano, rock salt, lime juice and vinegar. Simmer, covered for 20 minutes.

4. If storing, transfer to reaction-proof container, glass or ceramic. Do not store in metal container.

**Yield: a little over 2 cups**

# *Mojito* Sauce

*Mojito* goes well with just about everything. It can also rescue over-cooked fish or meat.

¼ cup *sofrito* (see index for recipe)

½ cup ketchup

1 tablespoon minced *aji dulce* or other sweet cherry pepper

3 tablespoons dry Sherry or dry red wine

2 tablespoons fresh lime juice

1. Combine all ingredients in a small bowl.

2. Allow to sit 30 minutes before serving with *tostones* and other finger foods.

**Yield: just under 1 cup**

# Saffron Parsley Seasoning
*Picada*

Picada is a seasoning paste whose key ingredient is saffron. Vibrant yellow and sultry, smoky in flavor.

**1 teaspoon saffron threads**
**6 garlic cloves, peeled**
**½ teaspoon black peppercorns**
**½ teaspoon pulverized rock salt**

**1 tablespoon paprika**
**½ cup chopped Italian parsley**
**1 tablespoon fresh lime juice**

1. Heat saffron in a small frying pan over moderate heat until crispy. Remove from heat and cool. Break up with your fingers. Set aside.

2. Grind garlic with a mortar and pestle until smooth. Add black peppercorns and rock salt; continue to pound with pestle.

3. Add paprika and saffron, breaking up saffron threads, and pulverizing.

4. Add parsley and lime juice, processing into a smooth paste.

5. Keeps for three to four days in refrigerator. Really best if refrigerated overnight to allow flavors to mingle.

**Yield: a little over ½ cup**

# Chimichurri Sauce
*Salsa de Chimichurri*

Traditionally used for Churrasco (beef tenderloin roast), this sauce adds a piquant garliky tang. Quick to make, too. Note: the traditional oil used is corn oil, but more flavorful olive oil is now preferred. Some cooks use half vinegar and half wine, so a little experimentation is in order. Use dried parsley to cut preparation time.

**2 bunches parsley, washed, patted dry and coarsely chopped**

**1 tablespoon salt**

12 large garlic cloves, chopped

1 ¾ cups extra-virgin olive oil

¾ cup sherry wine vinegar

1 tablespoon freshly cracked pepper

¼ teaspoon dried thyme

¼ teaspoon sugar

1. Combine parsley, garlic, oilive oil, vinegar, salt, pepper, thyme and sugar in food processor.
2. Pulse until just blended. Do not over process or you'll have parsley soup.
3. Allow to sit overnight in the refrigerator (in a covered container) before using.

**Yield: 3 + cups**

# Green Sauce
*Salsa Verde*

Serve Salsa Verde with Arroz con Pollo, pork or beef. To use with fish, substitute fish stock for the chicken. This recipe makes around 4 cups and will keep for 2 days in the refrigerator. Since it doesn't freeze well, cut recipe in half if smaller amount is desired.

4 tablespoons butter

4 tablespoons flour

2 ½ cups warm chicken broth (homemade is best, but canned is acceptable)

½ cup minced green bell pepper

½ small jalapeño pepper, seeded and minced

1 tablespoon freshly ground black pepper

¾ cup finely chopped parsley

¼ cup finely chopped cilantro

1. Melt butter in medium saucepan over low heat. Sprinkle in flour and stir with wooden spoon for 3 minutes until smooth to make a roux. Remove from heat.
2. Whisk in chicken broth until well combined.
3. Stir in bell pepper, jalapeño and black pepper. Return to low heat and simmer uncovered, stirring often, until thickened. Remove from heat.
4. Stir in parsley and cilantro. Serve at once.

**Yield: about 4 cups**

# Rub for Pork Roast

*Aliño para Carne de Cerdo*

Use this paste on a fresh leg of pork or any other pork roast. Note: cut slits into the skin, and rub the meat with the paste, allowing to marinate overnight for peak flavor.

¼ teaspoon salt

1 head garlic, peeled

1 tablespoon, plus 1 teaspoon
freshly ground black pepper

1/3 cup olive oil

2 tablespoon white wine vinegar

2 tablespoons fresh lemon juice

1 teaspoon ground oregano

1. Place all ingredients in a food processor or blender. Process until smooth.
2. Refrigerate overnight to allow flavors to mingle.

**Yield: enough rub for one 8- to 10-pound pork roast**

## Blenders

**Purchasing:** Blenders range in price from $20 to over $200. Consider how you'll use the appliance when selecting. If you'll be making a lot of frozen piña coladas and strawberry daiquiris, look for units that have 330- to 400- watts to crush ice efficiently. Otherwise, 290-watts is fine.

**Keeping kitchen clean:** Never blend more than 3 ½ cups in a blender. Use a food processor with its large capacity bowl instead.

**Processing hot liquids:** Yes, it can be done, albeit with caution. Always allow boiling liquids to cool down a bit by first removing from heat source, then sit for 30 minutes. Begin with lowest speed, half a cup at a time, with center of blender lid removed to allow hot air and steam to escape. Increase speed gradually. I prefer to use a glass blender as opposed to plastic for hot liquids.

**Cleaning:** Always rinse out immediately, sitting permits the mixture to cake and dry, making it nearly impossible to clean. Add warm water and a squirt of dish liquid, turn on blender at low setting and process for 10 seconds. Glass containers may go through dishwasher. Wash plastic by hand only, the same for the blades.

# Orange Garlic Sauce for Roast Pork

*Mojo Para Carne de Cerdo*

Note: regular orange juice may be substituted for the bitter Seville orange juice.

½ cup olive oil

½ cup minced yellow onion

8 large cloves garlic, peeled

1 tablespoon cracked black pepper

6 tablespoons red wine vinegar

½ cup, divided  Seville orange juice

1 teaspoon salt

1. Heat oil in a medium saucepan over moderate heat. Sauté onion and garlic until soft, but not browned.
2. Reduce heat, add remaining ingredients and ¼ cup of the orange juice. Simmer gently for 5 minutes. Set aside.
3. Pour off all the fat from the pan that held the roast. Deglaze the pan with remaining orange juice, scraping bottom of pan, scooping up brown bits. Stir this into sauce.

**Yield: about 2 cups**

## Tip–Hot Peppers

Be extra careful handling hot peppers. The volatile oils can burn skin and eyes badly. Use rubber gloves. To remove volatile oil, wash hands with soap and water, then rub with salt, washing again with salt and water.

When rinsing peppers, always use cold water and handle by stem. With the sharp tip of a knife, make four length-wise slashes. Carefully dig out the seeds, rinse pepper again and chop in bits. Most of the pepper's fire comes from the white ribs and the seeds. Leave a couple seeds in your recipes according to how hot you like it.

# Hot Pepper Onion Salsa

*Salsa de Ajíes Bravos y Cebollas*

Serve over barbequed chicken, fish, pork or meat.

1 medium yellow onion, sliced thinly

½ teaspoon salt

1 to 2 hot peppers to taste (jalapeños or habañeros)

½ teaspoon freshly ground black pepper

4 large garlic cloves, peeled and minced

1 *culantro* leaf, or ¼ cup chopped cilantro

¼ cup fresh lemon juice

¼ teaspoon thyme

2 tablespoons olive oil

1. Toss all ingredients in a large bowl until well coated with the olive oil.
2. Cover and refrigerate for up to two days.

**Yield: about 1 ¼ cups**

# Lime, Vinegar and Hot Chili Pepper Sauce
*Pique de Vinagre, Lima y Ajíes Bravos*

Use this recipe in the same manner as you would any commercial hot sauce. Keep in mind, the longer you allow it to steep, the hotter the sauce becomes.

2 tablespoons vegetable oil

1 medium yellow onion, minced

1 clove garlic, peeled and minced

12 fresh, hot peppers, seeded and chopped

12 black peppercorns

½ cup vinegar, preferably malt

½ cup fresh lime juice

1. Heat the vegetable oil in a medium saucepan over moderate heat. Sauté the onion and garlic until soft.
2. Stir in peppers and cook for 2 minutes. Remove from heat and add peppercorns. Allow to cool.
3. Pour mixture into a clean glass container with non-reactive lid. Stir in vinegar and lime juice.
4. Refrigerate, shaking bottle occasionally.

**Yield: 1 ½ cups**

# Avocado Lemon Dressing
*Aderezo de Aguacate y Limón*

Thick and rich. Serve over salads or as a sandwich dressing. The lemon juice prevents the avocado from discoloring.

1 medium ripe avocado, pitted, peeled and diced

4 tablespoons lemon juice

¼ cup minced onion

¼ teaspoon grated lemon zest

½ teaspoon salt

½ teaspoon freshly ground black pepper

¼ cup olive oil

1. Place avocado pieces in a ceramic or glass bowl. Pour lemon juice over top. Set aside.
2. Puree all ingredients except avocado in a food processor until smooth.
3. Add avocado and blend until lump-free. Serve at once.

**Yield: about 1 ½ cups**

## Avocado

The word 'avocado' comes from the Aztec word *abuacalt* from which the Spanish derived *abuacate* or *agucate*. There about a dozen types of avocado, including the popular Haas with its pebbly textured skin. Puerto Rico has its own variety of the fruit called 'del pais' (from the island). Round, the size of a large orange and bright green in color. Unlike the Haas, the skin is smooth, and the meat plentiful.

**Purchasing:** Select avocados that are heavy for their size, not too hard and free of black spots. Turn the avocado upside down. Gently press on the bottom with your thumb. If ripe, the skin will depress somewhat. Check the top of the fruit as it ripens first and make sure it is firm.

**Storing:** Keep unripened avocados at room temperature, out of the sun or heated areas. Ripe avocado stores up to 1 week in the refrigerator.

**Ripening:** Place avocado in a brown paper bag and twist closed. Do not refrigerate. Fruit will ripen in 1 to 3 days depending upon firmness of avocado. To speed the process up, add a whole apple to the bag. In an emergency, pierce avocado skin with a sharp fork and microwave on medium power for 30 to 60 seconds. Fruit will be sufficiently soft for guacamole.

**To slice open an avocado:** Pierce the top (elongated end) with a sharp knife, cutting from top to bottom, through the peel, down to the pit. Twist halves apart. Slide the tip of the knife under the pit, and flip out.

**To cube:** Make parallel cuts through the flesh of the pitted avocado.

Then score the fruit lengthwise, across the parallel lines. Insert a butter knife between the flesh and the skin to scoop out cubes.

**To prevent browning:** Drizzle with lemon or lime juice, or soak slices or cubes in acidulated water (6 tablespoons lemon or lime juice for each quart of water). Will prevent browning for up to 3 ½ hours.

**Serving:** Avocados are eaten raw, never cooked. Simply slice in half, pit and sprinkle lightly with salt and pepper. Very good in salads, sandwiches and as a soup topping. Nice stuffed with seafood or chicken.

**Nutrition:** Avocados are nearly 75% water, an excellent source of potassium, folic acid and vitamin B-6. Also contains Vitamin C, copper, niacin, iron, Vitamin A, zinc and magnesium.

# Avocado Dip
*Unto de Aguacate*

Avocados grow wild all over Puerto Rico and the Caribbean. If you have an avocado tree in your backyard, on a windy day it will rain avocados.

| | |
|---|---|
| 1 large ripe avocado, peeled, seeded and chopped | ¼ cup minced yellow onion |
| 1 small ripe tomato, peeled, seed, and minced | 1 garlic clove, peeled and minced |
| 1 tablespoon lime juice | ½ teaspoon salt |
| 3 tablespoons sour cream | 1 teaspoon freshly ground black pepper |

1. Puree all ingredients in a blender or food processor until smooth.
2. Chill for several hours before serving. Serve at once.

**Yield: 1 ½ cups**

# Instant Avocado Sauce
*Salsa de Aguacate*

This easy-to-make sauce begs to drizzled over grilled fish, chicken or meat. Double the amount of *recaíto* and you'll have a dressing for salad.

1 large ripe avocado, peeled, seeded and chopped    ¼ cup olive oil

½ cup *recaíto* (see index)

1. Puree all ingredients in a blender or food processor until smooth.
2. Chill for several hours before serving.

**Yield: 1 ½ to 2 cups**

# Tomato Sauce Island-Style
*Salsa de Tomate*

Serve over pasta or any meat or fish. The *culantro* leaf adds fresh taste and complexity to the sauce.

.3 tablespoons olive oil

1 medium yellow onion, chopped

1 clove garlic, crushed

1 medium green frying pepper, seeded chopped

2 medium sweet chili peppers, seeded and minced

3 pounds fresh tomatoes, peeled and chopped

¼ teaspoon ground oregano

¼ teaspoon dried thyme

1 culantro leaf, chopped, or ¼ cup chopped cilantro

2 tablespoons cider vinegar

2 tablespoons dry vermouth

¼ cup chicken broth

1 bay leaf

1 teaspoon salt

1 tablespoon brown sugar

1. Heat the oil in a medium saucepan over moderate heat. Sauté onion, garlic and peppers for 7 minutes. Do not brown.
2. Add remaining ingredients and bring to boil.
3. Reduce heat, cover and simmer for 1 hour. Remove from heat and allow to cool completely. Remove bay leaf.
4. Process in food processor in batches. Return to saucepan and simmer until sauce thickens, about 1 ½ hours. Stir frequently.

**Yield: a little over 3 cups**

# Guava Barbeque Sauce
*Salsa de Guayaba para La Barbacoa*

Guavas are found wild all over the island. The guavas we used in this recipe come from Anna's backyard. Brush this piquant sauce over ribs, chicken or fish. Note: frozen guava from your grocer's freezer section makes an excellent substitute for fresh.

2 tablespoons vegetable oil

1 medium onion, minced

1 cup frozen guava pulp, thawed

1 cup tomato sauce

½ cup white wine vinegar

¼ cup packed brown sugar

1 tablespoon molasses

2 teaspoons paprika

2 teaspoons chili powder

1 teaspoon salt

2 teaspoons freshly cracked black pepper

1. Heat oil in large, heavy-bottomed saucepan over medium heat. Add onion and sauté until lightly browned, 7 to 10 minutes.

2. Add remaining ingredients, reduce heat to lowest possible setting. Simmer, uncovered, until thickened, about 2 hours. May be refrigerated for up to 2 weeks.

**Yield: about 3 cups**

# Guava Jelly Glaze
*Glaceado de Jalea de Guayabas*

Lovely spooned over baked, broiled, or barbequed chicken or ribs.

6 tablespoons butter

¼ cup guava jelly

2 tablespoon Worcestershire sauce

1 teaspoon Dijon-style mustard

1 tablespoon lemon juice

1. Melt the butter together with the guava jelly in a small saucepan over low heat. Stir constantly until smooth.

2. Whisk in Worcestershire, mustard and lemon juice. Simmer for 3 to 4 minutes. Remove from heat and use at once.

**Yield: about ½ cup**

# LOW-CARB Cilantro-Onion Cream Sauce

Serve this rich garlicky and cheesey dip with celery or zucchini sticks, low-carb crackers, grilled fish, chicken or vegetables.

4 garlic cloves, peeled and coarsely chopped ½ cup freshly grated parmesan cheese

3 tablespoons minced green onion *culantro*

3 tablespoons minced cilantro or ¼ cup chopped fresh parsley

1 teaspoon freshly cracked black pepper

1 tablespoon Tabasco®

1 teaspoon salt

½ cup plain yogurt

2 ½ tablespoons fresh lime juice

¼ cup olive oil

½ cup cottage cheese

1. Puree garlic, onion, pepper, salt, lime juice, cottage cheese, parmesan, cilantro, parsley, Tabasco®, yogurt and olive oil in a food processor until smooth.

2. Scoop dip into a glass or ceramic bowl and seal with plastic wrap. Refrigerate overnight to allow flavors to mingle.

**Yield: about 2 ½ cups (6 servings)**

EACH SERVING PROVIDES APPROXIMATELY:
240 calories, **1.5 grams carbohydrates**, 2 grams of protein, 28 grams of fat

# LOW-CARB Curried Herb Dip

The addition of sour cream and yogurt keeps this dip from becoming too heavy. Enhances grilled fish, chicken or meat, or as a topping for vegetables.

1 cup mayonnaise

¼ teaspoon dried oregano

¼ cup plain yogurt

¼ teaspoon dried thyme

¼ cup sour cream

1 ½ teaspoons curry powder

1 ½ teaspoons cider vinegar

½ teaspoon cumin

1 garlic clove, minced

½ teaspoon salt

1 tablespoon minced green onion

½ teaspoon paprika

1 tablespoon minced fresh cilantro or *culantro* (see index)

½ teaspoon black pepper

1 tablespoon minced fresh parsley

1. Combine mayonnaise, yogurt, sour cream, vinegar, garlic, onion, cilantro, parsley, oregano, thyme, curry, cumin, salt, black pepper and paprika in a large bowl. Whisk until smooth.

2. Cover with plastic wrap and refrigerate four to five hours to allow flavors to meld.

**Yield: about 1 2/3 cups (8 servings)**

EACH SERVING PROVIDES APPROXIMATELY:
225 calories, **1 gram carbohydrate**, 2 grams of protein, 22 grams of fat

# LOW-CARB Hot and Spicy Roasted Pepper Sauce

You would never know this tangy, velvety smooth sauce was LOW-CARB.

2 red bell peppers, halved and seeded

2 tablespoons minced yellow onion

2 tablespoons minced green bell pepper

1 8-ounce package cream cheese, room temperature

1 small habañero pepper, seeded and coarsely chopped

1 tablespoon shredded fresh parsley

1 tablespoon shredded fresh cilantro

½ teaspoon oregano

4 cloves garlic, peeled and coarsely chopped

¼ cup light cream or half-and-half

½ teaspoon salt

½ teaspoon freshly cracked black pepper

1. Roast peppers on a baking sheet lined with aluminum foil and broil four inches from heat source for 20 minutes, until they begin to blacken and blister. Remove from oven and allow to cool for 5 minutes.

2. Place peppers in plastic bag and allow to sweat. After peppers have cooled down, slip off skins.

3. Puree roasted peppers, onion, green pepper, garlic, habañero, parsley, cilantro, oregano, cream cheese, light cream, salt and pepper in a food processor until smooth. You should have a lovely pink color.

**Yield: about 2 ½ cups (12 servings)**

EACH SERVING PROVIDES APPROXIMATELY:
102 calories, **3.5 grams carbohydrates**, 2.5 grams of protein, 10 grams of fat

# Fingerfoods and Appetizers

## Including

*Alcapurrias, Pastelillos, Frituras, Piononos,*
*Empañadas, Pinchos, Surullas, Pasteles and Pastelon*

## Appetizers and Finger Foods

I still remember my first visit to Puerto Rico. A photographer I had worked with before, Buddy Moffet, and I were producing a photo essay book on the island. I had prepared for the trip by memorizing *Fodor's Guide to Puerto Rico*. I made a list of every important historic site between Old San Juan, San German and Ponce. I could have given a tour of El Yunque rainforest, and I knew the location of every national chain hotel on the island.

All of this went out the window once we left the San Juan metro area. First, we became hopelessly lost. Road signs in Puerto Rico being sparse, and maps marginal at best. The further we traveled into the charming countryside, the more obvious it became we would be staying in a guest house, *parador*, not a four or five star hotel.

The hospitality and cleanliness of the *paradors* (Guest House) pleasantly surprised us, but what made the trip so memorable was the local food. Finger foods were sold at local beach hut restaurants and *kioskos* (roadside stands) all over the island. The road to El Yunque, the Caribbean National Forest has some particularly good *kioskos*. Each parador had its own kitchen or restaurant, serving up incredibly delicious local fare. This is when I began collecting Puerto Rican recipes.

Many of the following dishes come from that initial road trip Buddy and I took. Traditionally, Puerto Rican finger food is fried, a cooking technique borrowed from African slaves. Today Puerto Rico has some of the most advanced cardiac care units in the U.S., undoubtedly from the high consumption of saturated fats. Because of this, I have included more heart-healthy cooking instructions along with each recipe. Also, olive oil has been substituted for animal and saturated fats.

## Alcapurrias
## (Dumplings)

**Alcapurrias** are like stuffed dumplings, except the dough is made from green bananas and *yautía* (taro root) instead of flour. *Yuca* (cassava) may be substituted from the green bananas and *yautía*. Fillings vary from beef, chicken, and shellfish, which I am partial too. *Alcapurrias* may seem like a lot of work, but they are just so wonderful, it really is worth the effort. Wrap in aluminum foil, double bag in a plastic ziplock and freeze for up to three months.

# Basic Alcapurria Dough (Dumplings)

This is the first recipe Anna and I made together. While we grated the vegetables and our backs were turned, Tasuki, my daughter Roxanne's cat, ventured from his lair. Much to his consternation, his brand-new scratching post, the one he'd barely been able to try out, was in a playpen with a baby of all things. This was just too much, he thought. We heard Natalie giggle. Anna and I glanced at the playpen. My hands let go of a green banana. Tasuki had jumped in the playpen with Natalie. Go to *Basic Recipe for Stuffed Plantains* to find out what happened next.

| | |
|---|---|
| 1 quart water | 2 pounds of *yautía* (taro root) |
| 2 teaspoons of pulverized rock salt | 1 tablespoon achiote olive oil (annatto |
| 5 green bananas | colored, see Basic Sauces, Marinades, |
| 1 teaspoon vinegar | etc. chapter) |

1.  Fill a large bowl with 1 quart water and add salt.

2.  Peel bananas and taro root. Place into salt water. Allow to sit for 15 minutes.

3.  Grate bananas and taro with the fine side of a hand grater. Or, cut vegetables into small pieces and process in food processor until smooth.

4.  Mix banana/taro mixture with annatto-colored olive oil and vinegar. Transfer to glass bowl and cover with plastic wrap.

5.  Refrigerate overnight or at least three hours.

**Yield: enough for 16 *alcapurrias***

# Basic Yuca *Alcapurria* Dough

You can purchase cassava in the freezer section of Latino groceries. Thankfully, most times it comes peeled. This is one recipe where I recommend the food processor over hand grating.

**1/2 cup plain white rice**
**2 pounds *yuca* (cassava root)**
**2 teaspoons pulverized rock salt**

**1 tablespoon annatto-colored olive oil**
**1 egg, beaten**

1. Place rice in small bowl and cover with water and the two teaspoons salt. Soak for one hour. Drain.

2. To peel cassava root, slice off ends and cut the cassava in two. Use a paring knife and make four vertical incisions on the dark bark. Carefully peel. The flesh should be completely white, otherwise it is no good.

3. Grate the cassava by hand or in a food processor, until smooth. Add rice and puree.

4. Transfer grated cassava/rice mixture into a clean cheesecloth, and twist until all liquid has been removed.

5. Place cassava/rice into a large bowl. Add salt, olive oil and egg. Use your hands to knead into a dough.

6. Refrigerate for at least three hours.

## BAKING INSTRUCTIONS

1. Preheat oven to 375°F. Place a sheet of baking parchment on a sheet pan. Using an ice-cream scoop, place balls of dough, two inches apart, on the parchment.

2. Pressing down with the back of a teaspoon, make a ½-inch deep indention in each *alcapurria*.

3. Fill with 1 tablespoon of filling.

4. Press filling down with the back of a teaspoon and pinch the dough firmly shut over the filling.

5. Cover *alcapurrias* with aluminum foil and bake in preheated oven for 12 minutes. Remove foil, bake additional 12 to 15 minutes until *alcapurrias* are golden brown. Allow to cool for 5 minutes before removing from parchment paper.

## FRYING INSTRUCTIONS

For purists. Try and use olive oil, it's more heart-healthy. Also a good quality deep-fryer will allow you to quickly fry *alcapurrias*. The less time spent in the fryer, the less oil will be absorbed. The key is to purchase a cooking thermometer and heat the oil hot enough so the *alcapurrias* will cook quickly.

1.  Heat 2 cups of olive oil to 375°F.
2.  Cut off a large sheet of aluminum foil and baste lightly with olive oil. Place a scoop of the *alcapurria* dough on the foil. Depress center of dough with back of teaspoon and add a generous tablespoon of filling.
3.  Press filling down with back of teaspoon, and pinch the dough firmly shut over the filling.
4.  Using a spoon, gently glide the dough into the hot oil, being careful of splatters. Fry until golden. Drain on white paper towels.

**Yield: enough for 8 to 10 *alcapurrias***

# Beef Filling for *Alcapurrias*

This reminds me of beef turnovers (called patés) available at roadside stands in the U.S. Virgin Islands. Tantalizing flavor combination between the spices, olives and raisins.

**¼ cup olive oil**

**3 garlic cloves, peeled and minced**

**¼ cup minced onion**

**2 teaspoons fresh chopped oregano**

**1 pound extra-lean ground beef**

**1 small habanero or other hot chili pepper, seeded and minced**

**¼ cup chopped green bell pepper**

**3 tablespoons tomato paste**

**2 tablespoons apple-cider vinegar**

**¼ cup raisins**

**10 pimento-stuffed green olives, chopped**

**2 tablespoons capers**

**½ teaspoon pulverized rock salt**

1.  Heat olive oil over medium heat in a large skillet. Add garlic, onion, oregano, ground beef and habanero pepper. Stirring continuously, brown beef on all sides.
2.  Reduce heat and add green bell pepper, tomato paste, vinegar, raisins, olives, capers, and salt. Sauté for 8 minutes. Remove from heat and cool.

3. Fill *alcapurrias* with one generous tablespoon of filling.

**Yield: enough for 8 *alcapurrias***

## Chicken and Coconut Milk Filling for *Alcapurrias*

Chicken thighs will produce a moister filling.

¼ cup olive oil

3 garlic cloves, peeled and minced

¼ cup minced yellow onion

½ small fiery chili pepper such as
Serrano or Habanero, seeded and minced

1 teaspoon minced fresh ginger

1 pound boneless chicken breast or
thighs, skin removed and chopped

2 teaspoons fresh chopped cilantro

1 tablespoon fresh lime juice

½ teaspoon pulverized rock salt

½ cup unsweetened coconut milk
(canned is fine)

¼ cup minced red bell pepper

¼ cup minced green bell pepper

1. Heat olive oil in large skillet on low to medium heat. Add garlic, onion, chili pepper and fresh ginger. Sauté for 1 minute.
2. Add chicken and brown on all sides. Fold in cilantro, then lime juice, salt and coconut milk. Simmer 15 minutes, stirring constantly.
3. Add red and green bell peppers, continuing to cook over medium heat for 5 minutes. Chicken should be cooked through.
4. Remove from heat and allow to cool.
5. Fill *alcapurrias* with one generous tablespoon of filling.

**Yield: enough for 8 *alcapurrias***

## Pork Filling for *Alcapurrias*

½ pound ground pork meat

¼ cup minced cooking ham

2 tablespoons minced salt pork

¼ cup olive oil

2 tablespoons annatto-colored olive oil

1 tablespoon freshly chopped cilantro

4 large pimento-stuffed olives, chopped

3 green onions (scallion), chopped

2 tablespoons *recaíto* (see Basic
Sauces, Marinades, etc. chapter)

1 teaspoon freshly chopped oregano,
or ½ teaspoon dried

4 garlic cloves, peeled and minced

1 tablespoon capers

¼ cup chopped red bell pepper

¼ cup chopped green bell pepper

¼ cup fresh lime juice

¼ cup dry sherry

1. Brown the ground pork in a large skillet, then drain excess fat. Add minced cooking ham, salt pork, olive oil and annatto-colored oil and sauté over medium heat for 1 minute.

2. Add red bell pepper, green bell pepper, green onions, *recaíto*, cilantro, and oregano. Cook for 3 to 4 minutes until vegetables are just soft.

3. Fold in olives, capers, lime juice and sherry. Reduce heat and simmer for 5 minutes. Remove from heat.

4. Use 1 tablespoon of filling for each *alcapurria*.

**Yield: enough for 15 *alcapurrias***

## Saffron Lobster Filling for *Alcapurrias*

Shrimp or crabmeat make a lovely substitute for the lobster.

4 garlic cloves

¼ cup chopped green onions (scallion)

1 teaspoon fresh ginger

½ teaspoon saffron threads

½ teaspoon black peppercorns

1 teaspoon pulverized rock salt

1 teaspoon paprika

¼ cup capers

1 tablespoon fresh chopped cilantro or *culantro*

½ cup olive oil

1 teaspoon annatto-colored olive oil

¼ cup dry Sherry

½ cup chopped ripe tomato

½ cup chopped red bell pepper

½ cup chopped green bell pepper

1. Grind the garlic cloves, green onion and ginger in a mortar and pestle until a smooth paste forms. Add saffron, peppercorns, rock salt, and paprika. Still pounding into a paste, add cilantro.

2. Stir in olive oil, annatto-colored olive oil and Sherry.

3. Transfer to a skillet; sauté over medium heat for 3 minutes. Add tomato, red and green bell pepper and cook for another 5 minutes. Fold in capers and remove from heat, allowing to cool.

4. Fill *alcapurrias* with 1 generous tablespoon.

**Yield: enough for 8 *alcapurrias***

## Pastelillos (Meat Turnovers)

*Pastelillos* are small, flaky turnovers made from a flour dough, filled with seasoned ground beef, chicken, pork, seafood, cheese or guava paste. I love these. No wonder I had to spend two hours a day at the gym while working on this book. Baking, instead of frying (both techniques explained) helps with the waistline issue a bit.

Because they are usually fried, *pastelillos* come under the category of *frituras* (*frita* means fried). The term *fritura* includes all fried finger foods. *Frituras* are to Puerto Rico what the paté is to the Virgin Island West Indian, the egg roll to the Chinese, the taco to the Mexican and the calzone to the Italian.

Not to be confused with *pasteles* (made from a root vegetable dough, usually filled with pork, wrapped in banana leaves and boiled).

## Basic *Pastelillo* Dough (Flaky Turnover)

This is the shortening version, light and flaky. Melts in your mouth. The healthier, olive oil version follows.

3¼ cups, plus 3 tablespoons
of all-purpose flour
1 tablespoon salt
1 teaspoon baking powder
3 tablespoons, plus 2 teaspoon
   chilled vegetable shortening

1 egg, beaten
¾ cup cold water
   small amount of olive oil or any
   other vegetable (1 teaspoon is
   sufficient)
2 cups olive oil for frying

1. Sift flour, salt and baking powder into a large bowl. Using a fork or pastry cutter, cut shortening into flour. Mixture will be crumbly.

2. Whisk together egg and water in another small bowl.

3. Make a well in the center of the flour and add liquid. Stir at first with a fork, then grease your hands with oil, using your hands and fingers, knead dough until it forms a ball.

4. Transfer dough to floured cutting board, kneading for additional 5 to 7 minutes. Ball will be firm and smooth.

5. Divide dough into 12 pieces. Roll each piece individually with a rolling

pin until the size of a small plate. For *pastelillos* to serve with drinks as appetizers, cut the pastry circles in 2 ½ inch diameter.

6. Add a generous 1 ½ to 2 tablespoons of stuffing to center; fold in half. Secure edges by pressing with a fork dampened with water.

7. Heat the 2 cups of olive oil to 375°. Using a spatula, pick up each *pastelillo* and gently slide into oil, mindful of splatters. Fry until golden; draining on white paper towels.

**Yield: 12 *pastelillos*, or 24 of the appetizer size**

# Basic *Pastelillo* Dough II

This recipe uses olive oil instead of shortening, and is baked instead of fried. It's quite good, and much better for your arteries.

1 cup hot water (130°)          1 teaspoon annatto-colored olive oil
1 tablespoon sugar              3 cups flour
¼ ounce active yeast            1 teaspoon salt
2/3 cup olive oil

1. Mix water, sugar and yeast in a small bowl and let stand for 5 minutes. Yeast will then be activated and mixture should look bubbly. Gently stir in olive oil and set aside.

2. Combine flour and salt in a large bowl. Make a well in center and add yeast mixture. Using a wooden spoon combine until a dough forms, scraping sides of bowl often. Knead dough with hands until a ball forms.

3. Transfer dough to a cutting board and knead additional 5 minutes.

4. Place dough into a bowl greased with vegetable oil; cover with a dish towel, place in a warm place and allow dough to rise for 1 hour.

5. Punch down dough; transfer to cutting board and knead for 3 to 4 minutes. Divide dough in half with a knife. Roll into a 2-inch cylinder. Cut into six pieces.

6. Place all 12 pieces onto a lightly floured board, cover with a damp dish towel, and allow to rise 45 minutes.

7. Place each piece on a lightly floured surface or cutting board. Roll out each

piece with a rolling pin until 7 inches in diameter. For appetizer-size *pastelillos*, cut in 2 ½-inch circles.

8. Place 1 ½ to 2 tablespoons of filling in the center of each. Fold in two and fasten edges by pressing down with a fork.

9. Use a spatula to transfer the turnover to a non-stick baking sheet. Non-stick cookie sheets will do fine. Leave ½ inch between turnovers.

10. Baste with olive oil/egg wash. Recipe follows.

**Yield: 12 *pastelillos*, or 24 of the appetizers**

---

### Olive Oil Cayenne Egg Wash

Brush outside of pastelillos before baking.
**2 tablespoons olive oil**
**¼ teaspoon salt**
**1 egg**
**½ cup half-and-half cream**
**½ teaspoon cayenne, more or less to taste**

Place all ingredients in blender and combine at high speed. Or place all ingredients in a small bowl and whisk vigorously by hand.

---

# Beef and Olive Filling for *Pastelillos*

This might be cheating, but some days you just don't have time to make *pastelillo* dough from scratch. The Goya company makes these packages of frozen dough called *Dicscos*. They're quite good. I haven't been to the U.S. mainland in a while, but I understand you can find them in the freezer section of Latin groceries.

**1 tablespoon olive oil**

**2 tablespoons *sofrito* (see index)**

**3 cloves garlic, peeled and minced**

**1 teaspoon fresh chopped oregano**

**1 small fiery chili pepper, such as Habanero or Serrano, seeded and minced**

**1¼ pounds extra-lean ground beef**

**½ cup dry Sherry**

**½ cup fresh chopped tomatoes**

**1 tablespoons fresh chopped cilantro or *culantro***

**4 green onions (scallions), chopped**

**6 large pimento-stuffed olives, chopepd**

1. Heat oil in a skillet over medium heat. Add oil, *sofrito*, garlic, oregano, chili pepper and green onions. Sauté for 2 minutes until vegetables are just soft.

2. Add ground beef and brown. Add Sherry, tomato, cilantro and olives. Remove from heat. Season to taste with salt and pepper.

3. Use 1½ to 2 tablespoons filling for each *pastelillo*. Follow instructions in basic *pastelillo* dough for rolling out dough, sealing turnover, baking or frying.

**Yield: enough for 12 *pastelillos*, or 24 appetizers**

## Tangy Pork Filling for *Pastelillos*

Don't be afraid of pork. These days pork is bred to be extra lean, making it a nice change from chicken or red meat. Just be sure to cook it properly.

| | |
|---|---|
| 3 tablespoons olive oil | 1 tablespoon apple cider vinegar |
| ¼ cup minced onion | 2 tablespoons raisins, cut up |
| 1 garlic clove, crushed | 1 tablespoon capers |
| ½ pound lean ground pork | 8 pimento-stuffed olives, diced |
| 1 ounce ham, ground | 1 strip of cooked bacon, crumbled |
| 1 cup *sofrito* (see index) | salt and pepper to taste |

1. Heat the olive oil in heavy skillet over medium heat. Sauté onion and garlic until clear. Add pork and ham, cooking for 5 minutes, browning lightly on all sides until the pork meat is no longer pink.

2. Stir in *sofrito*, and vinegar. Reduce heat and simmer for 30 minutes. Add raisins, capers, olives and bacon, cooking for additional minute. Remove from heat and cool.

3. Use 1½ to 2 tablespoons filling for each *pastelillo*. Follow instructions in basic *pastelillo* dough for sealing turnover, baking or frying.

**Yield: enough for 12 *pastelillos*, or 24 appetizers**

## Chicken and Roasted Red Pepper Filling for *Pastelillos*

Chicken *pastelillos* freeze beautifully. Make a double batch and freeze to have on hand for guests who drop by unexpectedly for a drink.

¼ cup olive oil

3 tablespoons minced onion

3 garlic cloves, minced

¼ cup dry Sherry

1 can (2 ¾ ounces) *Paté de foie gras*

1½ pounds boneless, skinless, diced

1 large red bell pepper, roasted, seeds removed, skinned and diced

1/3 cup unseasoned breadcrumbs

1 teaspoon salt

1 teaspoon freshly cracked black pepper

½ cup fresh, diced mushrooms chicken breast

1 tablespoon fresh chopped *culantro*

1 egg, beaten

1. Heat oil in large deep skillet. Sauté onion, garlic, and mushrooms for 2 minutes, until just barely soft. Stir in Sherry and remove from heat.

2. Combine *Paté*, egg, breadcrumbs, salt, pepper, chicken and *culantro* in a large bowl until smooth.

3. Transfer to onion/mushroom mix and return heat to medium. Combine thoroughly and fold in roasted pepper. Cook for 2 minutes. Remove from heat and allow to cool before filling pastries.

4. Use 1½ to 2 tablespoons filling for each *pastelillo*. Follow instructions in basic *pastelillo* dough for sealing turnover, baking or frying.

Yield: enough for 12 *pastelillos*, or 24 appetizers

## Saffron Crab Filling for *Pastelillos*

Substitute chopped shrimp or lobster for crab.

2 tablespoons olive oil

1 teaspoon annatto-colored olive oil

¼ cup diced green bell pepper

1 sweet chili pepper, diced and seeded

3 cloves garlic, crushed

½ cup yellow onion, minced

1 pound crab meat, fresh or canned, shredded and cartilage pieces removed

1 teaspoon saffron threads

1 tablespoon chopped canned pimento

1 tablespoon capers

8 pimento-stuffed olives, chopped

1 teaspoon freshly cracked black pepper

1 teaspoon salt

1. In a deep skillet or medium saucepan, heat the olive oil and annatto-colored oil over medium heat. Sauté the green pepper, chili pepper, garlic and onion for 2 minutes until soft. Add saffron, pimento, capers, olives, pepper and salt, cooking additional 5 minutes.

2. Fold in crab, reduce heat and simmer for 10 minutes. Remove from heat and allow to cool before filling *pastelillos*.

3. Use 1 ½ to 2 tablespoons filling for each *pastelillo*. Follow instructions in basic *pastelillo* dough for sealing turnover, baking or frying.

**Yield: enough for 12 *pastelillos*, or 24 appetizers**

## Lobster and Wine Filling for *Pastelillos*

I like to add a splash of hot sauce to this quick, but impressive recipe.

| | |
|---|---|
| **1 tablespoon olive oil** | **2 tablespoons dry white wine** |
| **2 tablespoons minced onion** | **1 tablespoon dry Sherry** |
| **1 garlic clove** | **1 tablespoon cracker or breadcrumbs** |
| **2 tablespoons minced, canned pimentos** | **2 cups cooked and diced lobster meat** |
| **1 teaspoon salt** | **½ cup cream or evaporated milk** |
| **1 teaspoon Worcestershire® sauce** | **1 tablespoon freshly, chopped *culantro*** |

1. Heat the olive oil in a large skillet and sauté the onion and garlic for 2 minutes over medium heat until onion is just clear. Add pimentos, salt, Worcestershire®, wine and sherry, cooking for additional minute.

2. Fold in breadcrumbs and lobster. Reduce heat and gradually pour in cream or evaporated milk. Add cilantro and cook for 5 minutes until liquid portion has reduced. Remove from heat and allow to cool before filling *pastelillos*.

3. Use 1 ½ to 2 tablespoons filling for each *pastelillo*. Follow instructions in basic *pastelillo* dough for sealing turnover, baking or frying.

**Yield: enough for 12 *pastelillos*, or 24 appetizers**

### Did You Know?

Puerto Rico's northeast coast has a restored 19th century Spanish colonial light house know as El Faro. Also called **Las Cabezas de San Juan Nature Reserve.** Here you will find seven eco systems. The view is clear all the way to St. Thomas in the U.S. Virgin Islands. This 300+acre site is enveloped on 3 sides by Atlantic Ocean complete with cliffs, mangroves, lagoons, coral reefs, beaches, offshore cays (tiny islands) and boardwalk trails. Reservations required. Contact: 787-722-5882.

# Machengo Cheese and Sausage Filling for *Pastelillos*

True *Machengo* cheese is produced in La Mancha in central Spain. Made from 100% sheeps milk because the terrain in Spain is rocky, dry and unfriendly to cows, but perfect for goats and sheep. Wild herbs give this crumbly and somewhat dry cheese a zesty and exuberant taste. You can recognize *Machengo* by the zigzag pattern on the rind. The interior is a creamy white. Divine served with a dry white wine.

If you can't find *Machengo* cheese, check gourmet or Latin groceries. Sources at the back of this book list vendors. You can substitute aged, sharp white cheddar and parmesan (50/50) for *Machengo*.

¼ cup olive oil

¼ cup minced onion

4 garlic cloves, crushed

2 *aji-dulce* or sweet chili peppers, seeded and chopped

½ cup minced green bell pepper

¼ cup dry Sherry

14 ounces *Machengo* cheese, crumbled

¼ cup fresh chopped parsley

4 *chorizo*, Spanish-style sausages, diced

10 pimento-stuffed olives, chopped

Salt

Freshly cracked black pepper

1. Heat the olive oil in a large skillet over medium heat. Sauté onion, garlic, sweet chili peppers and green bell pepper for 2 minutes until onion is just clear. Add Sherry and cook for another minute.

2. Fold in *Machengo* cheese, parsley, sausage and stuffed olives. Season to taste with salt and pepper. Stir and cook for additional 2 to 3 minutes until cheese is completely melted. Remove from heat and allow to cool before filling *pastelillos*.

3. Use 1½ to 2 tablespoons filling for each *pastelillo*. Follow instructions in basic *pastelillo* dough for sealing and frying.

**Yield: enough for 12 *pastelillos*, or 24 appetizers**

## Chorizo

The Spanish introduced *chorizo* sausage to Puerto Rico. Compliments paella, rice dishes and pasteles and such.

*To make your own*, combine ½ pound ground pork, 1 tablespoon lemon juice, 1 tablespoon wine vinegar, 1 tablespoon chopped culantro or cilantro, 1 ½ tablespoons chili powder, ½ teaspoon dried oregano, ½ teaspoon ground cumin, ¾ teaspoon salt, and a splash of hot chili pepper sauce. Toss with a fork, combining well, refrigerate overnight. Sauté the next day, until no pink remains in the pork.

## Gallician Filling for *Pastelillos*

**1 cup shredded cheddar cheese**                    **½ teaspoon cracked black pepper**

1. Toss cheddar cheese with black pepper in a small bowl.
2. Use 2 tablespoons filling for each *pastelillo*. Follow instructions in basic *pastelillo* dough for sealing and frying.

**Yield: enough for 12 *pastelillos***

## Frituras (Fritters)

The difference between *frituras* and *pastelillos* is that *frituras* have small bits of meat, chicken, vegetables or fruits incorporated into the batter, instead of filled as a turnover. They melt in your mouth, and are a lot quicker to make them *pastelillos* or *alcapurrias*.

Each island in the Caribbean has its own version of *frituras*. The U.S. and British Virgin Islands have conch and coconut fritters; Jamaica has 'stamp and go'; Trinidad has 'acra'; and the French West Indies have 'acrat'. We owe are thanks to the African slaves for these fried delicacies. Serve fritters as appetizers, snacks, or even scrumptious breakfast fare. Also called *buñueolos* or *buñuelitos*.

## Cheese Fritters

*Buñuelitos de Queso*

Warning! Highly addictive. Serving with cold beer will worsen situation.

**3 large eggs, lightly beaten**                    **1 teaspoon salt**
**½ cup evaporated milk**                    **1 tablespoon sugar**

½ cup water
2 ½ cups flour
2 ½ teaspoons baking powder
½ teaspoon cayenne pepper

1 cup grated crumbly white cheese, such as *Machengo* or mild white cheddar
vegetable oil for frying

1. Stir eggs, evaporated milk and water together in large bowl.

2. Sift flour, baking powder, salt and sugar onto sheet of waxed paper or another bowl. Stir into egg mixture gradually until combined.

3. Fold in cheese and cayenne pepper.

4. Heat oil in deep fryer or skillet to 375°. Drop batter by spoonfuls, frying until golden.

5. Remove with slotted spoon and drain on white paper towels.

Yield: about 36

# Banana Fritters

*Jíbaritos*

¼ cup rum
3 tablespoons lime juice
1 teaspoon vanilla
2 tablespoons sugar
18 ripe *guineitos* (finger bananas)
1 cup flour
½ cup sugar

¾ teaspoon salt
¾ teaspoon baking powder
¼ teaspoon ground cinnamon
1/8 teaspoon ground nutmeg
1 cup water
½ teaspoon ground cinnamon

Serve with a scoop of vanilla ice cream and rum sauce. Nice for breakfast, minus the rum sauce and ice cream. Dust lightly with cinnamon sugar instead.

1. Combine rum, sugar, vanilla and lime juice in a cup. Set aside. Peel bananas and cut in half length-wise. Cut each half into 2 to 3 pieces, depending on size of banana. Place in flat, glass baking dish; pour rum mixture over top. Allow to sit for 1 hour.

2. Sift flour, sugar, salt, baking powder, nutmeg, cinnamon and baking powder into medium bowl. Gradually whisk in water until a smooth batter is formed.

3. In a deep fryer or skillet, heat vegetable oil to 375°. Dip banana slices in batter and gently slide into hot oil. Fry until golden. Remove with tongs, and drain on white paper towels.

4. To make cinnamon sugar: add ½ teaspoon ground cinnamon to ½ cup granulated white sugar; stir well.

**Yield: 6 servings**

# Rum Sauce for Fritters

*Salsa de Ron*

| | |
|---|---|
| **2/3 cup water** | **½ teaspoon ground cloves** |
| **1 cup sugar** | **½ cup dark rum** |
| **½ teaspoon ground cinnamon** | |

Boil the water with the sugar, cinnamon and cloves for 10 minutes. Cool to room temperature and stir in rum. Top each fritter with vanilla ice cream. Drizzle warm rum sauce over top.

**Yield: 1 ½ cups**

# Pumpkin Fritters

*Frituras de Calabeza*

Serve either as a sweet treat, or with a good hot sauce or mustard alongside fish or meat dishes. You can use pumpkin or winter squash interchangeably in this recipe.

| | |
|---|---|
| **1 cup all-purpose flour** | **¼ teaspoon ground nutmeg** |
| **2 teaspoons baking powder** | **½ teaspoon salt** |
| **1 tablespoon sugar** | **1 teaspoon fresh grated ginger,** |
| **¼ teaspoon ground cinnamon** | **or 1 teaspoon ground ginger** |
| **1 cup whole milk** | **3 cups mashed cooked pumpkin** |
| **vegetable oil for frying** | |

1. Sift flour and baking powder into large bowl. Stir in sugar, cinnamon, nutmeg, salt and ginger.

2. Fold in pumpkin. Stir in whole milk. You should have a batter of medium consistency.

3. Heat oil in deep fryer to 375°. Drop batter by spoonfuls into hot oil. Watch for splatters. Fry until golden. Remove with slotted spoon. Drain on white paper towels.

**Yield: 18 *frituras***

# Tanier Fritters

*Frituras de Yautía*

Man, oh man. Having touched little fried food over the past decade, I had no idea how addicting it could be. Be sure your cooking oil is at the proper high temperature. Too cool, and food will absorb twice as much oil.

| | |
|---|---|
| 2 pounds white *yautía*, washed and peeled | 1 tablespoon sugar |
| 1 large egg, lightly beaten | ¼ cup flour |
| 1 teaspoon salt | ½ teaspoon baking powder |
| 1 tablespoon milk | vegetable oil or shortening for frying |

1. Rinse *yautías* under cool water and run through a food processor until a smooth paste forms.
2. Stir in egg, salt and milk.
3. Combine sugar, flour and baking powder in small bowl. Fold into batter.
4. Heat oil to 375º in deep skillet or fryer. Drop by spoonfuls into hot oil, frying 2 minutes on each side until golden.
5. Drain on white paper towels.

# Breadfruit Fritters

*Frituras de Panapén*

| | |
|---|---|
| 1 medium breadfruit, about 3½ pounds, not too ripe | 2 large eggs, beaten |
| | 1 teaspoon salt |
| 1 tablespoon salt | 1 teaspoon freshly cracked black pepper |
| 2 tablespoons butter | vegetable oil for frying |

1. Slice off top and bottom of breadfruit.
2. Cut 6 vertical strips top to bottom using the sharp tip of knife.
3. Cut in quarters and slice off spongy core. Cut in 2 inch cubes.
4. Place in deep pot and cover with water. Stir in 1 tablespoon salt.
5. Boil for 30 minutes until soft. Drain and puree in food processor.
6. Pour oil into bottom of a deep fryer or deep kettle. Heat to 350º.

7. Meanwhile, stir in butter to warm breadfruit. Add egg, salt and pepper, combining well.

8. Carefully drop batter by spoonfuls into hot oil. Fry until golden.

9. Drain on white paper towels.

**Yield: about 12, 2-inch fritters**

---

### Plantains

Plantains belong to the banana family, but contain significantly more starch and cannot be eaten uncooked.

**Purchasing:** The color of the plantain selected depends upon how it is to be cooked. Plantains range in color from bright green (unripe) to black (very ripe). The fruit turns from green, to yellow, to yellow flecked with black, to half black to all black. Discard any that show signs of mold.

**Storing:** Maintain at room temperature. Once degree of ripeness is obtained for recipe, refrigerate.

**Peeling:** First, I always give plantains a bath in cold soapy water, submerging for 10 minutes to loosen dirt and dust from the grocery. Rinse with clear, cool water. Plantains have a thicker skin than bananas and are definitely not as easy to peel. Cut off plantain tips, slice in thirds, cross-wise, then make three or four vertical slits in peel. Fill a large bowl with warm water and submerge fruit for ten minutes. Peel should come off readily.

**Cooking:** Use green plantains like you would potatoes, adding to pot roast, stews and soups.

---

## Green Plantain Fritters

*Aranitas de Platano*

3 medium green plantains, peeled

1 teaspoon salt

1 teaspoon freshly grated black peppercorns

1 tablespoon annatto-colored olive oil

5 tablespoons olive oil

3 garlic cloves, crushed

1. Coarsely grate plantains into a bowl. Stir in salt and pepper. Set aside.

2. Heat the olive oils in a large skillet. Sauté the garlic over low heat for 1 minute.

3. Scoop up ½ cup of the grated plantain in your hands and form into a patty.

4. Fry the patties in hot oil until golden, turning once. Drain on white paper towels. Serve hot as a finger food or side dish.

**Yield: 8 to 10 patties**

# Eggplant Fritters
*Frituras de Berenjena*

Delicious with minced fresh or dried rosemary added to batter.

**2 pounds eggplant, peeled and cut into ¼-inch thick slices**

**1 teaspoon salt**

**1 ¼ cups flour**

**1 ¼ cups water**

**1 teaspoon salt**

**2 tablespoons annatto oil (see index)**

**½ teaspoon freshly cracked black pepper**

**¼ teaspoon nutmeg**

**vegetable oil or shortening for frying**

1. Place eggplant slices in flat casserole dish and cover with water and 1 teaspoon of the salt. Soak for 20 minutes. Then rinse and drain on white paper towels.

2. Blend flour, water, remaining 1 teaspoon of salt and annatto oil in a medium bowl, stirring into a smooth batter. Batter should be thick enough to coat eggplant slices. If not, add flour by tablespoonfuls until desired consistency is reach. Likewise if too thick, add water by teaspoonful until thinned out. Allow to sit for 20 minutes.

3. Heat one inch of oil or shortening in a deep skillet over moderate heat until 350° is reached.

4. Dip eggplant slices in batter and place in hot oil. Only fry one layer at a time of eggplant slices. Do not stack!

5. Fry 1 ½ minutes on each side or until golden. Remove from hot oil and drain on white paper towels. Serve warm. Sprinkle with black pepper and nutmeg.

**Yield: 8 servings**

# Sweet Rice Fritters

*Frituras de Arroz*

Serve at breakfast with hot, strong coffee or with afternoon tea.

| | |
|---|---|
| 1 cup cooked rice | 1 teaspoon baking powder |
| 2 medium eggs, lightly beaten | ½ teaspoon grated orange rind |
| ½ teaspoon salt | ¼ cup sweetened condensed milk |
| 1 tablespoon evaporated milk | ¼ cup milk |
| 1 tablespoon sugar | ½ teaspoon grated ginger |
| ¾ cup flour | ½ teaspoon grated cinnamon |
| vegetable oil or shortening for frying | |

1. Combine rice and eggs in medium bowl.
2. In small bowl, stir together salt, evaporated milk and sugar. Fold in flour and baking powder.
3. Fold in flour mixture into rice mixture. Add orange rind, sweetened condensed milk, milk, cinnamon and ginger, combining well.
4. Heat oil to 375° in a deep fryer or skillet. Drop by spoonfuls into hot oil. Fry two minutes on each side until golden.
5. Remove from oil with slotted spoon and drain on white paper towels. Serve warm.

**Yield: about 24, 1 ½ inch fritters**

# Cheese-Filled Rice Fritters

*Almojábanas*

Substitute *Machengo*, white cheddar or provolone for the Puerto Rican white cheese. The flavor will vary with the type of cheese used.

| | |
|---|---|
| ½ cup all-purpose flour | ½ cup, plus 2 tablespoons milk |
| 1 cup rice flour | 2 tablespoons melted butter |
| 1 teaspoon salt | 1 teaspoon fresh ground black peppercorns |
| 2 teaspoons baking powder | ½ pound Puerto Rican white cheese, grated |
| 3 eggs | vegetable oil for frying |

1. Sift the flours, salt and baking powder into a large bowl. Add milk, beat in eggs 1 at a time. Drizzle in melted butter. Add black pepper and cheese, combining well. Allow to sit at room temperature for 1 hour.

2. Heat oil to 375º in a deep fryer or skillet. Drop by spoonfuls and fry until golden. Drain on white paper towels. Serve as an appetizer with cold beer or alongside soups and main entrees.

**Yield: 36 to 40 fritters**

# Cornmeal and Cheese Fritters
*Almojábanas de Harina de Maiz y Queso*

My sister, Tanya and I sampled these at the Villa Cofresí Hotel in Ríncon, on the west coast of the island, just above Mayaguez. Ríncon is very popular with the surfing crowd.

| | |
|---|---|
| **1 ½ cups fine ground yellow cornmeal** | **3 medium eggs, lightly beaten** |
| **1 cup water** | **½ cup *Machengo* (sheep cheese from** |
| **¼ cup milk** | **Spain) or mild cheddar** |
| **3 tablespoons butter** | **1 jalapeño pepper, minced** |
| **1 teaspoon salt** | **¼ teaspoon ground nutmeg** |
| **vegetable oil for frying** | **¼ teaspoon ground cayenne pepper** |

1. Boil the yellow cornmeal in the 1 cup water for 1 minute. Remove from heat.

2. Stir in milk, butter and salt. Whisk in eggs, combining well.

3. Fold in cheese, jalapeño, nutmeg and cayenne.

4. Heat 1-inch of oil to 375°. Drop batter by spoonfuls into hot oil. Fry on each side for two minutes until golden.

5. Remove with slotted spoon and drain on white paper towels.

**Yield: approximately 30, 1 ½ inch fritters**

# Cornmeal Fritters
*Frituras de Maíz*

| | |
|---|---|
| **¾ cup water** | **1 teaspoon baking powder** |
| **1 teaspoon salt** | **2 tablespoons sugar** |
| **1 ½ cups fine ground yellow cornmeal** | **2 tablespoons milk** |

**3 tablespoons butter**                    **2 large eggs, lightly beaten**
**vegetable oil or shortening for frying**

1. Combine water and salt in a deep saucepan and bring to boil over medium heat. Remove from heat.

2. Whisk in cornmeal gradually until blended. Stir in butter and baking powder.

3. Combine sugar, milk and eggs in a small bowl. Stir into cornmeal mix slowly.

4. Heat two inches of oil in deep kettle or fryer to 350° over medium-high heat.

5. Drop by tablespoonfuls into hot oil. Do not overcrowd kettle. Fry two minutes on each side until golden.

6. Drain on white paper towels. Serve warm.

**Yield: 30, 1 ½ inch fritters**

## Codfish Fritters

*Bacalaitos*

You can find recipes for salt fish all over the Caribbean. Look for it the freezer section of Latin groceries. Some versions come in small wooden boxes or crates. The green onions add a delicate taste.

**½ pound salt codfish**                    **¼ cup chopped red bell pepper**
**2 cups all-purpose flour**                **¼ cup chopped green bell pepper**
**2 teaspoons baking powder**               **1 tablespoon fresh chopped *culantro***
**1 cup water**                             **or cilantro**
**1 tablespoon annatto-colored oil**        **1 teaspoon fresh cracked black pepper**
**¼ cup diced green onions**                **½ teaspoon salt**
**vegetable oil for frying**

1. Soak codfish in bowl of warm water for 2 hours to remove excess salt.

2. Sift flour and baking powder into medium bowl. Add water, annatto oil, stirring until smooth. Fold in onions, peppers, cilantro, pepper and salt.

3. Drain codfish and rinse. Remove any bones and skin. Shred into small pieces. Fold into batter.

4. Heat oil to 375°. Carefully drop batter by tablespoonfuls into hot oil. Fry until golden. Drain on white paper towels. Serve with cocktail sauce, hot mustard or hot pepper sauce. And a cold beer of course!

**Yield: 12 *bacalaitos***

# Shrimp Fritters
*Frituras de Camarones*

This is the Puerto Rican version of shrimp fritters. The addition of *culantro* to the batter distinguishes this recipe from its Virgin Island cousin.

2 cups all-purpose flour

2 teaspoons baking powder

1 cup water

1 tablespoon annatto-colored oil

¼ cup minced yellow onion

½ teaspoon salt

¼ cup chopped green bell pepper

1 tablespoon fresh chopped *culantro* or cilantro

1 cup diced, cooked shrimp

1 teaspoon fresh cracked black pepper

vegetable oil for frying

1. Sift flour and baking powder into medium bowl. Add water, annatto oil, stirring until smooth. Stir in onions, peppers, *culantro*, pepper and salt.

2. Fold shrimp into batter.

3. Heat oil to 375°. Carefully drop batter by tablespoonfuls into hot oil. Fry until golden. Drain on white paper towels. Serve with cocktail sauce, hot mustard or hot pepper sauce. And a cold beer of course!

**Yield: 18, 1 ½ inch fritters**

# Ham and Potato Fritters
*Frituras de Jamón y Papa*

These fritters are quite interesting, more like potato and ham sandwiches, deep fried in an egg batter. Delicious with cold beer. I like to dip them in habañero hot sauce.

2 pounds medium potatoes, peeled and halved.

1 tablespoon salt

¾ pound sliced, boiled ham

5 eggs, separated

vegetable oil or shortening for frying

1 garlic clove, crushed

1 teaspoon sugar

½ teaspoon salt

½ teaspoon freshly cracked black pepper

½ teaspoon crushed dried oregano

1. Place potatoes in a deep pot or kettle, cover with water and stir in 1 tablespoon salt. Cover and boil over moderate heat for 20 minutes. Potatoes will still be somewhat firm. Drain.

2. Cut cooled potatoes into ¼-inch thick slices.

3. Place a slice of ham between two potato slices and fasten with toothpicks. Set aside.

4. Beat egg whites in medium bowl until stiff peaks form. Fold in egg yolks, garlic, sugar, ½ teaspoon salt, black pepper and dried oregano.

5. Dip ham and potato sandwiches into egg mixture.

6. Heat one inch of oil in a deep skillet to 350°. Carefully lower sandwiches into hot fat, frying 1 to 2 minutes on each side until golden.

7. Remove from oil and drain on white paper towels before serving.

**Yield: about 16 fritters**

---

### Piononos (stuffed plantain rolls)

A popular specialty, *piononos* most likely made their way to Puerto Rico via Argentian and Italy. The origin of the name *piononos* is a mystery. *Pio* means pious and *nono* means ninth in Spanish. Another version has it that Pope Pious the IX was a glutton. He loved cakes with cream inside, thus Vatican cooks named the filled cake after him.

*Piononos* are made from ripe plantains cut lengthwise, filled with meat, seafood or chicken, then rolled into a circle and held together with a toothpick. You can find this delicious fingerfood at food stands along the beach, like at Luquillo or Pinones, just outside San Juan.

---

## Basic Recipe for Stuffed Plantain Rolls

*Piononos*

Tasuki and Natalie saga, continued from *Basic Recipe for Alcapurria Dough*. I nearly had a coronary when I saw the cat in the playpen with the baby. Tasuki can be quite cranky, especially if you touch him in the wrong way or place, he'll sink his teeth into your hand. Anna and I inched toward the playpen. We edged closer. The baby had a fistful of Tasuki's fur. My stomach dropped. A low rumble came from Tasuki's throat…go to the recipe for *Old Ladies' Bellies* to find out what happened next.

**3 large ripe plantains (see index to**                     **3 beaten eggs**

determine ripeness of fruit),
each cut into 4 lengthwise slices

1 teaspoon cayenne pepper
vegetable oil for frying

1. Heat the oil in a heavy frying pan and sauté the plantain until golden, turning once. Remove with tongs and drain on white paper towels.

2. When plantain slices are cool enough to handle, roll into a circle and fasten with a toothpick.

3. Heat oil to 375° in deep fryer. Stir cayenne into beaten egg. Fill the hole in center of ring with stuffing (see following recipes), dip in egg mixture. Fry until golden. Drain on white paper towels.

**Yield: servings6**

# Pork and Beef Filling for *Piononos*

2 tablespoons annatto oil

½ pound lean ground beef

½ pound ground pork

½ cup minced onion

2 garlic cloves, minced

¼ cup minced green bell pepper

½ cup diced ripe tomato

¼ cup diced ham

vegetable oil for frying

1 tablespoon fresh *culantro*

1 teaspoon fresh chopped oregano,
  or ½ teaspoon dried

6 pimento-stuffed olives, chopped

1 tablespoon capers

3 tablespoon raisins, chopped

3 eggs, beaten

1 teaspoon cayenne pepper

1. Heat annatto oil in deep skillet. Brown beef and pork. Drain excess fat. Add onion, garlic, pepper and tomato. Cook for 2 minutes until onion is clear.

2. Stir in ham, *culantro*, oregano, olives, capers and raisins. Cook for additional 5 minutes. Remove from heat.

3. Follow instruction #3 under Basic Recipe for Stuffed Plantain

**Yield: servings6**

# Machengo Cheese Filling for *Piononoss*

8 ounces of *Machengo* cheese cut in 1-inch cubes

1 clove garlic crushed

1 tablespoon fresh chopped *culantro* or cilantro

1. Toss the *Machengo* cheese, garlic and *culantro* in a small bowl.
2. Follow instruction #3 under Basic Recipe for Stuffed Plantain.

**Yield: servings6**

## Chicken Filling for Piononos

Freeze extra *sofrito* (see index) to have on hand when you have extra leftover cooked chicken or turkey meat. *Piononos* are a lovely treat when made with chicken. Quick and easy.

**1 cup *sofrito***

**1 ½ pounds cooked and diced chicken breast**

**8 pimento-stuffed olives, chopped**

**2 tablespoons capers**

1. Heat the sofrito in a deep skillet over medium heat. Add chicken, olives and capers. Cook for 10 to 15 minutes, until liquid is reduced by half. Chicken mixture should be dry enough to stuff plantain rings without falling out.
2. Follow instruction #3 under Basic Recipe for Stuffed Plantain.

**Yield: 6 to 8 servings**

## Shrimp Filling for *Piononos*

A visit to Puerto Rico is not complete without stopping at Piñones, just minutes outside of Isla Verde. The beach is long, white and sandy. Dozens of outdoor eating restaurants, painted in tropical colors rim the aqua blue sea. Piñones Forest is also home to the island's largest mangrove forest.

Substitute lobster or crab for the shrimp if desired.

**3 tablespoons annatto-colored olive oil**

**¼ cup minced green onion**

**½ small chili pepper, Serrano or Habanero**

**¼ cup minced red bell pepper**

**¼ cup *adobo* (see index)**

**1 tablespoon capers**

**1 pound cooked, shelled and deveined shrimp**

**1 teaspoon paprika**

**1 teaspoon saffron threads**

**¼ cup dry Sherry**

1. Heat the olive oil in a deep skillet over medium heat. Sauté the onion, chili pepper, red bell pepper, and *adobo* for 2 minutes until vegetables are soft.

2. Dice the shrimp and add to skillet. Stir in paprika, saffron, Sherry and capers. Reduce heat and simmer for 10 minutes.

3. Follow instruction #3 under Basic Recipe for Stuffed Plantain.

**Yield: 6 to 8 servings**

## Pinchos (Shish-kebabs)

*Pincho* translates to 'little thorn' or 'pointed stick.' *Pinchos* are the Puerto Rican equivalent of shish kebabs. Cooked on an outdoor broiler, you can find these at food shacks along the beach and roadside stands.

# Pineapple-Rum Marinated Beef *Pinchos*

For peak flavor, marinate the meat overnight in the refrigerator.

| | |
|---|---|
| ¼ **cup fresh pineapple juice** | 1 **tablespoon brown sugar** |
| ¼ **cup apple cider vinegar** | 4 **cloves garlic, crushed** |
| ¼ **cup Spanish dark rum** | 1 **teaspoon salt** |
| 1 **tablespoon molasses** | 1 **teaspoon cracked black pepper** |
| 1 **teaspoon fresh chopped oregano** | 2 **pounds beef filet, cut in 1-inch cubes** |

1. Combine pineapple juice, vinegar, rum, molasses, oregano, brown sugar, garlic, salt and pepper in large bowl. Add beef, toss gently. Cover and refrigerate at least 3 hours. Drain and reserve marinade.

2. Drop onions in boiling water for 5 minutes. Remove and slide off skins. Set aside.

3. Skewer 4 or 5 cubes of beef on stainless steel or bamboo sticks. Remember to soak bamboo sticks in water for 1 hour prior to using. Wrap ends of bamboo skewer in aluminum foil to prevent charring.

4. Preheat grill or indoor broiler. Baste skewers with marinade. Roast meat 4 inches from heat for ten minutes, turning several times. Baste again with marinade.

**Yield: 4 servings**

## Empañada (Meat Pie)

*Empañadas* are like pot pies. Each island in the Caribbean has its version of the meat pie. I know at Pusser's in Tortola I've had meat pot pies, made with ground meat and a layer of mashed potato. Puerto Rico has many different kinds: the pastry part made from flour, *yuca*, or corn; the filling could be seafood, chicken, beef or pork. Great way to recycle left-overs.

# Basic *Empañada* Crust

I did a good bit of experimenting with pie crusts. Making crust can be a simple procedure, but horror stories exist about dough that turns out hard, over-salted, tasteless, or too flaky. The most debatable ingredient is the fat. All butter crusts taste marvelous, but they're not flaky like shortening crust. Shortening lends excellent texture, but no taste. The following is a successful compromise.

2 ½ cups all-purpose flour,
   plus extra for dusting
½ teaspoon cayenne pepper
8 tablespoons vegetable
   shortening such as Crisco®
6 to 8 tablespoons ice water

1 tablespoons sugar
12 tablespoons unsalted chilled butter,
   cut into small pieces
¼ teaspoon nutmeg
1 teaspoon salt

1. Sift flour, cayenne pepper, nutmeg, salt and sugar into large bowl.

2. Toss in butter and work mixture with your fingers until crumbly. Cut in shortening with a fork or pastry cutter until flour resembles coarse cornmeal.

3. Sprinkle 6 tablespoons of ice water over mixture. Fold into flour with rubber spatula. Add up to 2 tablespoons of ice water if needed. You should have a stiff dough.

4. Wrap in plastic wrap and refrigerate for up to 2 days.

5. Divide dough into 2 balls. Dust cutting board or work surface with flour. Roll out both balls with rolling pin to 1/8-inch thick and 13 inches in diameter. Preheat oven to 450°.

6. Drape one dough circle over rolling pin and slide into 9-inch wide, 1 ½ inch deep pie dish. Press dough into pan.

7. Spoon filling into pan.

8. Dampen edges of dough with cold water. Fit second pastry over top of pie. Press down edges of dough with tines of a fork. Cut 4 slits in center of dough to allow steam to escape.

9. Reduce heat in oven to 350°. Slide pie into oven and bake for 45 minutes, until crust is golden.

**Yield: 4 to 6 servings**

# Chicken Filling for *Empañada*

Most Caribbean meat pies are made with beef. This chicken version makes a lighter, heart-healthy and welcome change.

**1 cup *sofrito* (see index)**
**¼ cup fresh lime juice**
**2 tablespoons apple cider vinegar**
**2 pounds boneless, skinless chicken, cubed**
**¼ cup minced onion**
**½ small Habanero pepper, seeded and minced**
**2 tablespoons chopped green olives**
**2 tablespoons capers**

**1 teaspoon fresh chopped oregano, or ½ teaspoon dried**
**1 bay leaf**
**1 chicken bouillon cube, crushed**
**8 pimento-stuffed olives, chopped**
**2 tablespoons capers**
**¼ cup minced green bell pepper**

1. Make basic *empañada* crust above. While dough is chilling, prepare the filling.

2. Combine the *sofrito*, lime juice and vinegar in a small bowl. Add chicken and toss to coat. Cover with plastic wrap and refrigerate, allowing to marinate for 2 to 3 hours.

3. Add onion, peppers, oregano, bay leaf, and bouillon cube to chicken mixture. Transfer to large skillet and cook over medium heat for 10 minutes. Stir frequently to break up bouillon cube.

4. Reduce heat and fold in olives and capers. Simmer for 10 additional minutes. Remove from heat and cool.

5. Follow instructions for filling pie and baking crust from Basic *Empañada* Crust #'s 5 through 9.

6. Cool pie on wire rack for 30 minutes before serving.

**Yield: 4 to 6 servings**

## Shrimp Filling for *Empañada*

3 tablespoons annatto-colored olive oil
¼ cup minced green onion
½ small chili pepper, Serrano or Habanero
¼ cup minced red bell pepper
¼ cup *adobo* (see index)
1 tablespoon capers

1 pound cooked, shelled and
    deveined shrimp
1 teaspoon paprika
1 teaspoon saffron threads
¼ cup dry Sherry

1. Heat the olive oil in a deep skillet over medium heat. Sauté the onion, red bell pepper, and *adobo* for 2 minutes until vegetables are soft.
2. Dice the shrimp and add to skillet. Stir in paprika, saffron, Sherry and capers. Reduce heat and simmer for 10 minutes.

Yield: approximately 1 ¼ to 1 ½ cups

## Pork and Beef Filling for *Empañada*

If you don't care for pork in this recipe, even though it is a leaner meat than ground beef, substitute an equal amount of ground beef. Likewise, all the beef may be eliminated and ground pork used in its place.

2 tablespoons annatto oil
½ pound lean ground beef
½ pound ground pork
½ cup minced onion
2 garlic cloves, minced
¼ cup minced green bell pepper
½ cup diced ripe tomato
¼ cup diced ham
vegetable oil for frying

1 tablespoon fresh *culantro*
1 teaspoon fresh chopped oregano,
    or ½ teaspoon dried
6 pimento-stuffed olives, chopped
1 tablespoon capers
1 tablespoon raisins, chopped
3 hardboiled eggs, chopped
1 teaspoon cayenne pepper

1. Heat annatto oil in deep skillet. Brown beef and pork. Drain excess fat. Add onion, garlic, pepper and tomato. Cook for 2 minutes until onion is clear.

2. Stir in ham, *culantro*, oregano, olives, capers and raisins. Cook for additional 5 minutes. Remove from heat. Fold in eggs.

**Yield: about 3 cups**

# Cornmeal Turnovers
*Empanadillas de Harina de Maíz*

**1 cup Beef and Pork Filling for Piononos (see index)**

**2 ¼ cups fine ground yellow cornmeal**

**1/3 cup flour**

**1 tablespoon cornstarch**

**vegetable oil for frying**

**½ teaspoon cracked black pepper**

**¼ teaspoon ground nutmeg**

**2 cups water**

**3 tablespoons milk**

**1 teaspoon salt**

1. Stir together cornmeal, flour, cornstarch, salt, pepper, nutmeg, water and milk in a medium saucepan. Simmer and stir over moderate heat until mixture separates from bottom and sides of pan. Remove from heat.

2. On a non-stick cookie sheet, spread a scoop the size of a golf ball and flatten to about 4 to 5 inches in diameter.

3. Heap 2 tablespoons of stuffing in center. Flip half of the cornmeal dough over to form a turnover. Press down on edges with fingers or fork.

4. Heat vegetable oil to 357°F.

5. Fry turnovers until golden, taking care not to crowd skillet. Drain on white paper towels.

**Yield: 18 turnovers**

## Pasteles

### *Steamed Meat Patties*

*Pasteles* are a part of being Puerto Rican. Not having *pasteles* at Christmastime is like not having gifts under the tree. *Pasteles* differ from *pastelillos* in that they are boiled in plantain leaves and not fried. The dough is made from grated root and other vegetables. Pork is the traditional filling, but seafood and chicken may also be used.

# Basic *Pastele* Dough and Assembly

*Masa*

Be sure to place vegetables in large pot of cold, salted water after peeling to keep them from turning black:

## DOUGH:

5 green bananas, peeled and grated
2 large green plantains, peeled and grated
6 tablespoons annatto-colored olive oil
1/3 cup milk
1 tablespoon salt
1 pound white *yautía* (taro) or
   Idaho potatoes, peeled and diced

1 cup pork stock (see index
   for recipe)
1 pound peeled and grated
   *yuca* (cassava), use frozen
   one if possible, it's more
   convenient

## WRAPPING:

12 banana leaves
12 sheets cooking parchment
water to boil *pasteles* r
affia (optional)

kitchen twine
2 teaspoons salt
1/3 cup annatto-colored olive oil

1. Fit food processor with grated blade. Have a large bowl handy to hold grated vegetables.

2. Drain water from vegetables. Process small amounts of the vegetables at a time. Add a little pork stock until the vegetables have the consistency of oatmeal. Once all the vegetables are pureed, place in large bowl.

3. Stir in any remaining pork stock, 6 tablespoons annatto oil, and the 1/3 cup milk. Use your hands to mix and remove any large chunks of vegetables. Batter should have a smooth silky surface.

## ASSEMBLING OF *PASTELES*

1. Wash and dry banana leaves. Trim to 8 by 8 inches with kitchen shears. Fill a deep baking dish with hot water and dip leaf in water until it wilts. Remove and place on a clean kitchen towel. Pat dry. Repeat process with all leaves.

2. Cut kitchen twine into 12, 30-inch pieces and set aside.

3. Set up an assembly area as follows: parchment paper; banana leaves; grated vegetable dough; pork filling and twine.

4. Place 1 sheet of parchment on a wood cutting board. Lay a banana leaf on top of the parchment. Spread 1 tablespoon of annatto oil over the leaf surface. Spoon ½ cup of the dough in the middle of the leaf. Smooth the dough with the flat side of a spoon to a 5 by 5-inch square.

5. Next spoon a generous ¼ cup of pork filling over the dough area.

6. To fold *pastele*: Grip the parchment and banana leaf together by the lower corners. Fold in half (away from your body) so that the filling is completely covered by the dough. Fold the ends in toward the middle. Fold in half in twice more. You should have a rectangle about 3 inches wide.

7. Tie *pasteles* in pairs with folded sides inside. Tie securely with twine.

8. Fill a large kettle or stockpot with water and bring to a boil. Add 2 teaspoons salt. Lower *pasteles* and bring back to a boil. Reduce heat and simmer for 45 minutes to 1 hour. Turn once during cooking period.

9. Remove from boiling water and drain. Open parchment paper and slide banana leaf rectangle onto plate. At this point, you may decoratively re-tie the pasteles with raffia (straw cord). Serve warm as a snack or main course.

DDD drawing needed of pastele assembly

**Yield: 12 pasteles**

# Traditional Pork Filling for *Pasteles*

**1 pound boneless pork roast,**
   **diced in ½-inch pieces**

**2 tablespoons *adobo* (see index for recipe)**

**2 tablespoons annatto-colored oil**

**2 tablespoons shredded,**
   **unsweetened coconut**

**1 cup recaíto (see index for recipe)**

**1 cup of tomato sauce**

**½ cup cooked chickpeas**

**½ cup raisins**

**½ cup smoked ham, diced finely**

1. Follow instructions for pasteles dough in previous recipe. Season pork with *adobo*. Heat annatto-colored oil in skillet and sauté the pork and ham over medium heat for 5 minutes until lightly browned on all sides.

2. Add *recaito* and reduce heat. Simmer for 3 minutes, then stir in tomato sauce, cooking additional 20 minutes. Pork should be cooked through.

# Traditional Pork Filling for *Pasteles*

1 pound boneless pork roast, diced in ½-inch pieces

2 tablespoons *adobo* (see index for recipe)

2 tablespoons annatto-colored oil

2 tablespoons shredded, unsweetened coconut

1 cup recaíto (see index for recipe)

1 cup of tomato sauce

½ cup cooked chickpeas

½ cup raisins

½ cup smoked ham, diced finely

1. Follow instructions for pasteles dough in previous recipe. Season pork with *adobo*. Heat annatto-colored oil in skillet and sauté the pork and ham over medium heat for 5 minutes until lightly browned on all sides.

2. Add *recaito* and reduce heat. Simmer for 3 minutes, then stir in tomato sauce, cooking additional 20 minutes. Pork should be cooked through. Fold in chickpeas, raisins and coconut. Heat through. Remove from stove and set aside.

3. Follow assembly instructions for *pasteles*.

# Lobster Filling for *Pasteles*

This is my favorite way to eat *pasteles*. This recipe may also be frozen for up to 2 months.

1 tablespoon annatto-colored olive oil

½ cup *sofrito* (see index for recipe)

¼ cup *alcaparrado* (see index for recipe)

¼ cup golden raisins

½ cup tomato sauce

1 ¼ pounds cooked lobster meat, diced

1 teaspoon salt

1 teaspoon freshly cracked black pepper

1. Follow instructions for dough from *pasteles* from preceding recipe.

2. Heat oil in deep skillet and sauté *sofrito* and *alcaparrado* for 2 minutes.

3. Stir in raisins, tomato sauce, lobster, salt and pepper. Cook over medium heat for 5 minutes. Remove from heat and cool before filling *pasteles*.

4. Follow assembly and cooking instructions from preceding recipe.

5. Serve *pasteles* hot with homemade ginger beer or Puerto Rican beer.

**Yield: 12 servings**

1. Soak plantain slices for 30 minutes in the salted water and garlic. Remove from water and pat dry with paper towels.

2. Heat 3 tablespoons of oil in deep skillet or frying pan. Sauté until soft, but do not allow to become crunchy on outside. Remove from hot oil with tongs, and drain on white paper towels.

3. Place a sheet of waxed or parchment paper over plantain slices and flatten. Dip into salted water and fry again until golden on all sides.

4. Drain on paper towels and salt to taste. Serve with *Mojito* Sauce (see index for recipe).

**Yield: 12 to 15 tostones**

# Shrimp-Stuffed Tostones

*Tostones Rellenos*

The first time I tasted these was at Luquillo Beach, the island's most popular stretch of sand. Dozens of concrete and tin-roofed eateries dot the beach. Forty-five minutes from San Juan just past the Caribbean National Forest, a.k.a. *El Yunque.*

**3 large green plantains, peeled and cut into diagonal slices ½-inch thick**

**3 quarts water**

**1 tablespoon pulverized rock salt**

**1 tablespoon annatto-colored olive oil**

**vegetable oil for frying**

**1 tablespoon tomato paste**

**2 tablespoons *sofrito* (see index for recipe)**

**½ pound medium shrimp, peeled, cleaned and tail removed**

1. Prepare plantains as for preceding traditional *tostone* recipe.

2. Heat the annatto oil in a medium skillet. Stir in tomato paste and *sofrito*.

3. Cook over medium heat for 2 minutes. Chop shrimp and fold into *sofrito*. Cook for 4 minutes until no longer pink. Remove from heat.

4. Scoop 1 teaspoon of the shrimp mixture on a *toston*. Top with another *toston* and secure with a toothpick. Serve immediately.

**Yield: 18 to 24 appetizers**

# Fried Plantain Chips

*Platanutre*

These are thin, like potato chips. Factories all over Puerto Rico produce these.

**shortening or vegetable oil**

**salt**

**4 large green plantains, peeled**

**cayenne or black cracked pepper**

**hot chili pepper sauce (optional)**

1. Heat vegetable oil in a deep skillet or fryer to 375°F.
2. Slice plantains cross-wise very thinly like potato chips. Note, *tostones* are much thicker and chewier.
3. Fry in hot fat until golden. Do not overload fryer as this will reduce temperature of oil and cause the chips to soak up unappetizing amounts of oil.
4. Drain on white paper towels. Season to taste with salt. I like to sprinkle a little cayenne or cracked black pepper on them as well. Goes nicely with ice-cold beer, even Chardonnay!

**Yield: about 16 ounces**

# Ricemeal Balls

*Bolitas de Harina de Arroz*

**¾ cup evaporated milk**

**¾ cup water**

**2 tablespoons butter**

**¾ cup ricemeal**

**vegetable oil or shortening for frying**

**1 cup grated crumbly white cheese, such as *Machengo***

**¾ teaspoon salt**

**½ teaspoon cayenne pepper**

1. Combine evaporated milk and water in a medium saucepan over medium heat, bringing to a boil. Remove from heat.
2. Stir in butter, ricemeal, cheese, salt and cayenne. Return to reduced heat, stirring constantly until mixture separates from sides and bottom of pan. Remove from heat and allow to cool.
3. Form into small balls, slightly smaller than a golf ball.

4. Heat oil to 375°F. Fry balls until golden. Remove with slotted spoon and drain on white paper towels.

**Yield: about 24 balls**

# Old Ladies' Bellies

*Barrigas de Vieja*

Tasuki and Natalie saga continued. The baby had a fistful of the cat's fur. A rumble came from Tasuki's throat, his tail twitched. The baby squealed in delight and grabbed onto the swinging tail. *Oh, my god.* Tasuki was famous for sinking his razor-sharp teeth into soft human flesh. The baby's mother, Anna dashed to the playpen and stopped. I skidded beside her. Then we both started laughing. Go to the recipe for *Vegetable Soup with Plantain Balls* to see what happened next.

| | |
|---|---|
| **2 cups flour** | **1 large egg, beaten** |
| **1 teaspoon salt** | **1 cup milk** |
| **½ teaspoon cinnamon** | **1 cup water** |
| **¼ teaspoon clove** | **vegetable oil or shortening for frying** |
| **¼ teaspoon ground ginger** | **sugar for dusting** |

1. Combine flour, salt, cinnamon, clove, ginger, egg, milk and water in large bowl. Stir until smooth and lump-free. Batter should be thin.

2. Heat oil in deep fryer or skillet until 375°F. Drop by spoonfuls into hot oil and fry on both sides until golden. Remove with a slotted spoon. Drain on white paper towels.

3. Sprinkle with sugar and serve at once.

**Yield: about 24**

## Surullos (Cornbread Sticks)

I bet you never dreamt so many treats came from Puerto Rico. If you haven't begun a good workout program, now may be the time to start.

Okay, a little background is needed here. Corn was a staple of the *Taino* Indian, who brought it with them when they came from South America. It found its way into candies, liquors, flours, breads and desserts. By the way, corn is also a good source of folic acid, magnesium, thiamine, iron and potassium, among other essential trace minerals and vitamins.

Anyway, *surullos* is another one of the delicious fritters made from a starchy vegetable (*yautía, malango,* plantains) you'll find in roadside stands. In early colonial days, peasants started their days with *surullos* made from corn or wheat flour, and steamed in corn husks or plantain leaves like *tamales.* The frying of *surullos* got its start with the African slaves.

## Surullos (Cornbread Sticks with Cheese)

*Machengo* is the best cheese for this, but Edam will work nicely as well.

| | |
|---|---|
| 2 cups water | 1 ½ cups yellow cornmeal |
| 1 teaspoons salt | 1 cup grated *Machengo* cheese or Edam |
| vegetable oil for frying | |

1. Combine water and salt in a saucepan. Heat to boiling and remove from heat. Stir in cornmeal, mixing well.

2. Return to stove and cook over medium heat until cornmeal mixture separates from bottom of pan.

3. Remove from heat again, and fold in cheese. Remove from heat and cool.

4. Heat oil to 375°F. Scoop cornmeal by spoonfuls and shape into cylinders 3 inches long.

5. Slide into hot oil and fry until golden on all sides.

6. ˙Drain on white paper towels. Serve warm.

**YIELD: about 24**

## Fried Bisquits
*Yani-Clecas*

*Yani-Clecas* are a flat biscuit served as a side dish to stews, chicken or meat dishes, or just by themselves drizzled with butter. Similar to baking biscuits, these are fried.

| | |
|---|---|
| 4 cups, plus 2 tablespoons all-purpose flour | 4 tablespoons vegetable |
| 1 tablespoon baking powder | shortening such as Crisco®, |

1 tablespoon sugar

1 teaspoon salt

2 tablespoons butter,
  chilled and cut up

1 egg, beaten

vegetable oil for frying

chilled and cut up

¼ teaspoon black pepper (optional)

¼ teaspoon paprika (optional)

1 cup whole milk

1. Sift flour, baking powder, sugar and salt into large bowl. Cut in shortening and butter with a pastry cutter or fork. Mixture should resemble oatmeal.

2. Stir in egg with a wooden spoon. Sprinkle in spices and slowly drizzle in milk, continuing to stir until a soft dough forms.

3. Turn out onto floured cutting board. Knead dough for 1 minute.

4. Shape into a 2-inch thick roll. Cut in ½-inch slices.

5. Heat oil to 375°F and deep dry buns until golden. Remove and drain on white paper towel. Serve with butter.

**Yield: 30 to 32 buns**

# LOW-CARB Cheddar Cheese Balls Island–Style

Double the batch for every six guests.

1 pound grated extra-sharp
  Cheddar cheese

1 8-ounce package cream cheese,
  room temperature

1 ounce feta cheese,
  room temperature

1 tablespoon minced onion

1 clove garlic, minced

1 tablespoon hot pepper sauce

¼ cup shredded cilantro or

4 large *culantro* leaves, shredded

1 teaspoon cracked black pepper

½ cup toasted walnuts,
  finely chopped

1. Grate the cheddar cheese while still chilled. Allow to come to room temperature.

2. Place grated cheddar, cream cheese, feta, onion, garlic, hot pepper sauce and cilantro in a food processor. Puree until smoothly blended.

3. Scoop into a dish, cover and refrigerate until firm.

4. Using an ice cream scoop, make small balls. Roll in crushed walnuts. Refrigerate again.

**Yield: 12 balls**

EACH SERVING APPROXIMATELY PROVIDES:

290 calories, **2.5 grams carbohydrates,** 15 grams of protein, 27 grams of fat

# LOW-CARB Hot Pepper Cheese Crisps

The trick to making these cheese crisps is to finely mince the hot peppers. I've gone so far as to puree them in the food processor.

**4 cups extra-sharp grated cheddar cheese (I prefer the Vermont kind)**
**¼ cup minced jalapeño peppers (jarred kind)**
**paprika**

1. Preheat oven to 425°F. Line a baking sheet with one of those new non-scorch baking sheets or parchment paper.

2. Toss together jalapeños and cheese until evenly blended. You don't want to bite into a huge, fiery chunk of hot chili pepper like Anna and I did. The flavor should be subtle and smooth.

3. Drop cheese by tablespoonfuls on top of the parchment, allowing about 2½ inches on either side for the cheese to spread. Sprinkle lightly with paprika.

4. Bake for 4 to 6 minutes until cheese turns golden. Do not burn. The flavor will be awful, like roasted gym socks.

5. Slide pan onto a wire cake rack to allow air to circulate underneath and cool the pan. After a few minutes, crisps should lift from pan with a spatula. Drain on white paper towels to absorb excess oil.

**Yield: 40 cheese crisps**

EACH CRISP CONTAINS APPROXIMATELY:

48 calories, **0.5 carbohydate,** 3 grams of protein, 5 grams of fat

# LOW-CARB Cilantro-Citrus Guacamole

Serve with LOW-CARB chips, celery sticks or bell pepper strips.

2 ripe avocados, peeled and pitted

2 teaspoons mayonnaise

2 tablespoons fresh lime juice

½ teaspoon freshly grated lime zest

1 tablespoon minced green onion

2 garlic cloves, peeled and minced

1 lime, halved

½ jalapeño pepper, seeded and minced

2 *culantro* leaves, minced or

2 tablespoons minced cilantro

½ teaspoon dried oregano

1 teaspoon salt

1 teaspoon freshly cracked black pepper

1. Combine mayonnaise, lime juice, zest, onion, garlic, jalapeño, cilantro, oregano, salt and pepper in a large glass or ceramic bowl.

2. Mash avocado into bowl using a potato masher, combining all ingredients until smooth. A couple lumps of avocado are attractive though.

3. Squeeze lime halves over top of avocado to keep from turning brown. Cover with plastic wrap (pressed into surface of dip) to further prevent oxidation.

**Yield: 8 servings**

EACH SERVING CONTAINS APPROXIMATELY:

99 calories, **5 grams carbohydrates**, 1 gram protein, 10 grams of fat

# LOW-CARB Baked Habañero-Tarragon Crab Dip

Instead of fat- and carbohydrate-laden chips or crackers, serve this with celery sticks, broccoli or cauliflower florets. Cucumber and zucchini sticks are surprisingly good also.

18 ounce can lump crabmeat, drained, picked over for bones and flaked

18 ounce package cream cheese, room temperature

1/3 cup mayonnaise

½ habañero pepper, seeded and minced

½ teaspoon dried tarragon

½ teaspoon salt

½ teaspoon freshly cracked black pepper

¼ cup grated parmesan cheese

1. Preheat oven to 300°F.

2. Puree crab, cream cheese, mayonnaise, parmesan, habañero, tarragon, salt and pepper in a food processor until smooth.

3. Scoop dip into a 1-quart ceramic or glass baking dish. No need to grease.

4. Bake until bubbly, about 25 minutes.

**Yield: about 2 ½ cup (12 servings)**

EACH SERVING PROVIDES APPROXIMATELY:

160 calories, **1.3 grams carbohydrates**, 5 grams of protein, 17 grams of fat

# LOW-CARB Curried-Garlic Shrimp Kabobs

My original recipe called for ¼ teaspoon of ground cinnamon. I doubled the amount-cinnamon is a known blood sugar stabilizer.

**¼ cup soy sauce**

**6 garlic cloves, crushed**

**1 tablespoon freshly minced ginger root**

**1 tablespoon minced cilantro**

**2 tablespoons minced green onion**

**2 tablespoons Splenda®**

**1 teaspoon olive oil**

**1 ½ teaspoons curry powder**

**¼ teaspoon cumin**

**½ teaspoon ground cinnamon**

**½ teaspoon freshly cracked black pepper**

**1 ½ pounds medium raw shrimp, peeled and deveined, tails on**

1. Combine soy sauce, garlic, ginger, cilantro, onion, Splenda®, olive oil, curry, cumin, cinnamon, pepper in a large ceramic or glass bowl.

2. Rinse shrimp under cool, running water and allow to drain. Place shrimp in bowl and toss until well-coated with soy/curry mixture. Refrigerate overnight, stirring occasionally.

3. Preheat broiler or barbeque. Thread shrimp on 8-inch steel or wooden skewers. Be sure to soak wood skewers in water for 45 minutes before using.

4. Place shrimp on broiler rack or directly on hot grill. Broil 3 to 4 inches from heat source, 3 to 4 minutes on each side. Shrimp should be pink and begin to curl. Do not overcook, i.e. shrimp are curled into a tight ball. They'll be tough.

**Yield: 4 servings (kebabs)**

EACH SERVING PROVIDES APPROXIMATELY:

225 calories, **7 grams of carbohydrates**, 37 grams of protein, 4.5 grams of fat

# Soups, Stews, and Broths

## Soups

Every island in the Caribbean seems to have its favorite soup, stew or chowder. Puerto Rico with its tropical climate and rich soil is perfect for growing corn, beans, vegetables and tubers—the base for soups.

Back in plantation days, slaves and indentured servants had an early version of the crock pot or *caldero*. Vegetables grown on their tiny plot of land were tossed into the pot, and then simmered all day over an open fire. If meat, poultry or seafood were available, that went in as well.

Soup on the island is served as a first course, or by a meal in itself. Glance at any good Puerto Rican restaurant menu and you'll find soup. And not just one entry, but several. *Asopao*, remarkably similar to gumbo (both have African origins) is made with rice. Every chef has his own recipe for this brothy soup. *Caldo* is more like a clear broth, often served as a first course, and *sopa* is thicker, a soup. If the budget is tight, *asopao de gandules* (beans) is filling and delicious. An incredible amount of vegetables, tubers, spices, herbs and meats go into *sancocho* a type of beef stew.

Several examples from each category of soup are included. Textures vary as well as cooking times. Although fresh is best, I often double a soup recipe and freeze half for those days when time is dear. A delicious and convenient way to prepare soup is in a crock pot. Most of the recipes in this chapter can be adapted by reducing the liquid by 1 cup.

Experiment with the amount of liquid in the recipes. Many of the vegetables may be substituted interchangeably. Personally I prefer to grind my own spices on the spot and use fresh herbs, but in a pinch do use dried or a combination of both. Vegetarians can substitute sautéed tofu, fish or seafood for the chicken, pork or beef.

Soups are versatile, nutritious and easy to prepare. And Puerto Rican recipes are especially delicious. Enjoy!

## Tip-Broths

In this modern age of food convenience, our grocery stores are crammed with canned and powdered soup stock—a boon to harried homemakers or to the wife who just spent eight hours slugging away at the office. However, if you do have the time, why not make your own stock and freeze some for future soups? The flavor dividend is more than ample trade off for any time involved.

Homemade stock adds flavor and complexity to soups and stews. Plus, it's an excellent way to use up leftovers and odds and ends from your vegetable crisper. Keep the following in mind:

- Stocks are not compost heaps. If you wouldn't eat that mushy onion or moldy carrot, don't put it in the stock. However, you can put in carrot, onion or garlic ends, potato parings, celery leaves, etc.

- Use a stockpot that is tall and narrow. A large pot, with a wider opening, will allow liquid to evaporate too quickly.

- Meat stocks require longer cooking times (1 ½ to 4 hours). Vegetable stocks lose flavor if over cooked. Simmer anywhere from 25 minutes to 1 hour.

- When cutting vegetables, cube no smaller than 1-inch pieces. The greater the surface area, the quicker the vegetables will release their flavor.

- Certain vegetables turn bitter in stocks. Avoid anything in the cabbage family (cabbage contains odoriferous sulfur compounds) broccoli, kale, cauliflower, brussel sprouts. Also avoid turnips, onions skins, or too much parsley or other greens.

# Vegetable Broth Island-Style
*Caldo de Vegetales*

For top flavor and to avoid bitterness from the herbs, Anna suggests the *recaíto* be added during the last 15 minutes of simmering.

| | |
|---|---|
| 1 tablespoon olive oil | 1 bay leaf |
| 1 large yellow onion, peeled | 2 teaspoons salt |
| 2 celery stalks, with leaves | 2 quarts cold water |
| 3 large carrots, peeled | ¼ cup *recaíto* (see index) |
| 6 cloves garlic, peeled and crushed | |

1. Cut vegetables in 1-inch pieces.
2. Heat the olive oil in a tall, narrow stock pot over medium heat until hot, but not smoking.
3. Sauté onion, celery, carrot and garlic over medium-high heat for 8 minutes, stirring constantly so vegetables do not burn.
4. Add bay leaf, salt and water. Bring to a boil, reduce heat, and simmer uncovered for 15 minutes.
5. Stir in *recaíto* for last 15 minutes of cooking.
6. Remove from heat and allow to cool for 20 minutes. Strain vegetables from broth and discard.

**Yield: about 1 ¾ quarts**

---

### Health Tip—Broth

♦ If your broth is too salty, toss in a couple slices of raw potato during cooking time. The potato will absorb much of the salt.

♦ To defat canned or homemade broth, store in the refrigerator overnight. Remove the lid and scoop off the fat. If time is of the essence, punch a hole in the top of the can and freeze for 30 minutes. Remove lid and skim off fat.

---

# Beef Stock
*Caldo de Res*

Beef stock should taste like beef, nearly as intense as pot roast jus and it shouldn't take all day to prepare. Anna and I began this soup after lunch and completed it in time for her to take home for dinner to her family.

| | |
|---|---|
| 2 tablespoons olive oil | 1 teaspoon salt |
| 4 pounds beef chuck | 6 fresh *culantro* leaves (wide coriander) |
| 2 pounds beef marrow bones | 1 fresh ear corn, peeled and chopped in |
| 1 large yellow onion, cut in half | pieces |

½ cup dry red wine

2 *aji dulce* (sweet cherry pepper), seeded and coarsely chopped

2 garlic cloves, crushed

2 quarts of water

1. Heat 1 tablespoon oil in kettle or heavy stockpot over medium high heat. Brown beef, bones and onion halves on all sides in batches. Add additional oil as needed. Remove meat, bones and onion and set aside.

2. Deglaze kettle with red wine. Simmer wine for 1 minute until syrupy. Return meat, bones and onion to kettle. Turn heat very low, cover and cook for 20 minutes. A dark liquid should be released.

3. Add 2 quarts of water, peppers, salt, *culantro*, corn and garlic. Turn heat up to medium high, bringing to a boil. Reduce heat and simmer for 1 ½ hours. Cool.

4. Scoop excess fat from top, strain. Use as a soup base. Season to taste with salt and pepper.

**Yield: 7 to 8 cups**

## Chicken Stock

*Caldo de Pollo*

Use a cleaver to hack the chicken parts small enough to richly flavor this broth. Stock may be kept for two days in the refrigerator or frozen up to two months.

2 tablespoons vegetable oil

1 large onion, quartered

6 garlic cloves, crushed

4 pounds whole chicken legs, cut into 2-inch pieces

2 quarts boiling water

1 celery stalk, cut up

1 carrot, peeled, cut up

2 teaspoons salt

1 bay leaf

6 fresh *culantro leaves*

1 teaspoon *sofrito* (see index for recipe)

1. Heat oil in kettle or heavy stockpot. Add onion and garlic, sautéing for 2 minutes until just clear.

2. Add half of the chicken to kettle, brown on all sides for 4 to 5 minutes. Transfer chicken to plate and sauté remaining chicken pieces. Return chicken to kettle, reduce heat to very low, cover and sweat chicken for 20 minutes until juices are released.

3. Add boiling water, turn heat to high. Carefully add celery, carrots, salt, bay leaf, *culantro* and *sofrito*. Reduce heat again, cover and simmer for 15 to 20 minutes. Remove from heat and cool.

4. Skim fat from top. Strain and discard solids.

**Yield: 8 cups**

---

## Which fish makes the best broth?

Blackfish, monkfish, red snapper (very popular in the islands) sea bass, cod and sole. You can also add an equal amount of lobster, shrimp or crab shells. Avoid oily fish such as mackerel, tuna, bluefish or salmon.

---

# Fish Broth
*Caldo de Pescado*

After *asapao, sopón de pollo con arroz* and black bean soup, *caldo de pescado* is the third classic soup of Puerto Rico. Made with head and tail intact, recipes vary from restaurant to restaurant. Traditionally it includes garlic, onions, tomatoes, sherry, vinegar and a bit Galician broth, which is made from salt pork, beans, and turnip tops. This recipe was handed down from Anna's great-grandmother who serves it for Sunday lunch.

2 ½ pounds fish trimmings, gills discarded, cut into pieces

1 large yellow onion, diced

1 celery stalk, diced

1 large carrot, peeled and sliced

6 garlic cloves, crushed

1 *aji dulce* (sweet red chili pepper) seeded and minced

1 tablespoon *sofrito* (see index for recipe)

½ cup chopped fresh parsley

1 small lime, cut in half

1 teaspoon cracked black peppercorns

1 teaspoon pulverized rock salt

1 cup dry white wine

¼ cup Galician broth (see index for recipe)

1 bay leaf

2 ½ quarts of water

1. Place all ingredients in kettle or heavy stockpot. Bring to boil over medium heat. Reduce heat and simmer for 1 to 1 ½ hours until meat fall off the bones. Occasionally skim scum from top.

2. Strain through sieve or 2 thicknesses of cheesecloth. Stock may be cooled and refrigerated for up to 3 days or frozen for 2 months.

**Yield: 8 to 10 cups**

## No time to make broth?

While homemade offers peak flavor, one must face reality at times. Not all store-bought broths are alike.

**Best flavor:** Avoid cans and look for the new ones in asceptic packaging. The boxes look like the kind your pre-schooler takes to school for fruit juice. Broths in these packages are heated and flash cooled, allowing what little flavor there is to remain. If you'll be simmering the soup for a while, use reduced-sodium to avoid over salting.

**MSG:** Bouillon cubes contain copious amounts of this dubious ingredient. Plus they're mostly brown-colored salt anyway.

**Improving flavor:** Toss in quartered onion, halved carrot and celery stalks, along with a pinch of fresh parsley while soup is cooking. Fresh chicken bones also impart terrific flavor. Remove vegetables and bones before serving. Another trick is to stir in a package of unflavored gelatin to cold broth. Gradually reheat. You'll get the texture of home-made broth.

**Gourmet shops:** Small speciality stores often carry condensed broths sold in tubs in the refrigerated section. They're quite good as far as store-bought goes. You can also order restaurant-quality broths on line.

**Too salty?:** Add a couple slices of potato during cooking. Remove when ready to serve.

## Garlic Broth

*Sopa de Ajos*

¼ cup olive oil

12 garlic cloves, minced

6 cups beef broth (see index)

3 tablespoons lemon juice

½ teaspoon cayenne pepper

6 eggs

6 slices toasted French or other
  chewy bread, buttered

½ cup grated parmesan cheese

1. Heat oil in a stock pot over low heat. Add garlic and sauté until golden.

2. Add beef broth, lemon juice and cayenne pepper. Cover and simmer for 15 minutes.

3. Drop eggs, three at a time into beef broth and poach. Remove with slotted spoon and set aside in small bowl.

4. Place a piece of toast in each soup bowl. Position one egg on top of toast. Pour one cup of hot soup over toast and egg. Sprinkle with parmesan. Serve hot.

**Yield: 6 servings**

# Bread and Egg Soup

*Sopa de Pan con Huevos*

This is a Puerto Rican version of French Onion Soup, with a bit of extra zest from the raw onion. You may substitute chicken, fish or vegetable broth for the beef. Note, you will need six soup bowls to serve this recipe.

**8 cups beef broth**
**6 thick slices crusty French bread**
**6 eggs**

**¼ cup minced red onion**
**1 cup grated parmesan cheese**

1. Simmer beef broth over low heat for 10 minutes.
2. Place one slice of French bread in each bowl.
3. Gently poach eggs, three at time in beef broth. Place one egg on top of each piece of bread.
4. Pour hot broth of eggs and bread. Sprinkle parmesan over top of each bowl. Garnish with minced onion. Serve at once.

**Yield: 6 servings**

## Egg and Fried Green Banana Soup

Anna and I experimented for two afternoons on this soup. The first time we used two garlic cloves. We knew something wasn't quite right when we tasted the soup. The cooled soup was stored overnight in the refrigerator and we tasted it again the next day. Better, the flavors had matured, but still lacking. We then doubled the amount of garlic, black pepper and a splash of vinegar for bite and piquancy.

| | |
|---|---|
| 6 green bananas, peeled and halved cross-wise | 8 cups soup stock (beef, chicken, fish or vegetable, see index) |
| 1 tablespoon salt | 8 eggs |
| vegetable oil for frying | 1 teaspoon freshly cracked black pepper |
| 4 garlic cloves, crushed | 2 tablespoons cider vinegar |

1. Soak banana halves in cold water and the 1 tablespoon salt for 15 minutes. Drain.
2. Heat vegetable oil in deep fryer or skillet to 350°F. Fry bananas and garlic for 10 minutes. Remove and drain on white paper towels.
3. Mash bananas and form into small balls, smaller than a golf ball.
4. Bring soup stock to a simmer in a deep kettle over moderate heat. Drop in banana balls. Carefully break open eggs and poach in beef stock for 3 minutes. Stir in cracked pepper and vinegar. Ladle into individual bowls. Garnish with *culantro*.

Yield: 6 servings

## Vegetable Soup with Plantain Balls
*Sopa de Vegetales*

Tasuki and Natalie saga continued. Anna and I nearly collided into each other as we raced over to the playpen. The baby clutched Tasuki's tail in one chubby fist, the other yanked on handfuls of fur. The cat's ears were flattened in annoyance. Our hearts hammering, we didn't want to move too quickly, afraid Tasuki, who had never seen a miniature human in his life, would hurt Natalie. We looked at each other, uncertain of our next move. Suddenly he flopped over on his back, startling the baby. I took a step forward. Tasuki was purring! Our shoulders sagged in relief. I figured Tasuki missed Roxanne, who had recently left for her first year at college, as much as I did. Apparently he decided that baby Natalie was as good as it was going to get playmate-wise for him. Go to the recipe for *Rice with Spareribs* for the continuing tale of Tasuki and Natalie.

1 large green plantain, peeled and
   cut in 1-inch slices (see index for
   peeling plantains and green
   bananas)
1 teaspoon salt
8 cups chicken, beef, fish or
   vegetable broth

¾ cup white *yautia*, peeled and cut
   in 1 inch cubes
2 medium carrots, peeled and cut in
   1 inch slices
½ pound fresh okra, cut in ½-inch pieces
4 garlic cloves, crushed
salt and pepper to taste

1. Place plantain in small saucepan and cover with water and the 1 teaspoon salt. Boil until tender. Drain, mash and form into small balls, about one inch in diameter.

2. Bring broth to a boil in kettle or deep soup pot. Add *yautia* and carrots. Simmer for 10 minutes.

3. Add okra, garlic and plantain balls. Simmer for 20 minutes until vegetables are soft.

4. Season to taste with salt and pepper. Tastes better if flavors are allowed to blend overnight.

**Yield: 6 to 8 servings**

# Chicken Soup
*Sopa de Pollo*

Everyone knows there's nothing like chicken soup for a cold. The addition of pungent *culantro* or cilantro seems to up the healing power of this broth.

4 pounds assorted chicken parts,
   cut up, skin removed
2 teaspoons salt
3 tablespoons olive oil
2 quarts chicken stock, or 1 quart
   chicken stock, plus 1 quart vegetable stock
1 tablespoon olive oil

1 large yellow onion, minced
4 garlic cloves, crushed
1 large green bell pepper,
   seeded and diced
2 *culantro* leaves, minced or
3 tablespoons minced cilantro
4 ounces thin spaghetti noodles

1. Sprinkle salt over chicken parts and allow to sit for ½ hour.

2. Heat the 2 tablespoons olive oil in large skillet and brown chicken on all sides. Remove from skillet.

3. Bring chicken stock to a boil in a deep kettle over medium-high heat. Add chicken pieces, returning to a simmer for 20 minutes. Scoop off any scum that forms on the top.

4. Sauté onion, garlic, pepper in the 1 tablespoon olive oil for 3 minutes in a small skillet over medium heat. Stir in *culantro* leaves. Stir into stock. Reduce heat, cover and simmer for additional 45 minutes.

5. Add noodles and cook for 10 minutes.

**Yield: 6 to 8 servings**

## Chicken Soup with Rice

*Sapón de Pollo con Arroz*

Next to *asopao* you can find this traditional soup on nearly every restaurant menu.

½ cup long-grain rice

1 cup water

2½ quarts of water

1 tablespoon salt

1 whole lime, cut in half

2 medium onions, halved

1 pound *calebeza* (West Indian pumpkin or butternut squash), peeled and diced

1 pound potatoes, peeled and diced

1 pound *yautía*, peeled and diced

1 3-pound chicken, wash, drained and sprinkled lightly with salt, cut in pieces

1 teaspoon *recaíto* (see index for recipe)

1. Rinse rice thoroughly with water and soak in the 1 cup of water.

2. Combine 2 ½ quarts of water, salt, lime halves, and onion halves in kettle or heavy stockpot. Turn heat on high and bring to boil. Add pumpkin, potatoes, *yautía* and chicken pieces. Reduce heat and simmer for 1 hour.

3. Remove chicken from kettle and set aside. Remove pumpkin, mash and return to kettle.

4. Drain water from rice and add to kettle. Add *recaíto*, stir and cover. Heat until just barely bubbly, reduce heat and simmer for 15 minutes.

5. Remove skin and bones from chicken and discard. Cut meat in bite-size pieces and return to kettle. Heat for additional 10 minutes. Remove lime halves.

6. Serve with crusty bread, a dry Spanish white wine or ice-cold beer.

**Yield: 8 to 10 servings**

# Chicken Soup Recipe I
*Asopao de Pollo*

*Asopao* is a very wet rice full of broth and pieces of seafood or meat. The world *asopao* comes form the Spanish word *sopa* meaning soup. Simple to prepare, yet elegant.

1 whole chicken (3 pounds), cut up
6 cups chicken stock (see recipe
 for chicken stock)
1 bay leaf
1 teaspoon salt
1 teaspoon freshly cracked black pepper
¼ cup chopped ham
1 6-inch *chorizo* (Spanish sausage),
 chopped

1 ½ cups rice
1 cup *sofrito* (see index)
10 pimento-stuffed green olives,
 chopped
2 tablespoons Spanish capers
1 tablespoon fresh chopped *culantro*
 or cilantro

1. Heat 4 cups water in a large stock or soup pot to a boil. Add chicken, bay leaf, salt and pepper. Return to boil, then reduce heat to simmer. Add ham and *chorizo*, cover and cook for 1 hour until chicken is tender.

2. Remove chicken from stock. Skin and bones may be removed if desired. Add rice and *sofrito* to broth, bringing to a boil. Reduce heat and cover; cook for 25 minutes until rice is soft.

3. Return chicken to pot. Stir in olives, capers and *culantro*. Heat through for 8 to 10 minutes.

4. To serve use large shallow soup bowls. Nice with *tostones*.

**Yield: 4 servings**

# Chicken Soup Recipe II

*Asopao de Pollo*

3 black peppercorns

2 teaspoons pulverized rock salt

3 cloves garlic, crushed

2 teaspoons fresh chopped oregano
 or 1 teaspoon dried

2 tablespoons olive oil

1 tablespoon apple cider vinegar

½ teaspoon paprika

1 whole chicken (3 pounds), cut up

2 ½ cups uncooked rice

8 cups of water

2 teaspoons salt

2 tablespoons olive oil

¼ cup lean, smoked ham, diced

2 tablespoons salt pork, diced

1 cup *sofrito* (see index for recipe)

1 can tomato sauce

1 ripe tomato, diced

10 pimento-stuffed olives, diced

1 6-inch *chorizo*

2 tablespoons capers

1 tablespoon, plus 1 teaspoon
 annatto-colored olive oil

1 cup fresh sweet peas, uncooked

1 large red bell pepper, seeded,
 and sliced

2 tablespoons fresh parsley

1. Grind the peppercorns, rock salt in a mortar and pestle. Add garlic and oregano. Pound using an up and down motion. Add olive oil, vinegar and paprika, grinding ingredients into a smooth paste.

2. Rub chicken with peppercorn/garlic mixture.

3. Rinse rice well, and soak in water for 1 hour.

4. In a large soup or stock pot, heat water and the 2 teaspoons of salt. Add chicken parts, cover and heat on medium-high for 15 minutes. Reduce to simmer, cooking additional 30 minutes. Remove chicken pieces from broth and set aside. Bones and skin may be removed from chicken; cut into bite-size pieces. Set aside.

5. In a *caldero* or heavy kettle, heat the 2 tablespoons olive oil and brown the ham and pork on all sides. Add *sofrito* and simmer for 8 to 10 minutes, stirring now and then.

6. Add tomato sauce, tomato, olives, *chorizo*, capers and annatto-colored olive oil. Sauté for 5 minutes.

7. Stir in chicken pieces and cook over medium heat until bubbly. Reduce heat, cover and cook additional 20 minutes.

8. Add broth from stock pot. Heat over high heat to boiling.

9. Drain and rinse rice. Add to broth, returning to boil. Reduce heat and simmer for 5 minutes. Stir in peas and red pepper. Stir occasionally and cook until rice is tender, about another 10 minutes. Serve at once in shallow soup plates.

**Yield: 6 to 8 servings**

# Chicken Soup Recipe III
*Asopao de Pollo*

2 cups long-grain rice

4 cups water, divided

2 cups of chicken stock (see index for recipe) or use canned

1 3-pound chicken, cut into serving pieces

¼ cup *adobo* (see index for recipe)

2 tablespoons annatto-colored olive oil

½ cup lean smoked ham, diced

½ cup diced red bell pepper

½ cup *alcaparrado* (see index for recipe)

½ cup *sofrito* (see index for recipe)

¾ cup tomato sauce

1 teaspoon salt

1 teaspoon freshly cracked black pepper corns

1 cup cooked green peas

1. Rinse rice well and soak in two cups of the water. Set aside.

2. Season chicken with *adobo* paste and refrigerate to marinate. Heat annatto-colored olive oil in a kettle or heavy stock pot. Brown the ham over medium heat. Add red pepper, *alcaparrado*, *sofrito*, and tomato sauce. Cook for 3 to 4 minutes.

3. Add chicken and remaining 2 cups of water and the 2 cups of chicken stock. Season to taste with salt and pepper. Bring to boil. Drain rice and add to kettle. Reduce heat and simmer for 30 minutes until rice is soft. Soup should be thick.

4. Serve hot in flat soup bowl and garnish with green peas.

**Yield: 6 to 8 servings**

# Chicken *Asopao* with Plantain Balls

Chickens run wild all over the island. Perhaps that is why there are so many versions of chicken soups—the over abundance of the birds.

2 cups uncooked rice

6 cups water, divided

1 3-pound chicken cut into pieces

¼ cup *adobo* (see index for recipe)

1 bay leaf

1 green plantain, peeled

1 tablespoon all-purpose flour

3 tablespoons olive oil

¼ cup minced yellow onion

4 cloves garlic, crushed

¼ cup dry Sherry

1 cup diced ripe tomato

6 cups chicken stock (see index for recipe)

1 cup fresh sweet peas

2 tablespoons fresh chopped cilantro or *culantro*

1 red bell pepper, roasted, skins removed and diced

1. Rub the chicken pieces with *adobo* and allow to marinate in the refrigerator for a couple hours.

2. Soak the rice in the 2 cups water for 1 hour.

3. Place 4 cups of water in deep kettle or stock pot. Heat to boiling and add chicken and bay leaf. Reduce heat, cover and simmer for 20 minutes. Remove from heat. Bones and skin may be removed from chicken. Cut chicken into bite-size pieces. Set aside.

4. Grate green plantain into shreds. Place a spoonful in palm of hand, add a pinch of flour and form into a ball. Set aside.

5. Heat olive oil in a skillet. Sauté onion and garlic. Deglaze pan with Sherry.

6. Drain rice, pour into kettle with chicken stock. Add chicken and onion/garlic/Sherry mixture. Add plantain balls. Bring to a boil, reduce heat and simmer for 13 minutes.

7. Add tomatoes and fresh peas. Simmer for additional 7 minutes. Stir in cilantro. Ladle into soup bowls, topping with roasted peppers. Serve hot with *tostones* and chilled beer.

Yield: 6 servings

# Chicken Stew

*Pollo Guisado*

Add a splash of Puerto Rican rum, 1 tablespoon of vinegar and 1 tablespoon of fresh lemon juice for additional depth of flavor.

2 pounds boneless, skinless chicken breast, diced

1 tablespoon annatto-colored olive oil

½ cup *sofrito* (see recipe for index)

8 ounces of tomato sauce

¼ cup *alcaparrado* (see index for recipe)

2 medium potatoes, peeled and cubed

1 red bell pepper, seeded and diced

1 bay leaf

2 cups of water

1. Heat the annatto oil in a kettle or deep pot. Sauté chicken for 5 minutes. Add *sofrito* and tomato sauce. Cook for additional minute.

2. Add *alcaparrado*, potatoes, bell pepper, bay leaf and water. Reduce heat, cover and cook for 45 minutes, stirring now and then. Remove bay leaf and discard. Serve with *tostones or yani-clecas*.

**Yield: 6 to 8 servings**

## Mussels

Mussels exist in marine coastal waters. Although they can be found anywhere, they prefer cold water. Nowadays, because of pollution, they are often farm-bred.

**Purchasing:** Mussels are sold fresh or canned. Never buy unshelled mussels unless they are still alive. Any open shells should close slowly when tapped, otherwise discard.

**Storing:** Fresh, unshelled mussels keep up to 3 days under refrigeration. Be certain to cover with a damp cloth. Shelled mussels must be stored in liquid and will keep about 1 ½ days. Freeze raw mussels up to 2 months.

**Preparing:** Wash and scrub mussels. You don't need to remove all the beard, just most of it as it does add flavor to stocks. Some mussels may be filled with mud or sand. Soak for an hour in salted water. To determine whether a closed mussel is dead, try moving the two halves of the shells back and forth. If they move, it's dead and needs to be tossed out. Discard any mussels that do not open when cooked.

**Nutrition:** High in B-complex vitamins, phosphorous, iron and zinc.

# Shellfish Stew

*Asopao de Mariscos*

If you like seafood, the fragrance of this shellfish stew is heady. Use the freshest ingredients possible and don't stint on the garlic. The extra time needed to prepare this stew is worth it.

| | |
|---|---|
| **2 cups long-grain rice** | **½ pound mussels, scrubbed, beards** |
| **2 cups of water** | **scraped away; or ¾ cup canned** |
| **1 ½ cups *sofrito* (see index for recipe)** | **1 cup fresh sweet peas, uncooked** |
| **6 cups chicken stock (see index for recipe)** | **2 tablespoons capers** |
| **1 lobster tail (1 pound), cut in pieces** | **8 pimento-stuffed olives** |
| **½ pound raw crabmeat, cartilage** | **½ cup dry Sherry** |
| **removed and flaked** | **2 pimentos cut in strips** |
| **½ pound shrimp, raw, shelled, and deveined** | |

1. Soak rice in the 2 cups of water for 1 hour.
2. Heat *sofrito* in deep kettle or *caldero* over medium heat for 3 minutes. Drain rice and add to kettle. Add chicken stock and bring to boil. Reduce heat and simmer for 10 minutes.
3. Fold in lobster and cook additional 3 minutes. Return to a boil, add shrimp, crab, mussels and peas. Cook 3 minutes. Remove from heat. Discard any mussels whose shells have unopened.
4. Stir in olives and capers. Add sherry. Allow to sit for 10 minutes before serving. Garnish with pimento strips.

**Yield: 6 servings**

# Seafood and Coconut Soup

*Caldo Santo*

The direct translation of *caldo santo* is saintly soup. Whether it means fit for a saint or the cook is a saint for taking the time to make the soup, the time expended is amply rewarded. If you can't find some of the root vegetables, substitute butternut squash, new potatoes and yams. Annatto seeds can be found at Latin groceries.

5 cups coconut milk, usweetened canned

¼ cup annatto seeds

1 cup *recaíto* (see index for recipe)

4 cups water

4 cups chicken broth (see index for recipe)

½ cup *alcaparrado* (see index for recipe)

½ cup peeled and diced *yuca* (cassava)

½ cup diced peeled and diced *yautía* (taro root)

½ cup diced *batata* (Puerto Rican sweet potato)

½ cup *calabaza* (West Indian pumpkin)

2 green plantains, peeled, grated and shaped into 1-inch balls

1 pound boneless fillet of red snapper, cut into 1 ½-inch pieces

½ pound lump crabmeat, picked over for cartilage

1 pound medium shrimp, peeled and deveined

½ pound *bacalao* (salt codfish), cooked and shredded

1 teaspoon salt

1 teaspoon fresh cracked peppercorns

1. Heat 1 cup of the coconut milk with the annatto seeds in a small saucepan over medium heat. When the milk turns bright red, remove from heat, strain and discard seeds.

2. Transfer annatto-colored milk, remainder of coconut milk and *recaíto* to kettle or heavy stockpot. Simmer over low heat for 5 minutes. Stir in water, chicken broth and *alcaparrado*. Cook for 1 minute.

3. Add *yuca*, *yautía*, *batata* and *calabaza*. Cook over medium heat for 25 minutes.

4. Stir in plantain balls and snapper. Cook for 5 minutes. Add crab and shrimp, cooking an additional 5 minutes. Fold in salt fish, cooking 2 minutes to heat through. Vegetables should now be soft.

5. Remove from heat and allow to cool for 10 minutes. Season to taste with salt and pepper. Serve hot with *surullos* or *frituras*.

**Yield: 6 to 8 servings**

## Chayote

Also known as christophene, the fruit was originally cultivated by the Mayans and Aztecs. Grows on a vine, preferring tropical and sub-tropical climates, the chayote resembles a pale avocado or a pear. Its thin skin is edible and varies in color from yellowish white to dark green.

**Purchasing**: Choose unblemished chayotes that are firm, but not rock hard as they will be tough.

**Storing**: Place unwrapped in the vegetable drawer of refrigerator for several weeks.

**Preparing**: Chayote needs to be peeled before or after cooking. Wear gloves as it secretes a sticky substance.

**Serving**: May be eaten raw in salads or cooked in creole-style dishes.

**Nutrition**: Raw chayote is a decent source of Vitamin C, folic acid, potassium, Vitamin B-6, copper and magenesium.

## Chayote Seafood Chowder

*Sopa de Chayote y Mariscos*

The rum in this recipe is optional, but it does add a mellowness and slightly smoky flavor.

1 tablespoon annatto-colored oil

1 tablespoon minced onion

1 small garlic clove crushed

2 medium chayotes, peeled and diced

1 celery stalk, diced

6 cups chicken stock (see index for recipe)

½ cup *sofrito* (see index for recipe)

1 cup light cream

1 large ear of corn, husked and cut in 1-inch pieces

1 lobster tail, chopped in 1-inch pieces with a cleaver

½ cup gold or dark rum

1 pound medium shrimp, peeled and deveined

12 mussels in shells, cleaned and checked for dead ones

1 cup water

1 teaspoon salt

1 teaspoon freshly cracked black pepper

1. Heat the annatto-colored oil in a small skillet. Sauté the onion and garlic for 1 minute until soft, but not brown. Set aside.

2. Heat the chayote, celery and 5 cups of the chicken stock in a medium soup pot over medium heat. Bring to a boil, reduce heat and add corn. Simmer for 20 minutes. Allow to cool for 20 minutes, then pour into a blender, a small amount at a time because the heat of the soup will expand. Puree until smooth; stir in cream and *sofrito*. Set aside.

3. Pour remaining cup of chicken stock, corn and the 1 cup water into a kettle or deep stockpot. Bring to a boil, reduce heat and add lobster. Simmer for 1 minute. Stir in rum, then add mussels and shrimp. Simmer for 4 to 5 minutes until mussels are open. Discard any that have not opened. Season to taste with salt and pepper. Serve with hot rice or *tostones*.

**Yield: 6 servings**

---

### Best Cut of Beef for Stew

Prepackaged stew beef at best is a hodgepodge of irregularly shaped pieces from different parts of the animal, which couldn't quite make the grade as steaks or roasts. Because of the difference in cuts and size, the cubes of beef will vary in cooking times, flavor and tenderness.

Cut your own beef stew pieces. **Chuck** is suited to long, slow cooking without becoming tough.

---

# Beef Stew

*Sancocho*

*Sancocho*, also known as *Ajiaco Criolla* (chili based stew) is usually served on special occasions. The preparation time is long, and the ingredient list is even longer. Enjoy this time in the kitchen with friends, an ice-cold beer or a refreshing libation made with smooth Puerto Rican rum.

3 tablespoons olive oil

6 garlic cloves

2 ½ pounds beef chuck, trimmed and cut into 1 ½ inch cubes

¼ pound smoked ham diced

½ cup minced onions

2 yellow plantains, peeled and sliced in 1-inch wheels

½ cup diced pumpkin (West Indian pumpkin or any other dry pumpkin or squash such as butternut)

1 cup peeled and diced yam

½ cup diced green bell pepper

¼ cup minced celery

1 *aji ducle* (sweet cherry pepper) seeded and diced

1 cup *sofrito* (see index for recipe)

1 cup tomato sauce

1 ½ cup diced ripe tomatoes

4 quarts beef stock (see recipe for index)

1 cup peeled and diced *yautía* (taro root)

1 cup peeled and diced cassava root

1 cup diced and peeled new potatoes

3 ears fresh corn, peeled and cut in 1 inch pieces

1 large chayote, peeled, cored and cubed in 1-inch pieces

1 tablespoon salt

1 tablespoon freshly ground pepper

1. Heat olive oil in a deep kettle (*caldero*), cast iron pot or heavy stockpot over medium heat.

2. Add garlic, beef, ham and onions. Stir and brown beef and ham on all sides. Fold in pepper, celery, sweet chili pepper and *sofrito*. Reduce heat and simmer for 5 minutes.

3. Add tomato sauce, tomatoes and 4 cups of the beef stock. Cook uncovered until liquid is reduced by half.

4. Add remaining stock, plantains, pumpkin, yam, *yautía*, cassava, potatoes, corn, chayote, salt and pepper. Cook another 30 minutes until meat and vegetables are tender. Serve with a crisp green salad and Puertorican beer such as *Medalla*.

**Yield: 6 servings**

## Browning

Browning is the result of sugar in food caramelizing, which produces an appealing texture, flavor and aroma. Anna told me that browning also kills surface bacteria on chicken, fish or meat, very important in hot Caribbean countries.

**Effective browning of meat:** You don't want to crowd the pan, otherwise food will end up steamed and mushy as moisture can't evaporate during the cooking process.

**Quick browning:** Use your broiler or grill set on high, with food three inches from heat source. Be careful though with very fatty cuts of meat. I learned the hard way with a couple of fire flare-ups. Likewise if meat is very lean, brush on a light coating of olive oil for a lovely brown sheen.

**For best flavor:** Avoid all coatings, such as flour or breadcrumbs. Rub meat lightly with inside of a cut lemon, then take a half cup of fresh herbs, roll into a ball and rub over meat surface. After browning deglaze pan with a bit of wine, water or stock, scraping up all brown bits. Use later for an intensely flavored sauce.

**Over-browned fried food?:** Drop any sugar called for in batter or coating recipe, and add a tablespoon of white wine, lemon or lime juice or vinegar to batter.

# Beef Stew

*Sopa de Res*

Anna took this stew home to her family for the taste test. Her grandmother suggested the addition of a ½ cup of sherry. It seemed like a lot of sherry, but it worked, adding an interesting undernote to the stew.

2 pounds lean beef, cut in 1-inch cubes (see Tip: The best cut of beef for stew)

2 tablespoons olive oil

2 quarts beef broth

4 garlic cloves, crushed

4 *culantro* leaves

2 sweet chili peppers, seeded, minced

½ pound *calabeza* (West Indian pumpkin) peeled in cut in 1 ½-inch cubes

½ pound green cabbage, coarsely chopped

2 carrots, peeled and cut in ½-inch slices

½ pound okra, trimmed and cut in 1-inch pieces

½ cup dry sherry

2 ounces thin spaghetti noodles

1. Heat olive oil in deep skillet and brown beef on all sides. Remove from skillet and set aside.
2. Bring beef broth to a simmer in deep soup pot. Add beef and cook for one hour, 15 minutes, scooping off any scum that rises to the surface.
3. Reduce heat, add garlic, *culantro*, chili peppers, pumpkin, cabbage, carrots and okra. Simmer for 20 minutes.
4. Stir in sherry. Add pasta and cook for additional 10 minutes. Vegetables should be tender. Remove *culantro* leaves. Ladle into soup bowls.

**Yield: 6 to 8 servings**

# Pork and Eggplant Stew

*Carne de Cerdo Guisada con Berenjena*

Keep extra *sofrito* on hand for quick and simple, tasty meals.

3 tablespoons olive oil

2 ½ pounds boneless pork roast,
   diced in 1-inch pieces

1 cup *sofrito*

1 cup tomato sauce

2 cups beef stock (see index for recipe)

1 bay leaf

2 cups peeled and diced eggplant

1 teaspoon salt

1 teaspoon fresh cracked black
   peppercorns

6 pimento-stuffed olives, chopped

1 tablespoon capers

1. Heat oil in kettle or large soup pot. Brown pork on all sides for 3 or 4 minutes.

2. Add *sofrito*, tomato sauce, beef stock and bay leaf. Bring to a boil, reduce heat, cover and simmer for 35 minutes.

3. Stir in eggplant, salt and pepper. Cook for 20 minutes. Fold in olives and capers, cooking for additional 5 minutes. Remove from heat and cool for 10 minutes before serving. Serve with pumpkin fritters.

**Yield: 6 servings**

# Ham Soup

*Sopa de Jamón*

This soup actually tasted better the next day. Low fat as well.

1 quart water

1 quart vegetable broth (see index)

1 small ham bone (about ½ pound)

1 ripe tomato, quartered

3 large, sweet chili peppers, seeded
   and quartered

3 *culantro* leaves

4 garlic cloves, slightly crushed, but
   left whole

10 ounces diced cooked ham

4 ounces thin spaghetti noodles

1. Bring water and broth to a boil in a large stockpot over moderate heat. Reduce heat, add ham bone and simmer for 45 minutes.

2. Add tomato, chili peppers, *culantro* and garlic, cover, cooking for additional 30 minutes.

3. Strain soup and return to pot, discarding ham bone and vegetables.

4. Add cooked ham and simmer for 10 minutes. Stir in noodles, cooking for additional 10 minutes.

**Yield: 6 servings**

# Creole-Style Tripe

*Mondongo*

If tripe is a little too adventuresome for you, substitute one pound roast pork, diced.

**8 whole peppercorns**
**2 teaspoons pulverized rock salt**
**2 cloves garlic, peeled and crushed**
**½ cup minced yellow onion**
**6 fresh *culantro* leaves**
**1 pound tripe, rinsed trimmed**
**1 quart water**
**2 pig's feet, rinsed and cut up**
**½ cup diced lean smoked ham**
**1 bay leaf**
**1 cup tomato sauce**

**¼ cup white table wine**
**½ cup *sofrito***
**1 cup peeled and diced *calabaza*** **(West Indian pumpkin or butternut squash)**
**1 cup peeled and diced *yautía*** **(tanier or Idaho potato)**
**1 tablespoon *alcaparrado***
**1 cup cooked white beans**
**½ teaspoon salt or more, to taste**

1. Crush the peppercorns and rock salt in a mortar and pestle. Add garlic and continue to pound in an up and down motion. Add *culantro* and onion to mortar and grind all ingredients to a paste. Set aside.

2. Place tripe in kettle or deep stockpot and add enough water to completely cover tripe. Bring to a boil, reduce meat to medium, and boil, uncovered for 10 minutes.

3. Remove tripe from kettle and drain water. Cut tripe into small pieces, approximately 1 to 1 ½ inches.

4. Add the 1 quart water to kettle. Add tripe, pig's feet, ham and bay leaf. Cover and boil for 1 ½ hours. Tripe should be tender.

5. Mix tomato sauce, white wine and *sofrito* in a small bowl. Pour into kettle. Add *calabaza* and *yautía*. Cook over medium heat for 20 to 30 minutes until vegetables are tender.

6. Fold in cooked beans and *alcaparrado*. Heat through for 5 minutes. Season to taste with salt.

7. Heat through for 5 minutes. Season to taste with salt.

**Yield: 6 servings**

## Galician Broth
*Caldo Gallego*

The addition of turnip or collard greens add calcium to this soup.

½ pound dried white beans, soaked overnight in water
1 ounce salt pork, rind removed
1 pound lean smoked ham, diced
2 6-inch *chorizos* (Spanish sausage)
2 small veal bones
½ cup minced yellow onion
2 teaspoons salt

1 teaspoon freshly cracked black peppercorns
1 teaspoon paprika
2 quarts of water
1 pound potatoes, peeled and cut in 1/2 -inch cubes
1 pound collard greens or turnip tops

1. Drain and rinse beans thoroughly. Place in kettle or heavy stockpot.

2. Add salt pork, ham, *chorizo*, veal bones, onion, salt, cracked pepper and paprika to kettle. Add water and bring to boil. Reduce heat, cover and simmer for 1 ½ hours.

3. Add potatoes and cook another 15 minutes. Toss in turnip green and simmer for 10 minutes until tender.

4. Remove bones. If a thicker sauce is desired, take out some of the potatoes and mash them, returning to broth. Remove *chorizos* and cut into ½-inch slices, returning to kettle. Serve hot. A bit spicy, so a cold beer or frosty glass of pinot grigio are in order.

**Yield: 6 servings**

# Soldier's Soup

*Racho*

Anna's great grandmother would begin this soup early in the morning, at 5:00 a.m. before the men went off into the cane fields to work. By mid-day this fragrant and nutritious soup would be ready.

1 pound lean stew beef, cut in 1-inch cubes

3 quarts water

2 *chorizos* (Spanish sausage), cut in ½ inch pieces

1 tablespoon salt

2 medium yellow onions, diced

1 green frying pepper, seeded and diced

2 tomatoes, minced

4 garlic cloves, minced

2 *culantro* leaves

1 pound dried chickpeas, boiled until tender or 2 one-pound cans of boiled chickpeas, rinsed and drained

1 pound green cabbage, quartered

1 pound pumpkin, peeled and cut in 1-inch cubes

½ pound potatoes, peeled and cut in 1-inch cubes

½ pound turnips, peeled and cut in 1-inch cubes

2 tablespoons tomato paste

1 tablespoon vinegar

1 teaspoon salt, or to taste

4 ounces thin spaghetti noodles

1. Rinse meat under cool water and pat dry. Place in deep soup pot or kettle, along with 3 quarts water, and 1 tablespoon salt and chorizos. Cover and bring to boil over moderate to high heat. Reduce heat, replace cover, and simmer for one hour.

2. Add onion, pepper, tomato, garlic, *culantro*, chickpeas and cabbage. Cover and simmer for 30 minutes.

3. Add pumpkin, potatoes, turnips, tomato paste, vinegar and salt. Cover and simmer for 35 minutes.

4. Break up spaghetti noodles and add to soup. Cook for 10 minutes. Discard *culantro* leaves. Ladle into soup bowls.

**Yield: 8 servings**

# Pigeon Pea Stew
*Asopao de Gandules*

Every one in the islands cooks with pigeon peas. My ex-husband's grandmother added them to rice dishes, soups, and casseroles. If you can't find pigeon peas, substitute black-eyed peas.

| | |
|---|---|
| 1 cup pigeon peas, canned or fresh | 2 cups *sofrito* (see index for recipe) |
| 8 cups water | 8 pimento-stuffed olives, chopped |
| 2 cups long-grain rice | 1 tablespoon Spanish capers |
| ¼ cup smoked ham, diced | 2 pimentos, cut in strips |
| ¼ cup salt pork, diced | 2 teaspoons salt |
| 3 tablespoons annatto-colored olive oil | 1 teaspoon fresh cracked black pepper |

1. Rinse pigeon peas under running water. Set aside. Rinse rice and soak in the 8 cups water for 1 hour.

2. Brown the ham and salt pork in a deep kettle or *caldero* over medium heat. Reduce temperature, add annatto-colored olive oil, *sofrito* and sauté for 8 to 10 minutes.

3. Add pigeon peas, olives and capers. Add rice, along with liquid to kettle. Bring to boil, reduce heat, cover and simmer for 20 minutes until rice is soft. Serve at once in flat soup bowls. Garnish with pimento strips. Season to taste with salt and pepper.

**Yield: 6 servings**

# Traditional Dried Bean Stew
*Habichuelas Secas Guisadas Tradicionales*

I have always enjoyed cooked beans. But, let's face it. Beans are very much dependant upon accompanying ingredients, i.e. spices, herbs, vegetables, meats. The Spanish sausage and olives add both a smoky and tangy note to the soup.

| | |
|---|---|
| 1 ½ cups dried beans | ½ cup *sofrito* (see index for recipe) |
| 2 quarts water | ½ cup tomato sauce |
| 2 cups peeled and diced (1-inch | 10 pimento-stuffed olives, chopped |

pieces) calabaza or winter squash

2 tablespoons annatto-colored
olive oil

½ cup diced smoked ham

1 *chorizo* (Spanish sausage) sliced
in ½-inch wheels

3 tablespoons capers

2 pimentos, chopped

1 cup peeled and diced *calabaza*
(West Indian pumpkin or butternut
squash)

1. Pick over beans, looking for twigs and stones, rinse several times under running water. Soak overnight, changing water a few times.

2. Drain beans and add to kettle along with the 2 quarts of water. Bring to boil, reduce heat and cook for 30 minutes. Add pumpkin and simmer for additional 30 to 45 minutes until beans are tender.

3. Meanwhile, heat oil over medium heat in heavy skillet. Add ham and *chorizo*, sautéing for 2 minutes. Fold in *sofrito* and tomato sauce. Cook for 8 to 10 minutes. Stir in olives, capers and pimentos.

4. Add *sofrito/ham* mixture to beans and pumpkin. Simmer uncovered for 20 minutes until pumpkin is soft. Serve hot with *tostones* or *surullos*.

## Healthy Tip

**For smoky flavor without the fat:** Substitute ¼ pound Canadian bacon and ¼ cup chopped, sun-dried tomato halves for salt pork, *chorizo* or other ham called for in a recipe. Or crumble a few slices of turkey bacon into a recipe for a lower-fat substitute.

**Yield: 8 servings**

# Basic Recipe for Black Bean Soup
*Frijoles Negros*

No good Latin cookbook would be complete without a version of Black Bean Soup. Smoky and piquant in flavor, Puerto Rico produces one of the best recipes. Vegetarians substitute olive oil, ½ teaspoon dried oregano and 2 teaspoons salt for ham bone and salt pork.

1 pound dried black beans, soaked, rinsed and picked over for small stones and broken beans

1 ½ quarts water

2 cups chicken broth

1 small ham bone, with some of the meat still on it

2 ounces diced salt pork

½ cup annatto oil

8 garlic cloves, peeled and crushed

¾ cup minced onion

4 sweet chili pepper, seeded and minced

1 tablespoon salt

1 tablespoon fresh minced oregano

1 bay leaf

½ teaspoon ground cumin

1 teaspoon freshly cracked black pepper

¼ cup dry sherry

1 tablespoon wine vinegar

1. Place soaked beans in a deep soup pot or kettle. Cover with the 1 ½ quarts water and 2 cups chicken broth. Add ham bone and salt pork. Cook for 45 minutes. Remove one cup of the black beans, draining liquid back into soup pot, and reserve the one cup beans.

2. Bring to a rapid boil. Reduce heat, cover and simmer for 45 minutes.

3. In a large frying pan or skillet heat annatto oil and sauté garlic, onion and chili pepper for seven to eight minutes, stirring occasionally. Add the one cup reserved black beans and mash into the skillet along with onion/garlic mixture.

4. Add skillet mixture to kettle, stirring in salt, oregano, bay leaf, cumin and black pepper. Cover and simmer over low heat for 45 minutes.

5. Stir in sherry and vinegar, cover and simmer for 30 minutes.

6. Remove cover and cook until soup thickens, another 20 minutes or so.

7. Best if allowed to cool and then refrigerated overnight. Remove ham bone and discard.

8. Ladle into individual bowls and garnish with fresh minced onion.

## Dried Beans

**Purchasing:** Buy beans from a busy market. Old beans will take longer to cook.

**Storing:** Never stores beans in their plastic bags. Bugs will eat through anything to get a meal. I had an army of red ants in my kitchen the other day that ate through two layers of garbage bags. Adding a dried chili pepper in with the beans helps keep bugs at bay.

**Preparing:** Spread beans out flat in a shallow baking dish. Discard any small stones, shriveled or broken beans. Pour beans into a large bowl and fill with water. Get rid of any that float to the top. Pour beans into a colander, rinse, and return to bowl, filling with water again. Pour beans into colander, rinse again, then pour into pot for soaking.

**Soaking:** Add 4 cups water for each cup of dried beans. Soaked overnight, beans should have increased to double their size. Drain and rinse. Be sure to discard soaking water as this causes gas.

**Cooking:** To avoid tough beans, do not add acidic ingredients such as tomatoes, vinegar or citrus juice to a bean recipe until the beans have cooked. Avoid adding salt during cooking as well, as this keeps the beans from absorbing water.

**Avoiding split skins:** Bring beans to a boil, then quickly reduce heat to low and cook uncovered.

**Avoiding bean mush:** Add a small amount of sugar to the recipe, i.e. baked beans with molasses, brown sugar etc. to help keep their shape. If you've overcooked the beans, mash with a potato masher to make bean dip. Add hot chili sauce for extra pizzaz.

**Nutrition:** Cooked beans are a good source of folic acid, potassium, and contain small amounts of Vitamin C, magnesium, copper, Vitamin A and iron. High in protein. Combine with other protein source to make a complete protein.

**Yield: 8 servings**

# Black Bean Soup II

Anna's cousin, Doritza Romano, brought us this recipe from her hometown, Ponce. Vegetarians may substitute vegetable broth in place of the chicken stock.

**2 cups soaked, rinsed black beans**

**4 cups chicken stock**

**4 garlic cloves, minced**

**1 teaspoon grated lemon rind**

| | |
|---|---|
| 2 cups water | ½ teaspoon cinnamon |
| 2 tablespoons olive oil | ½ teaspoon dried oregano |
| ½ cup minced yellow onion | 1 bay leaf |
| 1 large chili pepper, seeded and minced | ½ cup dry sherry |

1. Place the soaked beans in a large soup pot. Add chicken stock and water. Bring to boil, uncovered. Reduce heat, and simmer uncovered for 45 minutes until beans are nearly tender.

2. Heat olive oil in medium skillet. Sauté onion, pepper and garlic for 5 minutes until tender, but not browned.

3. Stir in lemon rind, cinnamon, oregano and bay leaf. Add this mixture to bean pot.

4. Add sherry and cook, covered, over low heat for 20 minutes. Add more water as needed. Soup should be thick, but not dry. Remove bay leaf before serving.

**Yield: 6 servings**

# Black Bean Soup with Shrimp

*Frijoles Negros con Camarones*

A sale on shrimp at the market resulted in the birth of this recipe. The addition of shellfish makes this soup a complete protein. Serve at lunch with hot rice and crusty bread, or as a first course at dinner.

| | |
|---|---|
| 5 ounces black beans, rinsed and picked over for stones and soaked overnight | 2 cloves garlic, crushed |
| | ¾ cup minced onion |
| | 2 medium tomatoes, chopped |
| 2 ½ cups water | 2 cups chicken stock |
| ½ teaspoon ground cumin | 1 pound cooked shrimp, tails removed, but left whole |
| ½ teaspoon dried oregano | |
| 1 bay leaf | ¼ cup dry sherry |
| 4 tablespoons annatto oil | |

1. Combine black beans, water, cumin, oregano, and bay leaf in a medium soup pot. Bring to boil over medium-high heat, reduce heat, cover and simmer for one hour. Remove from heat, take off cover and allow to cool for 30 minutes, stirring occasionally

2. Remove bay leaf and puree in food processor, one cup at a time.

3. Heat annatto oil in large skillet and sauté garlic and onion until just soft, but not browned. Add tomato and cook for another minute.

4. Add garlic mixture to food processor and puree. Add chicken stock, return to soup pot and bring to simmer. Fold in cooked shrimp and heat through another ten minutes.

5. Remove from heat and allow to sit for 15 minutes, covered. Stir in sherry and ladle into soup bowls.

**Yield: 4 servings**

## Did You Know?

The eastern islands of **Vieques** and **Culebra** are where Puerto Ricans go for their holidays. Sandy beaches and decent prices are the big attraction here. Charming Culebra is a throwback to the 50's, but Vieques is becoming one of the hottest destinations in the Caribbean. Vieques boasts of stylish inns, some 40+ white-sand beaches and is dotted with the ruins of many sugar and pineapple plantations. Much of Culebra has been designated as a wildlife refuge by the U.S. Fish and Wildlife Service.

# Cold Avocado Soup with Lobster
*Sopa Fria de Agucate*

Cooked, firm white fish, shrimp, or crab may be substituted for the lobster.

**4 large ripe avocados, peeled and diced**

**2 cups chicken stock**

**¼ cup *sofrito* (see index for recipe)**

**½ cup plain yogurt**

**¼ cup light cream**

**2 tablespoons lime juice**

**1 teaspoon apple cider vinegar**

**1 teaspoon salt**

**1 teaspoon cracked black peppercorns**

**1 whole lime, halved**

**1 cup chopped, cooked lobster**

**¼ cup chopped green onions (scallions)**

1. Combine the avocado, chicken stock, *sofrito*, yogurt, cream, lime juice, vinegar, salt and cracked pepper in a blender or food processor. Puree until smooth.

2. Transfer to glass bowl and squeeze lime halves over top to keep the avocado from turning brown. Cover with plastic wrap and refrigerate for at least 2 hours. When ready to serve, remove plastic wrap and fold in chopped lobster.

3. Serve chilled and garnish with chopped onions.

**Yield: 4 to 6 servings**

## LOW-CARB Chayote and Pork Soup

Note, cucumber may be substituted for the Caribbean vegetable, chayote.

2 tablespoons soy sauce

1 tablespoon dry white wine

1 tablespoon lemon juice

¼ teaspoon freshly grated lemon zest

2 garlic cloves, minced

2 tablespoons olive oil

½ pound lean pork, thinly slice

6 cups chicken broth

½ teaspoon Splenda®

1 small chayote, peeled and thinly sliced (or cucumber, peeled and chopped)

1 teaspoon salt

1 teaspoon freshly cracked black pepper

3 tablespoons chopped green onions

paprika

1. Combine soy sauce, white wine, lemon juice, zest and garlic in a small bowl. Add pork and marinate in refrigerator for 2 hours.

2. Heat olive oil a large saucepan over moderate heat. Stir fry pork, reserved marinade, for 5 to 6 minutes.

3. Stir in chicken broth and bring to a boil. Immediately reduce heat and add Splenda®, chayote or cucumber, salt and black pepper. Simmer for 20 minutes over low heat until chayote is soft.

4. Remove from heat and ladle into soup bowls. Sprinkle lightly with paprika and garnish with chopped green onions.

**Yield: 6 servings**

EACH SERVING PROVIDES APPROXIMATELY:
140 calories, **3.5 grams carbohydrates**, 10 grams of protein, 8 grams of fat

# LOW-CARB Curried Cauliflower Soup

Even my children like this soup. So, if you've never been a fan of cauliflower, now's the time to try it. Don't go overboard with the ginger. The flavor should be subtle, not choke you up.

1 tablespoon olive oil
¼ cup minced yellow onion
½ teaspoon freshly grated ginger
2 cloves garlic, peeled and
  coarsely chopped
3 cups chicken broth
1 head cauliflower, washed and
  broken into pieces

1 ½ teaspoons curry powder
¼ teaspoon cinnamon
1 teaspoon salt
½ teaspoon black pepper
½ teaspoon cayenne pepper
¼ cup light cream or half-and-half

1. Heat olive oil in a large skillet over moderate heat. Sauté onion, ginger and garlic for 5 minutes until soft, but not browned.

2. Pour in chicken broth and bring to boil over medium-high heat.

3. Add cauliflower, curry powder, cinnamon, salt, pepper and cayenne.

4. Bring to boil again, lower heat to simmer and cover. Cook for 20 minutes until cauliflower is soft.

5. Remove from heat and allow to cool for 30 minutes. You do not want to puree hot liquid in a blender or food processor, as scalds may result.

6. Puree cooled soup in batches until smooth. Return soup to saucepan over moderate heat.

7. Stir in light cream.

**Yield: 4 servings**

EACH SERVING PROVIDES APPROXIMATELY:
130 calories, **10 grams carbohydrates**, 5 grams of protein, 9 grams of fat

# LOW-CARB Spicy Roasted Red Pepper and Crab Soup with Saffron Cream

I served this at a dinner party for my writing group in San Juan. No one believed it was low-carb. Of course, this was my fiction writing group. Fiction writers have been known to stretch the truth. But, I swear—it's low-carb…really.

4 red bell peppers

¼ cup water

3 tablespoons dry white wine

2 garlic cloves, peeled and
  coarsely chopped

2 tablespoons olive oil

¼ cup chopped yellow onion

2 tablespoons chopped celery

1 teaspoon shredded cilantro

½ teaspoon cumin

¼ teaspoon allspice

1 cup chicken broth

1 cup lump crabmeat, shredded

1 teaspoon salt

1 teaspoon freshly cracked
  black pepper

1 cup half-and-half

SAFFRON CREAM:

¼ teaspoon crumbled saffron threads

½ teaspoon Spenda®

½ cup sour cream

1. Roast red peppers by placing them on an aluminum-covered baking sheet four inches from broiler. Broil for 20 minutes until slightly charred and blistered. Remove from oven and cool for 5 minutes. Place in tightly sealed plastic bag for 20 minutes. Slide off skins and reserve.

2. Puree water, wine, garlic, olive oil, onion, celery, cilantro, cumin and allspice in a food processor. Transfer to medium-size, heated saucepan. Sauté over moderate heat for five minutes.

3. Add chicken broth and bring to boil. Remove from heat and allow to cool for 20 minutes.

4. Puree, along with roasted peppers, in a food processor until smooth. Return to saucepan.

5. Stir in crabmeat, salt and pepper. Heat through over very low heat. Stir in light cream or half-and-half shortly before serving.

6. To make saffron cream: combine saffron, Spenda® and sour cream in a small bowl.

7. Divide soup into six equal bowls. Serve with a dollop of saffron cream.

**Yield: 6 servings**

EACH SERVING CONTAINS APPROXIMATELY:
260 calories, **11 grams carbohydrates**, 10 grams of protein, 20 grams of fat

# LOW-CARB Creamy Curried Chicken Soup with Sun-Dried Tomatoes

Spoon left over soup over pork chops or chicken breasts for another low-carb option.

3 tablespoons butter

2 teaspoons curry powder

¼ teaspoon ground cumin

1/3 cup minced yellow onion

¼ cup chopped celery

2 garlic cloves, peeled and minced

4 sun-dried tomatoes, soaked in hot water, and minced

1 cup chicken broth

1 cup half-and-half

1 cup cooked, diced, boneless, skinless chicken breast

6 tablespoons dry white wine

3 tablespoons lemon juice

1 teaspoon freshly ground black pepper

1. Melt butter in a large saucepan over moderate heat. Add curry powder and cumin, cooking for one minute. Stir in onion and celery, cooking for additional 3 minutes, until onions are soft, but not brown.

2. Add sun-dried tomatoes and chicken broth. Turn heat to medium-high and bring to a boil. Reduce heat and stir in half-and-half, chicken, white wine, lemon juice and pepper. Heat through.

3. Remove from heat and ladle into four bowls.

**Yield: 4 servings**

EACH SERVING PROVIDES APPROXIMATELY:
240 calories, **9.5 grams carbohydrates**, 11 grams of protein, and 16 grams of fat

# Salads

Twenty years ago, the only salad you could find in a Puerto Rican restaurant would be a couple leaves of iceberg lettuce, a tomato and a cucumber drizzled with oil and vinegar. As heart disease soared, the island became more health conscious—salads gained in popularity.

Which made sense, the fertile soil of Puerto Rico supplying an abudance of fruits and vegetables. Today, most salads on the island are served as main courses along with a plate of rice and beans. Salads are made from seafood, vegetables and meat. Avocado, bountiful on the island, is extremely popular, filled with seafood or as a chopped garnish.

When cooking some of the root vegetables, *yautía*, *tania*, taro or sweet potato, considering chilling and adding to your salads. Even though these vegetables are starchy, it will add some 'body' to the salad and valuable nutrients.

## Traditional Green Salad
*Ensalada Verde Tradicional*

If you travel in the country in Puerto Rico, this is a typical salad, simple, fresh and no frills.

2 cups lettuce, curly or romaine

2 medium tomatoes, thinly sliced

1 ripe avocado, peeled, pitted and sliced

½ teaspoon cracked black pepper

½ cup olive oil

4 tablespoons vinegar

½ teaspoon salt

1. Divide lettuce between two plates. Arrange tomato and avocado slices over lettuce.

2. Whisk together olive oil, vinegar, salt and pepper in a small bowl.

3. Drizzle over salad.

**Yield: 2 servings**

# Crab-Stuffed Avocado Salad

*Ensalada de Aguacate*

My ex-husband called this a ladies' luncheon entrée. I noticed it never stopped him from helping himself to my stuffed avocados.

1 pound fresh lump crabmeat, shredded
¾ cup mayonnaise juice of one lime
½ teaspoon cumin
1 tablespoon shredded *culantro* or
2 tablespoons shredded cilantro

1 garlic clove, minced
½ teaspoon salt
½ teaspoon freshly cracked black pepper
2 ripe avocados
Paprika

1. Mix together mayonnaise, lime juice, cumin, cilantro, garlic, salt and pepper in a large bowl until smooth.

2. Toss in crab, combining well.

3. Cut avocados in half and remove pit, discarding it.

4. Scoop crab mixture into avocado halves. Garnish with paprika.

Yield: 4 servings

# Tomato, Avocado and Chayote Salad in Citrus Vinaigrette

*Ensalada de Chayote*

Make a complete meal by adding chopped eggs, cheese, cold, cooked fish, steak or chicken breasts.

2 medium chayotes, peeled and quartered lengthwise
2 large ripe salad tomatoes, thinly sliced
1 large ripe avocado, peeled, pitted, and thinly sliced
1 tablespoon sherry vinegar

2 tablespoons fresh lemon juice
1 tablespoon orange juice
½ teaspoon salt
½ teaspoon freshly cracked black pepper
¼ cup extra-virgin olive oil
1 tablespoon recaíto (see index)

1. Fill a small pot with enough water to cover the chayotes. Bring to a boil over medium heat. Lower chayotes into boiling water, cook until soft, about 20 minutes. Drain and cool. Remove seeds and cut in bit-size pieces.

2. Divide avocado and tomato slices between plates. Arrange chayote over top.

3. To make dressing: whisk together olive oil, vinegar, lemon juice, orange juice, salt, black pepper and *recaíto* in a small bowl.

4. Drizzle over salad.

**Yield: 2 servings**

---

### Did You Know?

**Christopher Columbus,** on his second voyage to the New World, was the first European to set foot on Puerto Rico on November 19, 1493, near what would be later known as Aguadilla. The original name he gave the island was San Juan Bautista.

---

## Plum Tomato, Mozzarella and Red Onion Salad in Chardonnay Vinaigrette

*Ensalada de Tomate, Queso y Cebolla*

Be sure to use fresh basil instead of dried for maximum flavor.

2 pounds ripe plum tomatoes, thinly sliced
1 medium red onion, thinly sliced
1 pound mozzarella cheese (the hard kind,
   not the fresh), cut in ½-inch by 2-inch strips
¼ cup extra-virgin olive oil
½ teaspoon cracked black pepper

2 tablespoons chardonnay or other
   dry white wine
1 garlic clove, minced
½ teaspoon salt
2 tablespoons white wine vinegar
2 tablespoons shredded fresh basil

1. Divide tomatoes between four plates. Arrange onion slices and cheese over top.

2. To make vinaigrette: stir together olive oil, vinegar, wine, garlic, salt, pepper and basil.

3. Drizzle over salad.

**Yield: 4 servings**

# Potato Salad with Mango

*Ensalada de Papa*

Be careful not to overcook the potatoes. Twenty minutes should be plenty. You don't want them mushy.

2 pounds small waxy potatoes, peeled, diced, cooked and cooled

¾ cup mayonnaise

1 small red onion, minced

1 tablespoon *recaíto*

¼ cup diced fresh mango

½ teaspoon freshly cracked black pepper

1 green frying pepper, seeded and chopped

2 tablespoons shredded fresh parsley

4 eggs, hard-boiled and chopped

½ teaspoon salt

1. Combine mayonnaise, onion, *recaíto*, mango, frying pepper and parsley in a small bowl until well-combined.
2. Gently toss potatoes, eggs and mayonnaise mixture in large serving bowl. Chill for several hours before serving. Season to taste with salt.

**Yield: 6 servings**

## Healthy Tip

Instead of pouring calorie-laden dressing over your salad, combine olive oil and vinegar in a spray bottle. Shake well and spray over salad.

# Pigeon Pea, Carrot and Papaya Salad

*Ensalada de Gandules, Zanahorias y Lechoso*

Fresh pigeon peas are difficult to find stateside unless you grow your own. Try and find the frozen first if you can. They're better than the canned.

2 14-ounce bags of frozen pigeon peas or 2 14-ounce cans, drained

1 quart chicken stock (eliminate chicken stock and water if using canned)

1 quart water

1 cup olive oil

¼ cup cider vinegar

2 tablespoons dry white wine

1 garlic clove, minced

½ teaspoon dried tarragon

1½ pounds carrots, peeled and cut in thin slivers lengthwise

1 2-pound ripe papaya, cut in half and flesh scooped out in bite-size pieces

1 teaspoon salt

1 small red onion, minced

1 teaspoon freshly cracked black pepper

1. If using frozen peas, heat chicken stock and water to boiling in a deep kettle. Boil frozen peas for 20 minutes until soft. Drain and cool. Omit this step if using canned. Simply drain the peas and set aside.

2. Combine cooled peas, carrots, papaya and red onion in a large serving bowl. Toss gently.

3. Combine olive oil, vinegar, wine, garlic, tarragon, salt and pepper in a small bowl.

4. Drizzle over salad.

**Yield: 6 servings**

---

### Tip–Salad Gazpacho

Never throw out leftover green salad, even if it has wilted a bit. Puree 2 to 3 cups of vegetable cocktail juice along with 2 cups wilted salad, tightly packed, ½ cup chopped onion, 2 cloves garlic, peeled, 1 tablespoon hot chili pepper sauce, and croutons. Whirl all ingredients except croutons in blender until smooth. Season to taste with freshly cracked black pepper. Garnish with croutons. Voilá–a healthy and refreshing soup.

---

# Tangy Lobster over Spinach Greens

*Ensalada de Langosta*

Caribbean lobster is richer than Maine lobster, so less is needed for the recipe.

1 pound cooked lobster meat (1 ½ pounds if Maine lobster), cut in bite-size chunks

½ cup olive oil

3 tablespoons cider vinegar

2 tablespoons lemon juice

2 tablespoons lime juice

¼ cup minced onion

2 garlic cloves, crushed

½ teaspoon salt

½ teaspoon freshly cracked black pepper

2 cups fresh baby spinach leaves

12 pimento-stuffed olives

1 tablespoon capers

1. Combine olive oil, vinegar, lemon juice, lime juice, onion, garlic, salt and pepper in a small bowl. Reserve.

2. Place lobster in medium serving bowl. Drizzle with olive oil dressing. Toss to coat lobster. Set aside.

3. Arrange spinach leaves, dividing equally between four plates.

4. Top spinach with lobster. Divide olives and capers equally between plates.

**Yield: 4 servings**

## Codfish Salad over Mixed Greens

*Serenata*

Remember, the longer the soaking process for the fish, the less salty it will be.

**1 pound dried salt codfish**

**1 large yellow onion thinly sliced**

**2 large ripe tomatoes, thinly sliced**

**1 large cucumber, peeled, halved, then quartered**

**¾ cup olive oil**

**¼ cup white wine vinegar**

**2 cups mixed greens**

**4 tablespoons fresh lemon or lime juice**

**1 tablespoon sherry**

**¾ teaspoon salt**

**½ teaspoon freshly cracked black pepper**

**¼ teaspoon dried oregano**

**3 tablespoons capers**

1. Soak codfish in a pot of cold water for 4 to 5 hours, changing water every 1 ½ hours to remove salt. Rinse and drain.

2. Fill a pot with enough cold water to cover fish. Bring to boil, cooking fish for 15 minutes. Skim off any scum or skin. Drain, cool and remove bones. Shred fish.

3. Combine olive oil, vinegar, lemon juice, sherry, salt, pepper and oregano in a medium bowl.

4. Toss in fish, coating well. Add capers, tossing gently.

5. Arrange mixed greens on four plates, dividing equally. Arrange sliced tomatoes over greens. Top with codfish.

**Yield: 4 servings**

# LOW-CARB Shrimp, Goat Cheese and Walnut Salad

*Ensalada de Camarones y Queso*

A few toasted walnuts offer lots flavor bang for the buck.

½ cup extra-virgin olive oil

2 garlic cloves, minced

2 tablespoons white wine vinegar

2 tablespoon fresh lemon juice

½ teaspoon freshly grated lemon zest

¼ teaspoon Splenda®

½ teaspoon freshly cracked black pepper

4 ounces goat cheese, cut in 4 equal pieces

¼ cup chopped walnuts, toasted paprika

½ teaspoon salt

½ teaspoon dried cilantro

¼ teaspoon dried oregano

¼ teaspoon dried thyme

6 cups mixed baby greens

1 pound cooked shrimp, peeled, deveined, tails removed

½ teaspoon dry mustard

1. Combine olive oil, garlic, vinegar, lemon juice, zest, Splenda®, black pepper, dry mustard, cilantro, oregano and thyme in a small bowl.

2. Place shrimp in a medium bowl, drizzle dressing over top. Toss together with greens.

3. Divide salad equally between four plates. Arrange a slice of goat cheese on side of each plate. Toss walnuts over top. Sprinkle with paprika for garnish.

**Yield: 4 servings**

EACH SERVINGS PROVIDES APPROXIMATELY:
510 calories, 4.5 **grams carbohydrates**, 30 grams of protein, 42 grams of fat

# LOW-CARB Spicy Pork Tenderloin and Feta Salad in Toasted Hazelnut Vinaigrette

*Ensalada de Pernil y Queso*

This salad works well with any leftover pork, beef, or chicken, the more highly seasoned, the better.

¼ cup finely chopped hazelnuts

½ cup hazelnut oil

3 tablespoons white wine vinegar

1 teaspoon Splenda®

1 tablespoon habañero hot sauce or other spicy chili sauce

3 tablespoons fresh lime juice

2 garlic cloves, minced

1 teaspoon minced onion

1 teaspoon freshly ground ginger

1 ¼ pounds cooked pork tenderloin, thinly sliced

½ teaspoon salt

½ teaspoon freshly cracked black pepper

½ teaspoon cayenne pepper

4 ounces feta cheese, crumbled

6 cups mixed greens

1. Arrange chopped hazelnuts on a baking sheet four inches under a broiler. Broiler for 3 to 5 minutes until golden, but not burnt. Remove from heat and place in a ceramic bowl. Set aside to cool.

2. Combine hazelnut oil, vinegar, lime juice, garlic, onion, ginger, Splenda® and hot sauce in a small bowl. Whisk in salt, pepper, cayenne and toasted hazelnuts.

3. Arrange mixed greens over four plates. Divide pork slices evenly between plates.

4. Drizzle dressing over top. Sprinkle feta over plates.

**Yield: 4 servings**

EACH SERVING PROVIDES APPROXIMATELY:
625 calories, **6 grams carbohydrates,** 46 grams of protein, 50 grams of fat

# LOW-CARB Puerto Rican Beef and Cheese Salad in Citrus Vinaigrette

Doritza's father, who worked as a bank manager in Ponce, would bring this salad to lunch every Monday, the beef tenderloin left over from Sunday dinner.

1 tablespoons cider vinegar

2 tablespoons fresh lemon juice

2 tablespoons fresh lime juice

1 teaspoon grated zest of lemon or lime

¼ cup minced yellow onion

4 garlic cloves, peeled and minced

1 tablespoon minced cilantro

1 tablespoon minced green bell pepper

1 teaspoon cracked black pepper

1 teaspoon salt

½ cup olive oil

8 ounces beef tenderloin, thinly sliced

6 cups mixed greens

¼ pound Puerto Rican white cheese or mozzarella cheese, sliced in thin strips

1. Combine cider vinegar, lemon and lime juice, zest, onion, garlic, cilantro, bell pepper, black pepper, salt and olive oil in a medium bowl. Pour off and reserve half of vinaigrette in refrigerator.

2. Add beef and turn to coat well. Seal in plastic wrap and refrigerate overnight.

3. Sauté beef and marinade in a large non-stick skillet until desired doneness is reached. Remove from heat and cool.

4. Arrange mixed greens on four plates, dividing equally. Top with beef and cheese slices. Drizzle with remaining marinade.

**Yield: 4 servings**

EACH SERVING PROVIDES APPROXIMATELY:
520 calories, **5 grams carbohydrates**, 26 grams of protein, 43 grams of fat

# LOW-CARB Rosemary Chicken, Walnut and Cucumber Salad

*Ensalada de Pollo*

This salad explodes with fresh citrus flavor.

| | |
|---|---|
| 2 tablespoons chopped walnuts | 1 teaspoon crushed rosemary (fresh is best) |
| 4 tablespoons walnut oil | ½ teaspoon salt |
| 1 tablespoon cider vinegar | ½ teaspoon freshly cracked black pepper |
| 1 tablespoon lime juice | ½ teaspoon paprika |
| ½ teaspoon fresh grated lime zest | 6 cups mixed greens |
| 1 tablespoon minced onion | 4 boneless, skinless, chicken breasts (5 ounces each), cooked and thinly sliced |
| 1 garlic clove, crushed | 1 large cucumber, peeled, halved and quartered |

1. Arrange walnuts on a baking sheets and place four inches from broiler. Broil for 3 to 5 minutes until golden, but not browned. Remove from oven and baking sheet, placing in a heat-proof bowl.

2. Combine walnut oil, vinegar, lime juice, zest, onion, garlic, salt, black pepper, paprika and rosemary in a cup.

3.  Divide greens evenly between four plates. Arrange chicken slices over top. Arrange cucumber quarters artistically over chicken.

4.  Drizzle dressing over top.

**Yield: 4 servings**

EACH SERVING APPROXIMATELY PROVIDES:
475 calories, **6 grams carbohydrates,** 46 grams of protein, 32 grams of fat

# Rice Dishes: Arroz

One of the most important staples in the world, rice was known to be cultivated in China over 6,000 years ago. The Arabs introduced rice to the Greeks, and Alexander the Great brought it to India around 326 B.C. The scientific name *oryza* comes from the Greek word for rice. In A.D. 700, the Moors conquered Spain and brought rice with them. The Spanish conquistadors brought rice to the new world, the Americas, at the beginning of the 17th century. African slaves, imported to work the sugar plantations, also influenced the development of a rice-based cuisine.

The type of rice use will affect the flavor and texture of a dish. Short-grain and medium-grain rice take longer to cook, absorbing liquids slowly. Long-grain rice cooks faster and absorbs less. The texture of long-grain rice is fluffier. Note the small grains of sushi rice and how the rice clumps together.

In Puerto Rico, two sorts of rice are used: medium for brothy dishes like *asopaq* and sweet pudding-like desserts such as *arroz con dulce*. Long-grain rice works well for *arroz con pollo* (rice and chicken), *paella*, and *queso relleno con arroz con pollo* (stuffed cheese with rice and chicken).

## White Rice
*Arroz Blanco*

The secret to a light fluffy rice is to sauté the dried rice grains in oil, butter or pork fat. The oil slows down the abosorption of liquids, allowing the rice to cook slowly until tender. Stirring while cooking will result in a sticky rice, *amogollao*.

Any rice that sticks to the bottom of the pot is called *pegao*. This crispy, tasty is a delicacy and considered a treat. Be sure to use plenty of oil to make the best *pegao*.

**4 tablespoons butter or vegetable oil**     **1 teaspoon salt**

**2 cups long-grain white rice**               **4 cups cold water**

1. Place rice in a large bowl and add enough water to cover. Allow to sit for 2 minutes. Pour into a colander and rinse well under running water.

2. Heat oil or butter slowly in a kettle or cast iron stock pot. Stir in rice and salt, mixing well. Immediately pour in cold water. Stir, scraping bottom of pot.

3. Bring to a rapid boil, then reduce heat to medium. Cook uncovered until water cooks down and top of rice is bubbly.

4. Reduce heat to low and cover. Cook for 20 minutes.

5. Uncover, flip rice over with a fork from the bottom up. Cook for additional 5 to 8 minutes until all water is absorbed.

**Yield: serves 6**

# Garlic Rice

*Arroz con Ajo*

Garlic rice is quick to make, providing a nice change from blah, boiled rice.

**4 tablespoons olive oil or butter**  **2 cups long-grain rice**
**2 cloves garlic crushed**  **4 cups cold water**
**2 teaspoons salt**

1. Place rice in a large bowl and add enough water to cover. Allow to sit for 2 minutes. Pour into a colander and rinse well under running water.

2. Heat oil or butter slowly in a kettle or cast iron stock pot. Add garlic, rice and salt, mixing well. Immediately pour in cold water. Stir, scraping bottom of pot.

3. Bring to a rapid boil, then reduce heat to medium. Cook uncovered until water cooks down and top of rice is bubbly.

4. Reduce heat to low and cover. Cook for 20 minutes.

5. Uncover, flip rice over with a fork from the bottom up. Cook for additional 5 to 8 minutes until all water is absorbed.

**Yield: serves 6**

# Basic Seasoned Rice

You may substitute olive oil for the bacon or salt pork rind.

**1 slice bacon or 1 ½-inch cube of salt pork rind**  **2 cups long-grain white rice**
**1/3 cup *sofrito* (see index)**  **½ teaspoon salt**
**1 tablespoon annatto-colored olive oil**  **4 cups cold water**

1. Fry the bacon or salt pork rind in a kettle over medium heat until crispy. Remove meat. Crumble bacon and set aside Add *sofrito* and annatto oil and sauté for 5 minutes over moderate heat.

2. Stir in rice and salt, mixing well. Immediately pour in cold water and stir, scraping bottom of pot.

3. Bring to a rapid boil, then reduce heat to medium. Cook uncovered until water cooks down and top of rice is bubbly.

4. Reduce heat to low and cover. Cook for 20 minutes.

5. Uncover, flip rice over with a fork from the bottom up. Cook for additional 5 to 8 minutes until all water is absorbed.

**Yield: serves 6**

---

### Did You Know?

**Puerto Rico** is 3,435 square miles, about the size of Connecticut. It's north coast faces the Atlantic Ocean, while the East and South coast face the Caribbean Sea. The Virgin Islands are located to the east, and numerous small cays and islets dot its coast. Almost rectangular, the island is 111 miles east to west and 36 miles north to south.

---

## Basic Yellow Rice

Don't use an instant or Uncle Ben's type of rice with this recipe. It won't work.

| | |
|---|---|
| 4 tablespoons annatto-colored olive oil | 1 tablespoon sofrito (see index) |
| 2 ½ cups medium grain rice | 3 ½ cups water |
| 2 chicken bouillon cubes, crushed | 2 teaspoons salt |

1. Heat the olive oil in a medium saucepan over moderate heat. Sauté the rice for 2 minutes until glistening.

2. Add chicken bouillon and stir well until cubes are dissolved.

3. Stir in sofrito and cook for 1 minute.

4. Add water and salt and bring to boil over high heat.

5. Reduce heat once water has nearly evaporated. Stir a couple times and cover.

6. Simmer for 25 minutes until rice is tender.

**Yield: 4 to 6 servings**

# Basic Stewed Rice

*Arroz Guisado Básico*

To make a meal of this rice, add 2 cups of one of the following cooked ingredients: shrimp, crab, lobster, firm white fish, chicken, Vienna sausages or beans.

**1 ounce salt pork, rinsed and diced**
**1 ounces cured ham, rinsed and diced**
**3 tablespoons olive oil**
**1 tablespoon annatto oil**
**2/3 cup *sofrito***
**1 tablespoon tomato paste**

**2 tablespoons *alcaparrado***
**1 ¾ cups long grain rice, rinsed and drained**
**1 ¾ cups boiling water**
**salt and pepper to taste**

1. Brown pork and ham in a deep kettle or soup pot over medium heat.
2. Add olive and annatto oil and *sofrito*. Sauté for ten minutes over low heat, stirring now and then.
3. Stir in tomato paste and *alcaparrado*.
4. Add rice and sauté for 3 minutes, until rice glistens.
5. Pour in boiling water, stir, mixing well. Cover and cook over moderate heat until rice is dry. Resist the urge to stir.
6. Once rice is dry, flip it over from top to bottom with a large wooden spoon. Reduce heat and simmer for 15 minutes.
7. Flip rice again. Simmer additional 15 minutes. Season to taste with salt and pepper.

**Yield: 6 to 8 servings**

# Pigeon Peas and Rice

*Arroz con Gandules*

Christmas in Puerto Rico would not be the same without *arroz con gandules*.

3 slices bacon or 4 tablespoons
  vegetable oil (add 1 teaspoon salt
  if using oil instead of bacon)
½ cup *sofrito* (see index)
1 tablespoon *alcaparrado*

2 cups long-grain rice
4 cups cold water
½ cup diced lean smoked ham
1 ½ cups shelled pigeon peas
2 tablespoons tomato sauce

1. Fry the bacon or heat the oil in a kettle over medium heat. When bacon is crisp, remove, crumble and set aside.

2. Sauté the *sofrito* for 5 minutes. Add *alcaparrado* and rice. Immediately add water and stir.

3. Add ham, pigeon peas and tomato sauce. Return bacon to kettle. Stir well to mix.

4. Bring to a boil, then reduce heat to medium. Cook uncovered until water boils down and top of rice looks bubbly.

5. Reduce heat to low, cover and cook for 25 minutes.

6. Remove cover, fluff rice once with a fork from the bottom up. Cook for additional 8 to 10 minutes until all water is absorbed. Serve with roast pork, turkey or *ropa viejo*.

**Yield: serves 6 to 8**

## Pegao

The golden brown, crunchy rice that adheres to the bottom of a pot is called *pegao*. A favorite of Puerto Ricans, there's a true art to making it. I burnt the *pegao* several times before I became successful at it. Use extra oil and cook the rice, uncovered, for an extra 10 to 15 minutes. Keep in mind if you want a lot of *pegao*, you'll want a pot with a larger bottom, i.e. more *pegao*.

# Rice and Beans

*Arroz con Gandules*

Every Caribbean island has a technique for rice and beans. But the best tasting recipes come from Puerto Rico. I think it's the cilantro that makes the difference.

¾ cup sofrito (see index)

1 can tomato sauce

2 tablespoons, plus 1 teaspoon alcaparrado (see index)

4 tablespoons annatto-colored oil (see index)

2 cups long grain rice

3 cups hot water

1 16-ounce can pigeon peas

salt and pepper to taste

1. Sauté sofrito, tomato sauce, alcaparrado in the annatto-colored oil in a heavy stockpot or kettle over moderate heat for 5 minutes.

2. Add rice and hot water and cook uncovered, bringing to a boil until most of the water has been absorbed.

3. Once water has been absorbed, fold in pigeon peas, stirring gently a couple times from top to bottom. Do not stir after this point or the rice will go gummy or *amogollao*.

4. Cover and reduce heat to low. Simmer for 25 minutes. Season to taste with salt and pepper.

**Yield: 8 servings**

# Rice with Okra and Onions

*Arroz con Guingambós*

1 ounce diced salt pork

1 ½ ounces diced cured ham

1 tablespoon annatto oil

2 tablespoons olive oil

½ cup *sofrito*

1 large yellow onion, coarsely chopped

1 tablespoon *alcaparrado*

6 pimento-stuffed olives, chopped

2 tablespoons tomato paste

2 tablespoons dry sherry

½ teaspoon dried oregano

3 cups water

½ cup chicken stock

2 cups long-grain rice

2 cups fresh sliced okra or frozen

1. Brown the salt pork and ham in the annatto and olive oil in a deep kettle or pot over moderate heat.

2. Mix in *sofrito* and onion. Sauté until onions are soft, but not browned, about 5 minutes.

3. Stir in *alcaparrado*, olives, tomato paste and sherry. Cook for 3 minutes, then stir in dried oregano.

4. Pour chicken stock and water into kettle. Turn heat to high and bring to boil.

5. Stir in rice and bring to boil again. Reduce heat and cook uncovered until water reaches top of rice.

6. Fold in okra, flipping rice from top to bottom. Reduce heat and cook uncovered for 15 minutes.

7. Flip rice gently again. Cover and cook for 15 minutes.

**Yield: 6 servings**

# Buttered Rice with Vegetables and Vermouth

*Arroz con Mantequilla y Vegetales y Vermouth*

Anna's grandmother gave us this recipe. By now, I have noticed though that all of her recipes have some sort of liquor added to them.

**4 tablespoons butter**
**½ cup minced onion**
**2 cups long-grain rice**
**2 cups water**
**1 cup chicken broth**
**1 teaspoon *picada* seasoning (see index)**

**¼ cup dry vermouth**
**¾ cup finely diced carrot**
**¾ cup fresh or canned peas**
**2 teaspoons salt**
**½ teaspoon freshly cracked pepper**

1. Sauté the onion in the butter over moderate heat until soft, about 5 minutes.

2. Stir in rice and sauté 2 to 3 minutes until glistening.

3. Pour in broth and water, turn heat to high and bring to boil.

4. Stir in *picada* seasoning, vermouth, diced carrots and peas. Note, if using canned, do not add peas at this time. Stir in salt and pepper.

5. Bring to boil again, reduce heat and cook uncovered until rice is nearly dry.

6. Flip rice from top to bottom. If using canned peas, add at this time.

7. Reduce heat to low, cover and cook, covered for 15 minutes.

8. Flip rice again from top to bottom. Cook, covered for 15 minutes. Season to taste with salt and pepper.

**Yield: 6 servings**

# Rice with Vienna Sausage
*Arroz con Salchichas*

In the Virgin Islands, it seems everything has canned evaporated milk added to it. Probably something to do with the old days, lack of refrigeration and the difficulty in transporting milk to the islands. Here in Puerto Rico, I find Vienna sausage added to many dishes. I finally had to try them. Seasoned properly, they're actually quite good. Use in rice dishes and stews.

¼ cup *recaíto*
1 tablespoon olive oil
1 tablespoon annatto oil
¼ cup tomato paste
3 tablespoons dry sherry (optional)

1 9-ounce can of Vienna sausage, drained and cut in ½-inch pieces
¼ cup *alcaparrado*
3 cups chicken broth
1 ½ cups long-grain rice

1. Sauté the *recaíto* in the olive and annatto oil in a deep kettle or pot over moderate heat for 5 minutes.

2. Stir in tomato paste and sherry, reduce heat and simmer for 1 minutes.

3. Fold in sausage and *alcaparrado*, cooking for additional minute.

4. Pour in chicken broth, turn heat up and bring to boil.

5. Whisk in rice, reduce heat to moderate and simmer, uncovered until liquid level is almost to top of rice.

6. Fork rice over once from top to bottom. Cover and cook on low heat for 20 to 25 minutes until down. Fluff rice from top to bottom before serving.

**Yield: 6 servings**

## Squid

**Purchasing:** Purchase squid fresh, frozen, canned or dried. Keep in mind that fresh or defrosted squid is not always ready for cooking. Search out squid that is fresh and moist, with just a faint ocean smell.

**Storing:** Cooked or uncooked squid keeps for 1 to 2 days in the refrigerator. In fact, squid, recently caught, will tenderize if left to chill for a day or so.

**Preparing:** Remove transparent cartilage (the pen) and discard. Separate head from body and toss out. Lay out tentacles flat, slice off just below eyes and detach beaklike mouth from body. Rinse tentacles and body. Remove membrane by scraping with a paring knife. Slice in ½-inch pieces.

**Nutrition:** Squid is high in riboflavin and vitamin B12. Rich in protein and low in carbohydrates.

# Rice with Squid

*Arroz Con Negro*

If you're a fan of calamari, instead of cooking the squid with the rice, dip the squid pieces in a light batter and deep fry. Set aside and later fold into cooked rice recipe.

**1.5 pounds squid**

**4 tablespoons extra-virgin olive oil**

**1 tablespoon annatto-colored olive oil**

**4 large garlic cloves, crushed**

**1 large onion, minced**

**1 pimento, minced**

**1 tablespoon alcaparrado**

**1 chili pepper, minced**

**1/3 cup red wine**

**1 ripe, yet firm tomato, diced**

**1 tablespoon cilantro, minced**

**3 cups chicken or fish stock (better)**

**2 cups risotto rice**

**salt and pepper to taste**

**6 garlic cloves, peeled**

**¼ cup olive oil**

**2 teaspoons sea salt**

1. Follow instructions for cleaning squid above, but reserve the *pen*.

2. Heat olive oil and annatto-colored oil in the bottom of a covered casserole dish on the stove top over medium heat. Sauté onion and garlic for 3 minutes until just clear.

3. Toss in squid pieces and sauté for 5 minutes. Stir in pimento, alcaparrado, chili pepper, tomato and cilantro. Reduce heat and simmer for 35 minutes.

4. Bring broth to a boil in a small saucepan over medium heat.

5. Meanwhile, break up the ink sac in a small bowl with the red wine. Press through a sieve several times until most of the ink has been squeezed from the sac. Set aside.

6. Preheat oven to 325°F.

7. Pour boiling broth into squid mixture in casserole. Stir in rice and wine/ink mixture. Bring to a boil and cook for 10 minutes until rice is no longer swishy or soupy, but some liquid remains. Remove from heat.

8. Transfer casserole dish to oven. Bake for 15 minutes, uncovered. Remove from oven and place cover on dish. Allow to sit for 15 minutes.

9. Meanwhile, puree the 6 garlic cloves, ¼ olive and 2 teaspoons salt in a blender or food processor until smooth. Pour into small bowl.

10. Place rice and squid on dinner plates. Serve with garlic sauce on the side.

**Yield: 6 servings**

# Rice with Crab
*Arroz Con Jueyes*

Great land crabs exist all over the Caribbean. I'll never forget the time I was on a photo shoot on Grand Cayman, about a mile from where they filmed the movie *The Firm*. There were literally thousands of crabs crossing the roads. Our jeep couldn't move, so I jumped out to shoo them away. I felt so bad. All these cars were running them over. Eventually I gave up and we had no choice but to drive over the poor creatures to get to where we were going. Our island hostess later explained that the extraordinary crab sighting meant a hurricane later in the season. Later that year, Hurricane Marilyn struck.

Note: Lobster or shrimp may be substituted for the crab.

| | |
|---|---|
| 4 tablespoons extra-virgin olive oil | 2 tablespoons tomato paste |
| 1 tablespoon annatto oil | ¼ cup dry white wine |
| ¼ cup diced cured ham | 3 ½ cups water |
| ½ cup *sofrito* | 1 cup chicken broth |
| 2 green frying peppers, seeded and chopped | 3 cups long-grain rice, rinsed |
| ½ teaspoon dried oregano | 2 ½ cups cooked crabmeat |
| ½ teaspoon dried basil | salt and pepper to taste |
| 3 tablespoons *alcaparrado* | |

1. Brown the ham in a deep kettle in the annatto oil and olive oil over medium heat.

2. Stir in *sofrito* and frying peppers. Sauté for 5 minutes until peppers are just soft.

3. Fold in oregano, basil, *alcaparrado* and tomato paste, cooking 2 more minutes.

4. Pour in white wine, water and chicken broth. Turn heat on high and bring to boil.

5. Add rice and stir.

6. Reduce heat to medium, and cook uncovered until water reaches level of rice.

7. Fork over rice from top to bottom. Reduce heat to low, and cover uncooked for 10 minutes.

8. Fold in crabmeat, forking over rice again. Cover and cook over low heat for 20 minutes. Season to taste with salt and pepper.

**Yield: 6 servings**

# Rice with Salt Fish
*Arroz con Bacalao*

Preserved, dried codfish is popular all over the Caribbean as well. Soak and rinse the fish several times to reduce sodium content.

| | |
|---|---|
| 2 pounds salt codfish, thawed and cut in 1 ½-inch pieces | ½ teaspoon paprika |
| 2 tablespoons annatto oil | ½ teaspoon fresh cracked pepper |
| 1 tablespoon olive oil | 3 tablespoons *alcaparrado* |
| 1 ounce diced salt pork fatback | 1 tablespoon minced roasted pimento (canned is fine) |
| ¼ cup diced cured ham | 1 tablespoon dry vermouth |
| ½ cup *sofrito* | 3 ½ cups water |
| 1 teaspoon dried oregano | 2 ¼ cups long-grain rice |

1. Soak the salt codfish in cold water for 45 minutes. Drain and remove any skin and bones. Rinse and cover again with water. Set aside.

2. Heat annatto oil and olive oil in deep kettle over moderate heat. Brown the pork and ham on all sides. Drain excess fat.

3. Add *sofrito*, oregano, paprika and black pepper. Cook for 5 minutes.

4. Fold in *alcaparrado*, pimento and dry vermouth. Cook 5 minutes.

5. Add water and turn heat to high. Bring to boil. Stir in rice. Bring to boil, uncovered, then reduce heat to medium. Cook for 20 minutes. Liquid should be almost down to level of rice.

6. Rinse and drain codfish.

7. Fork over rice from top to bottom, folding in codfish. Cover, reduce heat and simmer for 25 minutes, until rice is dry. Fork over once while cooking.

**Yield: 6 servings**

---

### Tip—Rice

- To reheat cooked rice, place rice in an appropriately sized saucepan. Add 2 tablespoons water per cup of cooked rice. Cover and simmer over low heat until hot and all water is absorbed.

- To keep rice warm, place two layers of white paper towels under the lid. This will absorb steam and keep rice from becoming gooey.

- To cook a large amount of rice, use a pot with a large bottom, at least 10 inches in diameter.

---

## Saffron Rice with Seafood

*Arroz con Mariscos*

This makes a great buffet dish. To economize a bit, purchase smaller shrimp and double the amount of white, firm fish used.

¼ cup olive olive oil

½ cup minced yellow onion

2 large ripe tomatoes, peeled, seeded and chopped

2 green frying peppers, seeded and minced

1 pound raw shrimp, shelled and deveined

1 pound raw lobster medallions (crab is good also)

3 ½ cups fish stock

½ cup white wine

1 jalapeño pepper, seeded and minced

3 tablespoons *picado* seasoning

1 tablespoon tomato paste

½ pound firm white fish, cut in 1 ½ inch cubes (halibut is good, but swordfish is divine)

2 cups long-grain rice

1 pound raw clams, cleaned

1 pound raw mussels, cleaned and debearded

1. Heat olive oil in deep kettle or pot. Sauté onion, tomato and peppers over medium heat until soft, about 5 minutes.

2. Stir in *picado* seasoning and tomato paste. Cook for 1 minute.

3. Toss in fish, shrimp and lobster. Sauté for 2 minutes.

4. Add fish stock and white wine. Turn heat to medium high and bring to boil.

5. Stir in rice. Cook uncovered, heat reduced to moderate for 30 minutes. Liquid should be down to level of rice.

6. Fork over rice from top to bottom gently. Cook uncovered over low heat for 10 minutes.

7. Fork rice over again, folding in clams and mussels. Cover and cook for 10 minutes.

8. Remove from heat and allow to sit for 5 minutes. Discard any mussels or clams that haven't opened.

**Yield: 6 to 8 servings**

# Traditional Puerto Rican Paella

Spain's famous paella dish originated in the seaside port of Valencia. Along with many other culinary gifts from the Spaniards, paella made its way across the ocean to Puerto Rico. Annatto oil adds a beautiful pale orange color and smoky flavor.

2 pounds chicken pieces, rinsed and patted dry

2 teaspoons salt

2 cups long-grain rice

4 ½ cups chicken or fish stock

1 teaspoon freshly cracked pepper

½ pound lean pork, diced

¼ cup olive oil, divided

3 tablespoons annatto oil

1 cup minced yellow onion

2 green frying peppers, seeded
  and diced

6 large cloves garlic, minced

2 *chorizos*, cut in ½-inch pieces

2 tomatoes, peeled, seeded and diced

½ teaspoon saffron threads

2 pounds frozen raw shrimp

1 pound frozen raw lobster meat,
  shells removed and coarsely chopped

1 10-ounce can clams, drained

1 cup frozen or fresh green peas

1 seven-ounce can pimentos

1 bunch fresh asparagus, trimmed
  and cooked (you may use canned)

12 to 18 frozen mussels, ready to cook

1. Season chicken and pork with salt. Heat ¼ cup of the olive oil in a deep kettle or skillet. Brown chicken and pork on all sides over medium heat. Remove from skillet and reserve.

2. Preheat oven to 350°F. Drain olive oil from skillet and discard.

3. Add remaining ¼ olive oil to skillet along with annatto oil. Reduce heat slightly and sauté onions, peppers and garlic for five minutes.

4. Stir in chorizo and tomatoes. Remove from heat while crisping saffron.

5. In a small frying pan, dry heat saffron over moderate heat until crunchy. Remove from heat and cool. Crumble with hands into onion/pepper mixture and return to stove over moderate heat.

6. Add rice and ¾ cup of stock, along with cracked pepper. Cook for 5 to 6 minutes, stirring often. Add remaining stock, stirring well.

7. Transfer to oven-proof casserole or *paellera* (special paella dish)

8. Arrange chicken, pork, shrimp, lobster, clams and peas, so that they are covered by stock.

9. Cook for 45 minutes until all liquid has been absorbed.

10. Follow cooking instructions on package of mussels. If the paella has come out a bit dry, pour some of the seasoned liquid from the cooked mussels over the rice.

11. Garnish with cooked asparagus strips. Arrange mussels over top, discarding any that have not opened.

**Yield: serves 6**

# Spicy Seafood Paella

Paella takes its name from the traditional cooking utensil, *paellera*, a round, flat, tow-handled iron pan. A large casserole dish or heavy frying pan will do nicely as well. Vegetarians: substitute ¾ cup marinated spicy tofu, crumbled, for the *chorizo*. Add ½ small jalapeño pepper, seeded and minced, plus 1 teaspoon dried oregano.

¼ cup olive oil

2 *chorizo* Spanish sausages

2 green frying peppers, seeded
  and diced

1 large yellow onion, minced

6 large cloves of garlic, minced

1 teaspoon cayenne pepper

½ teaspoon saffron threads

2 cups long-grain rice

1 ¼ cups chicken stock or
  vegetable stock

1 ½ cups bottled clam juice

½ cup water

1 cup white wine

1 teaspoon freshly ground
  black pepper

1 tablespoon paprika

1 teaspoon salt

1 tablespoon fresh basil, chopped
  or 1 teaspoon dried

1 9-ounce package frozen peas

1 pound firm white fish, cut
  in 1-inch pieces

1 pound raw shrimp, shelled
  and deveined

12 small clams in shell, scrubbed

12 mussels in shell, scrubbed
  and debearded

1 pound raw lobster tails in shell,
  coarsely chopped

1 can pimento strips, drained and
  lightly heated in microwave

1 can asparagus, drained and
  lightly heated in microwave

1. Heat olive oil in 14-inch paella pan, heavy skillet or 4-quart ovenproof dish over moderate heat.

2. Remove casings from *chorizo* and crumble sausage into pan. If using tofu, do the same. Brown lightly, stirring often.

3. Add frying pepper, onion, garlic and cayenne pepper. Sauté until onion is soft, stirring often.

4. Preheat oven to 350°F.

5. Heat saffron threads in a small frying pan over moderate heat until crispy. Remove from heat and cool. Crumble into paella pan.

6. Stir in rice, chicken stock, clam juice, water and wine. Bring to boil over moderate to high heat. Add salt, paprika and pepper.

7. Remove from heat, cover and bake at 350°F for 30 minutes. Stirring twice during baking time.

8. Stir in basil and frozen peas. Fold in fish, shrimp, clams and mussels. Arrange lobster pieces on top. Cover and cook for 15 minutes until shrimp are opaque in center and clams pop open. Discard any clam or mussel that does not open.

9. Garnish with asparagus and pimento strips.

**Yield: 6 to 8 servings**

# Award-Winning Paella

This prize-winning recipe comes from Anna's cousin in Utuado (central mountains) who won first place in a local contest. You can use canned broths to save time, but homemade can't be beat. Next time you make chicken or fish stock, reserve some of the broth and freeze it for future use with paella.

¼ cup olive oil

¾ cup diced cured ham

4 ounces *chorizo* sausage,
  casings removed

2 pounds chicken parts,
  chopped into pieces

1 teaspoon salt

½ pound squid, diced

1 pound firm white fish
  such as halibut, diced

1 pound medium raw shrimp,
  shelled and deveined, tails on

1/2 cup yellow onion, minced

2 tomatoes, peeled, seeded
  and chopped

2 green frying peppers, seeded and minced

1 small red bell pepper, seeded
  and minced

½ cup *picada* seasoning (see index)

3 cups long-grain rice

3 cups hot chicken stock

3 cups hot fish stock

½ cup white wine

½ cup dry sherry

¼ cup fresh lime juice

¾ pound cooked clams, discard unopened
  ones

1 pound cooked mussels, discard unopened
  ones

1 pound cooked crab legs

1. Heat olive oil in large skillet (15-inch) or paella pan. Sauté ham for

2 minutes. Crumble *chorizo* into pan and lightly brown. Remove from pan and set aside.

2. Sprinkle chicken with salt. Sauté in pan over medium-high heat until browned on all sides. Remove from pan and reserve.

3. Add squid and halibut. Add another couple tablespoons olive oil if needed. Sauté for 4 minutes. Remove from pan and reserve.

4. Add shrimp and sauté until no longer pink, about 4 minutes. Remove from pan and reserve.

5. Add onion, tomato, green and red peppers. Sauté until onion is clear, about 4 to 5 minutes. Do not brown onions.

6. Stir in *picada* seasoning. Sauté for 2 minutes over moderate heat.

7. Stir in rice. Sauté for 2 minutes. Pour in chicken stock, fish stock and lime juice. Stir.

8. Turn heat to high and boil for 20 minutes without stirring. Fold in reserved chicken, fish and shellfish.

9. Reduce heat to very low, cover and simmer for 10 minutes without stirring. Mixture should be dry. Stir in white wine and sherry.

10. Arrange cooked clams, mussels and crab legs on top of rice. Cover and simmer for 10 more minutes.

11. Remove from heat and take off cover. Place a clean dish towel over pan. This will absorb excess liquid from rice. Allow to sit 10 minutes. Serve at once.

**Yield: 6 to 8 servings**

# Rice with Roast Pork

*Arroz con Lechón Asado*

Because of innovative new breeding techniques, pork is rapidly becoming the lean meat of the future.

| | |
|---|---|
| 1 tablespoon annatto oil | 1 pound roasted pork meat, cut |
| 1 tablespoon olive oil | in 1-inch cubes |
| ½ cup *sofrito* | 1 ¾ cups water |
| 3 tablespoons tomato paste | 1 ½ cups chicken broth |
| ¼ cup white wine or sherry | 2 cups long-grain rice, rinsed |

1. Heat the annatto oil and olive oil in a large pot or deep kettle. Sauté the *sofrito* for 5 minutes over moderate heat.

2. Stir in tomato paste and cooking wine. Cook for 3 minutes.

3. Fold in pork cubes and sauté for 3 minutes.

4. Add water and chicken broth, turn up heat and bring to boil.

5. Stir in rice and reduce heat to medium. Cook uncovered until water level reaches the top of the rice.

6. Stir rice from top to bottom with a fork or large spoon. Cover, reduce heat and simmer for 15 minutes.

7. Fluff rice again from top to bottom. Cover and cook for 15 minutes.

**Yield: 6 servings**

# Rice with Spareribs
*Arroz con Costillas*

Tasuki and Natalie saga continued from *Vegetable Soup with Plantain Balls*: A sharp cry from baby Natalie had Anna and I rushing to the playpen. The baby smiled up at us. Hmm, no Tasuki. Bewildered, we returned to the kitchen just in time to see Tasuki jump on the kitchen counter where a pot of rice and spareribs cooled. He stood on his hind legs, put his paws on the edge of the pot (I still can't believe it didn't flip over.) reached in and grabbed a sparerib. As he dashed away and secreted himself behind the washer, I had my first suspicion that Natalie and Tasuki were in cahoots. It was a week before I located the gnawed down bone. Go to the recipe for *Mashed Potatoes and Carrots* for more on Tasuki and Natalie.

1 ounce salt pork

2 ounces diced cured ham

1 tablespoon annatto oil

2 tablespoons olive oil

1 ½ pounds spareribs, washed
  and divided into 2-rib sections

½ cup *sofrito*

2 tomatoes, peeled, seeded and diced

2 tablespoons *alcaparrado*

6 pimento-stuffed olives, diced

1 teaspoon dried oregano

3 tablespoons tomato paste

¼ cup dry sherry or water

2 ½ cups water

½ cup chicken broth

1 ½ cups long-grain rice

1. Brown salt pork and ham over medium heat in the annatto and olive oil. Toss in spareribs and brown lightly. Pour off excess grease. Remove meat from pot and reserve.

2. Reduce heat and blend in *sofrito* and tomatoes. Simmer until soft.

3. Add *alcaparrado*, olives, oregano and tomato paste, along with sherry. Cover and simmer for 5 minutes.

4. Turn heat to high and add water and chicken broth, stirring once. Bring to a boil.

5. Mix in rice and bring to a boil. Reduce heat to medium and cook, uncovered until rice is nearly dry.

6. Fluff rice from top to bottom and fold in reserved meat. Reduce heat to low, cover and cook for 15 minutes.

7. Fluff rice again, cover and cook additional 15 minutes.

**Yield: 6 servings**

# Rice with Roast Pork and Beans

*Arroz Apastelado*

Note, any roast meat leftovers will work for this dish: lamb, veal or beef.

1 ¼ pounds lean pork meat, fresh ham or shoulder, rinsed and diced

1 quart water

¼ cup dry sherry

1 garlic clove, crushed

1 medium yellow onion, halved

1 small carrot, peeled and coarsely chopped

1 small ham bone, rinsed

1 tablespoon olive oil

¼ pound lean cured ham, rinsed and cubed

2 tablespoons tomato paste

1 tablespoon fresh chopped oregano or 1 teaspoon dried

1 teaspoon fresh chopped basil, or ½ teaspoon dried

2 tablespoons *alcaparrado*

1 tablespoon annatto oil

2 cups rice, rinsed and soaked for 1 hour

1 ½ cups cooked pigeon peas or canned

¼ cup lime juice

3 tablespoons raisins

½ cup *sofrito*

2 green frying peppers, seeded and chopped

2 tomatoes, peeled, seeded and chopped

salt

pepper

1 plantain leaf, rinsed and dried

1. Fill a deep saucepan with water and sherry. Cover and boil the lean pork meat, garlic, onion, small carrot and ham bone over moderate heat for 25 minutes. Discard vegetables and hambone, reserving pork meat and broth.

2. Heat olive oil in large kettle or cast iron pot. Brown cured ham over medium to high eat. Stir in *sofrito*, chopped tomato and peppers. Simmer for 7 to 8 minutes, stirring often.

3. Fold in tomato paste, oregano, basil, *alcaparrado*, and annatto oil. Cook for 3 minutes.

4. Add rice, stir and sauté for 2 minutes. Rice should be coated.

5. Pour in reserved broth and pork meat. Cook over low to medium heat, uncovered until rice is nearly dry, about 25 to 30 minutes.

6. Fold over top to bottom with a fork. Stir in pigeon peas, lime juice and raisins.

7. Cover with rinsed plantain leaf and simmer over low heat for 20 minutes. Flip rice again from top to bottom gently. Cover and simmer for additional 10 minutes. Season to taste with salt and pepper.

**Yield: 6 servings**

# Rice with Pork, Bacon and Black Beans
*Congri*

This actually tastes pretty good cold. Anna's husband takes this to work in an insulated thermos.

2 thick slices bacon

1 teaspoon annatto oil

¼ pound cured ham, diced

½ pound pork shoulder meat, cubed

½ cup *sofrito*

½ teaspoon dried oregano

¼ teaspoon dried basil

¼ teaspoon coriander

1 teaspoon salt to taste

1 ½ cups cooked black beans or canned

2 tablespoons tomato paste

2 tablespoons dry sherry

1 bay leaf

½ teaspoon cumin

2 cups water

1 cup chicken broth

2 cups long-grain rice, rinsed

1. Fry bacon in a deep kettle or soup pot until crunchy, but not burnt. Remove from kettle and cool. Crumble and reserve.

2. Brown the cured ham in the bacon drippings and annatto oil over moderate heat in the same kettle. Remove ham and set aside.

3. Brown pork meat in kettle. Reduce heat to low and stir in *sofrito*, cooking for 5 minutes.

4. Add tomato paste, sherry, bay leaf, cumin, oregano, basil, coriander and salt. Cook for 5 minutes.

5. Fold in beans and stir. Pour in water and chicken broth, stirring to combine.

6. Turn heat up, add reserved pork and ham. Bring to a boil.

7. Pour rice into kettle and stir. Reduce heat to medium and cook, uncovered, until nearly all the liquid has been absorbed.

8. Stir rice from top to bottom with a fork. Reduce heat to low and simmer, covered for 12 minutes.

9. Stir rice again from top to bottom. Cover and cook additional 15 to 20 minutes.

10. Fold in bacon bits. Remove bay leaf before serving.

**Yield: 6 servings**

## Yellow Rice with Great Land Crab

Different variations on this recipe can be found all over the island. Anna's grandmother gave us this recipe. It originally called for half a cup of rum. By now, we'd gotten used to *Abuela* adding liquor to everything. I toned it down with a ¼ cup of white wine instead.

3 tablespoons annatto oil

½ cup *recaíto*

2 tablespoons sofrito

3 cups boiling chicken stock

2 cups rice

12 cooked great land crabs, or

3 tablespoons tomato paste

¼ cup *alcaparrado*

¼ cup white wine (optional)

1 ½ pounds lump crab meat, or

12 frozen crab legs, thawed

1. Heat annatto oil in a deep kettle or soup pot over moderate heat. Sauté *recaíto* for 3 minutes.

2. Stir in tomato paste, *sofrito*, *alcaparrado*, and white wine. Simmer, uncovered for 1 minute.

3. Add boiling chicken stock. Stir in rice and crab. Cook, uncovered for 20 minutes until liquid reaches top of rice.

4. Fork rice over once from top to bottom. Reduce heat, cover and simmer for 25 minutes until all liquid is absorbed.

5. Fork rice over again from top to bottom to fluff before serving.

**Yield: 6 servings**

# Yellow Rice with Pigeon Peas

*Arroz con Gandules*

Economical and flavorful annatto, rather than saffron, make this rice yellow.

3 tablespoons annatto oil

½ cup *recaíto*

¼ cup *sofrito*

¼ cup tomato paste

2 medium *chorizo* sausage,
  casing removed

16 ounces pigeon peas, canned and
  drained, or frozen

3 cups boiling chicken broth

½ cup boiling water

2 cups long-grain rice

1. Heat annatto oil in a deep kettle or saucepan over moderate heat.

2. Sauté *recaíto* for 5 minutes.

3. Stir in *sofrito* and tomato paste. Cook for additional minute.

4. Fold in sausage and pigeon peas.

5. Pour in boiling broth and water.

6. Stir in rice, and cook, uncovered, for 20 minutes until liquid level has nearly reached top of rice.

7. Fluff rice over from top to bottom, cover and cook over reduced heat for 25 minutes. All liquid should be absorbed.

8. Fork over from top to bottom again.

**Yield: 6 servings**

# Yellow Rice with Shrimp and Vegetables
*Arroz Amarillo con Vegetales*

This dish bursts with aromatic garlic and *cilantro*, yet quick and easy to make. Keeps several days in the refrigerator, which brings out the mellow flavors.

**4 tablespoons annatto oil**

**½ cup *recaíto***

**¼ cup *sofrito***

**½ cup tomato sauce**

**2 pounds medium raw shrimp, deshelled and deveined, tails intact**

**1 ½ cups frozen mixed vegetables, thawed and drained, or assorted fresh seasonal vegetables, chopped in 1 1/2 -inch pieces**

**3 cups boiling chicken broth**

**¼ cup boiling water**

**¼ cup dry sherry (optional, otherwise increase water to ½ cup)**

**2 cups long-grain rice**

1. Heat annatto oil in deep kettle or soup pot. Sauté *recaíto* over moderate heat for 5 minutes.

2. Whisk in *sofrito* and tomato sauce. Cook additional minute.

3. Add shrimp and sauté until pink.

4. Fold in vegetables. Pour in boiling broth, water and sherry.

5. Stir in rice, and cook uncovered for 20 minutes until liquid nearly reaches top of rice.

6. Fold rice over once from top to bottom, cover and cook over reduced heat for 25 minutes. Rice should be dry.

7. Fork over rice again from top to bottom.

**Yield: 6 servings**

# Saffron Rice with Seafood

*Arroz con Mariscos*

This is another versatile buffet dish. Doritza's cousin served it at her daughter's wedding. Double or triple the amount of firm white fish, use smaller shrimp and reduce the amount of costly lobster.

¼ cup olive olive oil

½ cup minced yellow onion

2 large ripe tomatoes, peeled, seeded and chopped

2 green frying peppers, seeded and minced

1 jalapeño pepper, seeded and minced

3 tablespoons *picado* seasoning

1 tablespoon tomato paste

½ pound firm white fish, cut in 1 ½ inch cubes (halibut is good, but swordfish is divine)

1 pound raw shrimp, shelled and deveined

1 pound raw lobster medallions (crab is good also)

3 ½ cups fish stock

½ cup white wine

2 cups long-grain rice

1 pound raw clams, cleaned

1 pound raw mussels, cleaned and debearded

1. Heat olive oil in deep kettle or pot. Sauté onion, tomato and peppers over medium heat until soft, about 5 minutes.

2. Stir in *picado* seasoning and tomato paste. Cook for 1 minute.

3. Toss in fish, shrimp and lobster. Sauté for 2 minutes.

4. Add fish stock and white wine. Turn heat to medium high and bring to boil.

5. Stir in rice. Cook uncovered, heat reduced to moderate for 30 minutes. Liquid should be down to level of rice.

6. Fork over rice from top to bottom gently. Cook uncovered over low heat for 10 minutes.

7. Fork rice over again, folding in clams and mussels. Cover and cook for 10 minutes.

8. Remove from heat and allow to sit for 5 minutes. Discard any mussels or clams that haven't opened.

**Yield: 6 to 8 servings**

# Beans

## BEANS
## *LEGUMBRES Ó GRANOS*

Beans have been an important part of the human diet since ancient times. Highly nutritious, per 100 grams they supply six to nine grams of protein, 0.1 to 0.7 grams of fat, 18 to 28 grams of carbohydrates, 5 to 8 grams of fiber, and 100 to 140 calories. Also a good source of folic acid, potassium, iron and magnesium. Eat beans with a source of vitamin C, i.e. cabbage, citrus or bell pepper to increase iron absorption.

The protein in beans is incomplete, lacking certain amino acids. Therefore, always eat beans with a bit of other protein, cheese, rice, corn or other cereal grains.

There are two steps to cooking dried beans: soaking and cooking. **Soaking beans** allows the legumes to absorb water and being to break down the starches that can create stomach discomfort. Cooking makes them soft and easy on the digestion. Be sure to rinse after soaking as this will further reduce the gaseous starches. Lentils, split peas and black-eyed peas do not require soaking, though I like to soak them for 20 minutes and rinse once.

---

### Soaking and Cooking Beans

**Overnight Soak:** Cover 1 pound of beans in large bowl or stainless steel pot with 3 quarts of water. Cover, refrigerate and soak 7 to 8 hours. Drain and rinse.

**Quick Soak:** In large saucepan, bring 3 quarts water to boil. Add 1 cup dried beans and return to boil for 3 minutes. Remove from heat. Cover and allow to sit for 1 hour. Drain and rinse.

**Best Soak:** Developed by the California Bean Advisory board, this soak eliminates nearly all of the gassy starches. Good for low-carbers also! Follow instructions for quick soak. But allow to cool for 2 hours, then refrigerate overnight. Drain the following morning. This should reduce starches upwards of 75 percent.

When **cooking beans** do not add vinegar, salt, wine or tomato juice. This significantly slows down the cooking process and can make them tough on the stomach. Depending on the freshness of the dried beans and the type, cooking times will vary.

**To test for doneness:** Hold a couple beans between your two fingers and squeeze. They should mash easily.

**Stove cooking:**

- Place soaked beans in 5-quart saucepan. Cover with 3 times their volume in water. Herbs and spices, but no other condiments may be added at this time.
- Bring to a boil over medium heat, then reduce heat to a simmer. Cook, uncovered, stirring now and then. Do not boil. Add water as needed. Check for doneness around 45 minutes.
- Drain and use at once. Or rinse and drain, then divide into freezer packets. These homemade beans are much healthier than canned. Also more flavorful.

**Crockpot cooking:** This is one of the simplest and most convenient ways to cook beans. While the beans are cooking, you can finish preparing the rest of the meal.

- Method One: Place soaked beans in crockpot. Cover with 3 times their volume in water. Cover and cook on high until tender.
- Method Two: Place soaked beans in crockpot and cover with 3 times their volume in water. Cover and cook on high for two hours. Turn off crockpot and allow beans to sit for 8 hours. Add remaining ingredients, herbs, spices, vegetables or meat and place on low setting. Simmer for 8 hours until done.

# Basic Puerto Rican Stewed Beans
*Habichuelas or Guisantes Guisados*

While Hurricane Frances bore down on us, Anna and I made a huge pot of this stew to tide us over until the storm passed. We ended up sharing with all the neighbors. Unfortunately, the power grid on the island went down two hours into the storm. We ended up with no power for a week, eating at whatever fast-food restaurant had a generator.

1 pound dried beans, soaked

1 tablespoon annatto oil

1 ounce salt pork, diced

¼ cup diced cured ham

2 tablespoons dry sherry

½ teaspoon dried oregano

½ medium ripe plantain, peeled and
    cut in 1 inch slices

1 large sweet chili pepper, seeded and minced

½ cup *sofrito*

1 ½ tablespoons tomato paste

½ cup water

½ pound pumpkin, peeled, seeded, cubed and boiled until tender

1. Place the dried beans in a 5 quart saucepan. Cover 3 times bean volume with water. Bring to boil, uncovered. Reduce heat to simmer and continue to cook uncovered until tender. Test for doneness at 45 minute mark.

2. In a large skillet or frying pan, heat annatto and olive oil. Brown salt pork and ham on all sides.

3. Stir in pepper and sauté for 2 minutes. Fold in *sofrito*, tomato paste, sherry and oregano. Cook for additional 1 minute.

4. Stir *sofrito* mixture into bean pot. Add plantain and ½ cup water. Cover and simmer for 10 minutes.

5. Mash pumpkin and add to bean pot. Stir and cook, covered for another 10 minutes.

**Yield: 8 to 10 servings**

# Puerto Rican Black Beans

*Frijoles Negros*

This is often served as a side dish in Puerto Rico. Make an entire meal by filling bowls with hot white rice and top generously with beans, garnish with minced onions.

1 pound soaked black beans (see above for tips)

¼ cup olive oil

½ cup minced yellow onion

1 green frying pepper, seeded and minced

3 sweet chili peppers, seeded and minced

4 large cloves garlic, crushed

1 bay leaf

½ teaspoon dried oregano

1 ½ teaspoons salt

½ teaspoon cumin

½ teaspoon sugar

½ teaspoon cracked black pepper

½ cup water

¼ cup white wine

1 tablespoon vinegar

½ cup minced raw onion

1. Place soaked beans in a 5-quart saucepan. Cover with 3 times their volume with water. Bring to boil, uncovered. Reduce heat and simmer for 45 minutes. Do not boil as it will break their skins. Add water as needed. Test for doneness by rubbing a couple beans between your fingers to see if they will mash.

2. Heat olive oil in a heavy skillet. Sauté onions, peppers and garlic over moderate heat until onion is tender, about 5 minutes.

3. Add 1 cup of cooked beans and mash.

4. Add bay leaf, oregano, salt, cumin, sugar and black pepper. Stir and fold in remaining beans, water and wine.

5. Cover, turn heat to very low and simmer for 30 minutes. Add additional water as needed. Whisk in vinegar for last 10 minutes of cooking. Serve in bowls with hot rice. Garnish with minced raw onion.

**Yield: 6 to 8 servings**

## Stewed Chick Peas
*Garbanzos Guisados*

Vegetarians can omit the sausage and top with chopped, hard-boiled eggs if desired.

| | |
|---|---|
| 1 pound chickpeas, soaked | 2 *chorizo* Spanish sausages, |
| ¾ pound pumpkin, peeled, seeded | casings removed |
| and cut in 1 ½ inch cubes | ½ cup *sofrito* |
| ½ pound cabbage, cut in 2 inch pieces | 2 tablespoons tomato paste |
| 1 tablespoon annatto oil | 1 teaspoon salt |
| 1 tablespoon olive oil | 1 cup water |

1. Place soaked chickpeas in 5-quart saucepan or deep kettle. Cover with 3 times their volume in water. Bring to boil, uncovered, reduce heat and simmer about 1 hour.

2. Fold in pumpkin and cabbage. Cover and simmer for additional 30 minutes. Chick peas should be tender.

3. In a small frying pan, heat the annatto and olive oil. Crumble *chorizos* into hot oil and brown lightly. Drain excess fat.

4. Stir in *sofrito*, tomato paste and salt. Cook for 1 minute.

5. Stir *sofrito* mixture into kettle with garbanzos. Add 1 cup water. Cover and simmer for 20 minutes. Sauce should be thicker than that of black beans or stewed beans.

**Yield: 6 to 8 servings**

---

### Did You Know?

The most popular creature in Puerto Rico is the **coqui frog.** Only 1 ½ inches long, this tiny treefrog has huge eyes, webbed fingers and toes with suction cups. At night the coqui can be heard all over the island with its "kokee-kokee" song. It is believed that in the Caribbean National Forest, El Yunque, there are as many as 10,000 per acre.

---

## Stewed Fresh Pigeon Peas with Plantain Balls
*Gandules Frescos Guisados*

The plantain balls take a little while to make, but everyone needs to try them at least once—they're absolutely delicious.

1 small green plantain or
2 green bananas, peeled,
  boiled and quartered
1 pound fresh pigeon peas
1 tablespoon olive oil
1 tablespoon annatto oil (see index)
¼ cup *recaíto*

2 tablespoons tomato paste
1 teaspoon salt
1 teaspoon freshly cracked black
  pepper
½ pound pumpkin, peeled, seeded and
  cut into 1-inch pieces

1. Puree plantain in a food processor. Form into small balls about 1 ½-inches in diameter. Set aside.

2. Rinse peas under cool running water. Remove any broken or shriveled peas.

3. Fill a deep kettle with six cups water. Add peas. Bring to a boil over moderate heat. Reduce heat, cover and simmer for 45 minutes.

4. Heat olive and annatto oil in a medium skillet over moderate heat. Sauté recaíto for 5 minutes. Stir in tomato paste, salt and pepper. Set aside.

5. Add pumpkin to peas and cook additional 15 minutes.

6. Stir in *recaíto* mixture, cook for 5 minutes. Drop in plantain balls. Reduce heat and simmer until sauce has thickened to taste, about 30 minutes.

7. Serve with hot rice.

**Yield: 6 to 8 servings**

# Plantains, Green Bananas and Other Caribbean Vegetables

Plantains, bananas, *yautía*, taro and all other sorts of vegetables grow freely in Puerto Rico. For those islanders who live in high-rises in San Juan, the grocery stores burst with a colorful selection of produce.

If you can't find plantains at a stateside grocery, give green bananas a try. I encourage all to experiment with at least a couple of the recipes in this chapter. Even though some of the vegetables seem odd or unpalatable, true Puerto Rican fare has not been experienced until you've had chayote, one of the root vegetables or plantain.

## How to Peel Plantains and Green Bananas
### *Manera de pelar plátanos y guineas verdes*

1. Slice of both ends of banana or plantain. Note, if recipe does not call for whole banana or plantain, slice fruit in half cross wise, then proceed with steps two through four.
2. Slice banana or plantain vertically in 3 to 4 places using the sharp tip of a knife.
3. Remove skin by holding against knife and pulling down and off under cool running water to keep your hands or clothing from becoming sticky and stained.
4. Soak in cold salted water for 15 minutes.

## Boiled Green Plantains or Green Bananas
*Plátanos Verdes o Guineos Verdes Hervidos*

Green bananas were the first tropical side dish I had when I moved to the islands.

**2 large green plantains or
4 green bananas, peeled
and soaked in salt water**

**3 teaspoons salt
water**

1. Heat 2 quarts of water in large saucepan. Add salt and bring to boil.
2. Slice bananas in half, cross-wise. Slice plantain in thirds, cross-wise.
3. Lower plantains or bananas into salted water. Cook plantains 15 minutes, bananas 10 minutes.
4. Fruit should be soft, but not so soft as to be mushy or dissolve.

**Yield: 4 to 6 servings**

# Baked Plantain

*Plátanos Maduros (Amarillos)*

I have to admit I prefer ripe plantains and bananas as opposed to unripe ones. The sugar level in a ripe plantain or banana begins to caramelize when cooked. The sweetness of the fruit is a nice foil for fish, chicken, meat or spicy dishes. Watch out, they're addictive and not exactly low in calories.

Note: choose plantains where the entire skin is nearly black, even moldy looking. Believe it or not, this is what they look like when ripe.

**2 ripe plantains**

**aluminum foil**

**butter to grease foil**

1. Preheat oven to 350°F. Line a cookie sheet or shallow baking dish with aluminum foil. Butter foil lightly.
2. Wash plantains with light soapy water. A couple drops dish liquid is fine. Rinse and pat dry. Leave peel intact.
3. Slice off ends (tips). Cut a slit down the length of fruit to allow steam to escape.
4. Arrange fruit on cookie sheet and bake for 20 minutes.
5. Flip plantains over and bake additional 20 minutes. Serve with butter.

**Yield: 4 to 6 servings**

# Stewed Green Plantain Balls

*Albóndigas de Plátanos Verde Guisadas*

**1 ½ cups Beef and Pork Filling for Piononos**

**4 large green plantains, halved, peeled, soaked in salt water and grated**

**½ pound yautia, or ½ pound waxy white potatoes, peeled and grated**

**2 tablespoons olive oil**

**1 ounce salt pork, minced**

**1 large *chorizo*, casing removed and crumbled**

**3 garlic cloves, crushed**

**½ cup minced yellow onion**

**4 small chili peppers, seeded and minced**

**3 tablespoons tomato paste**

**3 tablespoons dry sherry**

**½ teaspoon paprika**

**2 tablespoons cornstarch**

1. Combine grated plantain with grated yautia or potatoes in large bowl. Set aside.

2. Sauté salt pork, *chorizo*, garlic, onion and chili peppers in the olive oil in a large skillet over medium heat. Onions should be soft, not browned.

3. Reduce heat and stir in tomato paste, sherry and paprika. Pour onion mixture into grated plantain mixture. Combine well.

4. Heat 2 quarts of salted water in a large saucepan to boiling.

5. Flour hands with cornstarch and scoop up a ping-pong size mound of plantain mash. Make a dent in center and fill with Beef and Pork filling. Add more plantain to top and pinch shut. Roll into ball shape, the size of meatballs.

6. Carefully lower into boiling water with a slotted spoon. Boil for 30 minutes.

7. Remove with slotted spoon and drain. Serve with butter.

**Yield: 4 to 6 servings**

## Plantains with Pork Crackling

*Mofongo*

Ten years ago I went on a week-long photo shoot in Puerto Rico. The photographer and I stayed at the most delightful *paradors* (guest houses modeled after those in Spain), each with its own restaurant. *Mofongo* was on every menu. Serve as a side dish to chicken, meat and fish dishes.

**3 large plantains, peeled and soaked in salted water (see index)**
**4 large garlic cloves, minced**
**1 tablespoon olive oil**

**¼ pound pork crackling (*chicharron*), well crumbled**
**1/3 cup chicken broth**
**vegetable oil or shortening for frying**

1. Slice plantains in diagonal 1-inch slices.

2. Heat oil to 350°.

3. In the meantime, sauté crushed garlic in olive oil, until soft, but not browned. Remove from heat.

4. Fry plantain slices a few at a time until golden, but still soft, not crunchy. Drain on white paper towels. Allow to cool slightly.

5. Run plantain slices through a food processor. Fold in garlic and pork crackling.

6. Form into small balls, about 1 ½ inches in diameter.

**Yield: about 8 to 10 balls**.

# Plantain Stuffed with Garlic Shrimp

*Mofongo Rellenos con Camarones*

Puerto Ricans love their garlic and this recipe is no exception.

**3 large plantains, peeled and soaked in salted water (see index)**

**1 large garlic clove, minced**

**1 tablespoon olive oil**

**¼ pound pork crackling, chicharrón, well crumbled**

**1/3 cup chicken broth**

**vegetable oil or shortening for frying**

STUFFING:

**3 tablespoons olive oil**

**½ cup minced yellow onion**

**4 garlic cloves crushed**

**¼ cup sofrito**

**3 tablespoons tomato paste**

**3 tablespoons dry sherry**

**2 pounds medium raw shrimp, deshelled, deveined and coarsely chopped**

1. Slice plantains in diagonal 1-inch slices.

2. Heat oil to 350°F.

3. In the meantime, sauté crushed garlic in olive oil, until soft, but not browned. Remove from heat.

4. Fry plantain slices a few at a time until golden, but still soft, not crunchy. Drain on white paper towels. Allow to cool slightly.

5. Run plantain slices through a food processor. Fold in garlic and pork crackling, with 1/3 cup chicken broth.

6. Form into small balls, about 1 ½ inches in diameter. Set aside.

7. STUFFING: Sauté the onion and garlic in the olive oil in a large skillet over moderate heat until soft, about 5 minutes. Do not brown.

8. Whisk in tomato paste, *sofrito* and sherry, simmering for 2 more minutes.

9. Drop in shrimp, and simmer, stirring constantly until shrimp turns pink. Remove from heat and allow to cool slightly.

10. Make a well in the center of each *mofongo* patty. Fill with shrimp, pinch *mofongo* shut over top.

11. Fry in hot oil (350°) until golden. Drain on white paper towels. Serve hot with *Mojito Sauce* (see index).

**Yield: about 10 balls**

## Traditional Shredded Green Plantain Fritters
*Arañitas*

Serve with Mojito Sauce (see index). If you don't have time to make it, serve with a mild or hot chili pepper sauce.

**4 large green plantains, peeled, soaked (see index) and grated in shreds**

**1 teaspoon salt**

**1 teaspoon cracked black pepper**

**3 large garlic cloves, minced**

**vegetable oil or shortening for frying**

### Plantain

Plantains are related to bananas and native to Malaysia. Unlike bananas, plantains are eaten cooked, either from unripe or ripe fruit. Unripe fruit is green, ripe is yellow, turning to black.

**Purchasing:** Choose firm, unblemished skin. Black plantains do not always indicate spoilage, they are merely ripe.

**Storing:** Keep at room temperature. Refrigerate only if excessively ripe. Peel ripe plantains, wrap and freeze.

**Serving:** Unripe, cooked plantain is served as a starchy vegetable in soups and stews or as a side dish. Cooked ripe plantain tastes similar to sweet banana. Use as an accompaniment to fish, chicken or meat dishes.

**Nutrition:** Like its cousin, the banana, plantains are high in potassium. Also contains Vitamin C, Vitamin B-6, Vitamin A, folic acid and magnesium.

1. Preheat oil to 350°F.

2. Combine the shredded plantain with the salt, pepper and garlic, mixing well.

3. Scoop up a ping-pong sized ball of plantain and flatten between your palms.

4. Lower into hot oil and fry until golden. Do not overcrowd skillet as this will lower cooking temperature and cause fritters to soak up too much oil.

5. Remove with slotted spoon and drain on white paper towels.

6. Serve warm with *Mojito Sauce*.

**Yield: about 12**

# Cheese-Stuffed Plantain Fritters

*Rellenos de Plátanos Maduros (Amarillos) con Queso*

Stuff these plantains with your favorite cheese. Puerto Ricans use a crumbly white cheese or a Spanish cheese made from sheep's milk *Machengo*. Sharp, distinctive cheeses work best, complimenting the sweetness of the plantain. I have used everything from cheddar, Edam, Swiss, even Brie.

**4 ripe plantains, unpeeled and cut in thirds**

**1 tablespoon sea salt**

**vegetable oil or shortening for frying**

**2 garlic cloves, crushed**

**½ pound sharp cheese, grated**

**1 tablespoon olive oil**

**1 teaspoon freshly cracked black pepper**

**2 tablespoons flour**

1. Heat 3 quarts of water and 1 tablespoon salt in a large saucepan over medium heat to boiling point. Gently submerge plantains, cover and without reducing heat, boil plantains for 18 minutes.

2. Remove from water and allow to cool for 10 minutes.

3. Heat olive oil in small frying pan. Sauté garlic for 5 minutes until soft, but not browned.

4. Peel plantains and mash. Fold in garlic and pepper, mixing well.

5. Dust hands with flour. Using an ice cream scoop or large spoon, scoop up a ping-pong size mound of plantain. Flatten and create a well in center.

6. Stuff with shredded cheese. Top with more mashed plantain and pinch edges shut.

7. Heat vegetable oil for frying in a deep kettle or skillet to 375°F.

8. Carefully lower a few plantain balls into hot oil. Do not over crowed as this will lower the temperature of the oil, causing the balls to cook slowly and absorb excess oil. Fry until golden.

9. Drain on white paper towels. Serve plain or with hot chili pepper sauce.

**Yield: about 12 stuffed plantains**

# Stuffed Plantain Fritters with Meat Filling

You can add any filling to this: shrimp, chicken, pork, etc.

1 ½ cups Beef and Pork Filling for Piononos (see index)

2 garlic cloves, crushed

2 tablespoons minced onion tablespoon olive oil

4 large ripe plantains, boiled and peeled (see index)

3 tablespoons melted butter vegetable oil for frying or 1 shortening

2 tablespoons cornstarch

1. Sauté garlic and onion in the olive oil in a small frying pan over moderate heat for about 5 minutes until onion is soft, but not browned.

2. Mash plantains. Fold in onion and garlic, combining well. Drizzle in melted butter and stir.

3. Heat vegetable oil or shortening to 375°F in a deep kettle or skillet.

4. Dust hands with cornstarch. Scoop up a ping-pong ball sized mound of plantain. Make a well in center and fill with a generous tablespoon of meat filling.

5. Top with additional plantain and pinch edges shut.

6. Lower into hot oil and fry until golden. Do not overcrowd kettle.

7. Drain on white paper towels.

Yield: 12 to 15 fritters

## Did You Know?

The **Caribbean National Forest**, a.k.a. **El Yunque**, is the only tropical forest in the U.S. National Forest system. Seventy-five percent of the remaining virgin forest in Puerto Rico can be found in its 27,846 acres. El Yunque contains 8 major rivers, four types of forest and 250 species of trees. More than 100 billion gallons of water drop on the forest each year. The walking trails are fabulous here, meandering past ferns, hot pink tropical impatiens flowers, and misty waterfalls. Personally, I believe the mountains (Luquillo Range) do a great deal to buffer the rest of the island from the devastating effects of hurricane force winds. For more information and to tour the rainforest call: 787-888-1880.

# Ripe Plantain Balls

*Albóndigas de Plátano Maduro (Amarillo)*

Make extra and freeze for future use.

**4 medium plantains, boiled and peeled (see index)**

**2 tablespoons butter, room temperature**

**½ teaspoon ground cinnamon**

**¼ teaspoon ground nutmeg**

**3 large eggs, lightly beaten**

**2 tablespoons evaporated milk**

**1 cup crushed soda crackers**

**2 tablespoons sugar**

**vegetable oil or shortening to fry**

**cornstarch for dusting hands**

1. Run plantains through a food processor or mash by hand.
2. Whip in melted butter, cinnamon and nutmeg.
3. Combine beaten egg with evaporated milk in a shallow dish. Combine sugar and cracker crumbs in another dish.
4. Heat vegetable oil or shortening to 375°F in a deep fryer or skillet.
5. Scoop up small balls the size of a ping-pong, roll in egg mixture, then roll in cracker crumb mixture.
6. Fry plantain balls until golden, taking care not to crowd fryer.
7. Drain on white paper towels.

**Yield: 24 balls**

# Plantain Cheese Pie

*Pastelón de Plátanos Maduros (Amarillos) con Queso*

One of the variations Doritza made on this recipe was to add cooked, chopped shrimp or cooked, cubed pork.

**6 large, partially ripe plantains**

**2 teaspoons salt**

**1 stick butter, chilled and chopped**

**½ cup, plus 3 tablespoons flour**

**1 teaspoon sugar**

**¾ pound sharp white cheese, grated**

**½ teaspoon fresh cracked pepper**

**1 tablespoon dry vermouth**

1. Preheat oven to 350°F. Grease a 9 or 10-inch glass pie dish generously with butter or shortening.

2. Slice plantains in half cross-wise, leaving peel on. Place in a large saucepan or kettle, cover with cold water, add salt and bring to boil over moderate heat. Cook for 20 minutes. Drain, allow to cool slightly. Mash or run through food processor.

3. Cut butter into the flour using a fork until crumbly and resembling sand. Add sugar and fold in mashed plantain, combining well.

4. Press half of the plantain mixture into bottom of pie plate.

5. Sprinkle with grated cheese. Dribble vermouth over cheese and dust with black pepper.

6. Top with remaining plantain, pressing down lightly.

7. Bake 25 to 30 minutes, until lightly browned.

**Yield: 6 servings**

## Plantain and Meat Pie

*Pastelón de Plátanos Maduros (Amarillos) con Carne*

Make two of these popular meat pies. They're sure to go fast.

1 ½ cups Beef and Pork Filling
    for Piononos (see index)
6 large, partially ripe plantains,
    cut in half cross-wise

1 teaspoon salt
1 stick butter, chilled and chopped
¾ cup flour
¼ cup dry sherry

1. Preheat oven to 350°F. Generously grease a glass 9 or 10-inch pie dish with shortening. Set aside.

2. Bring 2 quarts water to boil along with the 1 teaspoon salt. Add unpeeled plantain halves and boil for 20 minutes. Remove, drain and cool. Run through food processor or mash by hand.

3. Cut butter into flour with a fork until crumbly resembling sand.

4. Fold into plantain mash, combining well.

5. Press half of plantain mixture into bottom of pie plate. Top with meat filling. Sprinkle sherry over meat.

6. Press remaining plantain mash over meat filling.

7. Bake for 30 minutes until lightly browned.

**Yield: 6 servings**

# Plantain, Meat and String Bean Casserole

*Piñon*

Doritza's plantain tree in her back yard produced the sweet, delicious plantains for this recipe.

**2 cups Beef and Pork Filling for Piononos**
**½ cup tomato sauce**
**1 hard boiled egg, chopped**
**½ pound fresh string beans, trimmed, and chopped, or 1 pound canned, drained, or 1 pound frozen, cooked**
**4 large ripe plantains, peeled**

**4 tablespoons butter**
**6 large eggs, separated**
**olive oil to grease dish**
**1 tablespoon sherry**
**½ teaspoon salt**
**½ teaspoon paprika**

1. Preheat oven to 350°F. Grease a 9 to 10-inch heavy skillet or ovenproof dish with olive oil. Set aside.

   Heat Beef and Pork filling in medium saucepan over moderate heat. Add tomato sauce and stir. Cook for 2 minutes. Fold in chopped egg and remove from stove. Set aside.

2. Fill a medium saucepan with beans and 1 cup water. Bring to boil. Reduce heat and steam, covered, over moderate heat for 15 minutes. Remove from heat and drain. Set aside.

3. Slice plantains diagonally in 1-inch slices. Sauté in butter in a large skillet until lightly browned on both sides. Remove and drain on white paper towels.

4. Beat egg whites until stiff in medium bowl. Beat egg yolks in small bowl. Whisk into egg whites.

5. Set skillet or ovenproof dish on stove burner over very low heat.

6. Pour ¼ of egg mixture into dish. Layer with ½ of plantain slices.

7. Mix sherry, salt and paprika into meat filling. Scoop filling over plantain slices.

8. Layer string beans over meat filling. Place remaining plantains over this.

9. Pour remaining egg mixture over top. Cook on stove over very low heat for 5 minutes.

10. Bake in oven for 15 minutes.

**Yield: 6 servings**

# Plantain, Cheese and Ham Sandwiches

A sandwich without the bread!

**6 large plantains, ripe, but with some yellow on the skin**

**olive oil**

**½ pound baked ham, thinly sliced**

**½ pound sharp Cheddar, Swiss or smoked cheese, thinly sliced**

**3 large eggs, beaten**

**1 tablespoon evaporated milk**

**1 tablespoon dry sherry**

**½ teaspoon paprika**

**1 cup unseasoned breadcrumbs**

**1 teaspoon cracked black pepper**

**vegetable oil for frying**

1. Preheat oven to 350°F. Generously grease a glass baking dish with olive oil.
2. Peel plantains. Slice in half cross-wise, then in half lengthwise.
3. Bake plantain for 15 to 18 minutes. Plantain should not be fully cooked. Remove from oven and baking dish. Set aside to cool.
4. Whisk together eggs, evaporated milk, sherry and paprika in a shallow baking dish. Set aside.
5. Pound plantain slices to a ¼ inch.
6. Place a couple slices of ham and cheese on a plantain slice. Top with another plantain slice and fasten with toothpick.
7. Heat oil in deep fryer or skillet to 350°F.
8. Combine black pepper with breadcrumbs in shallow dish.
9. Dip plantain "sandwiches" in egg mixture, then in breadcrumbs. Repeat until all plantain slices have been used up.
10. Fry "sandwiches" a few at a time, on both sides, until golden. Drain on white paper towels.

**Yield: 6 to 8 servings**

# Plantains in Rum Syrup

*Plátanos Maduros (Amarillos) en Almíbar*

This treat really belongs in the desert chapter. Try adding a dollop of whip cream topping.

**4 large ripe plantains, peeled and soaked in salt water (see index)**

**3 tablespoons lime juice**

**1 teaspoon vanilla extract**

6 tablespoons butter

1 ¾ cups sugar

1 ¼ cups water

¼ teaspoon ground cinnamon

½ cup light Puerto Rican rum

1. Slice plantains diagonally in 1-inch pieces. Sauté plantains in the butter over moderate heat in a large skillet. Brown lightly.

2. Heat sugar, water and lime juice in a large saucepan over moderate heat. Bring to boil, reduce heat, cover and simmer for 30 minutes.

3. Remove cover and add plantains, cooking for another 20 minutes. Stir in vanilla and cinnamon, cooking until syrup has thickened.

4. Remove from heat and stir in rum.

**Yield: 6 servings**

## Plantains in Cinnamon Milk and Cheese

Anna ran this through a food processor and the baby loved it. High in potassium and protein.

4 large ripe plantains, peeled

5 tablespoons butter

2 1/2 cups milk

½ cup sweetened condensed milk

½ cup sugar

¼ teaspoon ground nutmeg

½ teaspoon grated lime rind

¼ pound sharp white cheese, sliced

1. Make a lengthwise slit along side of each plantain.

2. Melt butter in a large skillet over moderate heat and sauté plantains until lightly browned.

3. Combine milk, condensed milk, sugar, nutmeg and lime rind in small bowl. Set aside

4. Stuff plantain slits with sliced cheese.

5. Pour milk mixture over plantains. Cover, turn heat on very low and simmer for 20 minutes.

6. Remove cover and continue to cook over low heat for 30 minutes until soft.

**Yield: 6 servings**

# Coconut Plantain in Plantain Leaves

*Guanimes de Plátano*

If you don't have access to plantain leaves, parchment paper will do nicely.

**4 unripe plantains, peeled and soaked (see index)**

**½ cup fresh or canned, unsweetened coconut milk**

**¼ cup evaporated milk**

**½ cup sugar**

**½ teaspoon salt**

**½ teaspoon cinnamon**

**¼ teaspoon nutmeg**

**½ teaspoon grated lime rind**

**plantain leaves or parchment string**

1. Grate plantains and set aside.
2. Combine coconut milk, evaporated milk, sugar, salt, cinnamon, nutmeg and lime rind in a medium bowl.
3. Fold grated plantain into coconut milk mixture, combining well.
4. Rinse and pat dry plantain leaves.
5. Fill a 4 quart saucepan with salted water and bring to a boil over moderate heat.
6. Scoop a ball the size of a ping-pong into center of each leaf. Flatten into a square shape about 3/8" thick.
7. Fold up ends of leaves, then fold in sides, creating a rectangular package. Secure with string.
8. Lower packets into boiling water. Cover and simmer for 25 minutes. Drain thoroughly and serve at once in plantain leaves.

**Yield: 6 to 8 servings**

# Pickled Green Bananas

*Guineos Verdes en Escabeche*

Don't expect these green bananas to taste like sweet, ripe bananas. Use as you would a vegetable side dish.

**10 boiled medium green bananas (see index)**

**1 ½ cups olive oil**

**1 bay leaf**

**4 garlic cloves, minced**

**2 small yellow onions, thinly sliced**

½ cup good quality vinegar (not balsamic)

4 tablespoons lime juice

20 whole black peppercorns

½ cup *alcaparrado* (see index)

1 tablespoon dry vermouth

1 ½ teaspoons salt

1. Whisk together olive oil, vinegar, lime juice, peppercorns, bay leaf and garlic in a steel or enamel kettle or saucepan. Simmer over low heat for 30 minutes.

2. Add onion and simmer for additional 10 minutes.

3. Slice boiled bananas in diagonal 1-inch thick slices. Add to oil/vinegar mixture and simmer for 5 minutes. Remove from heat and cool. Stir in *alcaparrado*, vermouth and salt.

4. Cover and marinate 36 hours in refrigerator.

5. Serve as side dish or appetizer.

**Yield: 6 to 8 servings**

## Spicy Sautéed Green Bananas

I'm not a huge fan of green bananas, but this recipe finally won me over. Nice and spicy.

10 medium size green bananas, boiled (see index)

4 tablespoons olive oil

1 medium yellow onion, thinly sliced

4 garlic cloves, minced

1 jalapeño or habañero pepper, seeded and minced (habañero, a.k.a. scotch bonnet is much hotter than the jalapeño)

4 tablespoons tomato paste

¼ cup chicken broth

2 tablespoons vinegar

10 whole black peppercorns

10 pimento-stuffed olives, coarsely chopped

1 tablespoon capers

¼ cup pimentos, chopped (canned is fine)

1/3 cup water

1. Sauté onion and garlic in the olive oil in a large skillet over moderate heat until soft, about 5 to 6 minutes.

2. Add hot peppers, tomato paste, chicken broth and vinegar. Simmer for 5 minutes.

3. Stir in peppercorns, olives, capers, pimentos, and water, simmering for 10 minutes.

4. Add banana slices and simmer for additional 10 minutes.

**Yield: 4 to 6 serving**

## Sautéed Chayotes

*Chayotes Salteados*

Chayote tastes a lot like cucumber or green zucchini.

**4 medium chayotes, peeled cored, and sliced**

**1 tablespoon olive or vegetable oil**

**1 tablespoon butter**

**½ teaspoon salt**

**½ teaspoon cracked black pepper**

**2 tablespoons dry sherry**

1. Fill a medium saucepan with water. Bring to boil over high heat. Dip chayote slices into boiling water for 2 minutes. Remove at once and drain. Set aside.

2. Heat the olive oil and butter in a large skillet. Stir in salt, pepper and sherry.

3. Brown chayote slices lightly on each side. Serve warm with butter sherry sauce.

**Yield: 6 servings**

## Garlic Cheese Stuffed Chayotes

*Chayotes Rellenos con Queso y Ajo*

Now this is the way to eat chayotes! Serve with a green salad and crusty bread for lunch.

**3 large *chayotes*, cut in half, lengthwise**

**2 teaspoons salt**

**1 tablespoon olive oil**

**4 garlic cloves, minced**

**2 tablespoons minced onion**

**1 ¼ cups shredded sharp cheese, such as Cheddar or Gouda**

**½ cup unseasoned bread crumbs**

**2 tablespoons melted butter**

1. Fill a medium saucepan with water and salt. Bring to a boil and add *chayotes*. Reduce heat and boil for 20 to 30 minutes, until soft.

2. Remove from heat and allow to cool slightly. Remove pulp, discarding cores and stringy part. Reserve unbroken shells.

3. Mash chayote and set aside.

4. Preheat oven to 350°F.

5. Sauté garlic and minced onion in the olive oil in a small frying pan over moderate heat, until soft. Do not brown. Remove from heat.

6. Place cheese in a medium bowl and fold in garlic mixture, stirring well. Cut in shredded cheese, until combined.

7. Fold in mashed chayote.

8. Stuff shells with garlic/cheese/chayote filling.

9. Using the same frying pan for the garlic, add breadcrumbs and melted butter. Stir over low heat for 1 minute. Remove from heat.

10. Top stuffed shells with breadcrumb mixture.

11. Place in oven and bake for 30 minutes.

**Yield: 6 servings**

# Meat Stuffed Chayotes with Parmesan Cheese
*Chayotes Rellenos con Queso*

These keep well in the refrigerator, making for a tasty lunch the next day.

**3 large chayotes, cut in half, lengthwise**

**2 teaspoons salt**

**3 tablespoons olive oil**

**¼ cup *recaíto* (see index)**

**1 large green frying pepper, minced**

**1/3 cup cured ham, diced**

**½ pound lean ground beef**

**½ cup unseasoned breadcrumbs**

**2 tablespoons alcaparrado (see index)**

**2 tablespoons butter**

**½ cup grated Parmesan cheese (optional)**

1. Fill a medium saucepan with water and salt. Bring to a boil and add *chayotes*. Reduce heat and boil for 20 to 30 minutes, until soft.

2. Remove from heat and allow to cool slightly. Remove pulp, discarding cores and stringy part. Reserve unbroken shells.

3. Mash chayote and set aside.

4. Heat the olive oil in a large skillet. Sauté recaíto and pepper for 5 minutes until soft, but not browned.

5. Stir in ground beef and ham, browning lightly until no pink remains on the meat. Drain off any excess fat.

6. Stir in *alcaparrado* and simmer for 1 minute. Fold in mashed *chayote*, simmering for additional minute. Remove from heat and allow to cool for 15 minutes.

7. Melt butter in small frying pan over low heat. Toss in breadcrumbs and coat. Remove from heat. Fold in *alcaparrado*.

8. Fill chayote shells with stuffing. Top with buttered breadcrumbs. Sprinkle cheese over top.

9. Bake for 30 minutes.

**Yield: 6 servings**

# Chayote Hash
*Boronia de Chayote*

This recipe isn't in the low-carb section, but it could be.

**3 large chayotes, cut in half, lengthwise**
**2 teaspoons salt**
**2 tablespoons olive oil**
**1 teaspoon annatto oil**
**¼ cup diced cured ham**
**3 garlic cloves, crushed**
**½ cup minced yellow onion**
**1 medium green frying pepper,**
  **seeded and minced**

**3 sweet chili peppers,**
  **seeded and minced**
**1 tomato, peeled, seeded**
  **and chopped**
**¼ cup *recaíto***
**1 tablespoon tomato paste**
**1 tablespoon sherry**
**½ teaspoon cayenne pepper**
**6 large eggs, beaten**

1. Fill a medium saucepan with water and salt. Bring to a boil and add *chayotes*. Reduce heat and boil for 20 to 30 minutes, until soft.

2. Remove from heat and allow to cool slightly. Remove pulp, discarding cores and stringy part. Discard shells, and dice pulp.

3. Heat olive and annatto oil in large skillet over moderate heat. Sauté ham, garlic, onion and peppers until soft, about 5 minutes. Do not brown.

4. Stir in tomato, *recaíto*, tomato paste and sherry. Simmer over reduced heat for 3 minutes.

5. Fold in diced chayote.

6. Sprinkle in cayenne pepper and drizzle in beaten eggs, stirring constantly. Cook until eggs are done.

**Yield: 6 servings**

## Basic Recipe for Mashed Breadfruit

Breadfruit is a bowling ball-sized starchy vegetable that grows on trees. Use like potatoes.

**1 3-pound breadfruit, not overripe, nor unripe either**

**1 tablespoons salt**

**3 tablespoons butter**

**salt**

**pepper**

### Did You Know?

West Indian plantation owners, looking for a cheap food source for their slaves, read about Captain James Cook's discovery of breadfruit in the South Pacific. They implored King George III to sponsor Captain William Bligh on the M.S. Bounty on a breadfruit expedition. Of course, the Bounty was overthrown, but Bligh, not one to give up, hitched a ride back to England and located the breadfruit on his second voyage to Tahiti. To make a long story short, the slaves didn't care for the breadfruit and stuck to their more familiar and costlier rice. Nonetheless, breadfruit trees now grow all over the Caribbean. Thank you Captain Bligh.

1. Fill a 4-quart saucepan with water and 1 tablespoon salt. Bring to boil over medium high heat.

2. Meanwhile, wash breadfruit. Slice off ends. Cut into slices like a cantaloupe. Peel skin with sharp knife.

3. Boil for 25 minutes until soft.

4. Drain and mash. Serve with butter, seasoning with salt and pepper.

**Yield: 6 servings**

# Spicy Mashed Breadfruit with Parmesan Cheese

Good with beef tenderloin or pork, served with a gravy or mojito sauce.

| | |
|---|---|
| 3 ½ cups mashed breadfruit (see index) | ¼ cup evaporated milk |
| 4 tablespoons butter | 1 tablespoon dry sherry |
| 1 tablespoon flour | 4 egg yolks, beaten |
| ½ teaspoon cayenne pepper | ½ cup grated Parmesan cheese |
| ½ jalapeño or other fiery pepper, seeded and minced | 2 tablespoons butter |
| | ½ cup unseasoned breadcrumbs |
| 2/3 cup warm milk | |

1. Preheat oven to 350°F. Generously grease a shallow casserole dish with vegetable oil.
2. Melt butter in a small skillet over low heat. Sprinkle in flour and cayenne pepper, stirring constantly. Cook for 1 minute.
3. Add hot pepper, stir for additional 2 minutes.
4. Whisk in warm milk, evaporated milk and sherry, until well combined. Cooks until thickened over low heat.
5. Remove from heat and rapidly whip in beaten egg yolks.
6. Fold in mashed breadfruit and cheese. Press into greased casserole dish.
7. Melt butter in a small skillet over low heat. Toss in breadcrumbs, coating well.
8. Sprinkle over mashed breadfruit.
9. Bake for 30 minutes.

Yield: 6 to 8 servings

# Breadfruit Fritters

*Frituras de Panapén*

Be sure to serve this fritter at cocktail parties-it soaks up alcohol nicely.

| | |
|---|---|
| 2 cups warm, mashed breadfruit (see index) | 1 egg yolk, beaten |
| 1 tablespoon flour | salt |
| 3 tablespoons butter | pepper |
| 1 garlic clove, crushed | vegetable oil or shortening for frying |
| 2 large eggs, beaten | |

1. Melt butter in small skillet over low heat. Sprinkle in flour and garlic. Cook for 3 minutes, stirring constantly to make a roux.

2. Fill a deep fryer or skillet with oil. Heat to 350°F.

3. Fold roux into mashed breadfruit. Stir in eggs, combining well.

4. Drop by spoonfuls into hot oil. Be careful not too overcrowd pan.

5. Remove with slotted spoon. Drain on white paper towels. Serve as appetizer or side dish. Season to taste with salt and pepper.

**Yield: about 12 fritters**

# Breadfruit *Tostones*
*Tostones de Panapén*

Breadfruit tostones, tasty change from plantain tostones.

**1 3-pound breadfruit, not too ripe, nor too green**

**¼ cup olive oil**

**1 teaspoon annatto oil**

**½ teaspoon cayenne pepper (optional)**

**3 garlic cloves, crushed**

**salt**

**cracked black pepper**

**vegetable oil for frying**

1. Wash and rinse breadfruit. Slice off top and bottom with a sharp knife. Cut in half, then half again. Repeat until you have 8 segments. Remove core and discard. Peel skin.

2. Chop into 1 ½-inch pieces. Fill a large bowl with cold salted water. Submerge breadfruit for 20 minutes. Remove and drain.

3. Heat olive oil to 350°F in large skillet or deep fryer.

4. Fry breadfruit chunks for 8 minutes. Remove and drain on paper towels. Cool slightly.

5. Pound and flatten breadfruit until about 3/8-inch thick.

6. Fry again until golden. Remove and drain on white paper towels.

7. In small saucepan, heat olive oil, annatto oil, cayenne and garlic over moderate heat. Simmer for 10 minutes.

8. Drizzle over breadfruit tostones. Season to taste with salt and cracked black pepper.

**Yield: about 36 tostones**

# Breadfruit Chips
*Hojuelas de Panapén*

If you're on a low sodium diet, try sprinkling with Cajun seasoning.

| | |
|---|---|
| **1 3-pound breadfruit, not too ripe, nor too green** | **salt** |
| **1 tablespoon salt** | **pepper** |
| **2 cloves garlic, crushed** | **cayenne pepper (optional)** |
| **vegetable oil or shortening for frying** | |

1. Wash breadfruit. Slice off ends and cut in half. Cut in half again. Repeat until you have 6 to 8 segments, depending on size of breadfruit. Discard pulpy core.
2. Peel skin. Slice into thin slices with a sharp knife.
3. Fill a large bowl or pot with cold water and the 1 tablespoon salt. Soak breadfruit for 20 minutes. Drain.
4. Heat vegetable oil to 350°F in deep skillet or fryer. Drop in crushed garlic. Fry breadfruit one layer at a time, taking care not to overcrowd pan. Slices should be golden and crisp like potato chips.
5. Drain on white paper towels. Season to taste with salt, pepper and cayenne.

**Yield: 6 servings**

# Boiled Breadfruit Seeds
*Pepitas de Panapén Hervidas*

My low-carb guests love these peel and eat seeds.

| | |
|---|---|
| **2 ½ pounds breadfruit seeds** | **2 ½ tablespoons salt** |
| **9 cups boiling water** | |

1. Rinse breadfruit seeds well. Lower into salted, boiling water and cook for

30 minutes. Seeds should be soft.

2. Serve immediately. Peel to eat.

**Yield: 6 to 8 servings**

# Stuffed Breadfruit

Another tasty recipe courtesy of Anna's grandmother, Lucinda. This time she used a generous splash of vermouth.

**4 cups Beef and Pork Filling for Piononos (see index)**

**3 small breadfruits, cantaloupe-size, not too ripe, nor too green**

**¾ cup unseasoned breadcrumbs**

**2 tablespoons melted butter**

**¼ cup dry vermouth (optional)**

**¼ cup chopped chives**

1. Fill a large kettle or stockpot with cold salted water. Bring to boil over medium high heat.
2. Slice ends of breadfruit and halve, cross-wise. Scoop out centers to make room for filling. Discard centers.
3. Boil breadfruit for 30 minutes. Remove from heat and drain.
4. Preheat oven to 375°F.
5. Divide filling equally between breadfruit halves.
6. Melt butter in small skillet over low heat. Stir in vermouth and breadcrumbs until coated.
7. Top breadfruits with breadcrumbs, sprinkling chives over top.
8. Bake for 30 minutes until golden.

**Yield: 6 servings**

# Mashed Potatoes and Carrots

Tasuki and Natalie saga continued from *Rice with Spareribs*. Natalie had been teething for the past week, eating little. We had thought to tempt her with this sweet, orange-tinted mashed potato recipe. Unfortunately neither Natalie nor anyone else got to taste the dish. While Anna and I were outside wrestling bags of groceries from the car, Natalie's partner in crime, Tasuki vaulted up on the kitchen counter. By the time we arrived on the scene, an empty bowl was the only evidence of the cat's treachery. Eyeing his round stomach speculatively, I couldn't believe he ate all those vegetables. I was afraid he'd become ill later. He didn't, but slept in my bed all afternoon unable to budge. By the time I went to bed, he lifted listless eyes. I felt sorry for him and brought him a cup of water to lap up. Go to *Onion and Garlic Smothered Chicken* for more on Tasuki and Natalie.

**1 ½ pounds potatoes, scrubbed, peeled and halved**

**1 pound carrots, peeled and halved**

**1 tablespoon salt**

**2 large eggs, beaten**

**2 egg yolks, beaten**

**1 cup warm milk**

**4 tablespoons butter**

**½ cup unseasoned breadcrumbs**

**1 teaspoon salt**

**½ teaspoon cracked black pepper**

1. Fill a large kettle with cold water and the 1 tablespoon salt. Bring to boil over medium-high heat.

2. Add potatoes and carrots, cooking uncovered for 25 minutes. Remove and drain. Set aside.

3. Preheat oven to 350°F. Grease a square or oblong ceramic or glass baking dish with vegetable oil or shortening. Set aside.

4. Mash potatoes and carrots or run through a ricer (better).

5. Cut in beaten egg yolks, warm milk and butter until blended.

6. Press into greased dish.

7. Mix breadcrumbs with salt and pepper in a small bowl.

8. Sprinkle over potato/carrot mixture.

9. Bake for 20 minutes.

**Yield: 6 to 8 servings**

# Cheese Stuffed Potato Balls

*Rellenos de Papas con Queso*

If you haven't tasted *Machengo* cheese yet, try it in this recipe.

**2 pounds Idaho potatoes, peeled and diced**

**8 cups of water**

**1 tablespoon salt**

**1 tablespoon cornstarch**

**¼ cup all-purpose flour**

**6 ounces grated white Puerto**

1 tablespoon annatto-colored olive oil

3 tablespoons butter

1 egg, beaten

½ teaspoon salt

Rican or machengo cheese

1 teaspoon paprika

vegetable oil for frying

1. Combine 8 cups of water with the 1 tablespoon salt in a deep pot. Bring to boil, add potatoes, reduce heat and cook for 30 minutes until potatoes are soft. Drain and mash.

2. Stir in annatto oil, butter, egg, salt and cornstarch. Mix well and set aside. Allow to cool for 20 minutes.

3. Mix the cheese with the paprika in a small bowl.

4. Dust hands with all-purpose flour. Scoop up a golf ball-sized dollop of potato mixture. Flatten and make a small hollow or depression for filling. Fill with generous spoonful of cheese/paprika mixture. Bring potato mixture over top to cover filling completely. Dust again with flour. Repeat with remainder of potato mixture.

5. Heat oil to 375°. Drop in a few *rellenos* at a time and fry until golden. Do not overcrowd. Remove and drain on white paper towels.

**Yield: 6 servings**

# Ground Meat Stuffed Potato Balls

*Rellenos de Papas con Carne*

Many of the hotels on the Isla Verde beach strip in San Juan, serve this at their Sunday brunch buffet. The newly built Ritz-Carlton has one of the best buffets in San Juan, offering caviar, crab claws and divine chocolate mousse. Bring a fat pocketbook.

1 ½ cups meat filling (see index for Beef and Olive filling for *pastelillos*)

2 pounds Idaho potatoes, peeled and diced

8 cups of water

1 tablespoon salt

1 tablespoon annatto-colored olive oil

1 teaspoon paprika

vegetable oil for frying

1 egg, beaten

½ teaspoon salt

1 tablespoon cornstarch

¼ cup all-purpose flour

6 ounces grated white Puerto Rican or machengo cheese

3 tablespoons butter

1. Combine 8 cups of water with the 1 tablespoon salt in a deep pot. Bring to boil, reduce heat and cook for 30 minutes until potatoes are soft. Drain and mash.

2. Stir in annatto oil, butter, egg, salt and cornstarch. Mix well and set aside. Allow to cool for 20 minutes.

3. Mix the cheese with the paprika in a small bowl.

4. Dust hands with all-purpose flour. Scoop up a golf ball-sized dollop of potato mixture. Flatten and make a small hollow or depression for filling. Fill with generous spoonful of beef mixture. Bring potato mixture over top to cover filling completely. Dust again with flour. Repeat with remainder of potato mixture.

5. Heat oil to 375°. Drop in a few rellenos at a time and fry until golden. Do not overcrowd. Remove and drain on white paper towels.

**Yield: 6 servings**

# Zesty Potato, Cheese and Ham Sandwhiches

*Emparedados de Papa y Jamón Empanados*

The larger the potatoes, the easier it will be to make these "sandwiches".

¾ pound baked ham, sliced thinly
¾ pound sharp Cheddar, or smoked,
  semi-firm cheese, thinly sliced
8 large potatoes, peeled, boiled
  and sliced in ¼-inch thick slices
4 large eggs

½ teaspoon cayenne pepper
1 tablespoon white wine
1 tablespoon evaporated milk
½ teaspoon salt
1 ½ cups unseasoned bread crumbs
vegetable oil for frying

1. Place a couple pieces of ham and cheese between 2 potato slices. Fasten with toothpick. Repeat until all sandwiches have been made.

2. Heat oil to 350°F in deep skillet or fryer.

3. Whisk together eggs, cayenne pepper, white wine, evaporated milk and salt in a small bowl.

4. Pour egg mixture into flat casserole dish.

5. Dip "sandwiches" into egg mixture, then dredge in breadcrumbs.

6. Lower "sandwiches" into hot oil. Fry until golden on each side. Do not overcrowd skillet.

7. Drain on white paper towels.

## Meat and Potato Pie
*Pastelón de Papas*

It's interesting how many variations of the same dish exist on different Caribbean islands. My ex-husband, who was from St. Thomas, made his version of this meat pie with the addition of vinegar in the filling and a cheddar cheese topping. The British Virgin Islands have their own version of meat pie: Sheppard's Pie.

**2 cups meat filling (see index for Pork and Beef Filling for *Piononos*)**

**4 cups warm mashed potatoes**

**1 clove garlic, crushed**

**2 tablespoons minced onion**

**2 tablespoons olive oil**

**3 tablespoons butter**

**3 egg yolks, beaten**

**1 egg, beaten**

**2/3 cup grated Parmesan cheese**

**¼ cup chopped chives**

1. Preheat oven to 375°F. Generously grease a ceramic casserole or 10-inch glass pie dish with vegetable oil or shortening. Set aside.
2. Heat olive oil in small skillet over moderate heat. Sauté garlic and onion until soft, about 5 minutes. Remove from heat.
3. Whisk into mashed potatoes, along with butter and beaten eggs.
4. Press half of the potato mixture into casserole or pie dish.
5. Top with meat filling, then layer with potato mixture on top.
6. Sprinkle Parmesan cheese and chopped chives over potatoes.
7. Bake for 25 mintues, until cheese is lightly browned and bubbling.

**Yield: 6 to 8 servings**

## Potato Beignets
*Buñuelos de Papas*

Doritza served this fried delicacy with shrimp, green salad and plantains.

**1 ½ pounds potatoes, peeled and quartered**

**1 teaspoon salt**

**4 egg yolks, beaten**

**1 ¼ teaspoons salt**

| | |
|---|---|
| 4 tablespoons butter | ½ teaspoon cayenne |
| 2 tablespoons cornstarch | flour |
| 1 tablespoon flour | vegetable oil for frying |

1. Fill a medium saucepan with cold water and the 1 teaspoon salt. Bring to boil over medium-high heat.

2. Add potatoes, cover, reduce heat slightly, and cook for 20 minutes. Remove and drain. If you have a potato ricer, put potatoes through ricer, as this will keep the starches from breaking down and becoming a gluey mess. Otherwise, mash gently by hand.

3. Fold in butter, cornstarch, flour, eggs, salt and cayenne, combining well.

4. Heat oil to 350°F. Drop mixture in by tablespoonfuls and fry until golden. Remove with slotted spoon and drain on white paper towels.

**Yield: 8 to 10 appetizer servings**

## Rich Potato Pudding

*Papa Empanada al Horno*

Serve with roast chicken, turkey, or pork.

| | |
|---|---|
| 2 ½ pounds potatoes, peeled and halved | 5 eggs, separated |
| 1 tablespoon salt | 6 tablespoons butter |
| 1 cup warm milk | 1 teaspoon salt |
| ½ cup evaporated milk | 1 large potato, peeled and thinly sliced |

1. Fill a deep saucepan with cold water and the 1 tablespoon salt. Bring to boil over medium-high heat.

2. Boil potatoes, uncovered for 25 minutes. Drain and allow to cool. Run through a ricer or mash by hand gently.

3. Preheat oven to 375°F. Lightly oil a glass or ceramic baking dish. Set aside.

4. Stir in milk, evaporated milk, eggs yolks, butter and salt.

5. Beat egg whites until stiff peaks form. Fold into potato mixer until just barely combined. Turn into greased glass baking dish and garnish with potato slices.

6. Bake 25 minutes until golden.

**Yield: 8 servings**

## Cassava and Bean Stew

Surprisingly filling, but low in cholesterol.

**3 pounds cassava (yucca), peeled and dice in 1 ½-inch cubes**

**2 teaspoons salt**

**2 tablespoons olive oil**

**1 tablespoon annatto oil**

**1/3 cup *recaíto***

**1/3 cup *sofrito***

**3 firm, ripe tomatoes, peeled, seeded and coarsely chopped**

**1 cup tomato sauce**

**1 tablespoon tomato paste**

**1 cup tomato puree**

**2 cups cooked white beans, fresh or canned, drained**

**2 tablespoons capers**

1. Fill a large kettle or saucepan with cold water and the 2 teaspoons salt. Bring to boil over medium-high heat.

2. Boil cassava for 25 minutes until tender. Drain and set aside.

3. Heat olive and annatto oil in a large skillet or saucepan. Sauté recaíto for 3 minutes over moderate heat.

4. Stir in sofrito, tomatoes, tomato sauce and paste. Simmer for 5 minutes.

5. Stir in tomato puree. Simmer for 5 minutes.

6. Fold in beans and cassava. Cook, over low heat, for 10 minutes, covered. Garnish with capers.

**Yield: 6 to 8 servings**

## Garlic Pepper Cassava Fries

*Yuca con Mojo de Ajo*

These fries were habit forming. I made Anna take them all home with her.

**3 pounds cassava (yucca), peeled and cut in 3 ½-inch by 3/8-inch strips (fries)**

**1 tablespoon cracked black pepper**

**2 tablespoons olive oil**

**vegetable oil for frying**

**1 teaspoon salt**                                    salt

**5 large garlic cloves, minced**

1. Fill a deep kettle with cold water and the 1 teaspoon salt. Bring to boil over medium-high heat.

2. Boil cassava strips for 20 minutes. Do not overcook as "fries" need to be firm.

3. Heat olive oil in a small frying pan. Sauté garlic and black pepper for 5 minutes. Remove from heat and set aside.

4. Fill a deep skillet or fryer with vegetable oil. Heat to 350°F. Fry cassava strips, one layer at a time, taking care not to overload or crowd skillet. Remove when golden and drain on white paper towels.

5. Drizzle garlic/pepper oil over "fries." Season to taste with salt and pepper.

**Yield: 6 servings**

# Gingered Sweet Potatoes

*Batatas en Almíbar*

This is one of my favorite dishes to serve with roast turkey at holiday time.

**3 pounds sweet potatoes, scrubbed and rinsed**          **½ cup brown sugar**

**1 tablespoon freshly grated ginger root**               **¼ cup butter, melted**

**½ cup sugar**                                           **¼ teaspoon ground nutmeg**

1. Fill a large saucepan with water and bring to boiling point over high heat. Add sweet potatoes, reduce heat to moderate, cover and boil for 30 minutes. Remove and drain.

2. Preheat oven to 350°F. Lightly oil a glass or ceramic baking dish.

3. Arrange a layer of sweet potato across bottom of dish. Spread grated ginger evenly over sweet potato. Sprinkle sugars over top. Drizzle melted butter over sugar.

4. Bake for 30 minutes.

**Yield: 6 servings**

# Zesty Yam Fries

I realize these are high in calories, but they do make a make a rich in vitamin A alternative to French fries.

3 pounds yams, peeled and cut in 3 ½-inch by 3/8-inch strips ("fries")

2 teaspoons salt

1 tablespoon salt

2 teaspoons cayenne pepper

2 teaspoons black pepper

1 teaspoon onion powder

½ teaspoon garlic poweder

½ teaspoon dried thyme

vegetable oil for frying

1. Fill a deep kettle or saucepan with cold water and the 2 teaspoons salt. Boil the yam "fries" for 15 minutes. Do not overcook. Remove from water, drain and set aside.

2. Mix together the 1 tablespoon salt, cayenne and black pepper, onion, garlic powder and thyme. Set aside.

3. Fill a skillet or deep fryer with oil. Heat to 350°F. Fry one layer at a time of yams until golden. Remove from oil and drain on white paper towels.

4. Sprinkle with cayenne/salt mixture.

**Yield: 6 servings**

# Yam Beignets
*Buñuelos de Ñame*

Even though Puerto Rico and St. Thomas are only 40 miles apart, I never tasted anything like these yam beignets. Even my daughter Roxanne liked them.

1 ½ pounds yams, peeled and cut in 2-inch chunks

1 tablespoon salt

4 tablespoons butter

½ cup flour

2 large eggs, beaten

2 tablespoons evaporated milk

½ teaspoon salt

oil or shortening

1. Fill a large kettle with cold water and 1 tablespoon salt. Bring to boil over medium-high heat. Boil yams, uncovered, uncovered until soft, about 35 minutes. Drain, cool slightly and run through ricer or food processor until smooth.

2. Preheat oil to 375°F in a skillet or deep fryer.

3. Fold in butter, combining well. Sprinkle in flour a little at a time until incorporated.

4. Whisk in beaten eggs and milk. Sprinkle in salt, still stirring.

5. Drop by spoonfuls into hot oil, frying until golden. Remove and drain on white paper towels.

6. Serve plain as an accompaniment to chicken, meat or fish. Or, sprinkle with sugar and cinnamon.

**Yield: about 12 beignets**

# Puerto Rican Pumpkin Pudding
*Budín de Calabaza*

I serve pumpkin pudding as a side dish to roast turkey, beef or pork, along with a green vegetable, rice and salad.

**1 ½ pounds West Indian pumpkin, or any other dry pumpkin or orange squash (butternut)**

**1 tablespoon salt**

**6 eggs, separated**

**1/2 teaspoon ground ginger**

**¼ teaspoon nutmeg**

**¼ cup brown sugar**

**4 tablespoons butter**

1. Fill a deep kettle with cold water and 1 tablespoon salt. Bring to boil over medium-high heat.

2. Peel, seed and coarsely chop pumpkin. Boil pumpkin, uncovered, for 25 minutes until just tender. Remove from heat, drain and allow to cool somewhat.

3. Mash pumpkin or run through food processor. You will want a smooth, lump-free puree.

4. Preheat oven to 375°F. Butter a 2-quart glass or ceramic baking dish. Set aside.

5. Fold in beaten egg yolks, ginger, nutmeg, brown sugar and butter.

6. Beat egg whites until stiff peaks form.

7. Carefully fold into pumpkin mixture until barely blended.

8. Scoop into baking dish and bake for 30 minutes until golden.

**Yield: 8 servings**

# Spicy Yautía and Parmesan Fritters
*Frituras de Yautía y Queso Parmesano*

*Yautía* is the starchy root of a large-leaved tropical plant. Creamy yellow, it closely resembles flavor and texture of a Idaho potato, which may be used as a substitute for *yautía*.

**2 pounds yautía, scrubbed, peeled and washed**

**2 teaspoons salt**

**¾ cup grated Parmesan Cheese**

**¼ cup grated Puerto Rican white cheese,**
   **or other crumbly white cheese**
   **(cheddar is fine)**

**2 tablespoons flour**

**1 teaspoon cracked black pepper**

**1 tablespoon dry sherry**
   **(optional)**

**vegetable oil or shortening**

1. Quarter the yautía and run through the food processor to grate.
2. Fold in salt, Parmesan, white cheese, flour, black pepper and dry sherry.
3. Heat oil in deep fryer or skillet to 375°F.
4. Form flat 1 ½-inch in diameter patties. Fry one layer at a time, taking care not to overcrowd skillet. Remove when golden and drain on white paper towels.
5. Serve hot with hot chili pepper sauce, chutney or mustard as a side dish or appetizer.

**Yield: 18 fritters**

# *Yautía* and Cheese Beignets
*Buñuelos de Yautía y Queso*

Serve with sliced mango, pineapple and bananas and plenty of hot, strong coffee for Sunday brunch.

**1 ½ pounds *yautía*, peeled and**
   **cut in 2-inch chunks**

**1 tablespoon salt**

**2 tablespoons evaporated milk**

**½ teaspoon salt**

**¾ cup shredded sharp white**

4 tablespoons butter

½ cup flour

2 large eggs, beaten

cheese

oil or shortening

1. Fill a large kettle with cold water and 1 tablespoon salt. Bring to boil over medium-high heat. Boil *yautía*, uncovered, uncovered until soft, about 35 minutes. Drain, cool slightly and run through ricer or food processor until smooth.

2. Preheat oil to 375°F in a skillet or deep fryer.

3. Fold in butter, combining well. Sprinkle in flour a little at a time until incorporated.

4. Whisk in beaten eggs and milk. Sprinkle in salt and cheese, stirring until smooth.

5. Drop by spoonfuls into hot oil, frying until golden. Remove and drain on white paper towels.

6. Serve plain as an accompaniment to chicken, meat or fish or as an appetizer

**Yield: about 15 beignets**

## Cornmeal Guanimes

*Guanimes de Maíz*

If necessary, substitute parchment paper for plantain leaves.

2 cups fine ground yellow cornmeal

2 cups unsweetened coconut milk

½ cup milk

½ cup sweetened condensed milk

½ teaspoon ground anise

½ teaspoon salt

plantain leaves, rinsedand patted dry

string

1. Combine cornmeal, coconut milk, milk and condensed milk until smooth in a large bowl.

2. Stir in anise and salt.

3. Fill a deep kettle with cold, salted water. Bring to a boil over medium-high heat.

4. Cut plantain leaves or parchment into 8-inch squares.

5. Place 3 tablespoons of cornmeal paste into center and spread into square shape. You should still about a 2-inch border of parchment on all four sides.

6. Fold sides in, then fold over into thirds to form a packet. Tie with string.

7. Lower packets into boiling water and cook, covered for 35 minutes, over moderate heat.

8. Remove from water and drain. Serve in packets.

**Yield: about 24 *guanimes***

# Cabbage Pasteles
*Pasteles de Col*

Be sure to place vegetables in large pot of cold, salted water after peeling to keep them from turning black:

**WRAPPING:**

**1 large white cabbage, 3 to 4 pounds (white is traditional, but red looks quite attractive)**

**2 tablespoons salt**

**DOUGH:**

**5 green bananas, peeled and grated**
**2 large green plantains, peeled and grated**
**1 pound peeled and grated *yuca* (cassava), use frozen one if possible, it's more convenient**
**1 pound white *yautía* (taro) or Idaho potataoes, peeled and diced**

**1 cup pork stock (see index for recipe)**
**6 tablespoons annatto-colored olive oil**
**1/3 cup milk**
**1 tablespoon salt**

**TRADITIONAL PORK FILLING:**

**1 pound boneless pork roast, diced in ½-inch pieces**
**2 tablespoons adobo (see index for recipe)**
**2 tablespoons annatto-colored oil**

**1 cup recaíto (see index for recipe)**
**1 cup of tomato sauce**
**½ cup cooked chickpeas**
**½ cup raisins**

½ cup smoked ham, diced finely
twine or string, uncolored

2 tablespoons shredded,
unsweetened coconut

## WRAPPING:

1. Fill a deep kettle with cold water and the 2 tablespoons salt. Bring to boil over moderate heat. Remove any outer wilted leaves from cabbage. Lower entire head carefully into boiling water. Cook for 20 to 25 minutes. Remove and drain.

2. When sufficiently cooled, gingerly remove leaves one at a time from cabbage.

3. Gently pound spine of each leaf with a mallet until the leaf lays somewhat flat.

4. Reserve 18 to 24 best, intact leaves.

## PASTE (MASA OR DOUGH):

5. Fit food processor with grated blade. Have a large bowl handy to hold grated vegetables.

6. Drain water from vegetables. Process small amounts of vegetables at a time. Add small amounts of pork stock until vegetables have the consistency of oatmeal. Transfer to large bowl.

7. Stir in any remaining pork stock, the annatto oil and 1/3 cup milk. Use your hands to mix and remove any large chunks of vegetables. Batter should have a smooth silky surface. Set aside.

## FILLING:

8. Season pork with *adobo*. Heat annatto-colored oil in skillet and sauté the pork and ham over medium heat for 5 minutes until lightly browned on all sides.

9. Add *recaíto* and reduce heat. Simmer for 3 minutes, then stir in tomato sauce, cooking additional 20 minutes. Pork should be cooked through. Fold in chickpeas, raisins and coconut. Heat through. Remove from stove and set aside.

## ASSEMBLY:

10. Place a large cabbage leaf on a clean working surface. Scoop up 2 to 3 tablespoons of the paste and spread on leaf, not quite out to edges.

11. Place about 2 tablespoons of the pork filling on top of masa, flattened.

12. Roll up edges and fold leaves, making a packet. Tie with twine, so packets cannot unroll in cooking water. Repeat until all pastels are made.

COOKING:

13. Add fresh water to kettle and 1 tablespoon salt. Bring to boil over moderate heat.

14. Lower in pasteles, boil, uncovered for 40 minutes.

15. Drain and serve wrapped in cabbage leaves.

**Yield: 18 to 24 *pasteles***

# Asparagus Pudding

I always believed this recipe was Danish in origin. I was very surprised when I moved to San Juan and found it on a restaurant menu.

| | |
|---|---|
| 6 tablespoons butter | 2 10 1/2 -ounce cans asparagus tips, drained |
| 8 tablespoons flour | |
| 1 teaspoon salt | 8 eggs, separated |
| ½ teaspoon cracked black pepper | 2 tablespoons dry white wine |
| 1 cup warm milk | ¼ teaspoon nutmeg |
| ½ cup evaporated milk | paprika |

1. Preheat oven to 350°F. Generously grease a shallow glass baking dish with butter. Set aside.

2. In a medium saucepan, melt butter over very low heat. Gradually whisk in flour, salt and pepper to make a roux.

3. Drizzle in milk, stirring constantly, over moderate heat, until thickened. Remove from stove. Set aside.

4. Whirl egg yolks, wine, nutmeg and asparagus tips in a blender until smooth.

5. Stir egg yolk mixture into milk mixture.

6. Beat egg whites until stiff. Fold into asparagus mixture until just blended.

7. Spoon into greased baking dish.

8. Bake 45 minutes until golden. Garnish with paprika sprinkled over top. Serve at once while still puffy.

**Yield: 8 servings**

# Okra Stew

*Guingambós Guisados*

Until Anna introduced me to fresh okra, I had never developed a taste for it. Using fresh, instead of frozen, makes all the difference. It seems the frozen becomes extra slimy when cooked.

¼ pound salt pork diced, or 3 bacon strips

¼ pound ham, diced

1 tablespoon annatto oil

1 tablespoon olive oil

½ cup *recaíto*

2 tablespoons tomato paste

¾ cup minced yellow onion

1 pound tomatoes, peeled, seeded and chopped

1 ½ pounds okra, tips sliced off and cut in half cross-wise

1 ½ cups water

1 cup chicken broth

1. Sauté the pork and ham in the annatto and olive oil in a medium saucepan or kettle over moderate heat. Drain excess fat.

2. Add *recaíto* , tomato paste, onion, and tomato. Cook for 5 minutes.

3. Pour water and chicken broth in saucepan. Bring to boil. Add okra, reduce heat and simmer, covered for 30 minutes.

4. Uncover and cook until sauce has thickened, about 20 minutes.

**Yield: 6 servings**

## Health Tip

Choose **chayote** for some of your LOW-CARB meals. Each 100 grams contains: 93% water; 0.6 grams protein; **0.5 grams fat; 5.1 grams carbohydrates**; 0.7 grams of fiber and only 24 calories! Chayotes can be eaten raw in salads or cooked, added to soups and stews, stir-fried or stuffed. Replaces zucchini and cucumbers in most recipes. Note: wear gloves while peeling chayote, as it secretes a sticky resin.

# LOW-CARB Asparagus and Chayote Custard with Orange Glaze

Asparagus contains 4.2 grams carbohydrate per 100 gram serving.

½ pound asparagus, trimmed
   and cut into 2-inch pieces

½ pound chayote, peeled,
   pitted, and coarsely diced

1 tablespoon shredded parsley

2 tablespoons butter,
   room temperature

4 eggs

¼ cup light cream or half-and-half

¾ cup freshly grated Parmesan cheese

1 tablespoon chopped green onion

½ teaspoon salt

½ teaspoon freshly cracked black pepper

¼ teaspoon nutmeg

ORANGE GLAZE:

¼ cup butter

3 tablespoons fresh orange juice

1 tablespoon fresh lemon juice

¼ teaspoon Splenda®

1/8 teaspoon ground cinnamon

1. Preheat oven to 350°F. Coat a 1-quart glass or ceramic baking dish with non-stick vegetable spray.

2. Boil 1-inch of water in a medium saucepan over moderate heat. Boil asparagus and chayote for 3 ½ minutes. Remove from heat and drain.

3. Transfer for asparagus and chayote to a food processor. Add parsley, butter, eggs, and light cream. Puree until smooth.

4. Add Parmesan, onion, salt, pepper and nutmeg. Blend well.

5. Scoop into baking dish. Bake for 35 minutes.

6. To make glaze: melt butter in a small saucepan over moderate heat. Stir in orange and lemon juice, simmering for 1 minute. Whisk in Splenda® and cinnamon. Drizzle over Asparagus and Chayote Custard.

**Yield: 4 servings**

EACH SERVING (CUSTARD ONLY) PROVIDES APPROXIMATELY:
270 calories, 7 **grams carbohydrates**, 17 grams of protein, 20 grams of fat

EACH SERVING (ORANGE GLAZE ONLY)
140 calories, 3 **grams carbohydrates**, 1 grams of protein,, 12 grams of fat

# LOW-CARB Cauliflower and Cilantro "Mashed Potatoes"

Cauliflower tends to cook rather fast. Take caution in not over-cooking as it loses flavor and becomes grey and mushy.

| | |
|---|---|
| 1 pound cauliflower, rinsed, broken in small pieces, steamed for 15 minutes | 2 tablespoons shredded cilantro |
| | ¼ cup heavy cream |
| | 2 tablespoons butter, room temperature |
| 1 egg, beaten | ½ teaspoon salt |
| ¼ cup freshly, grated Parmesan cheese | ½ teaspoon freshly grated black pepper |

1. Preheat oven to 375°F. Spray a 1-quart baking dish with vegetable spray.
2. Transfer steamed cauliflower to bowl of a food processor. Add egg, Parmesan, cilantro, heavy cream, butter, salt and pepper.
3. Scoop into baking dish. Bake for 20 minutes.

**Yield: 4 servings**

EACH SERVING PROVIDES APPROXIMATELY:
160 calories, **8 grams carbohydrates**, 7 grams of protein, 11 grams of fat

# LOW-CARB Chayote, Zuccini and Goat Cheese Gratin

*Doritza's* husband Julio never discovered he was our guinea pig for the low-carb recipes. Oscar, who believes himself a gourmand, gave this recipe to all his pals in his cooking club.

| | |
|---|---|
| 1 pound zucchini, cut into ¼-inch circles | 6 ounces goat cheese |
| ½ pound chayote, peeled, pitted and thinly sliced | 2 tablespoons sour cream |
| | 1 teaspoon hot chili pepper sauce |
| 2 tablespoons olive oil | |
| ¼ cup minced green onion | 1 teaspoon salt |
| 2 garlic cloves, peeled and minced | 1 teaspoon freshly ground pepper |
| ¼ cup heavy cream | 2 tablespoons Parmesan cheese |

1. Preheat oven to 350°F. Boil zucchini and chayote in 2-inches of water in a medium saucepan for 3 minutes. Remove from heat and drain. Reserve.

2. Lightly coat a 1-quart baking dish with vegetable spray. Set aside.

3. Heat olive oil in a small skillet over moderate heat. Sauté onion and garlic for 5 minutes, until soft, but not brown. Remove from heat and reserve.

4. Place zucchini and chayote in bottom of dish. Top with onion and garlic mixture.

5. Heat heavy cream in a small saucepan over low-to medium heat. Break up goat cheese into small pieces and whip into cream, stirring constantly until cheese melts, about 4 minutes. Remove from heat and whisk in sour cream, hot chili sauce, salt and pepper.

6. Pour cheese mixture over vegetables. Sprinkle with Parmesan. Bake for 35 minutes.

**Yield: 4 servings**

EACH SERVING PROVIDES APPROXIMATELY:
290 calories, **9 grams of carbohydrate**, 12 grams of protein, 25 grams of fat

# LOW-CARB Chayote with Roasted Hazelnut Butter

Roasted hazelnuts transform this ordinary dish into the extraordinary.

**¼ cup toasted hazelnuts, finely minced**

**3 tablespoons butter**

**1 pound chayote, peeled and pitted**

**1 shallot minced**

**½ teaspoon salt**

**½ teaspoon freshly ground black pepper**

1. Preheat oven to 350°F. Arrange hazelnuts in a shallow pan. Toast for 10 minutes until golden. Do not burn. Remove from oven and set aside.

2. Melt butter in a small saucepan over low heat. Sauté shallot for 3 to 4 minutes. Stir in salt and pepper. Fold in hazelnuts.

3. Fill a medium saucepan with 1-inch of salted water. Bring to boil over medium heat. Boil chayote for 10 to 15 minutes. Drain.

4. Transfer chayote to a serving dish. Drizzle with hazelnut butter.

**Yield: 4 servings**

EACH SERVING PROVIDES APPROXIMATELY:
125 calories, **9 grams carbohydrates**, 2 grams of protein, 10 grams of fat

# Seafood

S eafood is available in abundance in Puerto Rico with the Atlantic Ocean on one side and the Caribbean on the other. Many of the typical seafood dishes show the Spanish heritage of the island, many using *sofrito* as their base.

Anna's cousin Livia, the artist, is responsible for many of these aromatic and traditional recipes.

## Fried Fish with Mojito Sauce
*Pescado Frito Con Mojito Isleño*

This traditional dish originated from the island's coastal towns, but has now gained popularity inland. Mojito Isleño comes from Salinas.

**3 ½ pounds firm white fish fillets (cod, snapper, flounder, turbo, etc.) ¾ inch thick**
**2 teaspoons salt**

Mojito:

¼ cup, plus 1 tablespoon olive oil
2 large yellow onions, thinly sliced
1 can (8 ounce) tomato sauce
4 tablespoons tomato paste
3 tablespoons cider vinegar
1 ¼ cups water
1/3 cup *alcaparrado* (see index)
1 large bay leaf

2 teaspoons freshly cracked
  black pepper
1 ½ teaspoons salt
2 roasted red peppers or pimentos,
  sliced in strips
vegetable oil for frying
2 cloves garlic, peeled and chopped
  coarsely

1. Rinse fish fillets under cold running water. Pat dry, season with salt. Set aside.

2. Heat olive oil in a large saucepan over medium heat. Sauté onion slices for 7 minutes. Do not brown. Remove from heat.

3. Stir together tomato sauce, tomato paste, vinegar and water in a medium bowl until well combined. Pour into sauce pan and stir.

176

4. Fold in *alcaparrado*, bay leaf, black pepper, salt and black pepper, roasted pepper or pimento strips. Return to low to medium heat, cover and simmer for 20 minutes. Uncover and simmer for additional 20 minutes. Remove from heat, cover and keep in a warm place.

5. Heat ½ inch of vegetable oil in a large skillet. Stir in garlic. Carefully lower fish fillets into hot oil. Do not overcrowd skillet. Fry over medium heat, 3 ½ minutes on each side. Fish should be cooked through in center, flaking easily with a fork.

6. Transfer to a serving platter, drizzling *mojito sauce* over top. Serve with plantains, okra and a green salad.

**Yield: 4 to 6 servings**

# Breaded Fish Fillets
*Filetes de Pescado Empanados*

Serve this basic recipe with any of the recipes from Chapter One.

**3 ½ pounds firm white fish fillets, 3/4 -inch thick**
**2 teaspoons salt**
**½ teaspoon freshly cracked black pepper**

**4 large eggs, beaten**
**2 cups unseasonsed breadcrumbs or cracker crumbs**
**¼ cup finely minced parsley**
**vegetable oil**

1. Rinse the fish fillets under cold running water. Pat dry. Season with salt and pepper.

2. Mix together breadcrumbs with parsley on large plate.

3. Dip fillets in beaten egg, then roll in breadcrumbs. Press breadcrumbs into fish. Set aside for 15 minutes to allow the coating to adhere.

4. Heat 1/2-inch of vegetable oil in a large skillet over medium-high heat. Fry fillets, taking care not over crowd pan, until golden, turning once.

5. Drain on white paper towels. Season with black pepper.

**Yield: 6 servings**

## Poached Fish in Hazelnut Butter Sauce

*Pescado Herbido*

Toasted hazelnuts and rum give this recipe an 'oh, wow' factor.

3 pounds firm, white fish fillets, 1-inch thick

8 tablespoons butter

½ cup chopped hazelnuts

½ teaspoon salt

3 tablespoons rum

2 tablespoons olive oil

½ cup minced yellow onion

1 small green frying pepper, seeded and minced

1 garlic clove, crushed

1 large *culantro* leaf or 1 tablespoon minced cilantro

1 cup chicken broth

¼ cup sweet white wine

1 cup water

1. Rinse fish fillets under cool running water. Pat dry and set aside.
2. Pulse together butter, hazelnuts and salt in a food processor until a dough-like consistency is attained. Scoop into a small saucepan and simmer over low heat until hazelnuts are lightly browned. Stir in rum, simmering for additional minutes. Remove from heat and keep in a warm place.
3. Heat olive oil in a large saucepan (large enough for the fillets to fit in one layer) over moderate heat. Add onion, green pepper and garlic, sautéing lightly for 3 minutes.
4. Add *culantro*, chicken broth, white wine and water. Bring to a boil.
5. Carefully place fillets in pan, making sure liquid covers fish. Simmer for 10 minutes or until fish flakes easily.

6. Carefully remove fish using a side spatula and place on serving dish.

7. Spoon hazelnut butter over top of fish.

**Yield: 4 to 6 servings**

# Shrimp and Herb-Stuffed Fish in Passionfruit Glaze

*Pescado Relleno*

Take care using too much celery. The flavor can overpower the rest of the dish.

**2 pounds firm white fish fillets, 1-inch thick**

**4 tablespoons butter**

**4 tablespoons minced green onion**

**2 tablespoons minced celery stalk**

**1 tablespoon minced green frying pepper or green bell pepper**

**1 *culantro* leaf or 2 tablespoons minced cilantro**

**2 tablespoons minced parsley**

**½ teaspoon dried whole oregano**

**¼ teaspoon dried thyme**

**½ cup cooked, finely chopped shrimp**

**1 cup fresh breadcrumbs**

**1 teaspoon salt**

**½ teaspoon freshly cracked pepper**

**1 egg, beaten**

## PASSIONFRUIT GLAZE

**4 tablespoons butter**

**2 tablespoons passionfruit syrup or puree**

**1 tablespoon pineapple juice concentrate (frozen kind)**

**2 tablespoons rum**

1. Preheat oven to 375°F.

2. Rinse fish under cool, running water. Slice open fillets lengthwise with the tip of a sharp knife, to make a pouch for stuffing.

3. Melt butter over moderate heat in a large skillet. Sauté onion, celery and peppers for 2 minutes. Add cilantro, parsley, oregano, thyme, shrimp, breadcrumbs, salt and pepper. Cook for 2 minutes over medium heat.

4. Whisk in beaten egg, cooking for 1 minute, stirring constantly. Remove from heat and allow to cool for 10 minutes.

5. Stuff fish fillets. Secure opening with wooden toothpicks.

6. Arrange fillets on buttered, glass baking dish. Bake uncovered for 30 minutes until fish flakes easily with a fork.

7. Meanwhile, to make glaze, melt butter in a small saucepan. Stir in passionfruit syrup and pineapple concentrate, cooking until bubbly. Whisk in rum. Remove from heat.

8. Carefully remove from dish using a wide spatula. Arrange on a serving plate. Spoon passionfruit glaze over top.

**Yield: 4 to 6 servings**


## Pickled Fish

*Pescado en Escabeche*

Pickled fish works well as an appetizer or served at lunch with mixed greens, hard-boiled eggs, and mango slices.

**3 pounds firm fish fillets, 1-inch thick**  **½ cup all-purpose flour**

**2 limes, halved**  **1 recipe *escabeche* sauce (see index)**

**1 teaspoon salt**  **vegetable oil**

**1 teaspoon cracked black pepper**  **2 garlic cloves, chopped**

1. Rinse fish under cool, running water. Pat dry. Squeeze lime halves over fish. Season with salt.

2. Mix black pepper into flour. Roll fillets in flour. Set aside.

3. Heat 1/2 -inch of vegetable oil in a large skillet along with garlic over medium heat.

4. Fry fish fillets, taking care not to overcrowd pan, six minutes on each side. Fish should flake easily in center if poked with a fork. Remove from heat and allow to cool completely.

5. In a deep glass baking dish, with cover, arrange fish slices. Pour *escabeche* sauce over top. Cover and refrigerate for at least 24 hours.

6. Serve chilled.

**Yield: 6 to 8 servings**

# Fish Sticks

*Palitos de Pescado*

Fried properly, at a high temperature, in an uncrowded pan, the fish will absorb little oil, resulting in a tasty, flaky crust. Avoid mincing the garlic. Chop coarsely for a more delicate flavor.

1 cup flour

1 teaspoon freshly cracked
  black pepper

1 cup seasoned breadcrumbs

3 pounds firm white fish, cut in
  strips 2-inches long, by ½-inch wide

4 eggs, beaten

vegetable oil for frying

1. Combine flour and cracked pepper on a large plate. Pour breadcrumbs onto another plate.

2. Dip fish sticks in egg, then roll in breadcrumbs, pushing crumbs into fish. Then dip in flour.

3. Heat ½-inch of oil in a large skillet over moderate heat. Fry sticks until golden, taking care not to overcrowd pan.

4. Drain on white paper towels. Serve with any sauce from Chapter One.

**Yield: 6 servings**

# Oven Baked Red Snapper in Brandy Garlic Sauce

*Pescado Al Horno y Ajo*

The traditional version of this recipe calls for whole snapper, leaving head, tail and bones intact. Any firm white fish may be substituted.

2 pounds snapper fillets

¼ cup olive oil

¼ cup brandy

3 tablespoons lemon juice

4 large garlic cloves, crushed

1 teaspoon salt

1 teaspoon freshly cracked
  black pepper

1. Preheat oven to 375°.

2. Rinse fish under cool, running water. Pat dry. Set aside.

3. Combine olive oil, brandy, lemon juice, garlic, salt and pepper in a small bowl.

4. Spoon a couple tablespoons of olive oil mixture into the bottom of a deep glass baking dish.

5. Arrange fish slices on bottom of dish. Drizzle remaining olive oil mixture over fish.

6. Bake uncovered for 30 minutes, until center of fish flakes easily with a fork.

**Yield: 4 to 6 servings**

---

### Did You Know?

**San Juan** is the second oldest city in the Americas, Santo Domingo in the Dominican Republic being the oldest. Old San Juan is delightful with its cobblestone streets and restored Spanish architecture. Nearby, the Condado and Isla Verde area glitters with hotels, nightclubs and mile-long beaches, resembling Miami Beach.

---

## Snapper Stewed in Lemon-Gingered Sherry and Tomato Sauce

This is one of my favorite lunch dishes. Light, lemony and fragrant with ginger. Serve with cooked, chilled vegetables.

2 pounds snapper fillets

½ cup olive oil

3 large garlic cloves, peeled and coarsely chopped

¼ cup minced yellow onion

1 ½ teaspoons freshly grated ginger

½ teaspoon dried oregano

1 teaspoon powdered chicken bouillon, or 1 cube, crushed

1 lemon halved

½ cup dry sherry

¾ cup tomato puree

½ teaspoon cayenne pepper

1 tablespoon *recaíto* (see index)

½ cup fresh, ripe tomatoes, peeled and diced

½ cup red bell pepper, seeded and cut in thin strips

½ cup green bell pepper, seeded and cut in thin strips

1. Rinse snapper until cool, running water and pat dry. Cut fillets into 1 ½ inch pieces. Set aside.

2. Heat olive oil in a deep skillet over medium heat. Sauté garlic, onion and ginger for 5 minutes, taking care not to burn onion or garlic.

3. Stir in oregano and chicken bouillon. Squeeze in lemon halves, reserving shells.

4. Whisk in sherry, tomato puree, cayenne and *recaíto*.

5. Carefully lower in diced fillets, stirring to coat fish evenly with tomato mixture.

6. Reduce heat until liquid begins to bubble. Fold in ripe tomatoes and bell peppers. Grate one teaspoon lemon zest from reserved lemon halves. Sprinkle in pan. Cover and simmer for 8 minutes.

7. Serve over hot white rice with sliced avocados.

**Yield: 6 servings**

# Zesty Stir-Fried Fish and Garden Vegetables
*Pescado con Vegetables*

The carb-conscious can omit the flour dredging on the fish, but it really does add a nice crunchy texture to the dish.

3 pounds firm white fish, cut in 1 ½-inch cubes

1 teaspoon salt

1 teaspoon freshly cracked black pepper

½ teaspoon paprika

½ teaspoon dried oregano

½ cup all-purpose flour

olive oil

3 garlic cloves, peeled and coarsely chopped

1 medium yellow onion

2 large green frying peppers, seeded and cut in strips

1 medium red bell pepper, seeded and cut in strips

2 large ripe tomatoes, peeled and cut in 1-inch cubes

1 teaspoon salt

1 teaspoon cayenne pepper

½ teaspoon cracked black pepper

1 tablespoon cider vinegar

1. Rinse fish under cool running water. Pat dry. Season with salt and pepper.

2. Combine oregano, paprika and flour. Dredge fish in flour mixture. Set aside.

3. Heat ½-inch of olive oil in a large skillet over medium heat. Add fish and brown lightly on all sides, for about 3 to 4 minutes.

4. Add garlic, onions, peppers and tomatoes. Cook for 3 minutes.

5. Stir in salt, cayenne, pepper and vinegar. Cover, reduce heat and simmer for 5 additional minutes.

6. Serve over hot rice.

## Fish Au Gratin with Ripe Tomatoes and Cilantro
*Pescado Au Gratin*

Kids of all ages love this quick and tangy recipe. Substitute chicken for the fish if you like. You may want to reduce the amount of cracked pepper by half for children

| | |
|---|---|
| **3 pounds firm white fish fillets** | **1 cup heavy cream** |
| **2 limes, halved** | **½ cup evaporated milk** |
| **½ teaspoon freshly cracked black pepper** | **1 tablespoon brandy** |
| | **1 cup grated parmesan cheese** |
| **1 ½ teaspoons salt** | **1 tablespoon minced *cilantro*, or** |
| **3 tablespoons unsalted butter** | **  *cilantro* (see index)** |
| **1 tablespoon minced green onion** | **1 large ripe tomato, thinly sliced** |
| **2 tablespoons flour** | **¼ cup unseasoned breadcrumbs** |

1. Rinse fish under cool running water. Pat dry. Squeeze lime halves over fish. Season with salt and pepper. Set aside.

2. Melt butter slowly in a large skillet over low heat. Stir in green onion, cooking for 2 minutes. Gradually blend in flour.

3. Slowly stir in cream and milk, stirring constantly over medium heat until sauce bubbles and thickens.

4. Reduce heat to low. Add brandy and parmesan cheese, stirring constantly until cheese melts. Stir in cilantro and remove from heat.

5. Arrange fish slices in a buttered glass baking dish. Top with sliced tomato. Pour cheese sauce over top.

6. Sprinkle with breadcrumbs and bake for 30 minutes. Center of fish should flake easily with a fork.

7. Serve with buttered hot peas and hot rice.

**Yield: 4 to 6 servings**

# Swordfish in Lemon-Garlic Sauce

*Pez de Espada con Salsa de Limón*

Any firm, white fish may be substituted for the swordfish.

**2 pounds swordfish steaks**

**1 teaspoon cracked black epper**

**3 garlic cloves, crushed**

**2 teaspoons salt**

**juice of one lemon**

**1 teaspoon fresh grated lemon zest**

**½ cup olive oil**

**1 large green pepper, seeded and**
    **cut in thin strips**

1. Rinse fish steaks under cool, running water. Pat dry.

2. Combine cracked pepper, garlic and salt. Stir in lemon juice, lemon zest and olive oil.

3. Drizzle 3 tablespoons of olive oil mixture in bottom of shallow, glass baking dish. Arrange fish fillets over top.

4. Spoon ½ of remaining marinade over fish. Reserve other half. Cover fish and allow to marinate for 1 hour.

5. Place fish and green pepper slices on a broiler rack and broil 4 inches from heat, 5 minutes per side.

6. Meanwhile, heat remaining marinade over moderate heat.

7. Remove fish and peppers from broiler pan and arrange on a serving dish. Spoon warm marinade over top. Serve with boiled green plantain and rice.

**Yield: 6 servings**

# Rich Fish Croquettes

*Croquetas de Pescado*

Goes nicely with a *Mojito* sauce or creamy au gratin sauce. To save on calories, instead of frying, place on a lightly greased baking sheet. Bake at 425°F until golden.

| | |
|---|---|
| 3 cups poached fish | ½ teaspoon cracked black pepper |
| 7 tablespoons unsalted butter | 2 tablespoons minced parsley |
| ¾ cup mashed potato | 3 large eggs, beaten |
| ½ cup evaporated milk | vegetable oil |
| 1 teaspoon salt | seasoned breadcrumbs |

1. Remove all bones and skin from fish.
2. Pulse fish, butter, potato, milk, salt, pepper, parsley and eggs in a food processor.
3. Scoop into a bowl and chill in refrigerator until firm.
4. Form fish mixture into croquettes. Roll in breadcrumbs. Refrigerate again until firm.
5. Heat 1/4 -inch of vegetable oil in a large skillet over medium-high heat.
6. Lightly fry croquettes on all sides until golden. Drain on white paper towels.

**Yield: 24 croquettes**

# Fish Pie in Paprika Cream Sauce

*Pastelón de Pescado*

Fish in cream sauce is always flavorful and the paprika adds an attractrive coral shade to the dish.

| | |
|---|---|
| 2 tablespoons butter | 1 cup mashed potatoes |
| 2 tablespoons flour | ½ pound firm, cooked white fish |
| 1 cup milk |   fillets, flaked |
| ¼ cup minced yellow onion | 4 tablespoons unsalted butter |
| ½ teaspoon paprika | 1 cup unseasoned breadcrumbs |
| ¼ teaspoon nutmeg | ¼ cup finely chopped hazelnuts |
| ½ teaspoon salt | ¼ cup grated parmesan cheese |
| ½ teaspoon cracked pepper | |

1. Preheat oven to 375°F.

2. Melt 2 tablespoons butter over low heat in a small saucepan. Sprinkle in flour, stirring constantly until lightly browned.

3. Drizzle in milk gradually. Add onion, paprika and nutmeg. Stir constantly until thickened. Remove from heat. Whisk in salt and pepper.

4. Butter the bottom of a glass pie dish. Arrange mashed potato evenly over bottom of dish, pressing down.

5. Top with flaked fish, pouring paprika cream sauce over top.

6. Melt 4 tablespoons butter in a small saucepan. Toss in breadcrumbs and hazelnuts, cooking for 1 minutes.

7. Sprinkle breadcrumb mixture over top of pie. Top with grated cheese.

8. Bake for 30 minutes or until bubbly.

**Yield: 6 servings**

## How to Use Salt Codfish

You can find salt codfish in the refrigerator section of Hispanic grocery stores. Before you can use it though, it needs to be soaked in water to get the salt out (a natural preservative).

- Cut the fish into 2-inch squares.

- Rinse under cool, running water and place into a large bowl. Fill bowl with cold water to cover fish.

- Place in refrigerator and soak for at least 6 hours, changing water about every 1 ½ hours. The more often you repeat the process, the less salty the fish will be

- Drain. Fill a saucepan with cold water. Bring to a boil over moderate heat and carefully lower in fish. Simmer for 15 minutes. A scum will rise to the surface. Skim this off.

- Remove pot from heat. Remove fish with a slotted spoon and place in a heat-proof container. Allow to cool completely.

- Remove any remaining skin and all the bones.

# Salt Codfish with Scrambled Eggs

*Bacalao Con Huevos Revueltos*

Like canned evaporated milk, salt codfish has been a staple for hundreds of years in the Caribbean—a food that kept well despite the lack of refrigeration.

| | |
|---|---|
| 2 tablespoons olive oil | 1 tablespoon tomato paste |
| 1 teaspoon annatto oil (see index) | ¼ pound dried salt codfish, prepared |
| ½ cup minced yellow onion | as above |
| 1 green frying pepper, seeded | 8 eggs, beaten |
| and minced | salt and fresh cracked black pepper |
| ½ teaspoon cumin | to taste |

1. Heat olive and annatto oil in a large skillet or frying pan over moderate heat. Add onions and frying pepper, sautéeing for 5 to 8 minutes until golden, but not black.
2. Stir in cumin and tomato paste until well-combined.
3. Flake in the codfish, stirring well.
4. Whisk in the beaten eggs. Reduce heat and stir until eggs are cooked as desired.
5. Season to taste with salt and pepper.

**Yield: 4 servings**

## Heathy tip

For a lower salt content, substitute any firm white fish: cod, turbot, halibut, swordfish or sea bass for salt codfish.

# Salt Codfish Stew with Sherry

*Bacalao Guisado*

Hundreds of years ago, you'd find this stew in lunchpails! I've added the brown sugar and the sherry (optional).

| | |
|---|---|
| 1 tablespoon olive oil | 3 tablespoons white wine vinegar |
| 1 tablespoon annatto oil (see index) | 1 bay leaf |

1 medium onion, thinly sliced

1/3 cup *recaíto* (see index)

¾ cup tomato puree

1 tablespoon tomato paste

1 tablespoon brown sugar

1 ½ pounds salt codfish, cooked and shredded (see above)

¼ sherry

1 large ripe tomato, diced

3 sliced hard-boiled eggs

1. Heat olive and annatto oil in a large saucepan over medium heat. Sauté onion for 5 minutes until soft, but not brown.

2. Stir in recaíto and cook for 3 minutes. Fold tomato puree, tomato paste, brown sugar and vinegar. Add bay leaf.

3. Fork in shredded codfish. Bring to a simmer, then reduce heat to low. Cook for 10 minutes.

4. Whisk in sherry, turn heat to medium and cook for 5 minutes. Garnish with diced tomato and hard-boiled egg slices. Perfect with rice, boiled root vegetables: yautía, breadfruit, yucca, green bananas or cooked ripe plantains.

**Yield: 4 servings**

## Stewed Shrimp

*Camarones Guisados*

Puerto Ricans love their garlic, and this recipe is no exception. Serve with crisp green salad and ice-cold beer.

5 whole black peppercorns

4 large garlic cloves, peeled and coarsely chopped

1 teaspoon salt

2 fresh *culantro* leaves or 2 tablespoons minced cilantro

2 tablespoons olive oil

1 medium yellow onion, minced

2 green frying peppers, seeded and minced

1 16-ounce can plum tomatoes, liquid and all

1 tablespoon tomato paste

3 tablespoons sherry

1 tablespoon apple cider vinegar

1 bay leaf

¼ teaspoon dried thyme

1 teaspoon salt

¼ cup *alcaparrado*

2 pounds raw shrimp, shelled and deveined

1. Grind together black peppercorns, garlic and salt in a mortar and pestle. For best results, use an up and down motion. Add cilantro, mashing well. Set aside.

2. Heat olive oil in a large skillet. Sauté onions and peppers for 2 minutes over moderate heat.

3. Stir in plum tomatoes, tomato paste, sherry, vinegar and bay leaf. Simmer for 5 minutes. Stir in thyme and salt. Fold in *alcaparrado*.

4. Add shrimp and cook, uncovered, until pink. Serve over rice.

**Yield: 6 servings**

## Tangy Marinated Shrimp

*Camarones en Escabeche*

I like to make a cold shrimp and rice salad with the marinated shrimp. Chill two cups of cooked rice, toss in marinated shrimp, add a cup of drained canned peas, toss gently with a fork.

| | |
|---|---|
| 2 pounds raw shrimp, shelled and deveined | ½ teaspoon freshly cracked black pepper |
| juice of one lemon | 1 small bay leaf |
| 1 cup olive oil | 2 garlic cloves, peeled and crushed |
| 1/3 cup white wine vinegar | 2 medium yellow onions, minced |
| ½ teaspoon salt | |

1. Rinse the shrimp and drain. Drizzle with lemon juice. Set aside.

2. Heat olive oil, vinegar, salt, pepper, bay leaf, garlic and onion in a non-reactive pot for 20 minutes over moderate heat. Remove from heat and cool completely.

3. Fill a pot with enough water to cover shrimp. Bring to a boil and cook shrimp for two to three minutes.

4. Remove from pot and drain. Allow to cool.

5. Toss with olive oil mixture, scoop into non-reactive (glass or ceramic dish), cover and refrigerate for 24 hours.

**Yield: 4 servings**

# Spicy Shrimp and Chorizo in Beer
*Camarones en Cerveza*

I don't think I've ever come across a cuisine or cookbook that didn't have sort sort of recipe for shrimp and beer. The *chorizo* gives it a Latin twist.

1 ½ cups beer

½ cup sofrito (see index)

1 6-inch chorizo, crumbled

2 pounds fresh or frozen shrimp,
  shelled, but tails on

2 tablespoons butter

2 tablespoons flour

1. Blend beer and sofrito in a large bowl. Stir in shrimp and chorizo. Marinate overnight.

2. Melt butter over low heat in a small saucepan. Sprinkle in flour, stirring constantly until lightly browned. Remove roux from heat and set aside.

3. Pour into large kettle and bring beer and shrimp to a boil. Whisk in roux, reduce heat, cook and uncovered for 10 minutes until sauce has thickened.

4. Serve over hot rice, with okra and plantains.

**Yield: 6 servings**

# Creamy Chili Ginger Shrimp
*Camarones*

Adjust the fieriness by adding more or less jalapeño peppers.

2 tablespoons olive oil

½ cup minced yellow onion

2 garlic cloves, minced

1 teaspoon freshly grated ginger root

1 jalapeño pepper, seeded and minced

2 pounds chopped cooked shrimp

2 cups heavy cream

2 tablespoons minced cilantro or
  *culantro* leaves

1 tablespoon brown sugar

1 teaspoon chili powder

½ teaspoon ground cumin

1 teaspoon salt

½ teaspoon cracked black pepper

1. Heat olive oil in a large saucepan over moderate heat. Sauté onion, garlic, ginger and jalapeño pepper for 5 minutes until soft, but not brown.

2. Stir in shrimp, heavy cream, cilantro, brown sugar, chili powder, cumin, salt and pepper. Simmer, uncovered, for 15 minutes. Remove from heat.

3. Serve over rice or pasta.

**Yield: 6 servings**

## Shrimp

Shrimp are small crustaceans (cousins to lobster and crab) that are found in salt water, as well as fresh and briny water. There are 160 species of these tiny creatures, although not all are as tasty as others. Americans consume more shrimp than any other country in the world—nearly 5 million pounds per annum.

**Purchasing:** The largest shrimp are the most expensive. But smaller shrimp are quite flavorful and make an economical alternative. Purchase shrimp with firm bodies and only a vaguely fishy smell. Avoid any that smell rank, are sticky or have black spots. When buying frozen, take care to avoid those covered with frost.

**Storing:** Thawed shrimp may be kept for 2 days or frozen 3 to 4 weeks.

**Preparing:** Shell a whole shrimp by holding its head in one hand and the body in the other. Pull on the head, removing any remaining bits of shell by hand. Or, if there is no head, with the tip of a sharp knife, cut a slit down the center back and remove the shell. You may also remove the black vein if you prefer. Use the shells to make fish stock or broth.

**Nutrition:** Shrimp are high in protein, Vitamin B-12 and niacin. Also low in carbohydrates.

## Brandied-Stuffed Jumbo Shrimp

*Camrones Relleno Al Horno*

Avoid over cooking the shrimp—10 to 15 minutes is plenty. Serve with hot, buttered rice or pasta.

18 jumbo shrimp, tails left on, but deveined

2 tablespoons olive oil

1 tablespoon butter

1 medium yellow onion, minced

2 *ají dulce* (sweet chili pepper) seeded and minced

2 green frying peppers, seeded and minced

3 garlic cloves, peeled and chopped coarsely

2 tablespoons brandy

1 cup seasoned breadcrumbs

2 tablespoons minced parsley

1 *culantro* leaf, minced or 1 teaspoon minced cilantro

¼ teaspoon ground cumin

olive oil

¼ cup brandy

1. Preheat oven to 375°F.

2. Cut a slit in the side of each shrimp, large enough to make a pocket for the stuffing. Set aside.

3. Heat olive oil in a large skillet over medium heat. Melt butter in oil. Sauté onion, peppers and garlic for 3 minutes. Do not brown.

4. Stir in brandy, breadcrumbs, parsley, cilantro and cumin. Reduce heat, cover and cook 3 minutes. Remove from heat and allow to cool for 5 minutes.

5. Stuff shrimp pockets with breadcrumb mixture.

6. Drizzle olive oil in the bottom of a glass baking dish and arrange shrimp over top. Pour brandy over shrimp.

7. Bake shrimp until they curl and turn pink, between 10 and 15 minutes, depending upon how hot your oven runs.

8. Arrange on a serving platter, with pasta or rice.

**Yield: 4 servings**

# Garlic Shrimp with Rum and Caramelized Onions

*Camarones con Cebolla*

This dish cooks up in no time at all and the rum contrasts nicely with the caramelized onions.

4 tablespoons extra-virgin olive oil

1 tablespoon brown sugar

2 medium onions, thinly sliced

6 garlic cloves, peeled and coarsely
chopped

2 pounds raw shrimp, shelled and
deveined

¼ cup dark Puerto Rican rum

juice of one lime

1 tablespoon minced *culantro* or
cilantro

1 teaspoon salt

1 teaspoon freshly cracked black
pepper

1. Heat oil in a large frying pan over medium heat. Add brown sugar and onions, sautéing until onions are brown.

2. Fold garlic and cook for another minute. Add shrimp, rum, lime juice, cilantro, salt and pepper. Cook, stirring constantly, until shrimp turns pink and curls.

3. Serve over hot rice, pasta or even potatoes.

**Yield: 4 servings**

## Boiled Crab Tropical Style

*Jueyes Hervidos*

*Jueyes* are land crabs, around the same size as Maryland crabs. They're found all over the Caribbean. I was on a photo shoot in Grand Cayman where literally thousands of land crabs dotted the roads. I felt so bad for the spiny creatures as cars were annihilating them. I got out of the jeep to shoo the crabs away, but there were just too many. Our hostess told us the phenomenon of land crabs meant a hurricane would come later in the season. It did—Marilyn.

2 pounds of live crabs

6 tablespoons salt, divided

1 large yellow onion, peeled and quartered

4 *aji dulce* (sweet chili peppers),
seeded and halved

2 small green frying peppers, seeded
and halved

6 garlic cloves crushed

4 *culantro* (see index) leaves or
3 tablespoons minced cilantro

4 whole black peppercorns

1 tablespoon cider vinegar

1. Fill a large kettle with cold salted (3 tablespoons) water (enough to cover crabs) over high heat. Bring to a rolling boil.

2. Plunge live crabs into boiling water until they stop kicking.

3. Remove crabs from water at once and drain. Rinse under cold, running water.

4. Fill pot again with water and remaining 3 tablespoons of salt.

5. Add onions, peppers, garlic and *culantro* leaves. Add peppercorns and stir in vinegar. Bring to a boil over high heat.

6. Lower crabs carefully and boil for 20 minutes. Drain and cool.

7. To open: place crabs on back. Using your thumb or knife remove apron or tail facing and discard.

8. Firmly twist off legs and claws. Crack open legs and claws as you would a lobster. Remove meat and reserve.

9. To separate body from shell use a knife like a crowbar and lift up. Scrape off spongy material at sides of body and any loose matter at center. Discard.

10. Holding sides of crab with each hand, crack body in half. Scoop out meat and reserve, avoiding bones.

11. Gingerly separate stomach and gall bag; discard. If you like, reserve liver and corals for other recipes.

12. Discard vegetables from cooking water.

**Yield: 4 servings**

# Crabs A La Salmorejo

*Jueyes Al Salmorejo*

I asked Anna what *Salmorejo* meant. She hadn't a clue and neither did her aunt. Nonetheless, once you've boiled the crab, the recipe is quick and tasty.

| | |
|---|---|
| 4 black peppercorns | 1 small yellow onion, minced |
| 3 large cloves garlic, peeled, coarsely chopped | 1 cup boiled crab meat |
| | 1 teaspoon sugar |

1 teaspoon salt

¼ teaspoon dried oregano

2 ½ tablespoons olive oil

4 *aji dulce* (sweet chili peppers)

1 small red bell pepper, seeded
and minced

¼ teaspoon nutmeg

¼ teaspoon allspice

3 tablespoons fresh lime juice

1 tablespoon dark rum (optional)

1 teaspoon cider vinegar

1. Crush peppercorns, garlic, salt and oregano in a mortar and pestle until finely ground. Set aside.

2. Heat olive oil in a large saucepan or kettle over moderate heat. Sauté sweet chili peppers, red bell pepper and onion for 5 minutes.

3. Add crab, sugar, nutmeg, allspice, lime juice, rum and vinegar. Add reserved black pepper mixture. Cover and cook for 8 to 10 minutes. Serve with rice or pasta.

**Yield: 4 servings**

# Crab Stewed in Marsala and Plum Tomatoes

*Jueyes Criolla*

If you don't have access to fresh crabmeat, canned will do in a pinch. Be sure to pick out any stones or cartilage.

5 black pepper corns

3 garlic cloves, peeled and
coarsely chopped

1 teaspoon salt

½ teaspoon oregano

¼ teaspoon cumin

¼ teaspoon nutmeg

2 tablespoons olive oil

1 teaspoon annatto oil (see index)

½ cup minced yellow onion

1 small green frying pepper, seeded
and minced

½ cup Marasala wine

1 16-ounce can plum tomatoes, ½ cup
liquid reserved

1 tablespoon tomato paste

1 ½ cups boiled crab meat

1. Grind the peppercorns, garlic, salt, oregano, cumin and nutmeg in a mortar and pestle until smooth. Set aside.

2. Heat olive and annatto oil in a deep kettle or large saucepan over medium heat. Sauté onion and pepper for 5 minutes until soft, but not brown.

3. Whisk in wine. Chop plum tomatoes coarsely and add to saucepan along with half a cup of liquid from can. Stir in tomato paste and simmer for 5 minutes.

4. Add flaked crab meat, stir, reduce heat, cover and cook for 12 minutes.

**Yield: 4 servings**

# Boiled Lobster

*Langosta Hervida*

I have never been one to enjoy the sight of a live lobster kicking and splashing when plunged into boiling water. My mother claims they actually scream. The purpose of using live lobsters is to ensure maximum freshness. A more humane way to kill the lobster is to place it in the freezer one hour before cooking.

**water to cover lobster(s)**             **lobster(s)**

**1 tablespoon salt for each quart of water**

1. Heat enough water to cover lobster in a large soup pot or kettle, along with 1 tablespoon salt per quart of water over high heat.

2. When water is boiling rapidly, plunge in lobster (see above for humane method), making sure it is completely submerged.

3. Cook lobster 12 minutes per pound, and one extra minute for each quarter pound.

4. Remove and drain.

5. Slit top side of lobster from head to tail with tip of a sharp knife. Split lobster in half, cutting the head lengthwise. Discard intestinal canal, stomach and any spongy matter. Liver and coral may be reserved to use in other recipes. Remove sand sac located near head.

6. Scoop out meat and crack claws to get to meat.

**Yield: each lobster equals one serving**

## Lobster with Roasted Peppers in Rum Cream Sauce

*Langosta a la Royal*

There's something about the flavor of roasted red peppers that dresses up any dish.

6 tablespoons butter

6 tablespoons flour

1 cup evaporated milk

½ cup water

¼ cup Puerto Rican rum

1 teaspoon salt

½ teaspoon cracked black pepper

1 small red bell pepper, roasted, skinned and cut in strips

1 pound boiled lobster meat, cut in ½-inch pieces

½ cup unseasoned breadcrumbs

2 tablespoons chilled butter, chopped in small pieces

1. Preheat oven to 350°F.
2. Melt butter in a large saucepan over very low heat. Sprinkle in flour gradually, stirring constantly, until lightly browned.
3. Stir in milk slowly, increase heat to moderate. Whisk in water and cook until mixture boils and thickens.
4. Stir in rum, salt, black pepper and roasted peppers. Cook for 1 minute and remove from heat.
5. Butter the bottom of a glass baking dish. Spoon lobster into dish.
6. Pour cream sauce over lobster. Sprinkle with breadcrumbs. Dot with butter, and roasted bell pepper strips.
7. Bake for 12 minutes.

Yield: 4 servings

## LOW-CARB *Sofrito* Marinated Salmon

If you prefer, use *recaíto*, which doesn't contain pork, instead of *sofrito*.

¼ cup *sofrito* (see index)

2 tablespoons dry white wine

2 tablespoons cider vinegar

4 6 ounce salmon fillets

1. Combine *sofrito*, wine and vinegar in a shallow baking dish. Add salmon, turning to coat with marinade. Cover and refrigerate 3 hours.

2. Preheat broiler. Spray a broiler pan with non-stick cooking spray.

3. Transfer salmon fillets to pan. Broil 5 inches from heat element, 4 to 5 minutes on each side. Salmon should be light pink, not red, in center when done. Serve at once.

**Yield: 4 servings**

EACH SERVING PROVIDES APPROXIMATELY:
280 calories, **6 grams of carbohydrates**, 36 grams of protein, 16 grams of fat

## LOW-CARB Citrus Swordfish with Olive, Pimento and Walnut Tapenade

Doritza's husband, our unsuspecting low-carb taste tester, suggested the addition of *alcaparrado* to this dish.

½ cup minced **alcaparrado (see index)**

2 tablespoons toasted walnuts, finely chopped

4 pimentos, minced

2 tablespoons extra-virgin olive oil

2 cloves garlic, minced

1 tablespoon minced red onion

½ teaspoon freshly grated lemon zest

1 tablespoon cider vinegar

½ teaspoon oregano

¼ teaspoon thyme

½ teaspoon freshly, cracked black pepper

4 9-ounce swordfish steaks

1 lemon, halved

1. Spray grill or broiler pan with vegetable spray. Preheat grill or broiler.

2. Combine *alcaparrado*, walnuts, pimentos, olive oil, garlic, onion, vinegar, oregano, thyme and black pepper in a small bowl. Set aside.

3. Broil fish 4 inches from heat source for 5 minutes on each, until no longer translucent in center. Remove from heat.

4. Squeeze lemons over fish. Top with tapenade.

**Yield: 4 servings**

EACH SERVING CONTAINS APPROXIMATELY:
460 calories, **9 grams carbohydrates**, 37 grams protein, 39 grams of fat

# LOW-CARB Puerto Rican Jerked Shrimp

You've heard of jerked chicken or pork. Well, this is jerked shrimp, island style, thanks to the cilantro.

2 tablespoons olive oil

1 tablespoon cider vinegar

1 tablespoon minced onion

1 tablespoon shredded *culantro* or cilantro

½ small habañero or other hot chili pepper, seeded and minced

2 teaspoons Splenda®

1 teaspoon salt

1 teaspoon cracked black pepper

1 teaspoon allspice

¼ teaspoon nutmeg

¼ teaspoon cinnamon

1 ½ pounds large, raw shrimp, peeled and deveined

1.  Combine olive oil, vinegar, onion, cilantro, hot chili pepper, Splenda®, salt, black pepper, allspice, nutmeg and cinnamon in a large zippered plastic bag. Add shrimp and toss well to coat. Refrigerate for several hours or overnight.

2.  Spray grill or broiler with vegetable spray. Thread shrimp onto metal skewers or wooden ones that have been soaked in water for 45 minutes. Grill 4 inches away from heat source for 3 minutes on each side. Remove from heat and serve at once, or cool and serve over mixed greens.

**Yield: 4 servings**

EACH SERVING PROVIDES APPROXIMATELY:
240 calories, **4 grams carbohydrates**, 36 grams of protein, 8 grams of fat

# LOW-CARB Crab with Creamy Habañero Sauce

If you like spicy and you like creamy, this is your signature dish.

½ cup non-fat cottage cheese

1 tablespoon olive oil

1 habañero chili pepper, seeded and minced

1 garlic clove, minced

1 tablespoon onion, minced

½ teaspoon dried oregano

¼ cup freshly grated Parmesan cheese

½ teaspoon salt

¼ teaspoon black pepper

2 cans (8 ounce) lump crabmeat, drained and flaked

1. Spray a 1-quart dish with vegetable spray. Preheat oven to 300°F.
2. Combine cottage cheese, olive oil, chili pepper, garlic, onion, oregano, Parmesan, salt and black pepper in a food processor until smooth. Fold in shredded crab by hand.
3. Scoop into glass baking dish and bake for 25 minutes until bubbly.

**Yield: 4 servings**

EACH SERVING PROVIDES APPROXIMATELY:
250 calories, **6 grams carbohydrate**, 45 grams protein, 9 grams of fat

# Chicken and Turkey

**D**id you know that more chickens than people exist in the world? Chicken is the world's largest source of animal protein, with the United States alone producing over 5 billion chickens are year. Probably a good thing when you consider how much of our natural resources are utilized to turn out a pound of beef.

At one time, most island homes had a chicken coop located near the house. This furnished the family with eggs and meat and a feathered 'watch-dog'. The sound of someone walking would rouse the entire chicken coop and alert the household.

Today, chicken coops have diminished in number. Coamo is home to the majority of the island's poultry-raising farms. However, chicken is still a staple of the Puerto Rican diet. The most well-known dish being *Arroz Con Pollo*.

## Basic Recipe for Baked Chicken
*Pollo Al Horno*

Roast chicken served in the Caribbean is more highly seasoned than the mainland version.

| | |
|---|---|
| 1 roasting chicken (about 7 pounds) | 1 onion, cut in half |
| 4 thin slices lemon | 2 sprigs fresh thyme, or 1 teaspoon |
| 4 cloves garlic, peeled |   dried |
| 1 teaspoon fresh cracked black pepper | 3 large, fresh sage leaves |
| 1 teaspoon sea salt | ½ teaspoon paprika |
| 1 teaspoon dried oregano | 1 tablespoon fresh chopped thyme |
| ¼ cup olive oil | 1 to 2 bottles of beer |

1. Preheat oven to 375°F. Pound garlic, pepper, salt and oregano using a mortar and pestle. Set aside.

2. Rinse chicken inside and out with cold running water. Pat dry.

3. Separate chicken skin from meat and bone of breast with fingers. Insert lemon slices under loosened skin.

4. Drizzle with olive oil and rub bird inside and out with garlic mixture.

5. Place onion halves, thyme and sage leaves inside cavity.

6. Sprinkle chicken with chopped thyme and paprika. Tie together drumsticks with string to enclose cavity.

7. Place chicken in shallow roasting pan, breast side up. Pour 1 bottle of beer into bottom of pan (chicken will be up on the rack). Wrap aluminum foil around legs as these tend to cook faster. Roast bird, basting occasionally with juice in pan, for about 2 hours. Add extra bottle of beer if needed. Remove foil from legs for last thirty minutes of roasting.

8. Chicken should be golden brown. Remove from oven and place on large platter. Allow to sit for 15 minutes for easier carving. Serve with rice, roasted potatoes and asparagus or broccoli.

**Yield: 8 servings**

---

## How to Check Chicken for Doneness

Chicken is cooked and safe to eat when a meat thermometer inserted into the thigh (not touching the bone) reads 175°F. Juices should run clear when thickest part of thigh is sliced with a knife.

---

# Basic Recipe for Fried Chicken
*Pollo Frito*

The batter coating makes a lovely, crunchy crust. Adjust seasoning to taste as island-inspired chicken can be spicy. Keep in mind the batter needs to be prepared 4 hours before using.

| | |
|---|---|
| **2 ½ to 3-pound chicken, cut in pieces** | **1 cup flour** |
| **2 cloves garlic, crushed** | **1 egg** |
| **1 teaspoon salt** | **1 tablespoon melted butter** |
| **1 teaspoon cracked black pepper** | **½ cup beer** |
| **1 teaspoon dried oregano** | **oil for frying** |
| **½ teaspoon paprika** | |

1. Whisk together flour, egg, butter and beer in a bowl until smooth. Refrigerate for 4 hours before using.

2. Run chicken pieces under cold water and pat dry.

3. Place chicken in a bowl and rub with garlic, salt, pepper, oregano and paprika.

4. Cover and set aside, or marinate in refrigerator over night.

5. Heat 3 inches of oil in a deep fryer or skillet to 375°F.

6. Dip chicken pieces in batter. Lower into oil carefully. Use tongs to move pieces around so they don't stick together. Do not overcrowd pan. Fry about 20 minutes, turning pieces often, until golden brown.

7. Drain on white paper towels. Serve hot.

**Yield: 4 servings**

# Roast Chicken with Pork, Chili Pepper and Raisin Stuffing

You may substitute ground beef for the pork in this recipe, although pork is more traditional in Puerto Rico.

*Stuffing:*

4 tablespoons olive oil, divided

1 pound lean ground beef or pork

2 ounces minced cured ham

1 teaspoon salt

¼ cup *recaíto* (see index)

½ cup minced yellow onion

4 sweet chili peppers, seeded and minced

2 garlic cloves, crushed

2 tablespoons dried parsley

½ teaspoon dried oregano

½ teaspoon dried thyme

¼ cup white wine

3 tablespoons apple cider or wine vinegar

1/3 cup raisins

1 3 to 4 pound roasting chicken, rinsed and patted dry

3 garlic cloves, crushed

1 tablespoon salt

1 ½ teaspoons cracked black pepper

1 teaspoon paprika

½ teaspoon dried oregano

10 pimento-stuffed olives, coarsely
  chopped
1 tablespoon large Spanish capers
2 tablespoons tomato paste

½ teaspoon dried thyme
2 tablespoons olive oil
2 bottles of beer or 1 cup white
  wine and 1 cup water

1. Stuffing: Heat 2 tablespoons of the olive oil in a large skillet over medium heat. Brown beef or pork lightly for 4 minutes.

2. Fold in ham and cook for another 2 minutes, until no pink remains on ground meat. Remove from heat and drain off excess fat. Sprinkle with salt.

3. Heat remaining 2 tablespoons of olive oil in another large skillet over moderate heat for 2 minutes. Fold in *recaíto*, onion, chili peppers and garlic. Sauté for 5 minutes until onions are soft but not browned.

4. Stir in parsley, oregano, thyme, olive, capers, tomato paste, wine and vinegar. Cook for 5 or 6 minutes, until liquid is reduced.

5. Fold in ground meat, cooking another 15 minutes over reduced heat, stirring now and then. Remove from heat and reserve.

6. Chicken: Rub chicken with crushed garlic. Sprinkle with salt, inside and out. Sprinkle with black pepper, paprika, oregano and thyme. Drizzle with 2 tablespoons of olive oil.

7. Stuff chicken with cooled meat filling.

**Yield: 4 to 6 servings**

## Cooking Times for Turkey

Cook 15 minutes per pound if bird weighs less than 16 pounds. Twelve minutes per pound if heavier.

# Roast Turkey with Criolla Stuffing
*Pavo Relleno a la Criolla*

Serve this highly-seasoned island bird with rice and pigeon peas, Puerto Rican style. Note: before you place turkey on a rack, cover the rack with heavily greased foil to keep the skin from tearing when you turn the bird.

**1 8 to 9 pound turkey**

**8 cloves garlic, peeled**

**2 teaspoons cracked black pepper**

**1 tablespoon dried oregano**

**1 tablespoon salt**

**¼ cup olive oil**

**2 tablespoons paprika**

**2 tablespoons fresh chopped thyme,**
  **or 1 tablespoon dried**

**3 tablespoons cider or wine vinegar**

**4 tablespoons olive oil**

**1 ½ pounds lean ground beef**

**1 cup minced onion**

**½ cup *sofrito* (see index)**

**¼ cup chopped *alcaparrado***
  **(see index)**

**½ cup seedless raisins**

**1 cup applesauce**

**3 hard-boiled eggs, chopped**

**2 bottles of beer**

1. Rinse and wash turkey, inside and out. Pat dry. Rinse and chop liver—this will be added to stuffing later.

2. Pound garlic, pepper, oregano and salt in a mortar until smooth. Mix in olive oil, paprika, thyme and vinegar. Rub garlic mixture inside and out of turkey. Cover turkey and refrigerate overnight.

3. Heat 3 tablespoons of the olive oil in a large skillet over medium heat. Brown meat lightly. Drain and set aside in a heat-proof dish.

4. Heat remaining tablespoon of olive oil over moderate heat. Sauté onions for 5 minutes until soft, but not browned. Stir in *sofrito*, *alcaparrado* and raisins, cooking for 5 minutes.

5. Return meat to pan and simmer for 5 minutes. Remove from heat.

6. Fold in applesauce and eggs. Allow to cool.

7. Preheat oven to 325°F. Remove turkey from refrigerator and stuff three-quarters full. Truss turkey.

8. Place turkey, breast down, on roasting rack, covered with heavily greased foil. Poke a couple of holes in the foil to allow the fat and juices to drain to the bottom of the pan.

9. Pour beer into bottom of pan. Roast turkey for 2 to 2 ½ hours. See note above for cooking times. Baste turkey every 20 minutes with beer and drippings.

10. Turn breast up after one hour. If you've chosen a bird heavier than 12 pounds, turn breast up after 1 ½ hours.

11. Turkey is down when the drumstick and thigh move easily. Or when the temperature of the breast meat (use a meat thermometer) reads 170°F and the thigh is at 180°F.

12. Place turkey on large platter and cover loosely with foil. Allow to sit 15 minutes before carving.

**Yield: 8 to 9 servings (figure one pound of bird per serving)**

## Chicken

A *chicken* is the male and female offspring of a hen that is at least 4 months old. Younger than that and the flesh is not ready. A broiler is a 7 week old bird and a roaster is 10 weeks old.

**Purchasing:** The cost per pound of whole chickens is less than chicken parts. Buy larger chickens because there is more meat on the bones.

**Serving:** Never eat chicken raw. Once cooked, it may be served hot or cold. Chicken may be marinated first, then baked, broiled, fried, sautéed or grilled. Either way, chicken is always tender and it is difficult to ruin chicken.

**Nutrition:** Chicken is high in protein, low in carbohydrates. Good source of niacin, Vitamin B-12, potassium, zinc and phosphorous.

# Basic Gravy

For perfect gravy, slowly brown the flour in the turkey fat drippings to make a roux. If you don't have enough fat, add butter.

Note: You can make gravy ahead and save a lot of last minute hassle. Purchase a couple inexpensive packages of turkey wings. Season with salt, pepper and garlic and roast until golden brown. Use these drippings to make the following recipe.

| | |
|---|---|
| **4 tablespoons fat from poultry pan drippings** | **½ teaspoon cracked black pepper** |
| **3 tablespoons flour** | **1 cup white wine** |
| | **1 cup chicken broth** |

1. Heat fat in small sauce pan over low heat. Sprinkle in flour and pepper. Blend, simmering over low heat until lightly browned, 3 to 5 minutes.

2. Pour in wine and broth slowly, stirring constantly over low heat until smooth and thickened, about 10 minutes.

# Onion and Garlic Smothered Chicken
*Pollo Encebollado y Ajo*

Tasuki and Natalie saga continued from *Mashed Potatoes and Carrots*. It was really getting to be too much, the conspiracy between the baby and the cat. They'd gotten the routine down pat. Natalie would let out a shriek from her playpen, we'd turn to check out the problem, Tasuki would lunge onto the kitchen counter, and tear out of the kitchen with a piece of hijacked food. We'd turn back to the baby, who would be all smiles and coos. It was one thing if he stole plain cooked food. But the morsels he snatched were all highly seasoned. I must say I lived in fear that afternoon of the garlic and onion upsetting his stomach.

4 pounds chicken pieces, rinsed and dried

6 garlic cloves, crushed

3 teaspoons salt

1 teaspoon cracked black pepper

1 teaspoon paprika

4 tablespoons olive oil

¼ cup vegetable oil

5 large onions, thinly sliced

3 large ripe tomatoes, peeled, seeded and coarsely chopped

4 tablespoons tomato paste

½ cup sweet white wine

½ cup chicken broth

1 bay leaf

1. Rub chicken with crushed garlic, then sprinkle with salt, pepper and paprika. Drizzle 2 tablespoons olive over chicken. Set aside.

2. Heat the vegetable oil in a large skillet over medium-high heat (too low heat will result in greasy, soggy chicken). Brown chicken on all sides. Remove from pan, and drain on white paper towels. Discard oil and wipe out skillet with paper towels.

3. Heat remaining 2 tablespoons of the olive oil in the same skillet over moderate heat. Sauté onions until soft, but not burnt, about 4 to 5 minutes.

4. Fold in tomatoes, tomato paste, wine, chicken broth and bay leaf. Simmer for 5 minutes.

5. Add chicken, cover and cook for 35 minutes until chicken is done, when a cut is made in the meat and juices run clear. Add additional wine as needed for sauce.

6. Remove from heat and serve with boiled new potatoes or hot white rice.

**Yield: 6 to 8 servings**

# Chicken in Sherry Sauce

Well, I can tell you that the Tasuki cat did not appreciate the liquor in this recipe. He stopped sneaking food for a couple of weeks after that.

3 ½ pounds chicken pieces, rinsed
 and dried

1 tablespoon *adobo* (see index)

¼ teaspoon dried thyme

½ cup olive oil, divided

4 tablespoons tomato paste

½ cup tomato puree

½ cup chicken broth

1 cup dry sherry

10 pimento-stuffed olives, coarsely
 chopped

1 tablespoon capers

1 tablespoon minced roasted pimentos,
 canned is fine

1 pound tiny white onions, peeled

1 ½ pounds tiny new potatoes, peeled

8 garlic cloves, crushed

4 tablespoons butter

6 tablespoons flour

1. Sprinkle chicken with *adobo* seasoning and thyme.

2. Heat ¼ cup of the olive oil in a large skillet over moderate heat. Brown chicken lightly on all sides. Remove from heat and set aside. Drain excess oil.

3. In another large skillet, heat remaining olive oil over medium heat. Stir in thyme, tomato paste, tomato puree, chicken broth and sherry until smoothly combined. Cook for 3 minutes.

4. Fold in olives, capers, pimentos, onions, potatoes and garlic cloves. Add chicken and bring to a boil. Reduce heat, cover and simmer for 35 minutes until chicken is tender.

5. Remove chicken from skillet and set aside.

6. Melt butter in a small frying pan or skillet over very low heat. Gradually sprinkle in flour, stirring constantly, cooking over reduced heat to make a roux. Remove from heat.

7. Whisk roux into sherry sauce, stirring constantly over moderate heat until sauce thickens. Serve sauce over chicken.

**Yield: 4 to 6 servings**

# Chicken Fricassee with Chili Pepper Olive Sauce
*Fricasé de Pollo*

This recipe calls for one cup minced sweet chili peppers. I like to use a slightly hotter pepper, such as jalapeño.

**4 pounds chicken pieces, rinsed and patted dry**

**5 garlic cloves, crushed**

**3 teaspoons salt**

**1 teaspoon cracked black pepper**

**½ teaspoon dried oregano (use 1 teaspoon fresh if you have it)**

**½ teaspoon paprika**

**¼ teaspoon dried thyme**

**4 tablespoons olive oil**

**¼ cup vegetable oil**

**¼ cup minced cured ham**

**1/3 cup *recaíto***

**4 mild chili peppers, seeded and minced (about 1 cup)**

**½ cup minced yellow onion**

**1 ¾ cups chicken broth**

**¼ cup dry sherry**

**¼ cup apple cider vinegar or wine vinegar**

**4 tablespoons tomato paste**

**8 pimento-stuffed olives, coarsely chopped**

**1 ½ teaspoons large Spanish capers**

**1 bay leaf**

**1 ½ pounds small red or new potatoes, peeled**

**¾ cup fresh or frozen (thawed) peas**

1. Place chicken in a shallow glass baking dish, large enough to hold the chicken in one layer. Rub chicken with crushed garlic. Sprinkle with salt, pepper, oregano, paprika and thyme. Drizzle with 2 tablespoons of the olive oil. Set aside.

2. Heat vegetable oil in a large skillet or deep kettle over medium-high heat. Brown chicken on all sides. Remove from pan and drain on white paper towels. Discard oil and wipe out skillet with paper towels.

3. Heat remaining 2 tablespoons olive oil in skillet. Brown ham lightly for 2 to 3 minutes. Stir in *recaíto*, chili peppers and onion. Sauté for 4 to 5 minutes.

4. Stir in chicken broth, sherry, vinegar and tomato paste. Cook for 1 minute.

5. Fold in olives, capers, bay leaf and potatoes. Add chicken and bring to a boil.

6. Reduce heat, cover and simmer for 35 minutes.

7. Fold in peas, cover and simmer for additional 5 to 10 minutes. Potatoes should be soft and chicken, when cut, should have clear juices run. You can add the peas a little earlier, but I like to wait until the end of the cooking time to avoid overdone peas.

8. Remove from stove and allow to sit for 10 minutes before serving.

**Yield: 8 servings**

# Chicken and Rice
*Arroz con Pollo*

Enjoy this traditional island recipe with fried plantain and sliced tomatoes drizzled with olive oil and vinegar.

| | |
|---|---|
| 1 3-lb chicken, cut into serving pieces | 1 tablespoon tomato paste |
| 2 tablespoons *adobo* (see index) | 1 tablespoon wine vinegar |
| 4 tablespoons olive oil, divided | 1 tablespoon dry sherry |
| 2 tablespoons annatto oil | 2 cups hot chicken broth |
| ½ cup *recaíto* | 1 ½ cups hot water |
| 1/3 cup *sofrito* | 3 cups long-grain rice |
| 2 ounces cured ham, diced | 1 10-ounce can pigeon peas or |
| 12 pimento-stuffed olives | green peas |
| 1 tablespoon, plus 1 teaspoon | ½ cup roasted pimentos, canned or |
| capers | bottled fine |

1. Rinse and pat dry chicken pieces. Rub with *adobo* seasoning.
2. Heat 2 tablespoons of the olive oil in a large skillet. Brown chicken on all sides. Remove from heat, drain and set aside.

3. Heat annatto and olive oil in a large saucepan or deep skillet over moderate heat. Sauté *recaíto* for 5 minutes, stirring occasionally.

4. Fold in *sofrito*, ham, olives, capers, tomato paste, vinegar and sherry, cooking for another 2 minutes.

5. Pour in chicken broth and water to *recaíto* mixture. Stir in rice, then peas, then chicken pieces.

6. Turn heat up to medium and cook, uncovered, until liquid reaches top of rice.

7. Fork over rice from top to bottom. Reduce heat, cover and simmer for 30 minutes.

8. Fork over rice again, cover and cook for 5 more minutes. Remove from heat. Garnish with pimento strips, cover and allow to sit for 5 minutes.

**Yield: 8 to 10 servings**

# Puerto Rican Chicken in Wine Glaze

Anna's grandmother serves this dinner for every one of her wedding anniversaries.

**4 pounds chicken pieces, rinsed
  and dried**
**3 tablespoons *adobo* (see index)**
**4 tablespoons olive oil**
**4 tablespoons butter**
**6 tablespoons flour**
**1 ½ cups hot chicken broth**

**2 bay leaves**
**1 cup minced yellow onion**
**2 pounds new potatoes, peeled
  (small, waxy potatoes work best)**
**1 cup dry white wine**
**2 tablespoons capers**

1. Trim any excess fat from chicken. Rub with *adobo* seasoning.

2. Heat olive oil in 4-quart saucepan or kettle over medium heat. Brown chicken on all sides. Drain excess fat.

3. Add chicken broth, bay leaves, onions and potatoes. Bring to boil over medium-high heat. Reduce heat, cover and simmer for 30 minutes. Add extra water, a ¼ cup at a time, if needed.

4. Heat butter in a small skillet over very low heat. Sprinkle in flour gradually, stirring constantly to make a roux, cooking for 2 minutes. Remove from heat and set aside.

5. Remove cover, add wine and simmer for additional 30 minutes.

6. Stir in reserved roux and capers, cook uncovered until sauce thickens.

**Yield: 6 to 8 servings**

# Chicken Croquettes with Roasted Red Peppers
*Croquetas de Pollo*

A wonderful way to use up leftover chicken or turkey. Run through a food processor instead of chopping by hand.

| | |
|---|---|
| 1 large red bell pepper | 1 tablespoon dry sherry |
| 1 tablespoon olive oil | 2 cups ground cooked chicken |
| 6 tablespoons butter | 3 large eggs, beaten |
| 1 tablespoon olive oil | 1 egg yolk, beaten |
| ¼ cup minced yellow onion | 1 ½ cups unseasoned bread crumbs |
| 1 medium green frying pepper, seeded and diced | 1 teaspoon cracked black pepper |
| | 1 teaspoon salt |
| ½ cup flour | ½ teaspoon dried oregano |
| ¾ cup hot milk | vegetable oil |
| ½ cup hot chicken broth | |

1. Preheat oven to 450°F.

2. Cut pepper in half length-wise, remove seeds and press halves down flat on glass baking dish greased with the 1 tablespoon olive oil. Bake peppers until skin is blackened. Remove from oven, cool for 10 minutes, then slide into brown paper bags for 20 minutes. Remove from bags and peel off skin gently. Mince and set aside.

3. Heat butter and olive oil in a large skillet over moderate heat. Sauté onions and green pepper for 5 minutes until soft, but not browned. Reduce heat, sprinkle in flour, whisking constantly to make a smooth roux.

4. Pour in hot milk, chicken broth and sherry. Turn heat to medium and simmer until sauce thickens and begins to separate from bottom and sides of pan.

5. Fold in chicken, stirring to combine. Cook for 1 minute. Remove from heat and pour into heat-proof dish.

6. Whisk together eggs and yolk. Set aside.

7. Combine breadcrumbs, black pepper, salt and oregano in a small bowl or dish.

8. Form chicken patties with your hands. Dip in egg mixture, then roll in bread crumbs. Place croquettes on waxed sheet and refrigerate 2 hours until firm.

9. Heat oil to 350°F in a deep skillet or fryer. Remove from heat and drain on white paper towels.

**Yield: 24 croquettes**

# Chicken Pie Criolla Style
*Pastelón de Pollo*

Comfort food—Puerto Rican style.

PIE CRUST:

2 ½ cups all-purpose flour, plus
   extra for dusting

¾ teaspoon salt

1 tablespoon sugar

12 tablespoons unsalted butter,
   refrigerated, cut in small ¼ pieces

8 tablespoons vegetable shortening,
   refrigerated

6 tablespoons ice water

FILLING:

1 ¼ pounds boneless, skinless chicken
   thighs, finely chopped

1 tablespoon annatto oil

2 tablespoons olive oil

1 ounce salt pork, minced

¼ cup white wine

¼ cup chicken broth

¼ raisins

¼ cup chopped prunes

1 tablespoon capers

2 ounces cured ham, minced

1 tablespoon *adobo* (see index)

¾ cup *recaíto* (see index)

1 tablespoon tomato paste

6 pimento-stuffed olives, minced

1 cup frozen peas, thawed and drained

½ teaspoon paprika

## CRUST:

1. Combine flour, salt and sugar in food processor (use lower blade only, remove grating blade).

2. Add butter pieces and pulse until flour is pebbly. Add shortening by teaspoonfuls and continue to pulse 4 or 5 more times.

3. Scoop flour mixture into medium bowl. Sprinkle ice water over top. Using an up and down motion with a large spoon, combine until you can form a smooth ball. Add an extra tablespoon of water if needed.

4. Divide dough into two and press into shape of a flat ball. Dust with flour and refrigerate for 30 minutes.

5. Sprinkle ¼ cup flour over work surface and rolling pin. Press down lightly on dough and roll back and forth. Rotate dough on surface and continue to roll out evenly, forming a circle. Diameter of dough should be 2 inches larger than pie plate.

6. Fold dough in half, than in half again. Place dough inside pie plate and unfold. Tuck pastry dough into corners of pie plate.

7. Trim dough down to ½ inch overlap of pie plate. Tuck dough under, so that a ¼ inch lip remains. Press down lightly.

8. Reserve remaining rolled out dough for top of pie.

## FILLING:

9. Rinse chicken, pat dry and rub with *adobo*. Set aside.

10. Heat annatto and olive oil in a deep skillet over moderate heat. Brown chicken for 2 to 3 minutes.

11. Stir in salt pork and ham, browning lightly for 2 minutes. Fold in *recaíto* and *adob*; reduce heat and cook for 2 minutes.

12. Whisk in tomato paste, wine, chicken broth and water. Bring to boil. Reduce heat, cover and simmer for 25 minutes. Remove from heat.

13. Preheat oven to 350°F.

14. Fold in raisins, prunes, capers, olives and peas. Sprinkle with paprika. Set aside.

15. Heap filling into bottom of pie crust. Position top crust over pie. Pinch edges shut with fingers or a fork.

16. Bake 35 to 40 minutes until crust is lightly browned.

**Yield: 6 servings**

# Island-Style Chicken Meat Balls
*Albóndigas de Pollo*

Another excellent and healthy way to use up leftover chicken or turkey.

| | |
|---|---|
| 1 ¾ cups ground chicken meat | 1 teaspoon cracked black pepper |
| 1 cup mashed potatoes | 1 teaspoon salt |
| 2 tablespoons *recaíto* | ½ teaspoon dried oregano |
| ½ cup unseasoned breadcrumbs | ½ teaspoon paprika |
| 4 large eggs, beaten | flour or cornstarch |
| 1 egg yolk, beaten | ¼ olive oil |
| ¼ cup evaporated milk | |

1. Combine chicken, mashed potatoes, *recaíto* and breadcrumbs in a large bowl.

2. Fold in eggs, egg yolks, evaporated milk, black pepper, salt, oregano and paprika until well combined. If mixture is not firm enough, add extra bread crumbs; if too dry, add a couple tablespoons regular milk.

3. Heat olive oil in a large skillet over medium heat.

4. Flour hands with cornstarch and make meat balls about 1 ½ inches in diameter.

5. Brown meat balls on all sides, for about 7 to 8 minutes. Break one open to test for doneness. Egg should be cooked and firm.

6. Serve with pasta along with a white or red sauce.

**Yield: about 30 chicken balls**

# LOW-CARB Turkey Patties with Lemon, Garlic and Cilantro

I always like to find new uses for turkey. Not only because of leftovers from holiday gatherings, but because turkey is produced with far fewer hormones than chicken.

Combining turkey with zesty Caribbean spices results in a highly flavored taste sensation. You can add extra heart-healthy garlic, but I prefer just a hint.

2 pounds ground turkey

1 garlic clove, minced

½ cup minced yellow onion

2 tablespoons minced green
  bell pepper

4 sun-dried tomatoes, finely snipped
  with scissors

2 ½ tablespoons shredded fresh
  cilantro

½ teaspoon dried whole oregano

½ teaspoon salt

1 tablespoon hot-pepper sauce

3 tablespoons olive oil

1 lemon, halved

1. Combine turkey, garlic, onion, pepper, sun-dried tomatoes, cilantro, oregano, salt and hot pepper sauce in a large bowl. Cover and refrigerate for 3 hours.

2. Divide turkey into six patties. Heat 1 ½ tablespoons of the olive oil in a large, heavy skillet over medium heat.

3. Add three of the turkey patties and sauté for 5 minutes on each side, until cooked in center. Drain on white paper towels. Keep in a warm place.

4. Pour remaining oil into skillet. Sauté last three patties 5 minutes on each side. Squeeze lemon halves over top of patties.

**Yield: 6 servings**

EACH SERVING PROVIDES APPROXIMATELY:
360 calories, **3.5 grams carbohydrates**, 31 grams of protein, 26 grams of fat

## Did You Know?

**River Camuy Cave Park** contains the third-largest underground river in the world. Located on the north east corner of the island, visitors descend through a 200-foot deep sinkhole into a chasm where tropical trees, ferns, flowers, birds and other wildlife flourish. Visitors then begin a 45-minute journey through a network of caves featuring stalagmites, stalactites and other enormous limestone outcroppings. For more information, call: 787-898-3100.

# LOW-CARB Curried Chicken Meatloaf

Liberal use of spices makes all the difference in flavor with low-carb dishes. Feel free to use extra herbs and spices. I've cut the raisins in half with scissors to reduce the amount of carbohydrates. You can omit them if you like.

2 tablespoons curry powder
½ teaspoon ground cumin
2 tablespoons olive oil
½ cup minced yellow onion
3 garlic cloves, minced
1 teaspoon freshly grated
   ginger root
1 teaspoon salt
1 teaspoon freshly cracked
   black pepper

1 ½ pounds boneless, skinless
   chicken breasts, cut in 2-inch
   pieces
1 egg, lightly beaten
1 tablespoon chopped pimento-
   stuffed olives
1 tablespoon capers
1 tablespoon raisins, cut in half
   with kitchen shears

1. Preheat oven to 325°F. Lightly spray a 9 × 5-inch loaf pan with vegetable spray. Set aside.

2. Heat curry powder and cumin over moderate heat for 1 to 2 minutes until lightly toasted and a pleasant aroma emerges.

3. Add olive oil and stir with a wooden spoon. Sauté onion, garlic and ginger until soft, about 3 to 4 minutes. Stir in salt and pepper and remove from heat.

4. Run the chicken pieces through a food processor until cut in small pieces.

5. Transfer to large bowl and combine with onion/garlic mixture. Using clean hands, work in eggs, olives, capers and raisins.

6. Press meat into loaf pan and bake for 60 minutes. Chicken should be cooked in center when done, not pink.

7. Remove from oven and drain off any fat. Cut into six serving slices.

**Yield: 6 servings**

EACH SERVING PROVIDES APPROXIMATELY:
260 calories, **3 grams of carbohydrates**, 21 grams of protein, 18 grams of fat

# LOW-CARB Chicken, Almond and Olive Terrine

Terrines can be served hot or cold. I like to slice them thinly and serve over a bed of mixed greens, red onions and hard-boiled eggs.

2 tablespoons olive oil

½ cup chopped yellow onion

1 garlic cloves, minced

1 pound chorizo or pork sausage, casing removed, minced

3 tablespoons shredded cilantro

3 tablespoons fresh parsley

½ teaspoon dried whole oregano

1 teaspoon salt

1 teaspoon freshly cracked black pepper

½ teaspoon paprika

¼ teaspoon nutmeg

2 eggs, lightly beaten

1 pound boneless, skinless chicken breasts, sliced in half lengthwise

3 tablespoons rum

2 tablespoons finely chopped almonds

3 tablespoons chopped pimento-stuffed olives

1. Preheat oven to 400°F. Lightly spray a 5 × 9-inch loaf pan with vegetable spray.

2. Heat olive oil in a large skillet over medium heat. Sauté onion and garlic for 3 minutes. Stir in sausage and cook until lightly browned. Remove from heat and drain off any excess fat.

3. Whisk in cilantro, parsley, oregano, salt, pepper, paprika, nutmeg and eggs. Reserve.

4. Pound chicken breasts, using a wooden mallet and cutting board, to ¼-inch thickness.

5. Place a layer of chicken in the bottom of the pan. Alternate with a layer of onion-sausage mixture. Sprinkle lightly with almonds and olives. Repeat, ending with sausage layer on top. Drizzle with rum.

6. Cover with foil and bake for 45 minutes. Remove foil and bake additional 45 minutes. Drain excess fat before servings. Cut into eight serving pieces.

**Yield: 8 servings**

EACH SERVING PROVIDES APPROXIMATELY:
400 calories, **4 grams carbohydrates**, 24 grams of protein, 29 grams of fat

# LOW-CARB Island Chicken with Butter-Lime Glaze

Serve leftovers chilled on a bed of mixed greens.

6 boneless, skinless 6 ounce chicken breasts, pounded to ¼-inch thickness

1 teaspoon salt

1 teaspoon freshly cracked black pepper

½ teaspoon whole dried oregano

3 tablespoons olive oil

1 clove garlic, minced

1 tablespoon dry white wine

4 tablespoons butter

3 tablespoons fresh lime juice

1 teaspoon freshly grated lime zest

¼ teaspoon Splenda®

½ teaspoon freshly cracked black pepper

¼ teaspoon salt

1 tablespoons chopped chives

1. Preheat oven to 300°F. Season chicken breasts with salt, pepper and oregano.

2. Heat olive oil in a large skillet over moderate heat. Add garlic, wine and chicken breasts. Sauté breasts until juices run clear when pierced with a fork, about six minutes. Remove chicken from skillet, cover and keep in a warm place.

3. Melt 4 tablespoons butter in the same skillet used for the chicken. Add lime juice, zest and Splenda®, scraping up any brown bits. Whisk in salt and pepper. Remove from heat.

4. Drizzle over chicken breasts. Garnish with chives.

**Yield: 6 servings**

EACH SERVING PROVIDES APPROXIMATELY:
450 calories, **1.5 grams carbohydrates**, 38 grams of protein, 33 grams of fat

# Beef and Pork

Pre-Colombian Puerto Rico did not have any livestock, except a few iguanas and small dogs. The Spaniards changed that when they brought over sheep, cattle, pigs, rabbits and fowl.

Beef and pork have been part of the Puerto Rican menu for centuries. Roast suckling pig is a national holiday tradition. Steak smothered in onions is an everyday delight. Stuffed pot roast is another favorite.

Serve these meat dishes alongside plantain and green banana recipes, rice, beans and other Caribbean vegetables.

Note: Be sure to check the index for other beef and pork recipes. You'll find many of them in the appetizer and soup chapters.

## Puerto Rican Steak and Onions

*Biftec Encebollado*

This is the traditional steak and onions dish Puerto Rico is famous for. Note: season the meat and marinate in the refrigerator for a couple days.

2 pounds boneless sirloin or
  beef round, thinly sliced
1 ½ teaspoons salt
1 teaspoon freshly cracked
  black pepper
4 garlic cloves, peeled and crushed

3 tablespoons olive oil
2 medium yellow onions, thinly sliced
extra olive oil for sautéing
2 tablespoons dry sherry

1. Trim any fat or gristle from meat. Pound lightly with a wooden mallet to thin. Rub with salt.

2. Combine pepper and garlic. Rub into meat. Arrange onion slices over top and drizzle with olive oil.

3. Cover and refrigerate for several hours, overnight if possible.

4. Heat about ¼-inch of the extra olive oil in a large, heavy-bottomed skillet over medium heat. Sauté meat slices one minute on each side. Set meat aside.

5. Drain nearly all the olive oil from pan. Sauté the onion slices until soft, about 5 minutes. Remove from pan and arrange on top of meat.

6. Deglaze pan by adding sherry, stirring up bits of brown. Simmer for 2 to 3 minutes.

7. Pour over meat and onions. Serve with hot white rice, plantains and okra.

**Yield: 6 servings**

# Pepper and Onion Smothered Steak

*Biftec Estofado*

This island-style steak is quick, simple and tasty. Select a superior cut of beef, otherwise you'll end up with shoe leather for dinner.

**2 pounds rib, rib-eye or Delmonico steak, trimmed and cut in 1 ½ inch cubes**

**1 teaspoon freshly cracked black pepper**

**1/4 teaspoon hot paprika**

**½ teaspoon salt**

**3 tablespoons red wine vinegar**

**2 tablespoons lemon juice**

**3 large garlic cloves, peeled and minced**

**¼ teaspoon ground oregano**

**1 small green frying pepper, seeded and minced**

**3 *aji dulce* (sweet chili peppers), seeded and minced**

**3 tablespoons olive oil**

**½ cup hot water**

**½ cup hot beef broth**

**2 tablespoons *recaíto***

**1 large yellow onion, halved and thinly sliced into half moons**

1. Rinse meat and pat dry with paper towels. Place meat in a large, flat glass baking dish. Sprinkle with salt, paprika and pepper on all sides. Set aside.

2. Combine vinegar, lemon juice, garlic, oregano and peppers in a small bowl, stirring to combine. Pour over meat. Refrigerate overnight.

3. Heat olive oil in a large heavy skillet over medium-high heat. Brown meat quickly on all sides.

4. Add vinegar/pepper marinade, along with hot water, broth, *recaíto*, and onion. Stir to combine.

5. Reduce heat to a simmer, cover and cook for 35 to 45 minutes. Beef should be fork tender.

**Yield: 4 to 6 servings**

# Shredded Beef Stew

*Ropa Vieja*

*Ropa Vieja* has echoes of the Spanish past. Despite the title, translating literally to 'old rags', this recipe yields a tender and flavorful beef stew. Note: Buy a steak or roast from the chuck and cube it yourself. Those prepackaged cuts of stew beef are made up of odds and ends of different muscle sections that couldn't be sold otherwise. Because of the inconsistencies, the meat will cook at different times. Cut all your own meat from the same cut to ensure even flavor and cooking times.

2 pounds beef chuck, trimmed and
   cut in 1 ½ inch cubes

1 carrot

1 large onion, halved

½ cup red wine

½ teaspoon salt

3 tablespoons olive oil

2 yellow onions, thinly sliced

2 cloves garlic, peeled and
   minced

1 large green frying pepper,
   seeded and minced

2 large tomatoes, peeled and
   chopped, about 2 cups

2 tablespoons tomato paste

1 bay leaf

¼ teaspoon ground allspice

¼ teaspoon ground oregano

   salt and freshly cracked black
   pepper to taste

1. Place the beef, along with the carrot, onion halves, red wine and salt in a large saucepan with sufficient water to cover. Simmer over low heat, covered, for 1 ½ hours. Remove from heat and allow to cool.

2. Shred meat, reserving stock. Set aside.

3. Heat olive oil in a large, heavy frying pan. Sauté onion, garlic and frying pepper until soft, but not brown.

4. Stir in tomatoes, tomato paste, bay leaf, allspice and oregano. Simmer until thickened, about 30 minutes.

5. Add 2 cups of reserved stock and shredded meat. Simmer for 15 minutes. Serve with rice and beans or mashed breadfruit.

**Yield: 6 servings**

# Puerto Rican Beef Stew

*Carne Guisada Puertorriqueña*

Recaíto adds a refreshing twist to an old standby.

2 pounds boneless beef chuck, trimmed
  and cut in 1 ½ inch cubes

2 teaspoons sea salt

4 large garlic cloves, peeled and minced

1 teaspoon chopped fresh oregano,
  or ¼ teaspoon dried

1 teaspoon freshly cracked black pepper

2 tablespoons olive oil

½ cup *recaíto* (see index)

½ cup *alcaparrado* (see index)

3 tablespoons tomato paste

1 bay leaf

2 ½ cups beef stock

½ pound potatoes, peeled and cubed

½ pound carrots, scraped and diced

vegetable oil

1. Make a rub for the beef by combining the sea salt, garlic, oregano, black pepper and olive oil. Allow the meat to marinate 1 hour, overnight in the refrigerator if possible.

2. Heat ¼ inch of the vegetable oil in a large kettle or stew pot over medium heat. Brown the beef on all sides and set aside.

3. Drain all but 3 tablespoons oil from the pan.

4. Reduce heat and sauté recaíto for 5 minutes. Stir in *alcaparrado* and tomato paste, simmering for 3 minutes. Add bay leaf.

5. Return meat to pan, add beef stock, cover and simmer over very low heat for 1 hour.

6. Add potatoes and carrot, cooking for additional 25 minutes.

**Yield: 6 servings**

## Which cut for pot roast?

For the best possible roast, choose cuts from the chuck. We found blade roast and under blade roast to be delicious, moist and tender. Chuck-eye roast has good marbling throughout, adding taste and moisture. Slightly fatty. Watch out for cone-shaped cuts labeled as chuck-eye. This is actually chuck fillet, an inferior and tougher cut. Avoid gritty shoulder roast.

# Stuffed Roasted Beef with Red Wine Glaze

*Lechón de Mechar Relleno*

When Anna and I experimented with the pot roasts, we wanted something that would not be tough and dry on the outside and rare inside. Roasting at 250° for the first hour cooked the meat on the inside. Turning up to 500° for 15 minutes, browned the outside nicely.

1 4-pound boneless beef roast, blade or
   under blade roast

1 small yellow onion, minced

4 medium garlic cloves, crushed

2 sweet chili pepper, seeded and minced

½ teaspoon ground oregano

¼ teaspoon ground thyme

1 teaspoon capers

1 tablespoon olive oil

1 tablespoon red wine vinegar

2 tablespoons sherry

1 teaspoon salt

1 teaspoon freshly cracked
   black pepper

¼ cup chopped, lean cured ham

2 hard-boiled eggs, chopped

¼ cup *alcaparrado*

twine to tie roast

2 tablespoons olive oil

salt and pepper to taste

½ cup red wine

1 cup beef broth

1. Trim meat, wash and pat dry. With the end of a sharp knife, make a long, deep pocket from both ends to center of meat.

2. Combine onion, garlic, peppers, oregano, thyme, capers, olive oil, vinegar, sherry, salt and pepper in a small bowl until smooth. Stuff slit with this mixture.

3. Refrigerate, uncovered for 4 days to age meat for optimum flavor.

4. Combine ham, eggs and *alcaparrado* in small bowl. Stuff into slit along with garlic/onion mixture.

5. Preheat oven to 250°.

6. Tie roast crosswise with twine every inch, then tied lengthwise a couple times.

7. Heat olive oil in a large oven-proof pot or Dutch oven over medium heat. Brown roast quickly on all sides, about 3 to 4 minutes.

8. Transfer meat to oven, and cook, uncovered, until a meat thermometer inserted into center reads 110°, about 45 to 55 minutes.

9. Turn up oven temperature to 500° and cook for additional 15 minutes. Insert thermometer into thickest part of cut. It should read 130°.

10. Remove roast from Dutch oven (reserving pan juices) and transfer to serving platter. Allow to rest for 25 minutes before serving.

11. Deglaze Dutch oven by adding red wine to pot, stirring up all bits of brown. Simmer on top of stove over medium heat for 2 to 3 minutes. Add broth and simmer additional minute.

12. Slice pot roast thinly and serve with wine glaze.

**Yield: 6 to 8 servings**

# Pot Roast in Sherry Glaze

*Lechón de Mechar en Jerez*

Thinly slice leftover meat for sandwiches the next day.

13-pound roast, blade or under
   blade roast

10 peppercorns

6 large garlic cloves, peeled
   and crushed

2 tablespoons minced yellow onion

½ teaspoon ground oregano

¼ teaspoon thyme

3 teaspoons salt

2 tablespoon olive oil

1 tablespoon vinegar

1 tablespoon vegetable oil

4 cups hot water

2 cups hot beef stock

2 small bay leaves

1 pound carrots, scraped and sliced
   in ¼ inch rounds

1 pound potatoes, peeled and cubed
   in 1 ½ inch pieces

½ pound tiny white onions, peeled

1 ½ teaspoons salt

½ cup dry sherry

¼ cup packed brown sugar

2 tablespoons cornstarch

½ cup sherry

1 tablespoon Grand Marnier (orange
   liqueuer)

1. Trim, wash and pat dry roast. Using a mortar and pestle, grind together peppercorns, garlic, onion, oregano, thyme, salt, olive oil and vinegar. Rub meat with this and refrigerate overnight.

2. Heat vegetable oil in a deep kettle or stew pot over medium high heat. Brown beef lightly on all sides.

3. Add hot water, beef stock and bay leaves. Turn up heat to high and bring to boil. Reduce heat to medium, cover and simmer for 2 ½ hours, stirring occasionally. Meat should be nearly fork tender.

4. Stir in carrots, onions, potatoes, salt, half cup sherry, and brown sugar. Turn up heat, returning to boil. Reduce heat, cover and simmer for 45 minutes. Meat should now be fork tender.

5. Dissolve cornstarch in sherry and Grand Marnier. Slowly stir into stew pot. Cook uncovered for 5 minutes until thickened.

6. Remove meat from pot, slice thinly and drizzle with sherry glaze.

**Yield: 12 to 14 servings**

## Succulent Pot Roast with Island Vegetables

*Lechón de Mechar con Vegetales de Isla*

Chop left over roast, chill and serve on a bed of lettuce with *mojito* sauce or your favorite dressing.

| | |
|---|---|
| 1 4-pound blade or under-blade roast | 3 ½ cups hot water |
| 10 peppercorns | 3 ½ cups hot water |
| 6 large garlic cloves, peeled and crushed | 2 small bay leaves |
| 2 tablespoons minced yellow onion | 1 ½ pounds yams, peeled and cut in 1-inch cubes |
| ½ teaspoon ground oregano | |
| ¼ teaspoon thyme | 1 ½ pounds cassava or sweet potato, peeled and cut in 1-inch cubes |
| 3 teaspoons salt | |
| 2 tablespoons olive oil | 2 medium yellow onions, diced |
| 1 tablespoon vinegar | 1 ½ teaspoons salt |
| 2 tablespoons olive oil | ½ cup dry sherry |
| ¼ cup packed brown sugar | |

1. Trim, wash and pat dry roast. Using a mortar and pestle, grind together peppercorns, garlic, onion, oregano, thyme, salt, 2 tablespoons olive oil and vinegar. Rub meat with this and refrigerate overnight.

2. Heat remaining 2 tablespoons olive oil in a deep kettle or stew pot over medium high heat. Brown beef lightly on all sides.

3. Add hot water, beef stock and bay leaves. Turn up heat to high and bring to boil. Reduce heat to medium, cover and simmer for 2 ½ hours, stirring occasionally and rotating meat so it will cook evenly on all sides. Meat should be nearly fork tender.

4. Add extra water as needed. Sauce should not fall below three-quarters from the top of the meat.

5. Stir in yam, sweet potato, onion, salt, sherry, and brown sugar. Turn up heat, returning to boil. Reduce heat, cover and simmer for 30 minutes. Meat should now be fork tender. Internal temperature of meat should be between 160° and 170°.

6. To serve, transfer meat to a cutting board and allow to rest for 25 minutes. Cut in 1/4 -inch thick slices. Place on platter and arrange vegetables around edge. Pour sauce over roast and vegetables.

**Yield: 6 to 8 servings**

# London Broil in Rum Glaze
*Biftec Al Horno*

London Broil is a recipe not a particular cut of beef. Supermarkets tend to sell top round and shoulder cuts the same way, as London Broil. Use shoulder steak. It's the most economical and has the least amount of fat. Don't drink rum? Not to worry. The alcohol burns off during the cooking process. Be sure to use dark rum, which imparts a faintly smokey flavor.

**1 boneless shoulder steak**
**(1 ½ to 2 pounds)**
**salt and black ground pepper**
**½ cup dark rum**

**3 tablespoons lime juice**
**3 tablespoons packed brown sugar**
**2 tablespoons olive oil**

1. Sprinkle meat with salt and pepper to taste. Transfer meat to shallow glass baking dish. Combine rum, lime juice, brown sugar and olive oil in a small bowl and pour over meat. Marinate overnight in the refrigerator. Turn meat a couple times.

2. Adjust oven rack to lowest position. Preheat oven to 500° for 30 minutes.

3. Heat a large, heavy, ovenproof skillet for 3 minutes over high heat. Add meat to pan and sear quickly on all sides.

4. Transfer pan to oven and pour remaining rum marinade over top. Cook 3 ½ minutes, then flip meat and cook additional 3 ½ minutes. Meat will read 125° on thermometer.

5. Remove from oven and pan. Place on cutting board (so meat does not continue to cook in pan). Allow to rest 5 minutes.

6. Cut thin slices on bias against grain. Pour rum glaze over top. Serve at once.

**Yield: 4 servings**

---

### Did You Know?

Seventy-eight miles southwest of San Juan and 26 miles west of Ponce lies a town called La Paguerra. It's principal attraction is the **Phosphorescent Bay**, which contains million of luminescent dinoflagellates (microscopic plankton). Boats leave nightly from the pier.

---

# Breaded Garlic Beefsteak

*Biftec Empanado*

Breaded beefsteaks are quite popular in island take-out places. They are either served on their own as an entrée with French fries and vegetables, or as a sandwich. Substitute chicken breasts or thighs if desired.

4 boneless tenderloin steaks (about 8-ounces per steak, ½-inch thick)

4 garlic cloves, peeled and minced

1 teaspoon salt

½ teaspoon freshly cracked black pepper

1 tablespoon vinegar

3 extra-large eggs beaten with ¼ teaspoon of salt

1 ¼ cups seasoned bread crumbs

vegetable oil for frying

1. Trim off excess fat or connective tissue from meat. Cut against the grain into ¼-inch thick slices. Pound the meat to flatten and thin slightly.

2. Rub meat with garlic, salt, pepper and vinegar. Cover and set aside for 1 hour.

3. Heat ¼ inch of oil in a large, heavy skillet over medium heat.

4. Dip each piece of meat into the beaten egg, then roll in bread crumbs. Press crumbs lightly into meat.

5. Fry for 2 minutes on each side, in a single layer. Do not overcrowd pan. Remove burnt bread crumbs and add extra oil if needed.

6. Drain on white paper towels.

**Yield: 4 servings**

## Breading

Breadcrumb coatings keep food moist while it cooks. Breadcrumb coatings have two parts: the moist part which helps the breadcrumbs adhere and the breadcrumbs. Use something with protein in it: eggs, buttermilk, yogurt, cream; the second part is the coating: bread crumbs, crushed nuts, cracker crumbs, cornmeal, a hard grated cheese, herbs, or four.

**Even browning:** Make sure food to be breaded is absolutely dry by patting with white paper towels. Any moisture left on the surface will form a steam pocket and cause the coating to break. First dip patted-dry food in flour or cornstarch, then in wet mixture, then in breading.

**To keep crust from dropping off:** Allow coated foods to sit for 20 minutes before frying.

**Crispiest crust:** Don't rely on extra frying time for a crisp crust. Start with crushed cracker crumbs or cornmeal.

**Flakiest crust:** No it's not the type of frying oil or shortening that makes a difference. Whisk in 1½ tablespoons oil to wet mixture, i.e. eggs, milk, yogurt, etc.

**Lightest crust:** Make your own fresh breadcrumbs.

# Creole Filet Mignon

*Filete Mignon a la Criolla*

1 beef tenderloin, trimmed and cut in slices 1 ½-inches thick

6 black peppercorns

2 large garlic cloves, peeled and crushed

½ teaspoon whole dried oregano

½ teaspoon salt

1 tablespoon vinegar

1 tablespoon lemon juice

1 medium yellow onion, minced

3 tablespoons olive oil

1 medium green bell pepper, seeded and cut in strips

1 medium red bell pepper, seeded and cut in strips

1 large yellow onion, halved and thinly sliced

½ cup dry sherry

1 tablespoon tomato paste

1 8-ounce can sliced mushrooms

1 large tomato, peeled and diced

4 tablespoons butter

1. Wash meat and pat dry with paper towels. Crush peppercorns, garlic, salt, oregano, vinegar, lemon juice and minced yellow onion in a mortar.

2. Transfer meat to a shallow glass baking dish. Rub meat with peppercorn mixture. Refrigerate for 1 hour or overnight. Stir occasionally.

3. In a heavy-bottomed skilled, heat olive oil over medium-high heat. Brown meat quickly.

4. Add peppers, sliced onion, sherry and tomato paste. Stir and cook for 3 minutes.

5. Stir in mushrooms, tomato and butter. Cook for 4 minutes. Serve with hot white rice and okra.

**Yield: 4 to 6 servings**

# Tropical Corned Beef with Garbanzos

*Carne de Pote con Garbanzos*

2 tablespoons butter (do not use margarine)

1 medium yellow onion, diced

3 tablespoons *sofrito* (see index)

1 tablespoon dark rum (optional)

½ teaspoon brown sugar

1 12-ounce can corned beef, shredded

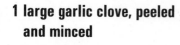

1 large garlic clove, peeled
and minced

1/8 teaspoon ground oregano

1 16-ounce can chickpeas, drained
and rinsed

¾ cup tomato sauce

1. Heat butter in large skillet or frying pan. Stir in onion, *sofrito*, garlic and oregano. Cook for 3 minutes. Add tomato sauce, stirring to combine. Cook 1 minute then add rum and brown sugar, cooking 1 minute.

2. Add shredded beef and stir. Fold in chickpeas. Cook uncovered, stirring often for 5 minutes. Serve with rice or potatoes.

Yield: 6 servings

## Caribbean Meatballs
*Albóndigas*

If you're tired of serving spaghetti and meatballs, try this revved up island version. Interestingly, meatballs are also served with rice in Puerto Rico or with potatoes or root vegetables such as sweet potato, yams or cassava.

1 ½ pounds lean ground beef

4 black peppercorns

2 garlic cloves, peeled and crushed

¼ teaspoon ground oregano

1 ½ teaspoons salt

2 tablespoons chopped parsley

1 cup seasoned breadcrumbs
2 large beaten eggs

1 cup tomato sauce

2 tablespoons olive oil

2 tablespoons malt vinegar

1/3 cup flour

vegetable oil

½ cup recaíto (see index)

½ cup minced yellow onion

2 tablespoons diced alcaparrado
(see index)

1. Place ground beef in a bowl.

2. Crush peppercorns, garlic, oregano, salt and parsley in a mortar. Stir in olive oil and vinegar.

3. Mix spices into meat, folding in breadcrumbs and vinegar. Form into 1 ½ inch balls using your hands.

4. Dip balls in beaten eggs, then roll in flour.

5. Heat ½ inch of vegetable oil in large, heavy-bottomed skillet over medium-high heat. Brown the meatballs all over and remove from pan. Set aside.

6. Drain off all but 2 tablespoons of the fat from the skillet. Sauté *recaíto* and onion over medium heat for 5 minutes. Add *alcaparrado* and tomato sauce, simmering for 5 more minutes.

7. Return meatballs to pan and heat through.

**Yield: 6 servings**

# Roasted Pepper, Beef and Noodle Casserole
*Picadillo de Carne con Pimientos Asados*

Serve with crusty white bread and a hearty red wine. Excellent as a leftover. The flavor improves after a day in the fridge.

**3 tablespoons olive oil**

**1 large green frying pepper,**
  **seeded and minced**

**1 medium yellow onion,**
  **seeded and minced**

**3 large garlic cloves, peeled**
  **and minced**

**1 ½ pounds lean ground beef**

**2 ounces diced fat back or 1**
  **bacon strip, fried and crumbled**

**1 teaspoon salt**

**1 teaspoon freshly cracked black pepper**

**1 28-ounce can tomatoes in sauce**

**½ pound macaroni, cooked al dente (firm)**

**2 large red bell peppers, roasted, peeled,**
**seeded and sliced into strips**

**3 large hard-boiled eggs, diced**

**½ cup *recaíto* (see index)**

**4 tablespoons *alcaparrado* (see index)**

1. Preheat oven to 400°. Generously grease a 2-quart glass baking dish. Transfer al dente macaroni to dish. Set aside.

2. Heat olive oil in a large, heavy-bottomed skillet over medium heat. Sauté frying pepper, garlic and onion until soft, about 3 to 4 minutes.

3. Add ground beef, stirring and breaking up any large chunks. Add fatback and cook until meat is no longer pink. Remove meat from pan and place in a steel colander. Rinse under hot water to remove excess fat.

4. Drain all but 2 tablespoons of fat from skillet. Sauté *recaíto*, *alcaparrado*, salt and black pepper.

5. Stir in tomatoes along with puree. Reduce heat and simmer for 2 minutes.

6. Return beef to skillet. Stir. Pour over macaroni.

7. Transfer to oven and bake for 10 minutes. Garnish with roasted pepper strips and chopped boiled eggs. Return to oven for 7 to 8 minutes.

**Yield: 6 to 8 servings**

# Caribbean Meat Loaf with Spicy Brown Sugar and Rum Glaze

*Butifarrón Sabroso*

### SPICY BROWN SUGAR AND RUM GLAZE

½ cup ketchup

5 tablespoons brown sugar

½ small jalapeño pepper,

2 tablespoons dark rum

2 tablespoons lime juice

½ small jalapeño pepper,
   seeded and minced

### MEAT LOAF

1 tablespoon olive oil

1 medium onion, minced

3 garlic cloves, minced

1 small green frying pepper,
   seeded and minced

2 large eggs

½ teaspoon whole dried oregano

1 teaspoon salt

1 teaspoon cracked black pepper

½ cup *sofrito* (see index)

2 ounces lean cured ham, diced

1 ounce salt pork, minced

1 pound ground chuck

½ pound ground pork

½ pound ground veal

1 tablespoon hot pepper sauce

½ cup milk

½ cup crushed saltine crackers

1/4 cup tomato sauce

1. For glaze, mix all ingredients in small saucepan and set aside.

2. Preheat oven to 350°. Heat oil in 10-inch skillet over medium heat. Sauté onion, garlic and frying pepper until soft, about 3 minutes. Remove from heat and set aside.

3. Combine eggs, oregano, salt, black pepper, *sofrito*, ham and salt pork in a large bowl. Fold in chuck, pork, veal, hot pepper sauce, milk, crackers and tomato sauce. Blend with fork.

4. Transfer meat to large cutting board or clean surface. Pat into a loaf, 9 by 5 inches.

5. Line a glass baking dish with foil and place loaf on top. Brush with half of glaze.

6. Bake until outside is crispy and a meat thermometer in center reads 160°, about 1 hour. Remove meat from oven and allow to sit for 20 minutes.

7. Slice in ½-inch pieces and drizzle with remaining glaze.

**Yield: 6 to 8 servings**

# Roast Pork Leg with Sherry Gravy
*Pernil Al Horno*

Instead of the traditional turkey that is served at Christmas or Thanksgiving on the mainland, Puerto Ricans prepare roast pork. Serve with rice and pigeon peas.

**1 4 to 6 pound pork leg**

**juice of one lemon**

**8 large garlic cloves, sliced**

**8 peppercorns**

**2 teaspoons dried whole oregano**

**2 tablespoons olive oil**

**2 tablespoons cider or malt vinegar**

**1 teaspoon salt for each pound of pork**

**½ cup dry sherry**

**¼ cup flour**

1. Rinse pork under cold running water. Pat dry with paper towels. Squeeze lemon juice over entire leg. This will do much to alleviate the 'porkish' odor.

2. Cut slits in the skin and fat using the tip of a sharp knife. Insert garlic slices into skin.

3. Crush peppercorns in a mortar. Mash in salt, vinegar and olive oil. Rub this into meat.

4. Refrigerate overnight. Remove from refrigerator ½ hour before cooking time. Preheat oven to 300°.

5. Transfer meat to a roasting pan. Insert a meat thermometer into center of meat. Bake for 2 hours. Meat should be golden.

6. Turn oven up to 350°. Bake for another 45 minutes. Thermometer should read 185°F. Remove from oven and place on large cutting board.

7. Meanwhile, to make gravy, drain liquid from roasting pan into a glass measuring cup. Skim off fat, measure off ¼ cup and reserve. You should have 2 ½ cups of juices left over.

8. If you don't have enough liquid, add water. If not enough fat, add butter to make up the ¼ cup.

9. Pour liquid into a medium saucepan, stirring in sherry over medium-high heat. Bring to a boil.

10. Heat fat in a small skillet and whisk in flour over medium-high heat to make a roux. Stir fat into hot liquid, smoothing out any lumps. Reduce heat and cook until gravy has thickened. Remove from heat. Pour over sliced pork roast.

**Yield: 6 to 8 servings**

## Pork Roast with Wine and Raisin Glaze

*Pernil con Vino al Caldero*

You can use a dry white wine for this recipe. But a sweet wine imparts a unique flavor.

| | |
|---|---|
| **4-pound leg of pork** | **4 teaspoons salt** |
| **juice of one lemon** | **2 tables-poons cider or malt vinegar** |
| **6 large peppercorns** | **2 tablespoons olive oil** |
| **6 garlic cloves, peeled** | **½ cup sweet white wine** |
| **1 teaspoon whole dried oregano** | **¼ cup raisins** |
| **¼ teaspoon dried thyme** | **1 tablespoon packed brown sugar** |
| **¼ teaspoon dried sage** | **2 tablespoons flour** |
| **¼ teaspoon dried rosemary** | |

1. Wash meat under cold running water. Pat dry with paper towels. Pour lemon juice over meat to get rid of odor.

2. Cut slits in pork using tip of a sharp knife.

3. Grind peppercorns, garlic, oregano, thyme, sage, rosemary, salt, vinegar and olive oil in a mortar.

4. Rub past into skin and under slits. 5

5. Refrigerate overnight. Remove from refrigerator ½ hour before cooking time. Preheat oven to 300°.

6. Transfer meat to a roasting pan. Insert a meat thermometer into center of meat. Bake for 2 hours. Meat should be golden.

7. Turn oven up to 350°. Bake for another 45 minutes. Thermometer should read 185°F. Remove from oven and place on large cutting board.

8. Meanwhile, to make gravy, drain liquid from roasting pan into a glass measuring cup. Skim off fat, measure off ¼ cup and reserve. You should have 2 ½ cups of juices left over. 9

9. If you don't have enough liquid, add water. If not enough fat, add butter to make up the ¼ cup.

10. Pour liquid into a medium saucepan, stirring in wine, raisins and brown sugar over medium-high heat. Bring to a boil.

11. Heat gravy in a small skillet and whisk in flour over medium-high heat to make a roux. Stir fat into hot liquid, smoothing out any lumps. Reduce heat and cook until gravy has thickened. Remove from heat. Pour over sliced pork roast.

**Yield: 6 to 8 servings**

# Roast Pork Shoulder with Guava-Orange Glaze
*Pernil de Cerdo al Horno con Glaceado de Guayaba*

Pork shoulder is often more convenient than pork leg. Serve instead of a traditional turkey for the holidays.

| | |
|---|---|
| **1 5-pound pork shoulder** | **½ teaspoon dried thyme** |
| **juice of one lemon** | **3 tablespoons malt vinegar** |
| **6 black peppercorns** | **3 tablespoons olive oil** |
| **5 teaspoons salt** | **1 cup guava jelly** |
| **2 large garlic cloves, peeled and crushed** | **¼ cup dark rum** |
| **1 teaspoon dried oregano** | **1 tablespoon Grand Marnier** |

1. Wash meat under cold running water. Pat dry with paper towels. Squeeze lemon juice over meat.

2. Cut slits in skin and fat with the tip of a sharp knive.

3. Crush peppercorns, salt, garlic, oregano and thyme in a mortar. Stir in vinegar and olive oil.

4. Refrigerate overnight. Remove from refrigerator ½ hour before cooking time. Preheat oven to 300°.

5. Melt guava jelly together with rum over low heat.

6. Transfer meat to a roasting pan. Baste meat with guava glaze, reserving 1/3 of glaze. Insert a meat thermometer into center of meat. Bake for 2 hours. Meat should be golden. Turn meat over.

7. Turn oven up to 350°. Bake for another hour. Skin should be crispy. Thermometer should read 185°F. Remove from oven and place on large cutting board and allow to rest 20 minutes.

8. Reheat reserved guava glaze in small saucepan. Pour over roast.

**Yield: 6 to 8 servings**

## Pork

There are numerous breeds of pigs, but due to the demand for leaner meat, new breeds are 30 to 50% less fatty than their ancestors. Pigs reproduce readily and will eat nearly anything, making them virtually maintenance-free for farmers.

**Purchasing:** The tenderest cuts of pork are loin, which are from the back. This includes loin chops, loin roast and loin fillet. Less expensive cuts are tougher, being cut from the shoulder and leg. Pork may be purchased fresh, salted or smoked. Ham comes from the leg; bacon comes from the loin or flank; salt pork from the shoulder.

**Storing:** Ground pork has the shortest life; refrigerate for 1 ½ days. Pork chops for 2 days, cooked pork for 3 days. Chops and roasts may be frozen for 6 months, bacon and ham for 1 month. Cooked meat for 1 month.

**Preparing:** Always cook pork to at least 150°F to kill any parasites. Do not overcook however. Cook at low temperatures (250°F) to keep from drying out. Do not microwave as it could leaves portions of the meat uncooked. Costly loin cuts are best cooked in the oven with dry heat. Less expensive cuts should be cooked in liquid. If you like, marinate pork for 24 hours before cooking for peak flavor.

**Nutrition:** Rich in protein, low in carbohydrates. Excellent source of B-complex vitamins, as well as potassium, zinc and phosphorous.

# Onion-Smothered Pork Medallions in Passionfruit-Rum Glaze

Passionfruit adds an exotic touch to this traditional dish. Purchase it canned in the freezer section of your grocer. To ensure even cooking, cut tenderloin slices to equal thickness.

1 teaspoon salt

½ teaspoon cracked black pepper

2 large garlic cloves, peeled and minced

   pork tenderloin (1 ½ pounds), silver skin removed, cut into 1-inch slices, pounded to ¾-inch thickness

2 tablespoons olive oil

2 medium yellow onions, halved and thinly sliced into half-moons

1/3 cup frozen passionfruit concentrate, thawed

3 tablespoons dark rum

2/3 cup chicken broth

1. Sprinkle pork medallions with salt and pepper. Rub with garlic.

2. Heat oil in large, heavy-bottomed skillet over medium-high heat. Oil should shimmer, not smoke.

3. Sear medallions on each side, about 1 minute, 10 seconds. Do not overcrowd pan. Transfer meat to a plate.

4. Heat olive oil in same skillet over medium heat. Sauté onion until lightly browned. You want the onions slightly caramelized.

5. Stir in passionfruit, rum and chicken broth, scraping bottom of pan to loosen brown bits. Cook for 2 ½ minutes.

6. Turn heat up and boil until liquid reaches consistency of maple syrup, about 3 minutes.

7. Reduce heat to medium, return pork medallions to skillet. Heat meat thoroughly, about 3 minutes.

8. Transfer to serving plate. Spoon onions and glaze over pork. Serve with hot white rice.

**Yield: 4 servings**

## TIP: Pork Chops

When purchasing pork chops, look for meat that is solid pink, rather than marbled with white. This is tough connective tissue. Always buy chops that are at least one-inch thick. The thinner ones cook too quickly and become tough.

There are five types of pork chops available. The two best are the 'center rib chop' and the 'center loin chop.'

What you don't want is the 'sirloin end chop' or the 'rib end blade chop.' The former contains a piece of hip bone and the meat looks all bunched up. The latter has a long thin blade bone.

The 'rib end pork chop' are a bit chewy, but moister than the coveted 'center rib chop.'

Be sure to score the fat on the ends of the pork chop so that they don't curl up while cooking.

# Fried Pork Chops

*Chuletas de Cerdo Fritas*

4 pork chops, ½-inch thick, trimmed of fat
1 ½ teaspoons salt
½ teaspoon cracked black pepper
½ teaspoon paprika
3 large garlic cloves, peeled and minced

¼ teaspoon dried thyme
¼ teaspoon ground oregano
1 teaspoon vinegar
vegetable oil

1. Rinse chops under cold running water. Pat dry.

2. Mix salt, pepper, paprika, garlic, thyme, oregano and vinegar in a small bowl. Rub into chops. Refrigerate for 2 hours.

3. Heat ¼-inch of vegetable in a large, heavy-bottomed skillet over medium heat.

4. Brown chops lightly on each side, for 2 minutes.

5. Reduce heat and cook 4 minutes on each side.

6. Drain on white paper towels. Serve with mashed breadfruit and a green salad.

**Yield: 4 servings**

# Egg-Dipped Ginger and Coriander Pork Chops
*Chuletas de Cerdo Rebozadas*

Serve leftover chilled chops, thinly sliced from the bone, over a bed of mixed greens and minced red onion.

**6 pork chops, ½-inch thick, trimmed**

**1 ½ teaspoon salt, or to taste**

**1 teaspoon cracked black peppercorns**

**½ teaspoon ground coriander**

**1 teaspoon grated fresh ginger root, or ½ teaspoon dried**

**1 tablespoon brown sugar**

**3 eggs, beaten**

**½ cup flour**

**vegetable oil**

1. Rinse chops under cold water and pat dry. Combine salt, pepper, coriander, ginger and brown sugar in a small bowl. Rub chops with this. Allow to stand 30 minutes.

2. Heat ¼-inch of vegetable oil in a frying pan set over moderate heat. Fry chops for 4 minutes on each side. Remove from pan and drain on white paper towels.

3. In a clean skillet, heat 4 tablespoons oil over medium heat.

4. Dredge in flour, dip into beaten egg, dredge in flour again.

5. Sauté chops for 1 ½ minutes on each side until golden. Drain on paper towels. Serve with Mango Chutney (see index), pigeon peas and rice and a green salad.

**Yield: 6 servings**

# Sugarcane and Ginger Pork Chops
*Chuletas de Cerdo Rebozadas con Jengibre*

Columbus brought sugar cane from the Canary Islands on his second voyage to the New World in 1493. Subsequently, slaves were brought over to work the sugar cane fields in the early 16th century. The rum industry was born on Puerto Rico.

6 pork chops, cut ½-inch thick, trimmed

4 garlic cloves, peeled and crushed

1 ½ teaspoons cracked black peppercorns

1 ½ teaspoons salt

¼ teaspoon ground cinnamon

¼ teaspoon ground cardamom

1 tablespoon butter

1 tablespoon olive oil

¼ cup minced yellow onion

½ cup packed light brown sugar

¾ cup chicken broth

¼ cup dark rum

¼ cup sweet white wine

1 tablespoon grated fresh ginger

2 tablespoons butter

1 teaspoon lemon juice

1. Rinse the chops under cold running water. Pat dry.

2. Combine the black pepper corns, garlic, salt, cinnamon and cardamom in a small bowl. Rub the meat with this. Allow to marinate 1 hour in the refrigerator.

3. Melt butter in a 10- to 12-inch skillet over medium-high heat. Add oil and swirl until fat browns slightly and begins to smoke.

4. Place chops in skillet and brown, about 1 minute. Turn and brown on other side for 1 minute.

5. Reduce heat to moderate, cover and cook for 4 minutes. Flip chops over and cook for 4 ½ additional minutes. Chops should be firm, but not hard. Transfer chops to serving dish and keep in a warm place.

6. Drain all but 2 tablespoons of the fat from the skillet. Sauté onion until soft, about 1 minute. Add sugar, stirring rapidly for 1 minute. Stir in broth, rum and wine. Boil until reduced by half, about 1 ½ minutes. Stir in ginger and cook for 3 minutes. You should have a syrup by now.

7. Remove from heat, swirl in 1 tablespoon butter. Drizzle in lemon juice, swirling again.

8. Spoon over pork chops.

**Yield: 6 servings**

# Breaded Pork Chops
*Chuletas de Cerdo Empanadas*

6 pork chops, ½-inch thick, trimmed

¼ cup lemon juice

1 ½ teaspoons salt

1 ½ teaspoon cracked black pepper

½ teaspoon paprika

1 large garlic clove, peeled and crushed

2 large beaten eggs

1 cup seasoned bread crumbs

vegetable oil

1. Rinse chops under cold running water. Pat dry. Rub with lemon juice.

2. Combine salt, pepper, paprika and garlic in a small bowl. Rub chops with this mixture. Allow to sit for 45 minutes in the refrigerator.

3. Heat ¼-inch of the vegetable oil in a large heavy-bottomed skillet over medium heat. Brown chops 3 minutes on each side. Drain on paper towels.

4. Drain oil from pan, wipe out with paper towels and heat a fresh ¼-inch of oil over medium-high heat.

5. Dip meat in beaten egg, then dip in breadcrumbs, pushing them into chops.

6. Fry chops 1 ½ minutes on each side. Drain on paper towels.

**Yield: 6 servings**

# Olive and Garlic Stuffed Pork Chops
*Chuletas Rellenas*

Doritza's sister, Mayra, generously parted with this family recipe.

6 pork chops, 1 ½-inch thick, trimmed

1 ½ teaspoons salt

1 teaspoon cracked black pepper

2 tablespoons olive oil

1 medium yellow onion, minced

½ cup flour

1 tablespoon malt, cider or wine vinegar

½ cup seasoned breadcrumbs

12 pimento-stuffed olives, minced

2 tablespoons raisins, snipped in bits with poultry shears

8 garlic cloves, peeled and minced

| | |
|---|---|
| 3 tablespoons butter | ¼ mild green chili pepper or jalapeño |
| vegetable oil | according to taste |

1. Rinse meat under cool running water. Pat dry. Slice chop lengthwise, but not all the way through, creating a pocket. Exercise caution so you don't cut your hand.

2. Season with salt and pepper.

3. Heat olive oil in a large, heavy-bottomed skillet over medium heat. Sauté onion, garlic and pepper until soft, about 3 minutes.

4. Stir in vinegar, bread crumbs, olives and raisins. Reduce heat and cook for 2 minutes.

5. Fill each chop pocket with ¼ cup of stuffing. Dredge each chop in flour. Fasten with toothpicks.

6. Wipe out skillet and melt butter. Add olive oil and swirl. Brown chops over moderate heat for 1 minute each side. Flip and then cook for 4 minutes each. Flip again and cook for 4 minutes each side.

7. Drain on white paper towels.

**Yield: 6 servings**

## Sautéed Pork Chops with Pineapple-Banana Salsa
*Chuletas Guisadas con Salsa de Piña y Plátano*

For those of you who enjoy nouvelle Caribbean cuisine with a bit of fire, add a dash of habañero hot sauce to the salsa.

| | |
|---|---|
| ½ teaspoon ground cinnamon | ¼ cup dark Puerto Rican rum |
| ½ teaspoon ground cumin | ¼ cup chicken stock |
| ¼ teaspoon coriander | 2 tablespoons dry sherry |
| 1/8 teaspoon allspice | 2 tablespoons packed brown sugar |
| ½ teaspoon black pepper | 1 cup diced pineapple, fresh or |
| ½ teaspoon salt | canned |
| 6 pork chops, 1-inch thick | 1 small, slightly unripe banana, diced |
| 1 tablespoon butter | ½ cup cubed ripe mango, or chopped |
| 2 tablespoons lime juice | canned peaches |

1 tablespoon olive oil

2 tablespoons minced red onion

½ teaspoon salt

1. Combine cinnamon, cumin, coriander, allspice, black pepper and salt in a small bowl. Rub into chops and refrigerate 3 hours.

2. Heat butter in a large, heavy-bottomed skillet over medium heat. Swirl in olive oil until butter is lightly browned and just begins to smoke.

3. Sauté chops for 1 minute on each side. Flip and sauté on other side for 1 minute.

4. Reduce heat to medium, cover and cook 3 ½ minutes each side. Transfer chops to a plate and warm area.

5. Drain off fat from skillet. Add rum, chicken stock and sherry. Over moderate heat, using a wooden spoon stir, scraping up brown bits. Cook 1 minute. Mixture will have cooked down by half. Stir in sugar, cooking 1 minute. Spoon over chops and serve with salsa.

6. TO MAKE SALSA: Toss pineapple, banana, mango, lime juice, red onion and salt. Serve chilled over warm chops.

**Yield: 6 servings**

# Spicy Pork Morsels

*Carne de Cerdo Frita*

Insert toothpicks into the morsels and serve at cocktail parties.

2 pounds boneless pork,
cut into 1 ½-inch cubes

3 large garlic cloves,
 peeled and pressed

vegetable oil

1 teaspoon salt

1 teaspoon cracked black pepper

1 small jalapeño pepper,
 seeded and minced into a pulp

½ teaspoon hot paprika

1. Trim off any fat from meat. Rinse under cold running water and pat dry. Rub with salt, pepper and garlic. Refrigerate 1 hour.

2. Heat ¼-inch of vegetable oil in a large, heavy-bottomed skillet over medium heat. Toss in hot pepper and sauté for 1 minute.

3. Add cubes, one at a time, stirring to prevent sticking to pan. Brown lightly on all sides about 2 minutes.

4. Reduce heat to medium-low, cover and cook for 12 minutes. Stir meat and cook for additional 12 minutes.

5. Remove cover and sauté for 20 minutes. Cubes should be golden. Drain on white paper towels. Serve with Mango Chutney (see index) Ajilimojili Sauce (see index) or Garlic Dipping Sauce. Sprinkle with paprika.

**Yield: 8 appetizer servings**

# Pork with Potatoes
*Carne de Cerdo con Papas*

2 pounds boneless pork, cut in
  1-inch cubes
1 ¾ teaspoon salt
1 teaspoon cracked black pepper
2 tablespoons olive oil
½ cup minced yellow onion
3 large garlic cloves, minced
3 *aji dulce* (sweet chili peppers)
vegetable oil

½ cup *sofrito* (see index)
¼ cup *alcaparrado* (see index)
½ cup tomato sauce
2 tablespoons dry sherry
2 cups hot water
1 ½ pounds potatoes, peeled
  and diced in ½-inch pieces
¼ cup minced parsley

1. Rinse pork under cold running water. Cut off any excess fat or membrane. Rub with salt and pepper. Set aside.

2. Heat olive oil in a large, heavy-bottomed skillet over moderate heat. Sauté onion, garlic and chili peppers for 2 minutes until soft, but not browned.

3. Toss in meat and brown on all sides, about 1½ minutes. Remove vegetables and meat. Reserve.

4. Drain all but 2 tablespoons of the oil in the skillet. Sauté sofrito for 3 minutes over moderate heat. Stir in *alcaparrado*, tomato sauce and sherry, cooking for 2 minutes.

5. Transfer meat, garlic and onions back to skillet. Stir in water, turn up heat and bring to boil. Cover, lower heat and simmer for 1 hour.

6. Fold in potatoes, cover and simmer over very low heat for 1 hour. Potatoes and meat should be tender. Garnish with minced parsley.

**Yield: 6 servings**

# Pork and Eggplant Stew
*Carne de Cerdo Guisada con Berenjena*

You guessed it-Grandma Lucinda, with her penchant for alcoholic ingredients, gifted us with this recipe.

1 tablespoon butter

1 tablespoon annatto oil (see index)

2 pounds lean pork shoulder, cut
   into 2-inch cubes

1 medium yellow onion, minced

3 garlic cloves, peeled and crusehd

1 large tomato, peeled, seeded and chopped

1 red bell pepper, seeded and
   minced

½ cup *recaíto* (see index)

1 tablespoon brown sugar

1 1-pound eggplant, peeled
   and diced

2 cups beer

1. Melt butter in a heavy-bottomed skillet over moderate heat. Add annatto oil and swirl pan. Lightly sauté pork cubes until golden, about 2 minutes. Remove cubes with a slotted spoon to an heatproof casserole.

2. Drain all but two tablespoons of fat from skillet. Sauté onion, garlic, tomato and bell pepper for 2 minutes until soft. Stir in *recaíto*, brown sugar and eggplant. Simmer for 10 minutes.

3. Return pork to skillet and stir in beer. Cover and simmer over low heat for 1 ½ to 2 hours until pork is tender. Sauce should be rich and thick. Serve with hot white rice and a green salad.

**Yield: 6 servings**

# LOW-CARB Hot and Spicy Pork Tenderloin

Puerto Ricans love their garlic. You can buy it at the local supermarket, already peeled, packed in oil, in huge, huge jars. I watched my friend Griselle, anoint a pork leg with what must have been a ½ pound of minced garlic. The aroma was out of this world. So was our breath.

3 tablespoons vegetable oil

2 tablespoons fresh lemon or

lime juice or cider vinegar

6 garlic cloves, minced

¼ cup minced onion

1 teaspoon freshly cracked
   black pepper

1 teaspoon salt

½ teaspoon cumin

½ teaspoon allspice

| 1 tablespoon freshly grated ginger root | ½ teaspoon oregano |
|---|---|
| 1 tablespoon hot chili pepper sauce | ¼ teaspoon ground rosemary |
| 1 tablespoon Splenda® | 1 ½ pounds pork tenderloin |

1. Combine vegetable oil, citrus juice, garlic, ginger, onion, pepper sauce, Splenda®, black pepper, salt, cumin, allspice, oregano and rosemary in a small bowl.

2. Rub tenderloin with three-quarters of garlic mixture, reserving the remainder. Place in a non-reactive bowl, cover and refrigerate overnight.

3. Preheat oven to 325°F. Lightly spray a roasting pan with vegetable spray.

4. Transfer marinated tenderloin to roasting pan. Bake for 45 minutes, or until a meat thermometer inserted in center reads 155°. Remove from oven.

5. Heat remaining marinade in a small saucepan over moderate heat. Sauté for 5 minutes until onions are soft, adding a couple tablespoons of water if needed.

6. Thinly slice pork and divide between four plates. Top with marinade.

**Yield: 4 servings**

EACH SERVING PROVIDES APPROXIMATELY:
265 calories, **4 grams of carbohydrates**, 38 grams of protein, 15 grams of fat

# LOW-CARB Orange and Jalapeño Marinated Flank Steak

The addition of orange zest and jalapeño peppers blend nicely with the smoky flavor of the rum.

| 1/4 cup fresh orange juice | 2 tablespoons Puerto Rican rum |
|---|---|
| 2 tablespoons fresh lime or lemon juice | 1 teaspoon salt |
| ½ teaspoon orange zest | ½ teaspoon freshly cracked |
| 2 jarred jalapeño peppers, minced | black pepper |
| 2 tablespoons minced yellow onion | ½ teaspoon cumin |
| 2 tablespoons minced red bell pepper | ¼ teaspoon coriander |
| ½ teaspoon ground oregano | 4 cloves garlic, minced |
| 1 tablespoon Splenda® | 2 tablespoons olive oil |
| 1 1 ½ pound flank steak. | |

1. Combine orange orange juice, lime juice, zest, jalapeños, onion, bell pepper, garlic, olive oil, rum, salt, black pepper, cumin, coriander, oregano and Splenda® in a shallow glass dish large enough for the flank steak. Cover and marinate overnight in the refrigerator.

2. Preheat broiler. Lightly spray a broiler pan with vegetable spray.

3. Transfer steak to broiler four inches from heat source. Broil 4 to 5 minutes on each side until desired doneness is attained.

4. Slice steak against grain (or it will be tough) into thin slices. Divide equally between four plates.

**Yield: 4 servings**

EACH SERVING PROVIDES APPROXIMATELY:
340 calories, 7 **grams of carbohydrates**, 37 grams of protein, 19 grams of fat

# LOW-CARB Garlic and Ginger Lamb

Lamb chops are lovely on their own, but Anna's aunt Doritza introduced me to this piquant island version.

**1 teaspoon whole black peppercorns**

**2 garlic cloves, coarsely chopped**

**1 tablespoon minced yellow onion**

**1 tablespoon olive oil**

**1 ½ pounds lamp chop (cut of your choice)**

**1 tablespoon grated ginger**

**2 *culantro* (see index)**
   **leaves, shredded, or**
   **1 tablespoon shredded cilantro**

1. Pound the peppercorns and garlic in a mortar and pestle. Add salt, onion, ginger, cilantro and olive oil until a smooth paste is attained. Rub paste onto both sides of lamb chops. Place in a non-reactive bowl, cover and refrigerate overnight.

2. Preheat broiler. Lightly spray a broiler pan with vegetable spray.

3. Place chops four inches from heat source. Broil 7 minutes on each side, or until a meat thermometer reads 150° to 160°F according to degree of doneness desired.

4. Divide chops between four plates.

**Yield: 4 servings**

EACH SERVING PROVIDES APPROXIMATELY:
189 calories, **2 grams of carbohydrates**, 25 grams of protein, 12 grams of fat

# LOW-CARB Creamy Curried Pork with Coconut

Hard to believe this is a low-carb recipe.

| | |
|---|---|
| **2 teaspoons curry powder** | **2 tablespoons heavy cream** |
| **½ teaspoon cumin** | **2 tablespoons water** |
| **1 tablespoon olive oil** | **1 teaspoon salt** |
| **2 tablespoons minced onion** | **½ teaspoon freshly cracked** |
| **1 teaspoon freshly grated ginger root** | **black pepper** |
| **2 tablespoons unsweetened coconut milk** | **1  1 ½ pound pork tenderloin** |

1. Toast curry powder and cumin lightly in a medium skillet over moderate heat until lightly toasted, about 2 minutes. Stir in olive oil, onion and ginger, sautéing for 2 minutes until onions are soft. Stir in coconut milk, heavy cream, water, salt and pepper. Remove from heat.

2. Drizzle marinade over pork and refrigerate several hours.

3. Preheat oven to 325°F. Lightly spray a shallow pan with vegetable spray.

4. Transfer tenderloin to pan, reserving marinade. Bake for 45 minutes, basting every 15 minutes. Cook until a meat thermometer inserted in center reads about 155°F. Remove pork from oven and allow to rest 10 minutes on a cutting board.

5. Slice thinly and divide between four plates. Stir remaining marinade in pan, whisking up any brown bits. Drizzle over pork.

**Yield: 4 servings**

EACH SERVING PROVIDES APPROXIMATELY:
295 calories, **6 grams carbohydrates**, 37 grams of protein, 12 grams of fat

# Flans, Custards, Puddings and Trifles

**P**uerto Rico has an incredibly varied selection of decadently rich flans and custards. It's no surprise as each wave of immigrants, Spanish, Danish, French and English, contributed recipes from their home country. Luscious tropical fruits, eggs from free-range hens, locally grown sugar cane and aromatic spices, inspired many new variations on old favorites.

This chapter contains a range of velvety desserts meant to be eaten with a spoon—everything from the island's most popular dessert, *flan*, to *tembleque*, a coconut custard to *islas flotante* (floating islands), a meringue garnished dessert.

Most custard or *flan* recipes call for eggs to provide thickness. Logically then, bread or rice provide the thickening agent (starch) for bread or rice pudding. Anna and I discovered, after many hours and *flans* served to my cat, Tasuki, that how the eggs are cooked makes a huge difference between a smooth custard and one that is lumpy and full of bits of 'scrambled eggs'.

Most *flans* are made from eggs and some type of milk: cream, half-and-half, or evaporated milk (popular in Puerto Rico and other southern Latin countries). The use of tinned or evaporated milk dates back to the days when it was difficult to keep fresh milk from spoiling.

As the *flan* is heated, protein molecules contributed by the eggs begin to unfold and stretch out. Picture a nest of pasta (a clump, not the straight kind in rectangular packages), dropped into hot water, unfurling its strands. The heat causes the protein molecules to bond with each other. In the process, water is trapped between them and the *flan* thickens. If *flan* is cooked to quickly, the protein molecules, instead of bonding at a leisurely pace, bond in a rapid, haphazard manner and form lumps, i.e. scrambled eggs—resulting in a grainy, lumpy custard. Anna told me this is why she always strains her flan. But why not get it right the first time I wondered?

Our goal was a *flan* that was fragrant, creamy, smooth, firm, but would still jiggle like Jello® when shaken. We also wanted a recipe that would not require two hours of kitchen time. After trying endless variations, we came up with recipe, *Perfect Flan*. The ingredient list was short, and the cooking technique simple and pared down.

For the purists, we included numerous *flan* recipes utilizing traditional Puerto Rican cooking methods and ingredients. But cooking is a science, which progresses over time, and we suggest that you give our *flan* recipe a try.

Anna and I consulted about two dozen recipes. No two were alike! Some called for yolks only or whole eggs, white or brown sugar and all sorts of milks, whole, light cream, heavy cream or evaporated milk. We discovered the most important things were the cooking method, time and temperature, the proportion of egg whites to yolks and the sort of dairy used.

We began with the ever popular Puerto Rican combination of whole milk, evaporated milk and sweetened condensed milk combined with sugar. We scalded the mixture and cooled it to room temperature. The eggs were then lightly beaten and poured into the scalded milk mixture. We then tried numerous cooking methods, which we will discuss shortly.

The *flan* made with the evaporated, sweetened and condensed, and whole milk was too rich and cloying on the tongue. Next we tried whole milk which produced a watery *flan*. Heavy cream by itself tasted like lard to us. While *flan* is not for the waistline conscious, we didn't feel like clogging our arteries unnecessarily. Half light cream and half whole milk was a lovely compromise, which resulted in a perfect, medium body custard.

Some recipes insisted that the perfect *flan* results from egg yolks only being used. Egg whites coagulate at a lower temperature than egg yolks and produce lumpy custard. This was not the case once we found once the proper cooking technique was employed. We tried recipes with whole eggs and an equal addition of egg whites added. While this *flan* unmolded beautifully, it was rubbery and needed to be eaten with a knife and fork. Too few egg whites, and the custard collapsed when unmolded—more *flan* for the cat. Finally we decided that four whole eggs and two yolks was an excellent combination.

Four different cooking techniques were employed: on top of the stove; on top of the stove in a double boiler, in the oven and in the oven in a water bath, called a *bain-marie*.

We quickly realized that the secret to creamy *flan* is slow, low and even heat. *Flans* heated too quickly, the protein molecules attach to each other in clumps-hence curdling. This happens when the *flan* reaches 185 degrees or more. When eggs are not heated slowly, they won't begin to thicken until around 170 degrees or higher—which brings you dangerously close to that 185 degree curdling temperature. Very little room for error here. However, when eggs are heated at a leisurely pace, thickening will begin at a lower temperature, around 150 degrees.

Even with a commercial gas range set on the lowest setting, it was nearly impossible to control the heat on a pan set directly on a burner. A stove top heats the eggs so quickly, they have little time to thicken before curdling. We thought we could solve this problem by using a double boiler. Since all the heat comes from the bottom, we had to stir the *flan* constantly to maintain an even temperature. This in effect ruined the eggs, keeping the protein molecules from bonding. We ended up with a thin custard—not at all what we wanted.

Then we poured the *flan* into individual ramekins and placed them on a glass baking dish in a 375° oven. It was like eating rubbery eggs. Water was then added to the glass baking dish, two-thirds up the side of the ramekins. Figuring that slower and lower heat was better, we reduced the temperature to 350° and extending the cooking time to 45 minutes.

We also played around with the temperature of the cream. A number of traditional Puerto Rican recipes call for scalding the dairy product—and we've left these recipes as is. However, recalling that heating the eggs too quickly results in a lumpy mess, we began with chilled cream and got a smooth, lump-free custard.

We've tried to keep this cookbook as time-honored and traditional as possible. Try the conventional *flan* recipes, such as *Traditional Flan I* and *Traditional Flan II* first. Then prepare the *Perfect Flan* recipe and compare the results.

# Traditional Flan I
*Flan Tradicionale I*

Technically speaking, a flan is an open tart with a sweet or tangy filling. But, in Puerto Rico, and in other Latin countries, *flan* is a baked custard. Often cooked in a *baine-marie*, the custard is poured into a mold, then placed and cooked in a pan of hot water reaching halfway up the sides of the mold.

**GLAZING CARAMEL**

**1 cup white granulated sugar**

**FLAN**

**1 cup whole milk**

**1 cup evaporated milk**

**1 cup sweetened condensed milk**

**¾ cup white granulated sugar**

**½ teaspoon salt**

**7 whole large eggs at room**
  **temperature, plus 1 additional yolk,**

**2 teaspoons vanilla extract**

**¼ teaspoon ground cinnamon**

**¼ teaspoon ground nutmeg**

1. *Glazing caramel*: place the 1 cup sugar in a heavy skillet over low heat. Stir continuously with a wooden spoon until sugar melts. Continue to stir and cook until sugar darkens. Do not make too dark as this imparts a bitter taste.

2. Pour caramel into 8 to 10 heat-resistant custard molds or ramekins. Tip the sides if desired, ensuring that caramel coats evenly. Set aside to cool.

3. Preheat oven to 350°. Add water to *baine-marie* mold or a large glass baking dish so that water reaches 2/3 up the sides of *flan* molds. Place in oven to begin heating water.

4. Whisk together milks, sugar and salt in a saucepan. Do not allow to foam. Scald over medium high heat. Do not boil. Remove from heat and set aside. Allow to cool to nearly room temperature.

5. Beat eggs and yolks lightly in a medium bowl. Do not allow to foam as this will result in a sandy-textured flan. Add scalded milk and strain for lumps.

6. Fold in vanilla, cinnamon and nutmeg. Pour into caramelized mold and set in the pan of hot water in oven.

7. Bake for 45 minutes until done. Flan that is done will jiggle like Jello® when done.

8. Remove from oven and pan of water. Cool for 2 hours before serving. Refrigerate covered.

9. To serve, invert onto a serving dish.

**Yield: 8 to 10 servings**

## Caramel

Sugar, heated, will turn to caramel, first a light golden color, then brown, then black (overdone). The darker the caramel, the more intense the flavor.

**Correct temperature:** For best results, use a candy thermometer between 320°F for a light flavor, 350°F for a deeper, more intense flavor.

**Even cooking:** Begin with low heat, and no stirring, until sugar has completely melted. Bring to a boil only after the sugar has melted. Do not stir once boiling has commenced. Shake pan back and forth while cooking. Once cooked, remove from heat and transfer to a clean, heat proof container. Place over a simmer pot of hot water to keep warm.

> **Caramelizing molds:** When glazing custard ramekins or molds, have a bowl of ice water on hand in case any of the melted sugar should spill on your hand. Anna and I discovered it's not necessary to tip and coat the sides of the molds. Dangerous at best. Once I ended up with a scorch mark on my stomach. Just pour a little extra caramel into the bottom of the ramekin. When the *flan* is inverted, it will run down the sides anyway.
>
> **Clean up:** Always the fun part. Do not let caramel cool and harden in pan. If it does, add water to pan and simmer over low heat.

## Traditional Flan II

Successfully substitute regular lime for the key lime.

**GLAZING CARAMEL:**

**1 cup granulated sugar**

**FLAN**

**6 large eggs, plus 6 yolks**

**3 cups whole milk**

**1 cup, plus 1 tablespoon granulated sugar**

**½ teaspoon salt**

**1 teaspoon grated zest of key lime**

**1 teaspoon vanilla extract**

1. Follow the glazing caramel instructions per *Traditional Flan I*, numbers 1 and 2.

2. Whisk whole eggs and yolk in medium bowl for 1 minute until just thickened. Add sugar and salt, stirring until dissolved. Beat in whole milk a little at a time. Whisk in lime zest and vanilla.

3. Pour mixture in caramelized ramekins or molds. Place in warm water bath in oven. Bake uncovered until *flan* is set, about 45 minutes.

4. Remove from oven and allow to cool for 2 hours before refrigerating. Chill in refrigerator, covered.

5. To serve, turn over custards onto a platter that will hold the liquefied caramel.

**Yield: 8 to 10 servings**

## Perfect Flan

Anna and I love the simplicity of this recipe. Traditional Puerto Rican recipes often call for one large flan. Small individual servings cook much faster and evenly.

GLAZING CARAMEL:

**1 cup sugar**

FLAN:

**4 whole large eggs, plus 2 yolks**

**2/3 cup, plus 1 tablespoon granulated sugar**

**¼ teaspoon salt**

**1 ½ cups whole milk**

**1 ½ cup light cream**

**1 teaspoon grated zest of key lime or lime**

**1 teaspoon vanilla extract**

1. Prepare caramel and glaze custard ramekins or molds as indicated in steps 1, 2 and 3 of *Traditional Flan I*.

2. Whisk whole eggs and yolks together in medium bowl. Stir in sugar and salt until dissolved. Gradually pour in whole milk and light cream. Stir in lime zest and vanilla extract.

3. Pour into prepared custard molds and place in water bath in oven. Cover pan loosely with aluminum foil and bake 35 to 45 minutes.

4. Test for doneness by jiggling baking dish. *Flan* should wiggle like Jello® and thin-blade knife inserted in center should come out nearly clean. Transfer *flan* to wire rack to cool for 2 hours. Cover with plastic wrap and refrigerate successfully for up to 2 days.

5. To unfold, run a wet knife around perimeter of each custard. Hold an individual serving plate, which can hold liquefied caramel, over top of custard and invert.

**Yield: 8 to 10 servings**

# Evaporated Milk Custard

*Flan de Leche Evaporada*

The use of evaporated milk in Latin and other southern countries has always been popular, historically due to lack of refrigeration. This flan recipe calls for only evaporated milk. No whole milk or cream whatsoever. Rich and dense to the palate and worth the effort.

**GLAZING CARAMEL:**

**1 cup sugar**

**FLAN:**

**6 eggs, plus 1 yolk**

**1 (13 ounce) can evaporated milk**

**1 teaspoon vanilla extract**

**1 cup sugar**

**¼ teaspoon sea salt**

1. Preheat oven to 350°. Fill a large shallow glass baking dish with hot water and place in oven.

2. Prepare caramel and glaze custard ramekins or molds as indicated in steps 1, 2 and 3 of *Traditional Flan I*.

3. Break eggs in a medium saucepan and lightly whisk in extra egg yolk, evaporated milk, vanilla, 1 cup sugar and salt.

4. Strain into caramelized custard molds. Carefully slide out glass baking dish and place custard molds in hot water bath. Bake 1 hour. Custards will be golden. Remove from hot water.

5. Cool custard molds on wire rack. Cover with plastic wrap and refrigerate until ready to serve.

6. To unfold, run a wet knife around perimeter of each custard. Hold an individual serving plate, which can hold liquefied caramel, over top of custard and invert.

**Yield: 8 servings**

## TIP—Eggs

- Store eggs in their carton. This keeps them from losing moisture and absorbing other smells.

- Keep eggs cool and fresher longer by storing on a refrigerator shelf, which is cooler than the door.

- To test for freshness, place a whole egg in a shallow pan of water. A fresh egg will sink to the bottom and stay there. A week-old egg will sink to the bottom, but bob a bit. A 3 week-old egg will stand on end; a rotten one will float on the surface.

- To remove an egg that is stuck to the carton, fill the slot with cool water and wait for 5 or 6 minutes. Remove egg.

# Almond Flan

*Flan de Almendras*

This is a nice alternative to heavy ice creams and cakes for dessert.

**1 cup granulated sugar to caramelize a mold**

**4 whole eggs, plus 2 yolks**

**¾ cup granulated sugar**

**¼ teaspoon salt**

**1 ½ cups whole milk**

**1 ½ cups light cream**

**1 teaspoon grated lime peel**

**½ cup ground almonds (process into powder in food processor or grinder)**

1. Caramelize a flan mold or 8 individual ramekins as instructed in *Traditional Flan I*, steps 1, 2 and 3.

2. Whisk whole eggs and yolks in medium bowl until slightly thickened. Stir in sugar and salt until dissolved.

3. Slowly pour in whole milk and light cream, combining well. Fold in grated lime peel and powdered almonds.

4. Pour into caramelized mold(s) and place in hot water bath in oven. Cover loosely with foil and bake individual ramekins for 45 minutes, or large *flan* mold for 1 ¼ hours or until a cake tester inserted in center comes out clean.

5. Remove from oven and cool on wire rack for 2 hours. Refrigerate covered with plastic rack for up to 2 days.

6. Serve by inverting custard cups onto a serving dish that will hold liquefied caramel.

**Yield: 8 servings**

# Pumpkin Flan
*Flan de Calabaza*

Flan made with West Indian pumpkin results in a surprisingly elegant and delicious dessert.

**GLAZING CARAMEL:**

**¾ cup granulated sugar**

**FLAN:**

**1 ½ pounds pumpkin, peeled, seeded and cubed in 1-inch pieces**

**½ teaspoon salt**

**1 12-ounce can evaporated milk**

**1 14-ounce can sweetened condensed milk**

**2 teaspoons vanilla extract**

**½ teaspoon ground cinnamon**

**½ teaspoon ground ginger**

**4 eggs, room temperature**

1. Glaze a 7- to 9-inch *flan* or custard mold with caramel, using the ¾ cup granulated sugar, as instructed in Traditional Flan I. Set aside.

2. Fill a large pot 2/3 full of water and the ½ teaspoon of salt. Bring to boil. Add pumpkin and cook until soft, about 15 to 20 minutes. Drain water and puree in food processor or place in large bowl and mash by hand. Set aside.

3. Preheat oven to 325°. Fill a large glass baking dish with enough water to reach 2/3 up the sides of *flan* mold. Place in oven to heat water.

4. Beat eggs lightly in another large bowl. Whisk in milks and vanilla without frothing. Fold in cinnamon and ginger. Add eggs one at a time. Fold in pumpkin.

5. Spoon *flan* mixture into mold. Set in water bath in oven.

6. Bake for 1 hour or until *flan* jiggles like jelly in mold.

7. Cool to room temperature. Run a wet knife around rim of custard and invert onto a serving dish. Slice into wedges to serve.

**Yield: 8 to 10 servings**

# Sweet Potato Flan
*Flan de Batata*

Very similar to pumpkin flan, just a bit drier. Use fresh grated ginger instead of ground for a nice bite.

**1 cup granulated sugar to caramelize a flan mold**

**1 pound sweet potatoes, peeled and quartered**

**¾ teaspoon salt**

**1 tablespoon freshly grated ginger root**

**¼ teaspoon ground cinnamon**

**¼ teaspoon ground cloves**

**½ teaspoon ground nutmeg**

**1 ½ teaspoons vanilla extract**

**8 large eggs, slightly beaten**

**2 tablespoons gold rum**

**1 ½ cups whole milk**

1. Caramelize a 7- to 9-inch flan or custard mold as per the Basic Vanilla Flan recipe. Set aside.

2. Place sweet potato in large pot and cover with water. Add salt and bring to a boil until soft, about 15 minutes. Remove from heat and drain.

3. Preheat oven to 325°. Fill a glass baking dish with water to reach 2/3 the height of the flan mold. Place in oven to heat water.

4. Puree sweet potatoes along with ginger, cinnamon, clove, nutmeg and vanilla.

5. Add eggs, rum and milk, processing until smooth.

6. Pour into flan mold and place in hot water bath in oven.

7. Bake for 1 to 1 ½ hours until a toothpick inserted in center comes out clean.

8. Cool for 2 hours then refrigerate covered for several hours.

9. Run a wet knife around rim of flan and invert on a serving platter. Cut into wedges.

**Yield: serves 8 to 10**

## Cheese Flan

*Flan de Queso*

Next to Pumpkin Flan, Cheese Flan is my favorite. I like to serve this with fresh raspberries.

¾ cup sugar to caramelize a mold

4 ounces softened cream cheese
 (room temperature)

½ cup granulated sugar

¼ teaspoon salt

6 ounces evaporated milk

6 ounces sweetened condensed milk

½ cup water

6 large eggs, room temperature

2 teaspoons vanilla extract

½ teaspoon ground ginger

1. Caramelize *flan* mold as instructed in Basic Vanilla Flan recipe. Set aside.
2. Preheat oven to 350°. Fill a large glass baking dish with water to come up 2/3 height of the *flan* mold. Set in oven to heat water.
3. Beat cream cheese and 1/2 cup sugar by hand or with an electric mixer set on low until smooth.
4. Combine salt, milks, water, eggs and vanilla in a separate small bowl. Stir in ginger.
5. Beat milk mixture into cheese mixture. Blend well. Spoon into mold.
6. Place into water bath and bake for 45 minutes. Cover with aluminum foil to prevent excessive browning of top and bake additional 45 minutes. A toothpick inserted in center should come out clean.
7. Cool for 2 hours and then refrigerate.
8. Run a wet knife around rim and invert onto a serving platter. Slice into wedges.

**Yeild: 8 to 10 servings**

# Pineapple Flan
*Flan de Piña*

Refreshing and light.

1 cup granulated sugar to
  caramelize a flan mold
1 cup fresh pineapple chunks
1 12-ounce can evaporated milk
½ cup granulated sugar

6 large eggs, plus 1 yolk, room
  temperature
¼ teaspoon salt
1 teaspoon freshly grated lime zest
  (rind)

1. Caramelize 7- to 9-inch flan mold as per Basic Vanilla Flan recipe. Set aside.

2. Preheat oven to 325°. Fill a glass baking dish with water so that it comes up 2/3 the height of the flan mold.

3. Puree all ingredients, except eggs, in a food processor until smooth. Allow foam to subside. Scoop off any excess. Add eggs, and blend briefly.

4. Strain into flan mold and set into water bath in oven.

5. Bake for 1 to 1 ½ hours until flan is set. Flan is done when it jiggles like Jello™.

6. Allow to cool for at least 2 hours before refrigerating.

7. When ready to serve, slide a wet knife around rim and invert on serving platter. Slice into wedges.

**Yield: 8 to 10 servings**

# Piña Colada Flan
*Flan a la Piña Colada*

Whenever I travel to the rainforest, just above the hamlet of Palmer, I stop at local fruit vendor, next to a gift shop called Louis N Sally, and pick up a fresh pineapple. Puerto Rican pineapples grow abundantly in the island's fertile soil and are exceptionally sweet. Coconut trees are found in nearly every backyard.

1 cup granulated sugar to carmelize flan mold

1 cup unsweetened pineapple juice
(if you can make it fresh yourself,
the effort is well worth it)

1 cup fresh coconut milk  or

1 ½ cups canned unsweetened coconut milk

1 cup granulated sugar

¼ teaspoon salt

9 large eggs, room temperature

¾ cup gold rum (don't use dark,
it will be too heavy)

¼ teaspoon ground nutmeg

1. Caramelize the 7- to 9-inch flan mold with the 1 cup granulated sugar as per instructions in the Basic Vanilla Flan recipe.

2. Preheat oven to 325°. Fill a glass baking dish water to cup up 2/3 the height of the flan mold.

3. Combine pineapple juice, coconut milk, sugar and salt in a medium bowl. Stir well.

4. Beat eggs and add to pineapple juice mixture. Stir in rum and ground nutmeg.

5. Strain into flan mold and spoon off foam. Place in water bath in oven and bake for 1 ½ hours until flan is firm. Flan should jiggle like jelly when done.

6. Cool for at least 2 hours before refrigerating.

7. To serve, run a wet knife around rim and invert onto serving platter. Cut into wedges.

**Yield: 8 to 10 servings**

---

### Did You Know?

Even though **Puerto Rico** has been part of the United States since 1898, if it hadn't been for the recent popularity of Puerto Rican music and film stars, most Americans wouldn't be aware it existed. Puerto Rico is lovely, a miniature Latin America set in America's Caribbean.

# Coconut Flan with Mango Sauce

*Flan de Coco con Salsa de Mango*

While on a photo shoot with my husband (now ex) and photographer Buddy Moffet, we stayed at the El Convento Hotel in Old San Juan. This was before it was remodeled. Buddy and Richard decided to hit the casinos in Isla Verde and I ordered room service. I ordered flan for the first time. The mango sauce served alongside began my love affair with flan.

1 cup granulated sugar to caramelize a mold

1 ¾ cups sugar

1 cup, plus 2 tablespoons water

2 ¼ cups freshly grated coconut

1 teaspoon freshly grated lime zest

9 eggs, room temperature and lightly beaten

2 medium mangoes, peeled, seeded, puréed, and pressed through a sieve to remove strings and fibers

1 tablespoon fresh lime juice

2 tablespoons dark or gold rum

1. Caramelize a 7- to 9-inch flan mold as per Basic Vanilla Flan recipe. Set aside.

2. Place water and sugar in a medium saucepan over high heat and bring to boil for 30 minutes. Mixture should be brought to a thread-stage syrup, about 230° on a candy thermometer. Remove from heat.

3. Preheat oven to 325° and fill a glass baking dish with water to come up 2/3 the height of the flan mold. Place inside oven to heat water.

4. Stir in coconut and lime zest to sugar mixture. Reduce heat enough so that eggs will not curdle when added. Add eggs, combine well, and strain into flan mold.

5. Set in hot water bath in oven and bake for 1 to 1 ½ hours until firm. A toothpick inserted in center will come out clean.

6. Allow to cool for 2 hours. Run a wet knife around rim, then invert on a serving platter.

7. Combine puréed mango, lime juice and rum. Pour over top of flan. Serve at once.

**Yield: 8 to 10 servings**

# Candied Milk

*Leche Costrada*

Quick and easy to make.

| | |
|---|---|
| **4 cups whole milk** | **4 eggs, plus 1 extra yolk** |
| **½ cup sugar** | **1 tablespoon brandy** |
| **½ teaspoon sea salt** | **1 teaspoon vanilla extract butter** |

1. Preheat oven to 350°. Fill a large shallow baking dish with 1-inch of hot water and place in oven. Butter 8 individual custard molds or ramekins.

2. Stir eggs and extra yolk lightly in a heat-proof bowl. Set aside.

3. Whisk together milk, sugar and salt in a large saucepan over medium-high heat. Bring to boil.

4. Pour hot milk mixture over eggs, stirring quickly. Fold in vanilla and brandy.

5. Strain into buttered custard molds. Place into hot water bath and bake 45 minutes, until golden brown and set.

6. Cool on wire baking rack and refrigerate.

7. To unmold, run a wet knife around edge of each custard mold and invert.

**Yield: 8 servings**

# Coconut Custard

*Tembleque*

The word tembleque translates to "shaky". I've had this desert in an Ocean Park (near Isla Verde and Condado in San Juan) restaurant served in a small plastic flower pot with a silk flower inserted in the center. The "soil" on top was made from crushed oreo cookies. This dessert is often served at Christmas.

| | |
|---|---|
| **4 cups fresh coconut milk or** | **2/3 cup sugar** |
| **unsweetened canned coconut milk** | **¾ teaspoon salt** |
| **1 teaspoon vanilla extract** | **6 tablespoons cornstarch ground nutmeg** |

1. Whirl all ingredients in a blender until smooth and free of lumps. Allow foam to subside and scoop off excess.

2. Pour into a medium saucepan and bring to a boil over medium heat.

3. Reduce heat and simmer until thickened, about 3 to 4 minutes. The custard should coat the back of a spoon when ready.

4. Pour into individual custard molds. Sprinkle lightly with nutmeg. Cover snugly with plastic wrap else a skin will form. Refrigerate over night.

**Yield: 6 servings**

## Stovetop Custard

*Natilla*

For an elegant touch, try substituting up to ½ cup *Framboise* (raspberry liqueur) or *Grand Marnier* (orange liqueur) for ½ cup of the whole milk.

| | |
|---|---|
| **6 tablespoons cornstarch** | **1 ½ cups light cream** |
| **½ teaspoon salt** | **1 ½ cups whole milk** |
| **1 cup sugar** | **3 eggs, plus 1 yolk** |

1. Sift together the cornstarch, salt and sugar into a large heavy-bottomed saucepan.

2. Slowly whisk in the whole milk and light cream into cornstarch/sugar mixture, followed by eggs.

3. Cook over medium heat, stirring constantly with whisk, scraping bottom and sides of pot until mixture coats a back of a spoon, about 15 to 20 minutes.

4. Pass custard through fine-mesh strainer into medium bowl. Press with back of large spoon. Discard clumps and residue in strainer.

5. Serve warm or cover surface with plastic wrap to keep skin from forming. Cool for 25 minutes, then refrigerate for up to 2 days.

**Yield: 6 servings**

## TIP—Cornstarch in Custards

♦ Custards made with cornstarch can be heated above 180° without curdling. Starch molecules keep egg protein molecules from clumping together.

♦ Use cornstarch with chocolate or other heavily flavored puddings only. The flavorings mask the cornstarch texture which can become somewhat grainy.

♦ Cornstarch sets custards quite firmly, so is not suitable for *flan*, which needs to be jiggly.

# Chocolate Custard
*Natilla de Chocolate*

Natalie and Tasuki saga continued from *Garlic and Onion Smothered Chicken*. Both the baby, Natalie, and the cat, Tasuki, enjoyed this treat. The chocolate did stain Natalie's cute yellow sundress, and Tasuki would have been fine except for a chocolate moustache thanks to Natalie's chocolate covered hands.

4 eggs, separated

¼ cup flour

2 cups whole milk

2 cups light cream

¾ cup sugar

¼ teaspoon salt

1 teaspoon vanilla extract

2 ounces grated, unsweetened
    chocolate ground cinnamon

1. Make a paste of the eggs yolks and flour, stirring with a small whisk until lump-free. Gradually whisk in 1 cup of the milk.

2. Combine the remaining 1 cup milk and 2 cups light cream with the sugar and salt in a medium saucepan and scald. Allow to cool for 20 minutes and then stir in vanilla extract.

3. Over very low heat, whisk in the egg/flour mixture to the 3 cups scalded milk. Add grated chocolate, cook very slowly, stirring gently until mixture thickens to custard-like texture. Remove from heat and cool to room temperature.

4. Beat egg whites until stiff peaks form. Fold into custard. Spoon into individual custard cups and refrigerate before serving.

5. Sprinkle tops with lightly with ground cinnamon.

## Sweet Potato and Coconut Pudding

Prick the top of this pudding and drizzle with rum. Serve warm with fresh whipped cream.

1 ¼ pounds white sweet potato, peeled and diced butter to grease a mold

2 cups coconut milk (see index)

½ cup granulated sugar

½ cup packed brown sugar

¼ teaspoon sea salt

¼ cup flour

½ teaspoon freshly grated ginger root

¼ teaspoon ground cloves

¼ teaspoon ground nutmeg

¼ teaspoon ground cinnamon

4 tablespoons melted butter

4 large eggs, lightly beaten

¼ cup rum

1. Boil the sweet potatoes in a deep pot for 20 minutes until soft.

2. Remove from water and mash in a large bowl until smooth.

3. Preheat oven to 375°F. Grease an 8- by 8-inch glass baking dish and set aside.

4. Gradually beat the coconut milk into the mashed sweet potatoes. Add sugars, salt, flour, ginger, cloves, nutmeg, cinnamon, and 4 tablespoons melted butter. Combine until smooth.

5. Fold in eggs, combining well. Scrape puree into glass baking dish.

6. Bake for 30 minutes. Reduce heat to 350° and bake additional 20 minutes or until cake tester inserted in center comes out clean.

7. Allow to cool in mold on wire rack for 45 minutes. Prick top of pudding with fork and drizzle the ¼ cup rum over surface. Serve while still warm with fresh, whipped cream.

**Yield: 8 servings**

# Sweet Polenta
*Funche Dulce*

Medium-grind cornmeal makes the best polenta. Finely ground cornmeal, the sort sold in many supermarkets, is too powdery and makes gummy polenta. Look for brands with a texture similar to granulated sugar. To make the smoothest polenta, you'll need a double-boiler.

| | |
|---|---|
| **3 cups boiling water** | **¼ cup seedless raisins** |
| **1 cup hot milk** | **½ cup sugar** |
| **½ teaspoon salt** | **¼ teaspoon cardamom** |
| **1 cup medium-grind cornmeal** | **3 tablespoons butter** |

1. Heat 2 inches of water to a boil in the bottom half of a double boiler. Reduce heat and maintain at a simmer.

2. Set top of double boiler over simmering water, and add the 3 cups boiling water and the 1 cup hot milk. Bring to simmer and stir in salt.

3. Whisk in cornmeal gradually, stirring constantly to avoid lumps. Fold in raisins, sugar and cardamom.

4. Cover and cook until polenta is soft and lump-free, about 1 to 1 ¼ hours, stirring every 15 minutes. Stir in butter when polenta is done. Serve at once.

**Yield: 4 servings**

# Coconut Polenta
*Funche Con Leche de Coco*

Canned, unsweetened coconut milk instead of fresh coconut milk may be substituted.

| | |
|---|---|
| **2 cups boiling water** | **1 cinnamon stick** |
| **2 cups hot coconut milk** | **¼ cup grated coconut (see index or** |
| **1 cup medium-grind polenta (not fine grind)** | **substitute packaged kind)** |
| **½ cup granulated sugar** | |

1. Bring 2 inches of water to a boil in bottom of a double boiler. Reduce heat to a simmer.

2. Add the top to the double boiler. Add boiling water and hot coconut milk and bring to a simmer.

3. Gradually whisking in the polenta, stirring constantly to avoid lump formation.

4. Stir in sugar and add cinnamon stick. Cover and cook until polenta is lump-free and smooth, about 1 to 1 ½ hours.

5. Remove from heat. Remove cinnamon stick and fold in grated coconut. Serve at once.

**Yield: 8 servings**

## Yellow Cornmeal Tembleque

*Tembleque de Maíz*

Serve this dense and rich dessert ideally after a light lunch or dinner.

| | |
|---|---|
| 2 cups coconut milk (see index or use canned) | ¼ teaspoon ground allspice |
| ½ cup sweetened, condensed milk | ¼ teaspoon vanilla extract |
| 1 ¼ cups medium-grind yellow cornmeal | ½ teaspoon salt |
| ½ teaspoon ground cardamom | ½ sugar |

1. Heat coconut milk and condensed milk in medium saucepan over moderate heat, stirring constantly until mixture just begins to boil.

2. Gradually whisk in cornmeal, cardamom, allspice, vanilla, salt and sugar. Stir constantly until mixture simmers and begins to pull away from sides of pan.

3. Pour into buttered 8- by 8-inch glass baking dish and allow to cool 45 minutes. Serve at once.

**Yield: 6 to 8 servings**

## Fried Milk

These slightly chewy squares are delicious with hot coffee and a liqueur after a light dinner.

2/3 cups sugar

½ cup cornstarch

¼ teaspoon ground nutmeg

¼ teaspoon ground cinnamon

2 cups whole milk

1 cup light cream

1 tablespoon butter

1 teaspoon almond extract

1 teaspoon grated lime peel

2 eggs, lightly beaten

¾ plain, dry bread crumbs vegetable
oil for frying powdered sugar

1. Sift sugar, cornstarch, nutmeg and cinnamon into medium saucepan.

2. Gradually whisk in whole milk and light cream. Bring to a boil over medium heat for 1 minute. Mixture should be thickened.

3. Remove from heat, stir in butter, almond extract and lime peel. Pour into ungreased 8- by 8-inch glass baking dish and refrigerate until firm.

4. Pour 1-inch of vegetable oil into deep fryer and heat until oil is hot, but not smoking.

5. Cut into 2-inch squares. Dip squares into beaten eggs, then roll in bread crumbs. Fry quickly until golden. Make sure oil is hot enough, or squares will absorb excessive amounts of oil.

6. Drain on white paper towels and roll in powdered sugar.

**Yield: 8 servings**

# Whipped Cream Dessert

Definitely not for the carb, fat or calorie conscious!

5 egg yolks

¾ cup sugar

½ cup shortening

1 ¾ cups flour

1 tablespoon, plus 1 teaspoon cocoa powder

3 teaspoon baking powder

1 ground cinnamon

¾ cup milk

5 egg whites

1. Beat egg yolks with sugar until light. Cream in shortening. Sift together flour, cocoa powder, baking powder and cinnamon.

2. Preheat oven to 350°.

3. Beat egg whites until stiff, but dry.

4. Whisk in milk slowly. Fold in beaten egg whites.

5. Grease a 9- by 12-inch baking dish. Bake 40 minutes until firm.

6. Cool for 1 hour and serve with fresh whipped cream.

**Yield: 6 servings**

# Floating Islands

*Islas Flotante*

This dessert takes a little extra time to make, but is well worth the effort. Drizzle with Cointreau liqueur for extra panache.

CUSTARD:

| | |
|---|---|
| **2 tablespoons, plus 1 teaspoon cornstarch** | **½ teaspoon salt** |
| **3 cups whole milk** | **¾ cup sugar** |
| **3 cups light cream** | **1 teaspoon almond extract** |
| **6 eggs, separated** | **½ teaspoon ground cinnamon** |

MERINGUE

| | |
|---|---|
| **6 egg whites, reserved from custard ingredients** | **1 tablespoon fresh lime juice** |
| **1 cup sugar** | **1 teaspoon grated lime zest** |

1. Sift cornstarch into medium bowl. Add a small amount of milk and stir, combining well. Beat in the 6 egg yolks and set aside.

2. Stir remaining milk and light cream along with salt, sugar, almond extract and cinnamon in medium saucepan. Bring to a boil over medium heat, stirring occasionally.

3. Slowly add egg yolk/milk mixture to saucepan. Reduce heat and continue to stir with wooden spoon until custard boils.

4. Strain through a mesh sieve into 12 individual custard cups.

5. Beat the 5 egg whites until stiff. Slowly whip in sugar, lime juice and lime rind. Beat until glossy stiff peaks form.

6. Garnish each custard cup with generous dollop of meringue. Chill at least 3 hours in refrigerator before serving.

**Yield: 12 servings**

# Cazuela

This was a very interesting and delicious dessert to make. It contains pumpkin, sweet potatoes, ginger, cinnamon and anise combined with fresh coconut milk—a heady combination.

Anna explained to me that a *cazuela* is an earthenware pot or casserole used to cook food. The clay actually imparts an earthenware taste to food. I know that certain health food aficionados advocate eating clay for its vital minerals and health benefits. Perhaps cooking in a clay pot does the same. Let's hope.

2 pounds pumpkin or butternut squash, peeled, seeded and cut into 2-inch cubes

2 pounds sweet potatoes, peeled, seeded and cut into 2-inch cubes

1 tablespoon salt

½ cup water

1 tablespoon freshly grated ginger

1 teaspoon freshly grated lime zest

1 teaspoon star anise or ½ teaspoon ground anise

1 cinnamon stick

4 whole cloves

¼ teaspoon ground nutmeg

6 tablespoon butter, softened

4 large eggs, beaten

1 ½ cups, plus 1 tablespoon sugar

5 tablespoons all-purpose flour

1 cup fresh coconut milk

1 teaspoon vanilla extract

1 teaspoon sea salt

¼ teaspoon black pepper

2 tablespoons butter plantain leaves (substitute parchment if not available), washed and patted dry

1. Fill a large pot with pumpkin and sweet potato. Fill and cover with water and the 1 tablespoon salt. Cover and bring to a boil over medium heat for 35 minutes or until vegetables are soft. Drain water.

2. Stir together the ½ cup water, ginger, lime zest, anise, cinnamon, cloves, and ground nutmeg in a small saucepot. Cover, bring to boil, reduce heat and simmer for 5 minutes. Strain through a mesh sieve. Reserve liquid and discard spices.

3. Mash slightly cooled pumpkin and sweet potato by hand. Stir in reserved spice liquid.

4. Fold in butter, eggs, and sugar. Whisk in flour, coconut milk, vanilla, salt and black pepper.

5. Preheat oven to 350°F.

6. Butter an 8- to 10-inch earthenware casserole dish with 1 tablespoon of the butter. Line the dish with the plantain leaves, buttering these as well.

7. Scoop pumpkin mixture onto leaves, cover loosely with foil and bake for 1 ½ hours.

8. Cool on wire rack for 2 hours. Invert on serving dish, removing plantain leaves.

**Yield: 12 servings**

# Bread Pudding

*Budín de Pan Sencillo*

Recipes for bread pudding are found all over Europe, especially England. Use French loaf bread (not the chewy kind with a tough crust) or white, American loaf bread from the bakery. The fine, dense texture of these two breads holds up well during cooking. Stale or fresh makes virtually no difference. This recipe yields a crisp, crunchy top and thick, silky custard.

5 large eggs, plus 2 yolks

2/3 cups sugar

2 cups whole milk

2 cups light cream

¼ cup dark rum

1 tablespoon vanilla extract

1 pound American or French style loaf bread, cut in 1-inch cubes

2 tablespoons melted butter butter for greasing a pan

3 tablespoons sugar

½ teaspoon ground cinnamon

¼ teaspoon ground ginger fresh whipped cream or vanilla ice cream

½ teaspoon salt

1. Preheat oven to 325°, placing oven to middle position. Butter a 9- by 13-inch glass baking dish and set aside.

2. Beat eggs lightly. Whisk in sugar, milk, cream, rum, vanilla extract and salt.

3. Line bottom of baking dish with two-thirds of the bread cubes. Pour egg/milk mixture over top, tossing gently to coat well. Let sit for 15 minutes.

4. Press remaining bread cubes over top, and push down. Some of the bread cubes will remain dry. Drizzle melted butter over top.

5. Mix the 3 tablespoons sugar with the cinnamon and ginger. Sprinkle over top of bread cubes.

6. Bake for 45 minutes until pudding is golden. Remove from oven and cool on wire rack for 35 minutes. Serve warm with whipped cream or vanilla ice cream.

**Yield: 8 to 10 servings**

## Coconut Bread Pudding
*Budín de Pasas con Coco*

Top with fresh, sliced mango and homemade whipped cream.

*glazing caramel:*

**1 cup sugar**
**6 tablespoons butter, melted**
**1 cup sugar**
**1 ½ cups coconut milk (see index or use canned)**
**½ cup sweetened, condensed milk**
**4 eggs, plus 2 yolks**

**1 pound firm, dense white bread, cut in 1 ½-inch cubes**
**½ teaspoon ground ginger**
**½ teaspoon ground cinnamon**
**¼ teaspoon allspice**
**1 cup whole milk**
**¼ cup unsweetened grated coconut**

1. Preheat oven to 375°F. Fill a large shallow baking pan with hot water and place in oven

2. Glaze an 8- by 8-inch glass baking dish with caramel using the 1 cup sugar and following instruction for *Traditional Flan I* steps 1 and 2, substituting the glass baking dish for the individual custard molds.

3. Combine coconut and condensed milk in a large bowl. Gradually beat in eggs and yolks.

4. Stir in butter, sugar, ginger, cinnamon, allspice and milk. Gently toss in ¾ of the bread cubes and allow to soak for 20 minutes. Add grated coconut and mix gently.

5. Scoop mixture into caramelized glass baking dish. Place dish in pan filled with hot water and bake for 2 hours, until firm. Remove baking dish from water.

6. Cool on wire rack for 45 minutes. Invert onto serving platter.

**Yield: 6 servings**

# Guava Bread Pudding

*Budín de Pan y Guayaba*

The fruit of the guava tree, native to tropical America, is part of the myrtle family, along with cinnamon, nutmeg and eucalyptus. It has a perfumey fragrance and a slight acid taste, making it a light and refreshing fruit. Guava is popular in many desserts in Puerto Rico.

3 cups whole milk

1 cups heavy cream

4 tablespoons butter

2 cups sugar

6 egg yolks, reserving whites
  for meringue

6 whole eggs

1 tablespoon dark rum

½ teaspoon salt

1 pound good quality white
  American loaf bread, crust
  trimmed and cut in 1-inch cubes

1 pound canned or jarred guava
  paste

6 egg whites

½ cup sugar

1.  Preheat oven to 275°. Grease a 13- by 9-inch glass baking dish generously with butter.

2.  Bring milk and heavy cream to a boil in medium saucepan. Remove from heat at once and stir in butter and sugar.

3.  Beat the 6 eggs yolks along with the 6 whole eggs slightly. Add rum and salt. Gradually pour into milk mixture.

4.  Line glass baking dish with bread cubes and pour milk/egg mixture over top. Bake 1 ½ hours. Remove from oven, but leave oven on.

5.  Slice guava paste into thin slices and arrange over top of pudding.

6.  Beat egg white until stiff, slowly whisking in the ½ cup sugar. Spoon over guava slice and return to oven. Bake for additional 30 minutes.

7.  Cool on wire rack. May be served with scoop of vanilla ice cream on side.

**Yield: 8 servings**

# Bread Pudding with Fruit Cocktail

Anna's uncle, Carlos, makes this bread pudding on birthdays, holidays and other special occasions.

| | |
|---|---|
| 1 tablespoon butter | 1 tablespoon dark rum |
| ½ cup whole milk | ½ teaspoon freshly grated ginger |
| ½ cup light cream | 1 pound firm, white sliced bread, |
| ½ cup coconut milk, unsweetened |   cut in 1-inch cubes |
|   fresh or canned | 2 cups fruit cocktail, drained |
| 4 eggs, lightly beaten |     fresh whipped cream |
| ½ cup sugar | |

1. Preheat oven to 350°F. Grease a 9-inch glass baking dish with the 1 tablespoon butter.
2. Whisk together the whole milk, cream and coconut milk. Gradually add the eggs, sugar, rum and ginger.
3. Line the bottom of the baking dish with the bread cubes. Pour milk/egg mixture over top. Fold in fruit cocktail.
4. Cover loosely with foil and bake for 30 minutes. Remove foil and bake for additional 15 minutes. Serve with fresh whipped cream.

**Yield: 8 to 10 servings**

# Bread Pudding with Rum

*Budín con Ron*

Avoid crusty French breads as they don't soften in the custard. A firm and dense, white American bread works best. Lovely topped with fresh, whipped cream. The crust remains crunchy in this recipe by reserving two cups of the cubed bread and pressing on top of the pudding shortly before baking.

**CINNAMON SUGAR:**

| | |
|---|---|
| 3 tablespoons white granulated sugar | ½ teaspoon ground cinnamon |

**CARAMALIZING GLAZE:**

**1 cup sugar**

**PUDDING:**

**4 large eggs, plus 2 yolks**

**¾ cup sugar**

**2 ¼ cups whole milk**

**2 ¼ cups heavy cream**

**1/3 cup light or gold rum**

**½ teaspoon vanilla extract**

**¼ teaspoon cardamom**

**¼ teaspoon nutmeg**

**½ teaspoon sea salt**

**8 cups bread cubes (about ½ loaf dense, firm white bread, cut in 1 ½-inch squares)**

**½ cup chopped seedless raisins**

**2 tablespoons unsalted, melted butter**

1. Caramelize a 13 × 9-inch glass baking dish following instructions for *Traditional Flan I* steps 1 and 2, substituting the large glass baking dish for the individual flan molds. Set aside.

2. For the cinnamon sugar, mix the 3 tablespoons granulated sugar with the ½ teaspoon ground cinnamon in small bowl or cup and set aside.

3. Preheat oven to 325º.

4. Whisk eggs, plus extra yolks and sugar in large bowl until fluffy. Whip in milk, cream, rum, vanilla, cardamom, nutmeg and salt.

5. Carefully fold in 6 cups of the bread cubes and the ½ cup of the raisins to soak up milk/rum mixture. Let sit for 15 minutes.

6. Scoop soaked bread cubes into caramelized glass baking dish. Gently press remaining 2 cups of bread cubes onto top of pudding, partially submerging.

7. Drizzle melted butter over top of pudding and sprinkle with cinnamon sugar.

8. Bake for 1 hour, then raise the oven temperature to 375º, baking for additional 10 minutes until golden brown. Pudding should puff slightly and jiggle in center when shaken.

9. Allow to cool on wire rack for 30 minutes. Serve while still warm with fresh whipped cream or vanilla ice cream.

**Yield: 8 to 10 servings**

# Spanish Toast with Rum

*Torrejas con Ron*

Instead of plain French toast, serve this Latin version (with its extra kick from rum) for Sunday or holiday brunch.

2 large eggs

1 ¾ cups milk

¼ cup light or gold rum

1 teaspoon vanilla extract

4 tablespoons sugar

½ teaspoon ground cinnamon

2 tablespoon all-purpose flour

½ teaspoon salt

10 to 12 slices firm, day-old French or Italian bread, cut ¾-inch thick slices

unsalted butter for skillet

1. Heat a 10- to 12-inch cast iron skillet over moderate heat for 5 minutes.
2. Beat eggs in shallow cake or pie dish. Whisk in milk, rum, vanilla, sugar, cinnamon, flour and salt until no lumps remain.
3. Soak slices of bread 30 seconds on each side. Set aside.
4. Melt 1 tablespoon butter in heated skillet. Add bread slices and fry until golden, turning once. Add additional butter as needed.
5. Serve at once.

**Yield: 10 to 12 slices**

# Simple Rice Pudding

*Arroz con Leche*

Use medium grain rice for this pudding. Long-grain, however, will do in a pinch.

1 cup medium grain rice

¼ teaspoon sea salt

4 cups whole milk

1 cup light cream

2/3 cup granulated sugar

1 teaspoon vanilla extract

1 3-inch cinnamon stick

1. Bring 2 cups of water and the ¼ teaspoon of sea salt to a boil in large, good-quality saucepan.

2. Add rice, stir, cover and simmer over reduced heat, stirring occasionally, for 20 minutes or until all water is absorbed.

3. Stir in whole milk, light cream, sugar and vanilla. Add cinnamon stick. Increase heat to medium and cook uncovered, stirring often, for about 25 minutes, until rice mixture thickens.

4. Reduce heat and continue to cook uncovered 10 to 15 additional minutes, stirring occasionally so rice does not stick and burn on bottom. Rice should be firm enough so that a spoon can stand up, unsupported.

5. Remove from heat, discarding cinnamon stick. Best if served warm, but may be refrigerated.

**Yield: 6 to 8 servings**

# Coconut Rice Pudding

*Arroz con Coco*

This is another traditional holiday dessert in Puerto Rico. All rice contains two sorts of starch, *amylase* and *amylopectin*. However, different types of rice, contain different amounts of these two starches. That is why sushi rice is sticky and long-grain rice is fluffy, the grains separate. Medium grain rice, neither too sticky or too loose, works best for rice pudding.

The addition of ginger and coconut make this pudding different from that found on the U.S. mainland.

| | |
|---|---|
| 1 cinnamon stick | 1 ½ cups half-and half |
| 5 whole cloves | 1 cup unsweetened coconut milk |
| ½ teaspoon salt | ¼ cup golden raisins |
| 1 cup medium grain rice | 4 tablespoons shredded unsweetened coconut |
| 2 ½ cups whole milk | 1 tablespoon fresh, grated ginger root |

1. Bring 2 cups water to a boil in large, saucepan. Add cinnamon stick and cloves. Pour the liquid through a colander into a bowl and discard spices.

2. Return liquid to saucepan. Add salt and rice, reduce heat, cover and simmer for 15 to 20 minutes. Stir once. Water should be nearly absorbed.

3. Add milk, half-and-half and coconut milk. Turn up heat to medium, bring to simmer, then reduce heat. Fold in raisins, shredded coconut and ginger. Cook uncovered, stirring often, until pudding begins to thicken.

4. Reduce heat further and cook additional 15 minutes. All the liquid should be absorbed.

5. Cool and serve at room temperature or chilled. When chilling, cover surface with plastic wrap and keep up to 2 days in the refrigerator.

**Yield: 6 servings**

# Rice Flour and Coconut Milk Pap
*Majarete con Leche de Coco*

2 ½ cups coconut milk (see index or use canned)

½ cup evaporated milk

½ cup sugar

½ teaspoon sea salt

1 teaspoon fresh lime zest

1 tablespoon butter

½ teaspoon vanilla extract

½ cup sifted rice flour

butter to grease 6 custard cups

1. Bring coconut milk, evaporated milk, sugar and salt to a boil in a medium saucepan. Reduce heat to simmer.

2. Remove from heat and gradually whisk in lime zest, butter, vanilla and rice flour.

3. Return to medium heat, cook, stirring until pap thickens. Remove from heat.

4. Pour into six, buttered custard cups and allow to cool for 45 minutes. Cover with plastic wrap and refrigerate until ready to serve.

**Yield: 6 servings**

# Ricemeal Pudding
*Manjar Blanco*

5 cups milk

1 ½ cups sugar

½ teaspoon salt

½ cup rice meal

½ teaspoon rose extract

½ teaspoon vanilla extract

1. Combine all ingredients in large saucepan over moderate heat, stirring constantly with a wooden spoon until mixture thickens and separates from bottom and sides of pot.

2. Pour into serving bowls and allow to cool.

**Yield: 6 servings**

## Corn Pudding
*Majarate*

| | |
|---|---|
| **4 cups whole milk** | **1 teaspoon orange flower water** |
| **4 cups fresh coconut milk** | **(agua de azahar)** |
| **(substitute canned, unsweetened)** | **3 cinnamon sticks** |
| **4 corn cobs** | **powdered cinnamon** |
| **¾ cup sugar** | |

1. Slice corn kernels from cobs using a sharp knife. Place in blender along with whole milk, coconut milk and sugar.

2. Pour into medium saucepan and cook over moderate heat until mixture boils. Stir constantly until thickened. Stir in orange flower water.

3. Remove from heat and discard cinnamon sticks. Pour into individual serving dishes while still hot.

4. Cool to room temperature. Sprinkle with powdered cinnamon and refrigerate for 3 hours.

**Yield: 6 to 8 servings**

## Sponge Cake Trifle with Coconut Cream
*Bien-Me-Sabe*

*Bien-me-sabe* translates literally to 'tastes good to me'. This dessert has its roots in Great Britain. The coconut adds a tropical flair.

**1 tablespoon butter, softened**

*CAKE:*

| | |
|---|---|
| **6 egg whites** | **1 teaspoon vanilla extract** |
| **½ cup sugar** | **¼ cup flour** |

**6 egg yolks**

*COCONUT CREAM:*

**2 cups unsweetened coconut milk,
  fresh or canned**

**1 cup sugar**

**6 egg yolks**

**¼ teaspoon ground ginger**

**¼ teaspoon ground cinnamon**

**4 tablespoons dark rum**

**1 teaspoon grated lime zest**

**3 egg whites**

**3 tablespoons sugar**

1. **Cake:** Preheat oven to 350° and place rack in lower third position in oven. Generously butter the bottom and sides of a 9 × 12-inch glass baking dish.

2. Beat the 6 egg whites with a hand beater or electric mixer until soft peaks form. Gradually add the sugar and continue beating until stiff.

3. In a separate bowl beat the 6 egg yolks with the vanilla until combined.

4. Fold the egg/sugar mixture into the egg whites with a wooden spoon. Avoid stirring, use an up and down motion.

5. Sprinkle in the ¼ cup flour and incorporate gently into the egg mixture. Do not over stir as this will result in a tough, leathery cake.

6. Pour batter into baking dish and place cake in the bottom third of oven. Bake for 30 minutes or until a toothpick inserted in center comes out clean.

7. Remove pan from oven. Allow to cool for 5 minutes in pan. Turn out on wire rack to cool.

8. **Coconut cream:** Combine 1 cup of the coconut milk with the 1 cup sugar in a medium saucepan. Bring to a boil over moderate heat, stirring constantly. A candy thermometer should read 320° or you can drop a small bit into ice water and a thread should form.

9. Beat the 6 eggs yolks with the ginger and cinnamon until frothy. Stir in remaining 1 cup coconut milk.

10. Stir in a couple tablespoons of the hot coconut cream mixture. Very slowly drizzle and stir in the egg mixture to the hot coconut cream. Simmer, stirring constantly, for 15 minutes. Do not overheat or allow to boil. Remove from heat and cool for 15 minutes. Fold in rum and lime zest.

11. **To put together:** Cut cake in 2-inch squares and arrange in the bottom of a glass serving dish. Round is very pretty. Spoon coconut cream over top.

12. Beat the 3 eggs whites in a small bowl until stiff peaks form. Gradually beat in sugar and continue to beat until stiff and glossy. Spoon over top of coconut cream. Refrigerate 3 hours before serving.

**Yield: 8 to 10 servings**

# Lady Fingers with Coconut Cream

*Bien-Me-Sabe Sencillo*

The difference between this recipe and the preceding one is that the egg whites for the meringue have a boiled sugar syrup added and the sponge cake is homemade, not store bought. Both are equally good.

| | |
|---|---|
| **1 cup water** | **24 lady fingers** |
| **2 ½ cups granulated sugar** | **2/3 cup granulated sugar** |
| **2 (8 ounce) cans coconut cream** | **¼ water** |
| **(the sweetened kind)** | **4 egg whites** |
| **10 eggs yolks, lightly beaten** | **1 tablespoon brandy** |

1. Heat the 1 cup water in a small saucepan to boiling. Quickly whisk in sugar and continue to boil over high heat without stirring until a light syrup is formed (candy thermometer 222°F).

2. Allow to cool 30 minutes. Stir in coconut cream, then fold in eggs, blending well.

3. Return saucepan to medium heat. Cook coconut cream/egg mixture for 5 minutes, returning to a boil. Remove from heat at once.

4. Place lady fingers on the bottom of a buttered 13 by 9-inch glass baking dish.

5. Pour coconut cream over lady fingers.

6. In another small saucepan, heat the ¾ cup sugar with the ¼ cup water until thickened (candy thermometer 240°F). Allow to cool 15 minutes.

7. Beat the 4 egg whites in a medium bowl until stiff peaks form. Gradually add brandy, then syrup. Beat until frothy.

8. Top lady fingers with meringue. Refrigerate for 3 hours before serving.

**Yield: 8 to 10 servings**

# Coconut Cream Dessert

*Bien-me-Sabe*

I found that adding passionfruit liqueur added a great deal of zip to this lovely dessert.

2 ¼ cups sugar

½ teaspoon ground cinnamon

¾ cup water, plus 2 tablespoons

2 cups fresh or canned (unsweetened)
   coconut milk

10 egg yolks, lightly beaten

24 store-bought lady fingers

6 egg whites

2/3 cup sugar

3 tablespoons passionfruit liqueur

1. Heat the 2 ¼ cups sugar and cinnamon with the ¾ cup water in a small saucepan over high heat (do not stir) until syrup thickens (222°F). Remove from heat and set aside to cool for 20 minutes.

2. Stir in coconut milk, gradually adding egg yolks.

3. Return saucepan to low to medium heat. Stir constantly and bring to boil.

4. Remove from heat and strain through mesh sieve.

5. Place lady fingers on the bottom of a large rectangular baking dish, about 13- by 9-inches wide. Pour coconut/egg mixture over top.

6. Beat the 6 egg whites with the gradually added 2/3 cups sugar until soft peaks form. Drizzle in passionfruit liqueur.

7. Place generous dollops of the whipped cream over ladyfingers and chill for at least 2 hours.

**Yield: 8 to 10 servings**

# LOW-CARB Flan

Yes, you can have your custard and eat it too.

½ cup Splenda®

3 large eggs

3 large egg yolks

3 cups milk

1 teaspoon vanilla extract

½ teaspoon rum extract

1 teaspoon freshly grated ginger root

¼ teaspoon salt

1. Preheat oven to 350°F. Lightly spray a 1-quart baking dish with vegetable spray. Set aside.

2. Whisk together Splenda® and eggs in a a medium bowl, beating until thick.

3. Heat milk in a medium saucepan over moderate heat. Bring to a boil and remove from heat at once.

4. Beat hot milk into egg mixture gradually. Whip in vanilla, rum extract, ginger and salt.

5. Pour into baking dish. Place dish in a larger dish filled with hot water. The hot water should reach three-fourths up the sides of the custard dish.

6. Bake for 40 minutes. Custard should jiggle slightly in center. Remove from oven and cool on a wire rack. Refrigerate overnight.

**Yield: 6 servings**

EACH SERVING PROVIDES APPROXIMATELY:
165 calories, **10 grams of carbohydrates**, 10 grams of protein, 11 grams of fat

# Cakes, Pies and Fruit Tarts

The sweet tooth of Puerto Ricans has been influenced by various immigrants over the centuries: the Spanish, French, Danish, even the British. European heritage can be seen in the custards, puddings and flans, cheese-based desserts and pastries.

Tropical fruits, always in abundance on the island, made its way into many of the recipes, adding a refreshing touch. The recipes here are easy to duplicate, many of the tropical fruits readily found in mainland grocery stores.

## Three Milk Cake

*Pastel Tres Leches*

Soaked in three different types of milk, this intensely flavored vanilla cake has suddenly taken the U.S. mainland, particularly Texas, by storm. The whipped cream topping, instead of a sugary frosting is divine.

Note: you'll need three medium-size mixing bowls and one large one. Rinse a medium bowl while the cake is baking for the whipped cream and chill it.

CAKE:

8 large eggs, room temperature

1 ½ cups, plus 1 tablespoon sugar

12 tablespoons butter, softened

1 ¾ cups, plus 3 tablespoons
   all-purpose flour

2 teaspoons baking powder

1 cup whole milk

2 teaspoons vanilla extract

1 teaspoon cream of tartar

THREE MILKS:

8 ounces light cream

1 5-ounce can evaporated milk, room temperature

1 14-ounce can sweetened condensed milk, room temperature

TOPPING:

2 cups heavy cream

¼ cup sugar

## CAKE:

1. Preheat oven to 350°. Generously grease bottom and sides of a 9 by 13-inch metal baking pan. Set aside.

2. Separate egg yolks from whites, setting white aside (do not refrigerate). Cream sugar and butter together in the large bowl using an electric mixer at medium speed until yellow and fluffy. Add egg yolks and beat 2 to 3 minutes until light.

3. Using a medium bowl, sift flour and baking powder together.

4. In the second medium bowl, combine milk and vanilla.

5. Slowly add the milk/vanilla mixture to the butter/sugar mixture. Alternate with the flour/baking powder. Beat well each time. Batter should be smooth, but do not overbeat as cake can fall apart. This happened to me one time. It looked like an earthquake split the Tres Leches cake in two.

6. In the third medium bowl, beat egg white with cream of tartar until soft peaks form.

7. Fold egg whites into batter carefully using a large spatula.

8. Pour in greased cake pan. Bake for 25 to 30 minutes until golden. Allow to cool completely.

## THREE MILKS:

1. Whisk light cream, evaporated milk and sweetened condensed milk together.

2. Prick top of cooled cake with a fork or toothpick. Pour over top of cake and allow to soak while whipping cream for topping. Invert on cake plate.

## TOPPING:

1. Whip heavy cream in a chilled medium bowl for 2 minutes. Gradually beat in sugar until stiff peaks form.

2. Generously ice top of cake with whipped topping. Serve at once.

**Yield: 10 to 12 servings**

# Cakes

Different cakes have different techniques for preparing and baking. But there are some basic rules for excellent cakes.

**Greasing:** Shortening really is best because it contains no water to make the cake stick to the pan. But butter adds a rich flavor. Be sure to use unsalted. Anna and I discovered this little problem, when our Tres Leches cake stuck to the bottom of the pan like cement.

**Heavy batters:** Some cakes are dense like pound or fruit cake and tend to be dry on the outside, while still unbaked on the inside. Solve this problem by using a tube pan, which allows the inside of the cake to bake evenly.

**Lightest cakes:** Use a light, shiny cake pan. Dark pan will make a thick, tough crust. Bake in bottom third of oven.

**Maximum flavor:** Baking extracts are wonderful. My mother always added a bit of orange extract to chocolate cake batter or chocolate frosting. Use lemon extract for trifles and almond for yellow or white cakes.

**Moistest cake:** Add an extra yolk for each two whole eggs. Substitute half the milk in a recipe with equal amounts of plain yogurt or buttermilk.

**Avoiding holes in batter:** Those ugly holes ruin the most tender and tastiest of cakes. Run a butter knife through the cake batter in a back and forth motion to eliminate holes.

**Rounded top?:** It's really tough to assemble a layer cake if the center has risen in your cakes. Moisten a clean dish towel with water and wrap around the outside of your cake pan, fastening with paperclips. This will keep the outside from baking too quickly.

**Getting it out of the pan:** Anna's aunt Doritza Romano taught us this neat trick. Place hot cake pans on a wet kitchen towel for a few minutes. The **steam will help release the cake.**

**Cooling:** Place cakes (already on wire racks) in the freezer for 20 minutes.

**Ants on your cake?:** We have a big problem with ants in the islands. Make a moat for your cake by taking a shallow glass baking dish or deep dinner plate and filling with at least ½ inch of water. Place a small cereal bowl, open and wider side up in the water. Top with cake set on a plate. The ants would have to swim through the water to get to the cake. By the way, this works well also for dry cat or dog food left out.

# Quick Tres Leches Cake

*This is perfect when you have company to impress, but not a lot of time.*

CAKE:

1 package yellow cake mix

¼ cup, plus 2 tablespoons vegetable oil

1 ½ teaspoons vanilla extract

1 cup water

5 medium eggs

THREE MILKS:

1 14-ounce can sweetened condensed milk

1 cup heavy whipping cream

1 5-ounce can evaporated milk

TOPPING:

1 cup heavy whipping cream

¼ teaspoon cinnamon

1/3 cup sugar

CAKE:

1. Grease a 9 x 13-inch metal cake pan and preheat oven as directed on back of cake package.
2. Follow remaining instructions on back of cake package, substituting the 1 cup water, vegetable oil, 5 eggs and vanilla for their additional ingredient list. Bake and cool as instructed. Invert on cake plate.

THREE MILKS:

1. Combine 1 cup of the heavy whipping cream with the evaporated milk and sweetened condensed milk.
2. Poke holes in top of cooled cake. Pour three milks over top and allow to soak in.

TOPPING:

1. Whip remaining heavy cream, adding sugar and cinnamon slowly until stiff peaks form.
2. Generously top cake. Serve at once.

**Yield: 10 to 12 servings**

# Fresh Orange Cake with Orange-Ginger Glaze
*Bizcocho de Chinas Frescas*

Instead of a sugary chocolate cake, I made this for a friend's 30th birthday.

| | |
|---|---|
| 1 ½ cups sugar | 1 teaspoon almond extract |
| 1 ½ cups cake flour | ½ teaspoon vanilla extract |
| ½ teaspoon baking soda | ½ cup vegetable oil |
| ½ teaspoon salt | 1 tablespoon melted butter |
| 7 eggs, 2 whole, 5 separated, room temperature | 2 tablespoons grated fresh orange rind |
| 2 egg whites, room temperature | ½ teaspoon cream of tartar |
| 2/3 cup fresh orange juice | |

GLAZE:

| | |
|---|---|
| 5 tablespoon unsalted butter, melted | 5 tablespoons fresh orange juice |
| 1 teaspoon freshly grated ginger or ½ teaspoon groun | 2 cups sifted confectioner's sugar |

Note: if you do not beat the egg white until very stiff, the cake will not rise properly, and be dense and wet.

1. Adjust oven racks to lower-middle position and heat oven to 325°F.
2. Whisk sugar, flour, baking soda and salt together in large bowl. Beat in 2 whole eggs, 5 egg yolks (setting whites aside), 2/3 cup orange juice, oil, melted butter, orange rind, vanilla and almond extract until smooth and lump-free.

3. Place remaining 7 egg whites in separate bowl with cream of tartar and beat 1 minute at low speed until foamy. Increase speed to medium high, beating whites until very stiff-9 minutes with a hand held mixer, or 6 minutes with a standing mixer.

4. Fold egg whites into cake batter. Pour batter into a greased and floured 9- by 3 ½-inch tube pan.

5. Bake 50 to 55 minutes until a cake tester inserted in center comes out clean. Set pan on wire rack for 5 minutes. If using a one-piece pan, bang on counter several times to loosen, then invert over serving plate. For two-piece pan, grasp tube and lift cake out of pan.

6. Serve at once, or wrap in plastic and store at room temperature for 2 days, or refrigerated for 5 days.

**GLAZE:**

1. Be certain to sift the confectioner's sugar before you use it, otherwise you'll have unattractive lumps.

2. Carefully scrape off loose crumbs from the top of the cake with a butter knife. Slip pieces of parchment or wax paper between the cake and serving plate to catch drips of glaze.

3. Whip butter, ginger, orange juice and sugar until smooth and lump-free using a handheld mixer at medium speed. Allow to sit one minute.

4. Gradually spread glaze over top of cake. Glaze should dribble prettily down sides. Allow glaze to harden, about 30 minutes.

**Yield: 12 servings**

# Rich Yellow Cake

Tasuki and Natalie saga continued from Chocolate Custard: As we end the book, the baby has three teeth and Tasuki, Anna, Doritza, Anna's aunt, and I have all put on at least five pounds. The cat's stomach is positively round. He enjoyed the flan-making experiments, but the remaining dessert chapters have interested him little. He's a year older and mellow, passing most afternoons sleeping in Natalie's playpen. Anna and I are grateful for this, because Natalie can walk now and Tasuki keeps her in the playpen. What will happen when we finish the book to these two good friends remains to be seen. Perhaps Tasuki will stay with Anna and Natalie when I fly to Massachusetts to visit my daughter Roxanne at college.

| | |
|---|---|
| **vegetable shortening to grease two 9-by 1½-inch cake pans** | **2 ¼ cups sifted cake flour flour for dusting** |
| **1 ¾ cups sugar** | **4 large eggs, plus 1 yolk, room** |
| **2 teaspoons baking powder temperature** | **½ cup whole milk, room temperature** |
| | **1 teaspoon vanilla extract** |
| **½ teaspoon salt** | **2 sticks (½ pound) unsalted butter,** |
| **1 teaspoon almond extract** | **room temperature** |

1. Place oven rack to lower-middle position. Preheat oven to 350°F.

2. Generously grease the two cake pans and cover bottoms with circle of wax paper or parchment. Grease the parchment, sprinkle pans with flour and shake out excess.

3. Beat eggs, milk, vanilla and almond extract in a small bowl by hand for 1 minute.

4. Mix together flour, sugar, baking and salt in another bowl with a mixer set on low speed for 1 minute.

5. Chop butter in 8 pieces and add one piece at a time while mixer is still running. Flour mixture should look crumbly and like coarse sand.

6. Slowly pour in 1 cup of the egg/milk mixture while mixer is running, beating on lowest speed for 30 seconds until combined.

7. Increase speed to high and beat for 1 minute until light. Add remaining milk/egg mixture and beat additional 30 seconds. Scrape sides and bottom of bowl.

8. Beat on high for another 20 seconds. Batter will be slightly bubbly, resembling buttermilk.

9. Divide batter between the two pans. Bake until golden and a cake tester inserted in center comes out clean.

10. Cool in pans on wire rack for 10 minutes. Run a butter knife or spatula around edges to loosen cake. Place plate over top of cake and invert. Invert again and place on lightly greased rack. Remove parchment paper.

11. Cool completely before frosting. See following for various frostings.

**Yield: 12 servings**

# Coffee-Rum Butter Cream Frosting

If you'd rather not use the raw eggs, the texture will be less smooth. Note, with the ever growing concern over salmonella, a bacteria that contaminates eggs, poultry and meat, government officials recommend that immuno-compromised patients, the very young and elderly (those most severely affected if stricken with the bacteria) should not eat raw or undercooked eggs. I've included several other frostings that do not use raw eggs.

**1 ½ tablespoons instant coffee**
**¼ cup light or golden rum**
**1 teaspoon vanilla extract**
**3 cups confectioner's sugar, sifted**

**2 sticks butter (½ pound), room temperature**
**2 eggs yolks or 6 tablespoons milk or light cream**

1. Combine coffee, rum and vanilla in small bowl until coffee is dissolved. Set aside.

2. Beat butter in another bowl using an electric mixer set a medium speed for 1 minute until light and fluffy.

3. Reduce speed and gradually add sugar, beating away all lumps. Increase speed to medium and beat for 2 minutes until smooth.

4. Gradually beat in rum/coffee mixture until incorporated. Add eggs (or milk), beating for 4 minutes until fluffy. Use at once, or cover and refrigerate for up to one week, bringing to room temperature before frosting cake.

**Yield: 3 cups**

VARIATIONS

### Amaretto Butter Cream

Follow recipe for *Rum-Coffee Butter Cream Frosting*, omitting instant coffee, rum and vanilla, substituting ¼ cup Amaretto.

### Chocolate Butter Cream

Melt 4 ounces semi-sweet chocolate and 2 squares unsweetened chocolate in a double boiler. Remove from heat and allow to cool for 10 minutes. Follow instructions for *Rum-Coffee Butter Cream Frosting*, omitting instant coffee, rum and eggs, substituting the melted chocolate for the rum in step 1.

**Lemon Butter Cream**

Follow recipe for *Rum-Coffee Butter Cream Frosting*, omitting the instant coffee and rum, substituting 1 ½ tablespoons fresh lemon juice and 1 ½ tablespoons water. Add 1 tablespoon fresh grated lemon rind.

**Intense Vanilla Butter Cream**

Follow recipe for *Rum-Coffee Butter Cream Frosting*, omitting the instant coffee and rum, substituting 1 tablespoon vanilla extract and 2 tablespoons water.

---

## Baking

**Baking in glass pans:** Reduce oven temperature by 25°. I prefer to bake in glass as opposed to non-stick pans. I still don't quite trust those coatings not to come off onto the food. Use sufficient shortening and flour to coat dish.

**Even baking:** Foods in an oven cook by being surrounded by hot air. So if you overcrowd the oven racks, you'll have unevenly baked and possibly burnt food. Convection ovens circumvent this problem by using a fan that distributes the air to avoid hot or cold spots. When baking, try not to place one pan directly above another, stagger and rotate pans instead.

**To mix dry ingredients:** Use a wire whisk instead of a wooden spoon to save time and distribute ingredients evenly.

---

# Rum Cake

Make an extra one of these cakes. Store in a glass dish with a tight fitting lid. Once a week for a month, drizzle a quarter cup of rum over the top. The result will be a decadently potent rum cake.

**½ pound butter, room temperature**

**1 ½ cups sugar**

**5 large eggs, plus 2 yolks, room temperature**

**¼ cup dark rum, plus another ¼ cup for soaking**

**1 teaspoon vanilla extract**

**2 cups cake flour**

**½ teaspoon salt**

**½ teaspoon mace**

1. Adjust oven rack to center position. Preheat oven to 325°F. Grease a 9- by 5- by 3 1/2 -inch loaf pan with vegetable shortening. Line bottom and sides with parchment paper.

2. Cream the butter in a medium bowl using an electric mixer set on medium-high for 20 seconds until smooth and shiny. Slowly beat in sugar until light and almost white, about 4 minutes, scraping sides of bowl often.

3. Add eggs one at a time, beating well. Stir in rum and vanilla. Sift in flour, salt and mace, incorporating gradually.

4. Spoon into greased pan and bake for 1 ¼ to 1 ½ hours, or until toothpick comes out clean.

5. Cool in pan for 5 minutes. Lightly prick top of cake with a fork and pour the ¼ cup of rum over top. Allow to sit additional 5 minutes before turning out onto rack. Discard parchment and reinvert so rum-soaked top is face up.

**Yield: 8 to 10 servings**

### Did You Know?

Only two regions in the United States produce **coffee**, Hawaii and Puerto Rico. Originally from the Dominican Republic, Puerto Rico has been producing high-quality coffee for over 300 years. Coffee has three qualitities, the top ranking one being: café super premium. Only 3 coffees in the world qualify for this distinction: Kona coffee from Hawaii; Blue Mountain coffee from Jamaica; and Alto Grande from Puerto Rico.

## Rum Chocolate Cake

Rich and moist, this intensely chocolate-flavored cake is perfect for beginning bakers as it is mixed right in the saucepan that melts the chocolate.

| | |
|---|---|
| vegetable shortening to grease two 8 1/2- by 4 ½- by 2 ½-inch loaf pans | 2 teaspoons vanilla extract |
| | ½ teaspoon almond extract |
| 2 tablespoons unsweetened cocoa powder | 2 cups sifted cake flour |
| 8 ounces unsweetened chocolate | 1 ½ cups sugar |
| ¾ cup butter | 1 teaspoon baking soda |
| 1 cup strong coffee | ¼ teaspoon salt |

**¾ cup dark rum, plus additional**
**½ cup to soak cake**

**¾ cup semi-sweet chocolate bits**
**2 eggs, plus 1 yolk**

1. Preheat oven to 275°. Grease the two loaf pans and dust with the 2 tablespoons cocoa powder. Using the cocoa powder instead of flour avoids a white-floured appearance to the chocolate cake.

2. Melt chocolate and butter in a heavy-bottomed 4-quart pan over low heat, stirring constantly. Whisk in coffee and ¾ cup rum, stirring until incorporated. Remove from heat and cool for 10 minutes.

3. Beat in eggs, vanilla and almond extract.

4. Sift flour, sugar, baking soda and salt together. Gradually beat in flour mixture to chocolate egg mixture using a wooden spoon or wire whisk for 4 to 5 minutes until smooth. Fold in chocolate bits.

5. Divide batter between two pans. Bake for 55 minutes or until a toothpick inserted in center comes out clean.

6. Remove from oven and lightly prick top of loaves with a fork. Drizzle remaining ½ cup of rum equally over the still warm cakes. Allow to sit for 15 minutes in the pans.

7. Invert on greased rack, then flip over so that rum-soaked side faces up. Serve warm with whipped cream.

**Yield: two 8 ½- by 4 1/2- by 2 ½-inch loaves**


# Key Lime White Cake

**1 ½ cups sugar**

**1 ½ cups cake flour**

**½ teaspoon baking soda**

**1 teaspoon almond extract**

**½ teaspoon vanilla extract**

**7 eggs, 2 whole, 5 separated,**
**room temperature**

**2 egg whites, room temperature**

**3 tablespoons fresh key lime or lime juice**

**1 tablespoon, plus 1 teaspoon**
**fresh grated lime rind**

**½ teaspoon salt**

**2/3 cup water**

**½ cup vegetable oil**

**1 tablespoon melted butter**

**½ teaspoon cream of tartar**

Note: if you do not beat the egg white until very stiff, the cake will not rise properly, and be dense and wet.

## Frosting

Frosting a cake successfully need not be daunting if you follow a few simple tips.

**Cool cake first** otherwise the frosting will liquefy from the cake's heat and run down the sides.

**Crumbs in frosting:** Freeze cakes for 20 minutes. Ice with a thin layer of frosting, return to freezer for 10 minutes, then finish frosting cake.

**Smooth finish:** Use your blowdryer over the tops and sides of cake like the pros do.

**Avoiding a mess:** Place narrow strips of waxed paper between the cake and the plate. Remove wax strips and discard after frosting.

1. Adjust oven racks to lower-middle position and heat oven to 325°F.

2. Whisk sugar, flour, baking soda and salt together in large bowl. Beat in 2 whole eggs, 5 egg yolks (setting whites aside), 2/3 cup water, lime juice, lime rind, oil, melted butter, vanilla and almond extract until smooth and lump-free.

3. Place remaining 7 egg whites in separate bowl with cream of tartar and beat 1 minute at low speed until foamy. Increase speed to medium high, beating whites until very stiff-9 minutes with a hand held mixer, or 6 minutes with a standing mixer.

4. Fold egg whites into cake batter. Pour batter into a greased and floured 9- by 3 ½-inch tube pan.

5. Bake 50 to 55 minutes until a cake tester inserted in center comes out clean. Set pan on wire rack for 5 minutes. If using a one-piece pan, bang on counter several times to loosen, then invert over serving plate. For two-piece pan, grasp tube and lift cake out of pan.

6. Serve at once, or wrap in plastic and store at room temperature for 2 days, or refrigerated for 5 days.

**Yield: 12 servings**

# White Cake with Passionfruit Filling and Rum Lime Frosting

I think this is my favorite chapter in this cookbook. Anna, Doritza and I certainly enjoyed preparing and tasting the cakes. I didn't enjoy the extra gym time as much.

shortening to grease two 9- by 1 ½-inch round cake pans

1 cup milk, room temperature

6 extra large egg whites, room temperature

1 tablespoon white rum

1 teaspoon almond extract

1 teaspoon vanilla extract

1 ½ cups, plus 2 tablespoon sugar

3 ½ teaspoons baking powder

¼ teaspoon baking soda

1 teaspoon salt

1 ½ sticks unsalted butter, room temperature

1 teaspoon fresh grated lime rind

2 ¼ cups cake flour

FROSTING:

2 sticks unsalted butter, room temperature

½ teaspoon almond extract

¼ teaspoon salt

1 tablespoon fresh lime juice

4 cups confectioner's sugar

1 tablespoon rum

FILLING:

¼ cup frozen passionfruit concentrate, room temperature

1/3 cup apricot preserves

1. **CAKE:** Adjust oven rack to center position. Preheat oven to 350°F. Generously grease cake pans and line bottom with parchment or wax paper. If you don't have either paper, sprinkle 2 tablespoons of flour into bottom of cake pans, shake to coat bottoms and toss out excess flour. Set aside.

2. Blend together milk, egg white, vanilla and almond extract and rum in small bowl. Set aside.

3. Sift flour, sugar, baking powder, baking soda and salt into a large bowl. Beat in butter with an electric hand-held beater until mixture resembles wet crumbs. Fold in lime rind.

4. Slowly pour in milk/egg mixture into flour/butter mixture and beat 2 minutes at medium speed. Beat on high for 20 seconds.

5. Divide batter between two prepared pans. Bake for 25 until toothpick inserted in center comes out clean.

6. Allow to cool in pans for 5 minutes. Invert onto greased cake rack. Allow to cool completely, for 1 hour or more.

7. **FROSTING:** Beat butter, sugar, lime juice, rum, almond extract and salt together in a small bowl using a hand-held electric mixer at low speed until creamy. Place in refrigerator while making filling.

8. **FILLING:** Stir passionfruit concentrate into apricot preserves in a small bowl.

9. Spread 2 tablespoons of frosting on bottom of cake plate to anchor cake. Set down one cake layer. Spread top with passionfruit preserve mixture. Place second layer of cake on top. Frost top and sides of cake.

**Yield: 12 servings**

# Fresh Coconut Cake

*Bizcocho de Coco*

Light, tender and moist. Use freshly grated coconut meat for best flavor and texture. The addition of lemon to both the cake and the following frosting adds a lovely dimension to an otherwise typical coconut cake.

| | |
|---|---|
| shortening to grease two | 2 teaspoons baking powder |
| 9-inch round cake pans | ½ teaspoon baking powder |
| 2 tablespoons flour | ½ teaspoon salt |
| 1 teaspoon fresh lemon rind | ¾ cup milk |
| ¾ cup vegetable shortening | 3 tablespoons fresh lemon juice |
| 1 ½ cups sugar | 3 cups fresh grated coconut |
| 3 eggs, separated, plus 1 extra white, | ¼ cup cream of coconut |
| room temperature | (the canned kind used |
| 2 ¼ cups flour | to make piña coladas) |

1. Preheat oven to 375°F. Generously grease and flour (using the 2 tablespoons flour) the two cake pans.

2. Cream shortening in large bowl using a hand mixer set on medium for 1 minute until glossy. Beat in sugar until light and smooth.

3. Beat in egg yolks one at a time, stirring in lemon rind.

4. Sift flour, baking powder, baking soda and salt together onto a piece of waxed paper.

5. Beat in one third of the flour mixture while mixer is still running. Alternate with cream of coconut, milk and lemon juice until all dry and wet ingredients are incorporated and smooth. Fold in grated coconut.

6. Rinse off beater blades and beat egg white (4) in a separate small bowl until stiff, glossy peaks form (but not dry).

7. Gently fold egg whites into cake batter 1/3 at a time.

8. Divide batter equally between two cake pans.

9. Bake for 25 to 30 minutes until a toothpick inserted in center comes out clean. Cool in pans for 10 minutes.

10. Gently invert on greased cake rack. Allow to cool completely before frosting with *Fluffy Coconut Frosting*.

**Yield: 12 servings**

# Fluffy Coconut Frosting
*Azucarado Esponjoso de Coco*

1 ½ cups sugar

¼ teaspoon salt

¼ cup water

1 teaspoon vanilla extract

¼ teaspoon cream of tartar

3 egg whites

1 teaspoon fresh grated lemon rind

½ cup fresh grated coconut (see index, if you absolutely must, you may use the packaged kind, but only for the frosting, not the cake)

1. Fill the bottom half of a double boiler with 1 ½ inches of water. Bring to a simmer.

2. Combine sugar, cream of tartar, salt, egg whites and water in top of double boiler. Before placing over hot water, beat with a handheld mixer on low speed for 30 seconds until blended.

3. Place top of double boiler over water and beat continuously over low heat until frosting stands in peaks, about 5 to 7 minutes.

4. Remove from heat at once and continue to beat for 2 minutes until thick.

5. Fold in lemon rind, vanilla and grated coconut before frosting cake.

**Yield: about 3 to 4 cups**

---

### Heathy tip

**To reduce fat in batter:** Substitute up to one third of the butter or oil in a recipe with fat-free sour cream. Use cake flour instead of regular flour, which will give the illusion of lightness without using extra fat. Add a teaspoon of orange or almond extract to batter for richer flavor.

**To reduce fat in frosting:** Use instant pudding and beat in 1 cup reduced fat milk until thick. Fold in 1 ½ cups non-dairy whipped topping.

**To reduce sugar and fat in frosting:** There are some good low-carb instant pudding mixes available. I've found the vanilla to be better than the cholocate. Beat in 1 cup reduced fat milk until thick. Fold in 1 ½ cups non-dairy whipped topping.

---

## Piña Colada Cake
*Bizcocho de Piña Colada*

Add tropical pizzazz to the conclusion of a dinner party with this lucscious treat.

1 ½ cups coconut milk (see index or use unsweetened canned)

½ teaspoon salt

butter to grease an 8-by 8-inch glass baking dish

½ cup granulated sugar

½ cup confectioner's sugar

½ teaspoon cardamom

½ cup all-purpose flour

1 teaspoon vanilla extract

½ cup coconut cream (Coco Lopez or other sweet and thick syrup used for piña colada drinks)

½ cup crushed canned pineapple, completely drained

¼ cup dark rum

½ cup ground almonds

1 teaspoon fresh grated lemon rind

6 egg whites

½ cup melted butter

1. Stir together coconut milk and coconut cream in a medium saucepan over moderate heat, bringing to a boil. Reduce heat and simmer until liquid is reduced to just less than 1 cup. Stir in rum. Set aside.

2. Grease a glass baking dish and line bottom with crushed pineapple. Set aside.

3. Combine sugars, almonds, cardamom, lemon rind and flour in a bowl.

4. Preheat oven to 375°F.

5. In a separate bowl, beat egg whites until soft glossy peaks form. Fold egg whites into sugar/almond mixture. Stir in melted butter and salt.

6. Pour batter over crushed pineapple. Bake for 35 minutes until golden. Remove from oven and cool on wire rack for 5 minutes.

7. Prick top of cake all over with fork. Pour reserved coconut milk over hot cake. Slice and serve at once with vanilla ice cream or whipped cream.

**Yield: 4 to 6 servings**

# Sponge Cake with Pastry Cream

*Bizcocho Esponjoso con Crema Repostera*

One finds this cake all over in Puerto Rico, one bakery outdoing the other. A bakery near the Hotel El San Juan in Isla Verde serves a particularly rich version.

In a perfect world, sponge cake is lighter than the basic butter-based layer cake. The texture is delicate, yet springy and holds up well to a rich custard or jam filling.

Anna and I began by making a traditional sponge cake that we found in a classic Puerto Rican cookbook. The recipe added no fat or butter, relying on beaten eggs only to offer lift and structure. The cake had a pleasing light texture, but was tasteless, dry and a bit chewy. Fat was definitely needed and we added a small amount of melted butter and hot milk. The end result was much better.

We also tried different types of flours and settled on a combination of all purpose and cake flour for the best texture. Too many eggs produced an eggy texture and taste, while too few left a flattened cake. After ten ingredient and preparation variations, the following is our best recipe.

shortening to grease two 9-inch pans
½ cup cake flour
¼ cup, plus 1 tablespoon
  all-purpose flour
1 tablespoon baking powder
½ teaspoon salt
3 tablespoon milk

3 tablespoon butter
1 teaspoon vanila
5 large eggs, room temperature
4 tablespoons sugar
1 teaspoon fresh lime juice
½ teaspoon fresh grated lime rind
¼  teaspoon mace

## Heathy tip

**To bake with less fat:** Fill a small, clean spray bottle with cooking oil and spray pans instead of greasing heavily with shortening. Replace up to 25% of the fat in a recipe with applesauce. Instead of adding high-fat chocolate chips or nuts to batter, fill cake or cupcake tins, then sprinkle chocolate chips or nuts lightly over the top.

**To use fewer eggs or dairy products:** Dairy and eggs can add a hefty wallop of fat to recipes. Replace each whole egg with two whites. For peak flavor and texture, try and leave in at least one whole egg in the recipe. Cut amount of cream cheese in a recipe in half, replacing other half with reduced-fat, fat-free sour cream or non-fat cottage cheese (whisked through a blender until smooth). Replace whole milk with partially reduced fat milk or buttermilk.

**Choosing correct flour for low-fat baking:** Fat added to recipes imparts tenderness by coating the flour and limiting gluten development. That's why they tell you not to over beat batter, as this increases gluten development. Now you know why your chocolate sponge cake tasted like shoe leather. Use a low-protein flour, such as cake or pastry flour. With low-protein flour there's less chance for gluten to develop. The resulting baked good will be more tender, as if you had added fat. Soy flour, extremely popular with the low-carb crowd, has a higher fat content and may be used to replace up to 50% of the flour in a recipe.

**To reduce fat from chocolate:** Cut the amount of unsweetened baking chocolate in half and substitute unsweetened cocoa powder.

**To cut fat from nuts:** Cut the amount of nuts in a recipe in half and toast them for intense flavor.

PASTRY CREAM:

2 cups milk

7 eggs yolks

½ cup sugar

¼ teaspoon salt

4 tablespoons cornstarch

1 teaspoon vanilla extract

2 tablespoons dark rum

confectioner's sugar

1. Adjust oven rack to lower-middle position. Preheat oven to 350°F. Generously grease cake pans and cover bottoms with rounds of parchment paper.

2. Sift cake flour, all-purpose flour, baking powder and salt onto a piece of waxed paper.

3. Heat milk and butter in small saucepan over lowest heat. Stir in vanilla and remove from heat.

4. Separate 4 of the whites from the eggs, reserving yolks. Beat whites in medium bowl using electric mixer set on low until foamy. Increase speed to medium and beat in 4 tablespoons of the sugar until soft peaks form. Do not beat dry.

5. Beat remaining eggs and yolks in separate bowl with remaining sugar and confectioner's sugar for 5 minutes until thick. Fold into beaten whites. Stir in lime juice and rind.

6. Gently add flour mixture to egg mixture, folding in with a rubber spatula, 10 to 12 strokes. Sprinkle in mace.

7. Drizzle in heated milk/butter mixture, folding gently until mixture is incorporated, another 6 or 7 strokes.

8. Divide between prepared cake pans. Bake about 15 minutes or until light brown and cake springs back from touch.

9. Remove from oven and run a butter knife around edge of pan to loosen cake. Place plate over top of cake and invert. Remove and discard parchment. Reinvert cake and allow to cool before filling and assembling.

## PASTRY CREAM:

1. Heat milk in small saucepan. Do not allow to simmer. Remove from heat. Remove ½ cup of milk and whisk in cornstarch. Return to remaining milk in saucepan, stirring until smooth.

2. Whisk egg yolks, sugar and salt in a large saucepan using a wire whisk for 3 minutes until lemon colored.

3. Slowly stir in hot milk mixture to egg yolk mixture. Cook over low heat, stirring constantly, scraping sides and bottom of pot, for 10 minutes until mixture thickens. It should resemble pudding. Remove from heat.

4. Stir in vanilla and rum. Pour into a glass bowl and cover with plastic wrap or a thin layer of cold milk to keep a skin from forming on top of the pastry cream.

5. Refrigerate until firm. Pour off milk before using.

## TO ASSEMBLE CAKE:

1. Place strips of wax paper beneath one cake layer set on a cake platter to catch any drips from cream filling.

2. Carefully spoon cream filling over top of cake. Arrange second layer of cake on top.

3. Lightly sift confectioner's sugar over top.

**Yield: 8 servings**

# Gypsy's Arm Sponge Roll with Guava Filling

*Brazo Gitano con Guava*

Anna's aunt, Doritza Romano, provided this recipe for the best sponge-cake jelly roll I ever had. The cornstarch gives it a firm, springy texture that won't break apart when rolled. The filling is clear with the delicate, perfumey taste of guava.

SPONGE ROLL:

5 eggs, separated

2 teaspoons vanilla extract

½ teaspoon lemon extract

½ teaspoon salt

½ cup granulated sugar

1/3 cup sifted cornstarch

1/3 cup sifted all-purpose flour

confectioner's sugar

FILLING:

1 cup sugar

3 tablespoons cornstarch sifted

½ teaspoon salt

¾ cup water

¼ cup guava paste, chopped

½ cup fresh lemon juice

SPONGE ROLL:

1. Preheat oven to 357°. Grease a 10 ½ by 15 ½-inch jelly-roll pan and line with wax paper. Grease and flour the wax paper also.

2. Beat egg yolks with vanilla and lemon extract in a medium bowl. Set aside.

3. Beat egg whites until foamy. Add salt and keep beating until soft peaks form. Sprinkle in granulated sugar and beat until stiff, but not dry peaks form.

4. Scoop egg whites on top of egg yolks. Sift flour and cornstarch over top. Cut in gently with a rubber spatula until blended.

5. Spoon onto prepared pan. Bake for 10 to 12 minutes until a toothpick inserted in center comes out clean. Do not over bake, otherwise the cake will crack when rolling.

6. Dust a clean kitchen towel (non terry cloth) generously with confectioner's sugar.

7. Separate edges of cake from pan using a butter knife. Turn jelly roll out onto towel, removing the wax paper. Trim off any hard edges of cake.

8. Roll up cake lengthwise in the towel and allow to cool on a wire rack for 25 minutes.

9. Unroll carefully and spread with pastry cream or Guava Filling. Roll again without the towel, pressing lightly. Wrap in wax paper for 20 minutes, then unwrap and place on serving platter. Dust with confectioner's sugar. Slice with a bread knife.

## GUAVA FILLING:

1. Stir together the sugar, cornstarch, salt, water, guava paste and lemon juice. Bring to a boil.

2. Reduce heat and simmer for 1 minute, stirring constantly. Filling should thicken.

3. Remove from heat and chill in refrigerator until firm.

4. Follow instruction number 9 from above.

**Yield: 14 to 16 slices**

# Chocolate Sponge Cake with Chocolate Cream Filling

*Bixcocho Esponjoso de Chocolate con Crema Repostera de Chocolate*

For a richer, more complex taste, add a teaspoon of powdered, instant coffee to the filling.

½ cup cake flour
¼ cup, plus 1 tablespoon all-purpose flour
1 teaspoon baking powder
2 tablespoons, plus 1 teaspoon butter
1 teaspoon vanilla extract
5 large eggs, room temperature

1 teaspoon vanilla extract
½ teaspoon salt
3 tablespoons milk
3/4 cup sugar
1 tablespoon confectioner's sugar
1 teaspoon lime juice

| | |
|---|---|
| 1 teaspoon fresh grated lime rind | ¼  teaspoon mace |

7 ounces unsweetend melted chocolate (melted in double boiler)

CHOCOLATE CREAM FILLING:

| | |
|---|---|
| 2 cups milk | 4 tablespoons cornstarch |
| 7 eggs yolks | 1 teaspoon vanilla extract |
| ½ cup sugar | 2 tablespoons dark rum |
| ¼ teaspoon salt | 3 ounces unsweetened chocolate, melted |

1. Adjust oven rack to lower-middle position. Preheat oven to 350°F. Generously grease cake pans and cover bottoms with rounds of parchment paper.

2. Sift cake flour, all-purpose flour, baking powder and salt onto a piece of waxed paper.

3. Heat milk and butter in small saucepan over lowest heat. Stir in vanilla and remove from heat.

4. Separate 4 of the whites from the eggs, reserving yolks. Beat whites in medium bowl using electric mixer set on low until foamy. Increase speed to medium and beat in 4 tablespoons of the sugar until soft peaks form. Do not beat dry.

5. Beat remaining eggs and yolks in separate bowl with remaining sugar and confectioner's sugar for 5 minutes until thick. Fold into beaten whites. Stir in lime juice and rind.

6. Gently add flour mixture to egg mixture, folding in with a rubber spatula, 10 to 12 strokes. Sprinkle in mace.

7. Drizzle in heated milk/butter mixture and melted chocolate, folding gently until mixture is incorporated, another 6 or 7 strokes.

8. Divide between prepared cake pans. Bake about 15 minutes or until light brown and cake springs back from touch.

9. Remove from oven and run a butter knife around edge of pan to loosen cake. Place plate over top of cake and invert. Remove and discard parchment. Reinvert cake and allow to cool before filling and assembling.

### CHOCOLATE CREAM FILLING:

1. Heat milk in small saucepan. Do not allow to simmer. Remove from heat. Remove ½ cup of milk and whisk in cornstarch. Return to remaining milk in saucepan, stirring until smooth.

2. Whisk egg yolks, sugar and salt in a large saucepan using a wire whisk for 3 minutes until lemon colored.

3. Slowly stir in hot milk mixture to egg yolk mixture. Cook over low heat, stirring constantly, scraping sides and bottom of pot, for 10 minutes until mixture thickens. It should resemble pudding. Remove from heat.

4. Stir in vanilla, rum and melted chocolate. Pour into a glass bowl and cover with plastic wrap or a thin layer of cold milk to keep a skin from forming on top of the pastry cream.

5. Refrigerate until firm. Pour off milk before using.

### TO ASSEMBLE CAKE:

4. Place strips of wax paper beneath one cake layer set on a cake platter to catch any drips from cream filling.

5. Carefully spoon cream filling over top of cake. Arrange second layer of cake on top.

6. Lightly sift confectioner's sugar over top.

**Yield: 8 servings**

# Fruit Cocktail Cake
*Bizcocho de Frutitas Surtidas Enlatadas*

The best way to describe this cake is as a sponge cake trifle. I added a splash of rum to make it more interesting.

| | |
|---|---|
| ½ cup sugar | 1 can (1 pound 14 ounces) fruit cocktail |
| 1 Sponge Cake with Cream Filling | ¼ cup light rum recipe (see index) |

1. Prepare sponge cake according to instructions and cut in 1 ½ inch cubes. Set aside.

2. Preheat oven to 350°. Fill a shallow baking dish with 1 inch of hot water and place in oven.

3. Caramelize an 8- by 8- by 2-inch square glass pan by melting the ½ cup in the pan over medium heat on the stove. Be sure to use oven gloves. Tip pan to coat sides. Set aside on heat-proof surface.

4. Prepare cream filling as for sponge cake recipe, but do not refrigerate.

5. Drain can of fruit cocktail, reserving fruit.

6. Arrange sponge cake cubes on bottom of caramelized pan. Alternate with layers of pastry cream and fruit.

7. Place pan in water filled baking dish. Bake 1 hour until firm. Remove from water and cool on wire rack. Sprinkle rum over top.

8. Serve warm with whipped cream or chill overnight in refrigerator.

**Yield: 8 to 10 servings**

## Ginger and Spice Pound Cake

Delicious with fresh, whipped cream or crème fraiche.

| | |
|---|---|
| **vegetable shortening to grease A 9- by 5- x 3 ½-inch loaf pan** | **¼ teaspoon cardamom** |
| | **1 ½ cups cake flour** |
| **2 tablespoons flour to dust pan** | **2 tablespoons candied minced ginger** |
| **½ pound unsalted butter, room temperature** | **1 1/3 cups sugar** |
| | **1 tablespoon freshly grated ginger root** |
| **4 large eggs, plus 2 yolks, room temperature** | **¼ teaspoon ground mace** |
| | **½ teaspoon salt** |
| **1 teaspoon vanilla extract** | **¼ teaspoon nutmeg** |
| **½ teaspoon almond extract** | **2 tablespoons evaporated milk** |

1. Adjust oven rack to center position. Preheat oven to 325°. Grease and flour loaf pan. Set aside.

2. Whip butter with hand-held mixer set at medium-high until smooth and shiny, about 20 seconds.

3. Slowly beat in sugar until light in color and fluffy, about 4 minutes.

4. Mix eggs, vanilla extract, almond extract and evaporated milk in a separate bowl.

5. Slowly drizzle egg mixture in sugar/butter mixture.

6. Sift salt and flour together. Using a rubber spatula, slowly fold in flour into

egg/sugar/butter mixture, until just smooth. Stir in candied ginger, grated ginger root, ground mace, nutmeg and cardamom. Do not over mix batter.

7. Pour batter into greased loaf pan.

8. Bake 60 to 70 minutes until cake is springy to touch, a sides have shrunken slightly away from pan. Insert a cake tester in center, ensuring it comes out clean.

9. Allow to cool on wire rack for minutes, then invert cake onto rack and remove pan. Store at room temperature.

**Yield: 8 to 10 servings**

# Mango Upside-Down Cake
*Bizcocho de Mango*

To be honest, I've never been a big fan of pineapple upside down cake. But, I do love mangoes, with their peach-like flavor and consistency. Mangoes grow in wild abundance in Puerto Rico and the rest of the Caribbean.

A well-made upside down cake should have the perfect proportion of caramelized topping and fragrant fruit resting on top of a flavorful and buttery cake that would be firm enough to hold up under the weight of the fruit and topping. It also needed to be dry enough to soak up the fruit juices without becoming a soggy mess.

As always, Anna and I were in a time pinch and looked for baking shortcuts. Use a cast-iron skillet and save both on time and cooking utensils.

## CARAMEL TOPPING:

5 tablespoons unsalted butter
¾ cup brown sugar
2 medium, ripe, yet still firm mangoes, peeled, pitted and cut in ¼ inch slices
1 ½ cups all-purpose flour
2 tablespoons cake flour
3 tablespoons cornmeal
½ teaspoon salt

6 tablespoons butter
¾ cup, plus 2 tablespoons sugar
3 eggs, separated, plus extra yolk
2 teaspoons vanilla extract
½ cup plus 2 tablespoons milk
3 tablespoons light or dark rum

**TOPPING:**

1. Melt butter in bottom of cast-iron skillet over low heat. Turn heat to medium and add brown sugar, stirring for 4 minutes, until sugar is melted. Remove from heat.
2. Arrange mango slices in bottom of skillet.

**CAKE:**

1. Adjust oven rack to lower-middle position. Preheat oven to 350°F.
2. Combine all-purpose flour, cake flour, cornmeal and salt in a medium bowl. Set aside.
3. In another, larger bowl, cream butter with an electric mixer set a medium speed until light and fluffy. Slowly add ¾ cup sugar, continuing to beat. Add egg yolks and vanilla, scraping sides of bowl often.
4. Turn down speed and add one third of flour mixture, then one third of milk. Continue to alternate until flour and milk are used up. Beat until batter is smooth.
5. Beat egg whites in a clean bowl until soft peaks form. Add remaining 2 tablespoons sugar and beat until stiff.
6. Fold one third of the egg whites into cake batter using a rubber spatula. Gently fold in remaining egg whites.
7. Pour batter on top of mango slices.
8. Bake in skillet for 50 minutes until top is golden and a toothpick inserted in center of cake comes out clean. Remove from oven.
9. Allow cake to cool 5 minutes in pan. While still hot, drizzle rum over top. Slide a butter knife around outside of skillet to loosen cake. Place a cake platter (that can hold the caramel glaze) over top of cake and invert. Replace any fruit that has stuck to bottom of skillet.

**Yield: 8 to 10 servings**

**VARIATIONS**

**Pineapple Upside-Down Cake**     **1 small ripe, yet still firm pineapple**

There's no need to use canned pineapple for this recipe. Slice off the top of the pineapple, peel, quarter, then core. Cut into pieces 3/8" thick. Arrange as you would the mango in preceding recipe.

# Fruit Cake

*Bizcocho con Frutitas Abrillantadas*

Every kitchen should have a recipe for a dark and tender fruit cake fragrant with island spices. Unlike many stateside recipes that preserve the cake with brandy, this recipe uses Puerto Rican rum.

When I lived in St. Thomas, my ex-husband's grandmother began her Christmas fruitcake the first week of November. Weekly she sprinkled it with Virgin Islands rum, to preserve it and keep it moist. The cake was to-die-for. It sure did pack a wallop though.

**butter and flour to grease pans**

| | |
|---|---|
| **¼ pound unsalted butter** | **¼ teaspoon cloves** |
| **1 cup dark brown sugar, firmly packed** | **¼ teaspoon cardamom** |
| **2 large eggs** | **¼ teaspoon nutmeg** |
| **¼ cup molasses** | **½ teaspoon salt** |
| **¼ cup, plus additional ½ cup dark Puerto Rican rum and extra for soaking** | **½ cup milk** |
| | **2 cups mixed candied fruit** |
| **2 cups flour** | **½ cup candied citron** |
| **½ teaspoon baking soda** | **1 tablespoon fresh grated** |
| **½ teaspoon baking powder** | **lemon rind** |
| **½ teaspoon ground cinnamon** | **½ cup golden raisins** |
| **½ teaspoon allspice** | **½ cup chopped dates** |
| **½ teaspoon mace** | **½ cup chopped walnuts** |

1. Preheat oven to 325°F. Butter and flour two 9-by 5-inch loaf pans. Set aside.

2. Cream butter with wooden spoon for 1 minute. Add brown sugar and beat until light.

3. Add eggs, continuing to beat. Stir in molasses and ¼ cup of the dark rum.

4. Sift together flour, baking soda, baking powder, cinnamon, allspice, mace, cloves, cardamom, nutmeg and salt onto waxed paper.

5. Gradually beat flour mixture into butter/egg mixture. Stir in milk, combining until smooth.

6. Fold in candied fruit, lemon peel, raisins, dates and nuts, mixing well.

7. Divide batter between two pans and bake for 1 to 1 ¼ hours, until a toothpick comes out clean.

8. Remove from oven and lightly score tops of loaves with a fork. Pour remaining rum over top. Allow to soak for 15 minutes.

9. Turn out onto greased wire racks to cool. Store in airtight containers, sprinkling once a week with rum, for up to 2 months.

**Yield: two 9- by 5-inch loaves**

# Guava Cheese Cake

*Bizcocho de Queso*

I like to crush my own graham crackers for crumbs. That way I know they're fresh. You can substitute mango, pineapple or any other preserve for the guava.

| | |
|---|---|
| **1 cup graham cracker crumbs** | **1 teaspoon vanilla extract** |
| **3 tablespoons melted butter** | **1 tablespoon fresh lime juice** |
| **1 ¼ cups granulated sugar** | **1 teaspoon freshly grated lime rind** |
| **4 eggs, separated** | **1 pound cream cheese, room** |
| **1 cup sour cream** | **temperature, cut in pieces** |
| **3 tablespoons flour** | **12 ounces guava preserves** |

1. Preheat oven to 325º. Combine crumbs, melted butter and ¼ cup of the sugar in a small bowl. Butter a 9-inch springform pan and press crumb mixture into bottom and up sides, 1 inch. Refrigerate.

2. Beat egg yolks in medium bowl with electric mixer until thickened and lemony.

3. Beat in sour cream, flour, vanilla, lime juice, lime rind and ¾ cup of the sugar until blended.

4. Beat in cream cheese one piece at a time until no lumps remain.

5. Beat egg whites in a separate bowl until foamy, then add remaining ¼ cup of the sugar, continuing to beat until stiff.

6. Fold egg whites into cream cheese mixture.

7. Scoop guava preserves on top of graham crust.

8. Spoon cheese mixture over guava preserves. Bake 1 hour. Cool on wire rack, then chill in refrigerator.

# Sweet Potato Cake

*Bizcocho de Batata*

This cake tastes much better than it sounds. The spices add a lovely complexity, and the sweet potato a hint of richness.

**2 teaspoons salt**

**2 pounds sweet potatoes, scrubbed and cut in pieces**

**1 cup all-purpose flour**

**½ teaspoon salt**

**½ cup evaporated milk**

**1 pound butter**

**1 ½ cups sugar**

**6 eggs**

**1 tablespoon fresh grated ginger root**

**1 ½ cups cold whole milk**

**½ teaspoon ground cardamom**

1. Place sweet potatoes in deep kettle. Cover with cold water and stir in 2 teaspoons salt. Cover and boil for 25 to 30 minutes until tender. Drain water and set aside.

2. Preheat oven to 350º. Grease a 9-inch round cake pan with shortening and flour lightly.

3. Sift together flour and remaining salt on wax paper. Combine with 1 cup of the whole milk in small bowl until well blended. Stir in remaining milk and evaporated milk.

4. Mash sweet potatoes or run through a potato ricer (best) into a large bowl.

5. Fold milk/flour mixture into mashed sweet potatoes.

6. Slowly cut in butter, sugar, eggs, ginger and cardamom until batter is smooth.

7. Scoop batter into prepared pan. Bake for 1 ½ to 1 hour 45 minutes until toothpick inserted in center comes out clean.

**Yield: 12 servings**

# Guava Cakes

*Guava, like passionfruit, adds a hint of citrus, vanilla, and almond flavor.*

**8 tablespoons butter**

**2 tablespoon vegetable shortening**

**½ teaspoon baking soda**

**¼ teaspoon salt**

1 teaspoon vanilla

¾ cup sugar

1 ¾ cups flour

2 ½ teaspoons baking powder

4 medium eggs, beaten

1 teaspoon fresh grated lime rind

1 pound guava paste, sliced in ¼-inch thick slices

1. Preheat oven to 350ºF. Grease a square glass baking dish, 8 by 8 by 2-inch.

2. Cream butter, shortening, vanilla and sugar until fluffy and almost white in large bowl.

3. Sift flour, baking powder, baking soda and salt on wax paper. Cut flour mixture into butter, combining well.

4. Gradually stir in eggs and lime rind, mixing until smooth.

5. Pour half of batter into greased dish. Top with guava slices. Spoon remaining batter over top.

6. Bake 35 minutes or until golden. Cool on wire rack.

**Yield: 12 servings**

# Hojaldre

Hojaldre keeps very well, if covered tightly, and actually improves in flavor as it ages.

¾ cup butter

1 cup firmly packed brown sugar

4 large eggs

2 cups all-purpose flour

1 ½ teaspoons baking powder

1 ½ teaspoons cinnamon teaspoons nutmeg

1 ½ teaspoons nutmeg

½ teaspoon ground cloves

¼ teaspoon cardamom

¼ teaspoon salt

1/3 cup whole milk

1/3 cup sweet red wine

confectioner's sugar, sifted 1 ½ (for garnishing)

1. Preheat oven to 350ºF. Generously grease and flour a 9-inch by 3 ½-inch tube pan.

2. Cream butter and sugar, beating until fluffy and nearly white. Whisk in eggs.

3. Sift together flour, baking powder, cinnamon, nutmeg, clove, cardamom and salt on wax paper. Repeat process twice more.

4. Add ¼ quarter of the flour mixture at a time to the egg mixture, combining well. Repeat until all of flour is incorporated, alternating milk and wine. Batter should be smooth.

5. Pour batter into prepared pan and bake for 55 to 60 minutes until a toothpick inserted in center comes out clean.

6. Remove from oven and cool in pan on wire rack for 8 minutes. Invert cake on greased wire rack. Flip again so top is facing up and cool until room temperature, about 60 minutes.

7. Place on cake platter and dust with confectioner's sugar.

**Yield: 8 to 10 servings**

# Basic Pie Crust

2 ½ cups all-purpose flour, plus extra for dusting

¾ teaspoon salt

1 tablespoon sugar

12 tablespoons unsalted butter, refrigerated, cut in small ¼ pieces

6 tablespoons ice water

8 tablespoons vegetable shortening, refrigerated

1. Combine flour, salt and sugar in food processor (use lower blade only, remove grating blade).

2. Add butter pieces and pulse until flour is pebbly. Add shortening by teaspoonfuls and continue to pulse 4 or 5 more times.

3. Scoop flour mixture into medium bowl. Sprinkle ice water over top. Using an up and down motion with a large spoon, combine until you can form a smooth ball. Add an extra tablespoon of water if needed.

4. Divide dough into two and press into shape of a flat ball. Dust with flour and refrigerate for 30 minutes.

5. Sprinkle a ¼ cup flour over work surface and rolling pin. Press down lightly on dough and roll back and forth. Rotate dough on surface and continue to roll out evenly, forming a circle. Diameter of dough should be 2 inches larger than pie plate.

6. Fold dough in half, than in half again. Place dough inside pie plate and

unfold. Tuck pastry dough into corners of pie plate.

7. Trim dough down to ½ inch overlap of pie plate. Tuck dough under, so that a ¼ inch lip remains. Press down lightly.

**Yield: 2 unbaked pie crusts**

## Basic Meringue Topping

Creating meringue is much easier than it seems.

2 ½ teaspoons cornstarch, sifted

¼ cup water

¼ teaspoon cream of tartar

¾ cup sugar

5 large egg whites

1. Combine cornstarch and water in small saucepan over medium heat. Bring to simmer, stirring constantly until translucent. Remove from heat to cool.

2. Preheat oven to 325°. Combine sugar and cream of tartar in small bowl.

3. Beat egg whites in a medium bowl using an electric mixer at high speed until whites are frothy. Add sugar mixture 1 tablespoon at a time, beating until soft peaks form.

4. Slowly beat in cornstarch mixture until stiff peaks form.

5. Top pie filling with meringue, by placing spoonfuls of meringue around edge of pie, then filling in center. Spread the meringue to the edges of the pie crust with the back of a spoon. Be sure the meringue overlaps the crust slightly or the meringue will shrink during baking and leave an unsightly gap.

6. Bake 15 to 20 minutes until golden. Serve within 12 hours.

**Yield: topping for 1 pie**

## Basic Whipped Cream with Rum

You can omit the rum if you like from this recipe, substituting vanilla, almond or orange extract. Grand Marnier, Cointreau, Kirsch liqueuer or brandy may also be used in place of rum.

1 ¼ cups heavy cream, chilled

2 tablespoons sugar

1 tablespoon rum

1. Just before serving pie or cake, whip the cream and sugar in chilled bowl using an electric mixer set at medium speed. Beat until soft peaks form.
2. Stir in rum, beating until stiff.

**Yield: topping for 1 pie or cake**

# Coconut Pie
*Pastel de Coco*

**1 prepared Basic Pie Crust**
**½ cup grated coconut (this is the one time to use the sweetened, packaged kind)**

FILLING:

**6 tablespoons cornstarch, sifted**

**1 ¾ cups whole milk**

**6 egg yolks**

**½ cup coconut milk (see index)**

**¼ teaspoon lemon extract**

**¾ cup sugar**

**½ teaspoon salt**

## PIE CRUST AND TOPPING:

1. Adjust oven rack to middle position. Preheat oven to 375°. Prick dough in several places.
2. Press 12-inch square of aluminum foil inside pie shell. Weigh down dough with pie weights. Bake for 18 minutes. Remove from oven and left foil at edges, carefully removing pie weights. Allow crust to cool.
3. Spread grated coconut onto a lightly buttered cookie sheet. Broil for 5 to 7 minutes until golden. Remove from oven and cool.

## FILLING:

1. Dissolve cornstarch in small amount of milk. Pour into medium sauce pan.
2. Stir in egg yolks and blend well. Add remaining milk, coconut milk, lemon extract, sugar and salt.
3. Cook over medium heat, stirring constantly with a wooden spoon until

mixture thickens.

4. Reduce heat slightly and continue to stir until simmer. Remove from heat and allow to cool for 5 minutes.

5. Stir several times, then pour into cooled shell.

6. Top with toasted coconut.

**Yield: 1 pie, serves 12**

# Butter Pie
*Pastel de Mantequilla*

**Lovely with strong, hot Puerto Rican coffee.**
**1 prepared Basic Pie Crust**

FILLING:

| | |
|---|---|
| **½ cup sugar** | **¾ cup evaporated milk** |
| **¼ cup cornstarch, sifted** | **1 teaspoon vanilla extract** |
| **¼ teaspoon salt** | **5 tablespoons unsalted butter** |
| **6 medium egg yolks, lightly beaten** | **2 teaspoons rum** |
| **1 ¾ cups whole milk** | **¼ teaspoon ground cardamom** |

PIE CRUST:

1. Prepare and bake basic pie crust as per steps 1 and 2 of *Coconut Pie*. Allow crust to cool.

FILLING:

1. Combine sugar, cornstarch and salt in medium saucepan. Whisk yolks, one at a time.

2. Stir together milk and evaporated milk. Slowly stir into yolk mixture. Cook over moderate heat, stirring constantly until mixture thickens and begins to bubble.

3. Reduce heat and simmer for 1 minute, still stirring.

4. Remove from heat and stir in vanilla, butter, rum and ground cardamom.

5. Pour filling into flat glass baking dish. Place plastic wrap directly over filling to prevent skin from forming.

6. Cool 20 minutes. While filling is still *warm*, pour into cooled pie crust. Press fresh plastic wrap directly onto filling. Note, at this point, you may top with meringue topping (see index). But do so while the filling is still hot or the meringue won't set properly.

7. Refrigerate until firm, 3 to 4 hours.

**Yield: 8 servings**

# Chocolate Pie

*Pastel de Chocolate*

**1 prepared *Basic Pie Crust***

FILLING:

½ **cup sugar**

¼ **cup cornstarch, sifted**

**2 tablespoons, plus 1 teaspoon unsweetened cocoa**

¼ **teaspoon salt**

**6 medium egg yolks, lightly beaten**

**1 ¾ cups whole milk**

¾ **cup evaporated milk**

**5 ounces semi-sweet chocolate bits**

**1 teaspoon vanilla extract**

**4 tablespoons unsalted butter**

**2 teaspoons rum**

¼ **teaspoon ground cinnamon**

PIE CRUST:

1. Prepare and bake basic pie crust as per steps 1 and 2 of *Coconut Pie*. Allow crust to cool.

FILLING:

1. Combine sugar, cornstarch, unsweetened cocoa and salt in medium saucepan. Whisk yolks, one at a time.

2. Stir together milk and evaporated milk. Slowly stir into yolk mixture. Stir in chocolate bits. Cook over moderate heat, stirring constantly until mixture thickens and begins to bubble.

3. Reduce heat and simmer for 1 minute, still stirring.

4. Remove from heat and stir in vanilla, butter, rum and ground cinnamon.

5. Pour filling into flat glass baking dish. Place plastic wrap directly over filling to prevent skin from forming.

6. Cool 20 minutes. While filling is still *warm*, pour into cooled pie crust. Press fresh plastic wrap directly onto filling.

7. Refrigerate until firm, 3 to 4 hours. Top with chilled whipped topping.

**Yield: 8 servings**

# Lime Pie

*Pastel de Limón*

Many people prefer the flavor of key limes when making a lime pie. Anna and I tried key limes and found them difficult to squeeze, being thin-skinned and full of seeds. Use regular limes. To us, the flavor was nearly identical and we needed far fewer limes.

LIME FILLING:

**1 tablespoon fresh grated lime zest**

**¼ teaspoon ground ginger**

**6 large egg yolks**

**1 14-ounce can sweetened condensed milk**

**½ cup fresh lime juice (3 to 4 limes)**

GRAHAM CRACKER CRUST:

**1 ¼ cups fresh graham cracker crumbs (use a food processor)**

**3 tablespoons, plus 1 teaspoon granulated sugar**

**4 tablespoons unsalted butter, melted**

WHIPPED CREAM:

**¾ cup heavy cream, chilled**

**2 tablespoons granulated sugar**

**1 tablespoon Cointreau liqueur**

FILLING:

1. Whip lime zest and ground ginger with egg yolks for 1 minute with an electric hand mixer set on low. Beat in milk. Slowly drizzle in lime juice, combining well. Set aside. Mixture will thicken at room temperature (see How Key Lime Thickens below)

## GRAHAM CRACKER CRUST:

1. Place oven rack in center position. Preheat oven to 325°F.
2. Combine graham crumbs, butter and sugar in small bowl. Press into bottom and sides of 9-inch pie pan.
3. Bake for 12 minutes until lightly browned. Remove and cool on wire rack for 30 minutes.

## TO ASSEMBLE PIE:

1. Preheat oven again to 325°F. Lime filling should be thickened by now. Pour into cooled crust.
2. Bake for 15 to 20 minutes until firm in center (will still jiggle when shaken).
3. Cool on wire rack for 45 minutes.
4. Refrigerate until well chilled.

## TOPPING:

1. Whip cream in chilled medium bowl with electric hand mixer set on moderate speed until soft peaks form.
2. Beat in sugar a little at a time. Add liqueur, beating until stiff peaks form.
3. Spoon topping over refrigerated pie.

**Yield: 1 pie, 8 servings**

## HOW LIME PIE FILLING THICKENS

When I first made this pie, Anna didn't believe that the filling would thicken on its own at room temperature. But everything in cooking is based upon science and specific heat and chemical reactions.

The high acid content of limes, along with the protein and sugar in sweetened condensed milk is responsible for this thickening action.

Canned, sweetened condensed milk is produced by boiling much of the water content from fresh milk, then adding sugar. The lime juice then curdles the milk, which is now thick enough to thicken into a sliceable filling.

Okay, so why isn't the filling lumpy with curdles? Well, the sugar plays an important part in maintaining a smooth filling. The sugar separates the protein strands by ensuring they don't cling together.

Sweetened condensed milk is the only milk that will produce this smooth, thickened result. Fresh milk doesn't contain enough sugar, and cream doesn't work because its high fat content blocks the lime juice from curdling the milk.

## Rum Apple Pie

*Pastel de Manzanas y Ron*

I'm sure by now you've guessed that I've added rum to most of the traditional Puerto Rican recipes in this cookbook. Let's be fair, some of them already contained rum. Honestly, I am not a rum drinker. But adding rum to island recipes just does something magical and tropical…

**1 recipe Basic Pie Crust**

**4 pounds tart apples (Granny Smith is popular in the islands because its lower sugar content helps the apple hold up longer)**

**¾ cup sugar**

**2 tablespoons lemon juice**

**1 tablespoon dark rum**

**1 tablespoon fresh lemon zest**

**1 tablespoon fresh grated ginger root**

**½ teaspoon salt**

**¼ teaspoon ground nutmeg**

**¼ teaspoon ground cinnamon**

**¼ teaspoon ground allspice**

**¼ teaspoon ground cardamom**

1. Prepare basic pie dough as directed. Adjust oven rack to center position. Preheat oven to 425°F.

2. Roll one dough ball into a 12-inch circle. Fold dough in half, then in half again. Place inside deep dish pie plate.

3. Unfold dough and press into corners. Place plate in refrigerator.

4. Peel, core, and slice apples into ½ inch slices. Place in a medium bowl and toss with sugar, lemon juice, dark rum, lemon zest, grated ginger, salt and spices. Allow to sit for 20 minutes. Remove unrolled dough ball from refrigerator and allow to soften slightly.

5. Remove pie plate from refrigerator and heap fruit into center. Press down slightly, leaving a slight mound in middle.

6. Roll out second dough disk and place over top of filled pie.

7. With clean chicken scissors, trim dough to ½ inch beyond pie edge. Tuck excess underneath, pressing down with edges of fork to seal.

8. Prick top of crust otherwise pie may blow up.

9. Bake for 25 to 30 minutes until golden. Reduce heat to 350°F. Remove pie from oven carefully and cover edges with aluminum foil to prevent excessive browning. Bake for 30 additional minutes. Remove from oven and cool on wire rack for 3 hours. Serve plain or with vanilla ice cream.

**Yield: 8 servings**

# Mango Pie
*Pastel de Mango*

If by some chance you have leftover pie, freeze it as it keeps well.

| | |
|---|---|
| 1 recipe for *Basic Pie Crust* | 1 teaspoon fresh grated ginger root |
| ¼ cup granulated sugar | ¼ teaspoon nutmeg |
| ½ cup brown sugar | ¼ teaspoon cinnamon |
| 3 tablespoons tapioca | ¼ teaspoon cardamom |
| 1 tablespoon lemon juice | ½ teaspoon salt |
| 1 teaspoon grated lemon zest | 6 cups peeled, pitted and sliced mango |

1. Prepare *Basic Pie Crust* as directed.

2. Adjust oven rack to center position. Preheat oven to 400°F.

3. Roll one dough ball into a 12-inch disk. Fold dough in half, then in half again. Place in center of deep dish pie plate. Unfold and press dough into corners.

4. Combine sugars, tapioca, lemon juice, lemon zest, grated ginger, spices and salt in a large bowl. Add mango and toss gently to coat. Allow to sit for 10 minutes.

5. Scoop fruit into center of pie shell, pressing down gently, but leaving fruit slightly mounded in center.

6. Roll out second dough ball into 12-inch disk. Place over filling.

7. Trim top within ½ inch of edge and tuck underneath. Press down with tines of fork to seal.

8. Bake until golden, about 25 minutes. Reduce heat to 350°F and bake additional 25 minutes.

9. Remove from oven and place on wire rack to cool, about 2 hours. Serve at once.

**Yield: 8 servings**

## Pineapple Pie

*Pastel de Piña*

This is a quick and easy recipe. And, the canned pineapple is absolutely delicious, intense and fragrant.

Note: you'll need a candy thermometer for this one.

**2 one-pound cans crushed pineapple**　　**1 tablespoon fresh grated lime rind**
**1 ½ cups sugar**　　**4 tablespoons light rum**
**1 tablespoon fresh lime juice**　　**1 *Basic Pie Crust* recipe**

1. Simmer the pineapple and sugar in a medium saucepan over moderate heat until temperature attains 220°F on candy thermometer.

2. Remove from heat. Stir in lime juice, lime rind and rum. Set aside to cool.

3. Prepare pie crust as per steps 2 and 3 of *Mango Pie*.

4. Scoop pineapple into center of pie crust and press down lightly. Fruit should be slightly raised in center.

5. Roll out second ball of dough into 12-inch cylinder. Place over top of fruit and trim down to ½ inch on sides. Tuck excess dough underneath and press down with tines of fork.

6. Bake in 400°F oven for 35 minutes until golden.

7. Remove from oven and cool on wire rack for 2 hours.

**Yield: 8 servings**

# Mango Tart
*Tarta de Mango*

A fruit tart is different from a fruit pie. Instead of a shortening crust, butter and eggs are used. Tart dough is rested and chilled, which helps limit gluten development and prevents excessive drying out and toughness. Unlike a pie, the crust is spread with a egg and milk-based pastry cream, then topped with raw fruit.

Assemble just before serving, avoiding a soggy crust.

PASTRY SHELL:

1 ¼ cups all-purpose flour, plus extra for dusting

2 tablespoons, plus 1 teaspoon sugar

6 tablespoons unsalted butter, chilled, cut into ½-inch pieces

¼ teaspoon salt

1/8 teaspoon baking powder

1 large egg, beaten with 1 tablespoon rum

PASTRY CREAM:

3 tablespoons, plus 1 teaspoon sugar

2 tablespoons all-purpose flour

1/8 teaspoon salt

½ cup whole milk

¼ cup evaporated milk

1 tablespoon dark Puerto Rican rum

1 large egg, plus 1 egg yolk

½ teaspoon vanilla extract

½ teaspoon almond extract

1 tablespoon unsalted butter, room temperature

GLAZED FRUIT:

6 cups peeled, pitted, ripe mango, cut in ¼ inch thick slices

¼ cup apple jelly

1 tablespoon 151 proof rum

## PASTRY SHELL:

1. Combine flour, sugar, salt and baking powder in a food processor. Toss butter over flour. Pulse until mixture resembles gravel or peas. Place mixture in medium bowl.

2. Add egg/rum mixture, using a wooden spoon to mix. Shape dough into a ball, kneading with hands. Flatten into a flat ball, dust with flour, then wrap in plastic and refrigerate for 2 hours.

3. Remove dough ball from refrigerator and allow to stand for 15 to 20 minutes at room temperature. Roll dough on lightly floured surface until 12 inches in diameter and ¼ inch thick.

4. Slide dough onto lightly buttered cookie sheet. Fold sides up to make a lip to contain pastry cream and fruit. Prick dough lightly with a fork, otherwise it will blow up. Cover with plastic and place in freezer for 15 minutes.

5. Place oven rack at center position. Preheat to 400°F. Place pastry shell in oven and reduce heat to 350°F. Bake until golden. Cool on wire rack.

## PASTRY CREAM:

1. Combine sugar, flour and salt in a medium saucepan. Whisk in whole milk, evaporated milk and eggs. Turn stove to low heat, stirring constantly, until thickened. Simmer, stirring constantly for 30 seconds. Remove from heat.

2. Stir in vanilla, almond extract and butter. Scoop pastry cream into a glass bowl and pour cold milk over top. Refrigerate for 2 hours or overnight.

3. Pour off milk and stir in rum.

## TO ASSEMBLE:

1. Spread pastry cream evenly over cooled pastry crust.

2. Heat apple jelly in a small saucepan over low heat until liquid. Stir in 151 proof rum. Set aside, keeping warm.

3. Arrange fruit over pastry cream.

4. Spoon jelly lightly and evenly over fruit. Chill for 1 hour in refrigerator. Serve at once.

**Yield: 8 servings**

# VARIATIONS:

Substitute ripe pineapple or papaya slices for the mango.

## LOW-CARB Banana-Ginger Cake

Yes, happily there is such a thing as a low-carb tropical cake!

1 cup vanilla whey protein powder

½ cup almond flour

2 ½ teaspoons baking powder

½ teaspoon salt

¼ teaspoon ground mace

¼ teaspoon ground cinnamon

½ cup sour cream

2 tablespoons heavy cream

3 large eggs

1 cup Splenda®

1 ½ teaspoons vanilla extract

¾ cup mashed ripe bananas

1 tablespoon freshly grated ginger root

8 tablespoons butter, room temperature

1. Preheat oven to 350°F. Lightly coat an 8 or 9-inch round or square cake pan with vegetable spray. Set aside.

2. Whisk together protein powder, almond flour, baking powder, salt, mace and cinnamon in a medium bowl. Set aside.

3. Beat butter in a large bowl using an electric beater set at medium speed until fluffy. Whisk in eggs, Splenda® and vanilla, beating for 4 to 5 minutes.

4. Reduce speed to low and gradually add dry ingredients to egg mixture. Beat one minute.

5. By hand, fold in vanilla, banana, ginger, sour cream and heavy cream, until just blended. Do not over mix.

6. Transfer batter to cake pan. Bake for 25 minutes until a toothpick inserted in center comes out clean.

7. Remove from oven and cool on a wire rack for 10 minutes. Invert onto rack and cool completely.

**Yield: 12 servings**

EACH SERVING PROVIDES APPROXIMATELY:
201 calories, **11 grams carbohydrates**, 9 grams of protein, 14 grams of fat

# LOW-CARB Cinnamon, Pecan and Chayote Coffee Cake

I realize this recipe sounds odd, but it is quite delicious and moist.

## PECAN FILLING:

¾ cup finely chopped pecans

1/3 cup Splenda®

¾ teaspoon ground cinnamon

¼ teaspoon ground ginger

## COFFEE CAKE:

1 ½ cups vanilla whey protein powder

½ cup almond flour

1 ½ teaspoon baking powder

1 teaspoon baking soda

½ teaspoon salt

8 tablespoons butter, room temperature

3 large eggs

1 cup Splenda®

1 ½ teaspoons vanilla extract

½ teaspoon lemon extract

1 cup sour cream

1 pound chayote (or zucchini) peeled and thinly sliced

1. Preheat oven to 350°F. Lightly spray a 9-inch round, glass baking dish with vegetable spray.

2. Combine pecans, Splenda®, cinnamon and ginger in a small bowl. Set aside.

3. Combine protein powder, almond flour, baking powder, baking soda and salt in a medium bowl.

4. Beat butter in a large bowl using an electric mixer at medium speed until fluffy. Beat in eggs, then Splenda® for 2 minutes. Do not overbeat or you'll have large, dry holes in your coffee cake. Whisk in vanilla, lemon extract and sour cream.

5. Beat in dry ingredients gradually until just blended.

6. Transfer half the batter into pan. Sprinkle with half the pecan mixture. Top with remaining batter. Layer chayote or zucchini slices on top. Finish with remaining pecan mixture.

7. Bake for 25 minutes until a wooden toothpick inserted in center comes out clean.

**Yield: 12 servings**

EACH SERVING PROVIDES APPROXIMATELY:
210 calories, **9 grams carbohydrates**, 12 grams of protein, 16 grams of fat

 **13** ## Cookies, Candies and Coconuts

## Shortbread Cookies
*Mantecaditos*

Sandy and crumbly as perfect shortbread should be:

½ pound butter, room temperature

1 ½ teaspoons almond extract

½ cup confectioner's sugar

2 tablespoons granulated sugar

2 cups all-purpose flour

¼ teaspoon salt

1. Preheat oven to 350°F.

2. Cream butter with almond extract in a medium bowl, gradually whipping in sugars until and fluffy.

3. Sift flour and salt onto a wax paper. Gradually fold into butter mixture until well-combined.

4. Flour a rolling pin and roll out the dough until ¼ inch thick. Cut into rectangles, squares or use a cookie cutter.

5. Place on ungreased cookie sheets. Prick each cookie with a fork and bake for 20 minutes or until golden on the edges.

6. Slide off cookie sheet immediately and cool on wire rack.

**Yield: 24, 1 x 2 inch cookies**

## Almond Cookies
*Polvorones*

These cookies resemble Viennese Crescents and the generous use of butter makes them melt in your mouth. Doritza and I made this recipe one afternoon. I lined a cookie tin with wax paper and filled it with the *polvorones*. The next day I drove to the rainforest to meet my friend Lisette for a hike. I had fully intended to give her the tin of cookies for her grandmother who had generously shared many of her recipes with me. After the hike, we stopped in at the Westin for cappuccino. Foolishly I brought the tin along. I'm embarrassed to admit we demolished nearly half the tin before we came to our senses.

½ pound butter, room temperature
1 egg yolk
2 cups flour
1 cup ground almonds

¾ confectioner's sugar, plus extra dusting cookies
1 teaspoon almond extract

1. Preheat oven to 300°F.
2. Cream butter in a medium bowl with a hand whisk until shiny. Whisk in egg and almond extract. Gradually beat in sugar, beating until light and fluffy.
3. Whisk in flour and ground almonds, combining thoroughly.
4. Shape into 2-inch crescents with your fingers. Roll in confectioner's sugar and bake on ungreased cookie sheets for 12 to 15 minutes, until lightly browned.
5. Slide off cookie sheets at once and cool on wire racks. Dust again with confectioner's sugar before serving.

Yield: 36 to 48 cookies

# Petit Merengues
*Merenguitos*

4 egg whites room temperature
¼ teaspoon salt
1 cup, plus 2 teaspoons sugar

1. Preheat oven to 225°F.
2. Beat egg whites with a hand mixture until soft peaks form. Do not over beat.
3. Add salt and gradually beat in sugar, except for the 2 teaspoons. You should have stiff peaks now. Sprinkle in remaining sugar.
4. Fill a pastry bag with a fancy tip and squeeze out 1 ½ inch rounds on non-stick cookie sheet.
5. Bake for 1 ½ hours. Meringue should be crunchy, not brown.

Yield: about 72 meringues

# Snowballs

*Bolas de Nieve*

Make these with your kids-they're so much fun to create.

| | |
|---|---|
| ½ cup water | 2 egg whites, room temperature |
| 2 ½ cups sugar | 1 teaspoon almond extract |
| 1 teaspoon grated lemon rind | |

1. Combine water, sugar and lemon rind in a medium saucepan over medium heat until mixture boils. Do not stir. Syrup should be at hard ball stage, 265°F. Remove from heat.
2. Beat egg whites with an electric beater set a high until stiff peaks form. Slowly pour syrup, still beating on high.
3. Continue to beat until mixture thickens. Stir in almond extract. Shape into small 1 ½ inch balls and wrap in wax paper.

**Yield: about 36**

# Coconut Macaroons

*Macaroons de Coco*

You haven't tried macaroons until you've had them made with fresh coconut, instead of canned.

| | |
|---|---|
| 1 ½ cups fresh grated coconut (see index) | ¼ teaspoon salt |
| ¾ cup sugar | 3 egg whites |
| 4 tablespoons flour | 1 teaspoon almond extract |

1. Preheat oven to 325°F. Place rack in center position in oven.
2. Combine coconut, sugar, flour and salt in large mixing bowl.
3. Beat egg whites with almond extract with electric beater set on low for 1 minute.
4. Fold egg whites into coconut mixture. Drop by teaspoonfuls on lightly greased or non-stick baking sheet.
5. Bake 20 to 25 minutes until edges are golden. Remove from baking sheets at once and place on greased wire rack.

**Yield: 18 to 24 cookies**

# Coconut-Guava Cookies (Galletitas de Coco y Guayaba)

*Galletitaqs de Coco y Guayaba*

| | |
|---|---|
| 2 sticks unsalted butter at room temperature | 2 tablespoons flour |
| 2/3 cup sugar | ½ teaspoon salt |
| 1 teaspoon almond extract | ¾ cup guava preserves |
| 3/4 cup sweetened flaked coconut (store-bought kind) | |

1. Beat butter and sugar in a large bowl until fluffy and almost white.
2. Stir in almond extract, coconut, flour and salt. Refrigerate 1 hour until dough is firm.
3. Preheat oven to 350°F. Shape into balls using a tablespoon to measure.
4. Place on ungreased cookie sheet, 1 ½ inches apart.
5. Press a small indention in center of each cookie using your thumb.
6. Bake until golden, about 15 to 20 minutes. Cool on wire rack.
7. Fill center of each cookie with guava preserves.

**Yield: 24 cookies**

# Coconut Milk

Coconut milk can be purchased canned, but fresh is quick and easy to make. If you don't have a blender, grate the coconut by hand, then pour the hot water over the top. If you can't find coconut, substitute fresh milk and ¼ cup dried, unsweetened coconut per cup milk. Whirl in blender, or beat with hand mixer until smooth.

**meat from 1 fresh coconut, cut into chunks**

**3 cups very hot, but not boiling water**

1. Place coconut chunks and hot water in a blender. Purée for 2 to 3 minutes, then stop. Allow to stand for 20 to 30 minutes.
2. Strain through clean cheese cloth into bowl. Squeeze out as much liquid as possible.
3. Use at once or refrigerate for up to 3 to 4 days.

## TIP—HOW MUCH COCONUT MILK FROM ONE COCONUT

- ◆ 1 large coconut equals 1 pound coconut meat
- ◆ 1 pound coconut meat equals 4 cups grated coconut
- ◆ 4 cups grated coconut equals just under ½ cup coconut milk

### Coconut

The best coconuts are available between October and December. This is the time those of us in the islands tread carefully beneath coconut trees, as they tend to drop like cannonballs without warning.

**Purchasing:** Select coconuts that are heavy in proportion to their size. Shake them. They should be full of liquid. If you don't hear anything, it probably has dried up inside.

**Storing:** Unopened, coconuts, can be kept in a cool, dry place for up to three months. Refrigerate for up to a week once open. You may also freeze for 4 months.

**To quickly grate:** Save time and effort by placing peeled small pieces of coconut meat into a food processor. Pulse to grate.

# Grated Coconut

*Coco Rallado*

This is the coconut to use for recipes that call for grated coconut as an ingredient, not as a garnish. The dehydrated packaged kind is just not the same thing.

The easiest way to open a coconut is to throw it down on a cement or rock surface like the monkeys do. Don't try this on your good kitchen floor. Or, you can do the following.

**1 ripe coconut**

1. Shake the coconut to make sure it is full of liquid. If dried up, it's old and needs to be discarded.

2. Pierce a couple of the eyes with a screwdriver or an icepick. Drain the liquid through a mesh sieve into a cup. The liquid is wonderful chilled with rum.

3. Smash the coconut open with a hammer. Break into several smaller pieces. About this time, I give the coconut pieces a good rinse under running water to remove bits and pieces of brown shell.

4. Pry the meat from the shell using a short and sharp knife.

5. Peel the brown skin from the white meat.

6. Cut meat into 1-inch pieces.

7. Fit a food processor with the grating blade and feed in chunks of meat in small batches until grated. The industrious may use a hand grater.

**Yield: about 3 to 4 cups**

# Sugar Frosted Coconut Fruits

*Fruitas de Coco Azucardas*

Kids enjoy decorating the 'fruits.'

**3 cups grated coconut (see index)**
**3 cups granulated sugar**
**1 tablespoon fresh lime juice**
**1 teaspoon grated lime rind**
**3 medium eggs, lightly beaten**
**candied leaves**
**nutmeg for dusting**

**¼ teaspoon salt**
    **food coloring**
**1 ½ cups granulated sugar**
    **(for rolling)**
**whole cloves**
**½ teaspoon vanilla**

1. Combine grated coconut and the 3 cups sugar in a medium saucepan.

2. Whisk together lime juice, rind, eggs, vanilla and salt in a small bowl. Stir egg mixture into coconut mixture.

3. Cook over medium heat, stirring constantly, until mixture boils.

4. Reduce heat immediately, stirring occasionally, and simmer for 30 to 40 minutes. Mixture should be nearly dry and 240°F on a candy thermometer.

5. Scoop out mixture into 5 small bowls. Tint each bowl with several drops of the food color, i.e. red, blue, yellow, etc.

6. Roll each 'color' into 8 to 10 balls. Of course, for bananas, you'll want a banana shape instead of a ball.

337

7. Pour remaining 1 ½ cups sugar into a shallow dish. Roll each 'fruit' in the sugar and top with a clove to mimic the stem.

8. Garnish with candied leaves. Dust wherever appropriate with nutmeg, i.e. to resemble brown flecks on a banana, etc.

**Yield: about 24 fruits**

## Love Powder
*Polvo de Amor*

Old cookbooks list this coconut treat as a topping for desserts, but it also makes a delicious chutney for fish or chicken.

**2 cups shredded coconut**
**¾ cup granulated sugar**

1. Combine grated coconut and sugar in a deep kettle or saucepan over medium-high heat, stirring constantly for 5 minutes.

2. Reduce heat to medium and cook another 8 to 10 minutes until coconut turns brown and cruncy.

**Yield: approximately 2 cups**

## Coconut Squares
*Cocada*

As you can tell, coconut candies, cakes and cookies are big on the island. It's no wonder. Coconut trees grown everywhere. Even the city of San Juan has coconut palms within its limits.

**3 cups grated coconut**          **½ teaspoon salt**
**3 cups water**                   **4 large eggs, lightly beaten**
**3 ½ cups sugar**                 **4 tablespoons butter, room**
**1 teaspoon fresh grated ginger root**   **temperature**
**½ teaspoon fresh grated lime rind**     **½ cup crushed almonds butter**

1. Bring grated coconut, 3 cups water, 3 ½ cups sugar, ginger, lime rind and salt to boil in a heavy saucepan.

2. Reduce heat to low and cook for one hour without stirring. You should be at the light syrup stage (222°) on a candy thermometer.

3. Remove from heat and cool to room temperature.

4. Butter an 8 by 8-inch glass baking dish. Preheat oven to 375°F.

5. Stir eggs and butter into coconut mixture. Fold in crushed almonds.

6. Turn into glass baking dish. Press coconut/almond mixture down lightly.

7. Bake for 55 minutes. Remove from oven and place on wire rack. Cool to room temperature.

8. Cut into 2 inch squares.

**Yield: 12 squares**

# Coconut Crunch

*Turroncitos de Coco*

One finds this candy all over Puerto Rico, even at the 24-hour gas stations!

**2 cups coconut milk (see index)**  
**3 cups sugar**  
**½ teaspoon almond extract**

**½ teaspoon vanilla**  
**1/8 teaspoon mace**

1. Boil coconut milk, sugar, almond extract, vanilla and mace in a deep kettle or pot. Reduce heat to medium and cook without stirring until syrup thickens into hard ball stage (258°F, candy thermometer).

2. Grease a marble slab and pour candy mixture over it to allow cooling.

3. When beginning to firm, but not harden, pull as for taffy. Pull out, bring back, then pull out again. Keep going until candy whitens.

4. Without wasting a moment, roll candy into long logs, about 1 ½ inches thick. Slice into 2 inch pieces. Best if wrapped in wax paper.

**Yield: about 48 pieces**

# Coconut Kisses

*Besitos de Coco*

**3 cups grated coconut (see index)**
**½ cup all-purpose flour**
**¾ cup sugar**
**½ teaspoon salt**
**butter**

**1 tablespoon vegetable oil**
**1 teaspoon fresh grated ginger root**
**1 tablespoon brown sugar**

1. Preheat oven to 325°F. Generously butter a cookie sheet.
2. Combine coconut, flour, sugar, brown sugar, vegetable oil, ginger and salt in a large bowl.
3. Form into 1 ¼ inch balls with your hands.
4. Place on cookie sheet, flattening slightly and bake for 30 minutes until edges begin to brown.
5. Remove from oven and cool on wire cookie rack.

**Yield: 24 to 30 cookies**

# Coconut Candy Bars

*Dulce de Coco en Barras*

**3 cups fresh grated coconut (see index)**
**2 ¾ cups sugar**
**1 ¾ cups whole milk**
**¼ cup evaporated milk**
**½ teaspoon fresh grated lime rind**

**½ teaspoon fresh grated ginger root**
**½ teaspoon salt**
**½ teaspoon white vinegar**
**½ teaspoon vanilla**
**¼ teaspoon ground mace**

1. Combine all ingredients in a heavy saucepot or cast iron pot over medium heat. Bring to a boil.
2. Reduce heat and simmer for 40 to 45 minutes until mixture separates from sides and bottom of pot. Watch for hot splatters. Stir for 20 seconds.
3. Pour onto marble slab or greased surface. Using rubber spatulas dipped in water, shape into a ½ inch thick square.
4. Cool for 30 minutes, then slice into 1 ½ by 3-inch bars.

**Yield: 12 bars**

# Sweet Potato and Coconut Candy Bar

*Dulce de Batata y Leche de Coco*

**1 pound white sweet potato**
**½ cup, plus 1 tablespoon coconut milk (see index)**

**1 1/3 cups sugar**
**¼ teaspoon salt**

1. Peel sweet potato, coarsely dice and cover in cold salted water. Boil until tender. Drain.
2. Mash the potatoes in a heavy saucepan or cast iron pot caldero. Stir in coconut milk, sugar and salt.
3. Cook over moderate heat, stirring constantly until mixture separate completely from bottom of pot. Be careful of hot splatters.
4. Remove from heat and cool for 10 minutes. Scoop onto marble slab or any dampened hard and smooth surface.
5. Shape into a square about ½-inch thick. Allow to cool for 1 hour.
6. Slice into 1 ½ inch by 3-inch bars.

**Yield: 10 to 12 bars**

# Sweet Potato Sapodillas

*Nísperos de Batata*

**1  pound white sweet potato**
**½ cup, plus 1 tablespoon coconut milk (see index)**
**½ teaspoon salt**

**1 egg yolk, beaten**
**ground cinnamon for rolling**
**1 ½ cups sugar**
**whole cloves**

1. Scrub, peel, wash and quarter sweet potatoes. Place in deep kettle or cast iron pot, cover with cold, salted water and cook over medium heat until soft. Drain and put through ricer or mash.
2. Stir in coconut milk, sugar, salt and egg yolk.
3. Turn heat on medium and bring to boil, stirring constantly. Reduce heat when mixture separates from bottom and sides of kettle.

4. Remove from heat and cool 30 minutes. Shape mixture into small balls.

5. Roll in ground cinnamon and top each ball with a whole clove.

**Yield: 16 to 20 balls**

# Cream Caramel Candy

*Dulce de Leche*

Quick and simple to make.

**2 cans sweetened-condensed milk**
**1 ½ teaspoons vanilla**

1. Cook the condensed milk in a heavy saucepan over medium heat until mixture forms a soft ball in cold water, 235°F on candy thermometer.

2. Remove from heat and add vanilla. Beat until creamy.

3. Pour into two buttered bread pans. When cold, slice in 1-inch cubes.

**Yield: approximately 72 pieces**

# Cream Caramel II

*Dulce de Leche II*

**1 ¼ cups sugar**            **3 tablespoon butter**
**½ cup glucose**            **2 tablespoons, plus 1 teaspoon flour**
**2 cups evaporated milk**            **1 teaspoon vanilla**
**1 egg yolk**

1. Combine sugar, glucose and 1 cup of the evaporated milk in a medium saucepan over moderate heat until mixture begins to simmer.

2. Beat egg yolk with remaining evaporated milk in small bowl. Gradually stir into boiling sugar/cream mixture. Cook until mixture forms a soft ball when dropped in cold water, 235°F on candy thermometer.

3. Cream butter in another small bowl. Slowly beat in flour. Gradually stir into candy mixture. Cook until 240°F. Remove from heat.

4. Stir in vanilla and pour into Criscoed™ shallow, glass baking dish.

5. When cold, slice into 1-inch cubes.

**Yield: approximately 100 pieces**

# Coconut Caramels

*Dulce de Leche con Coco*

Once you eat caramel with coconut, you'll never go back to plain caramel candy again.

| | |
|---|---|
| 1 cup grated coconut (see index) | ½ teaspoon salt |
| 1 cup evaporated milk | ¾ cup Crisco™ |
| 1 cup sweetened condensed milk | 1 teaspoon almond extract |
| ½ cup packed brown sugar | ½ teaspoon rose extract |

1. Soak coconut in evaporated milk for 1 hour. Place in medium saucepan along with sweetened condensed milk, brown sugar, salt and 1/3 of the Crisco™. Stir in almond and rose extract.

2. Cook over moderate heat until mixture forms a soft ball in cold water, 235°F on candy thermometer.

3. Stir in remaining Crisco™ and cook until mixture reaches 250°F.

4. Scoop candy into buttered or Criscoed™ shallow glass baking dish.

5. Slice into 1-inch squares when cool. Wrap each caramel in wax candy.

**Yield: approximately 100 pieces**

# Latin Caramels with Almonds

*Dulce de Leche con Almendra*

| | |
|---|---|
| 2 cups granulated sugar, divided | 1 cup finely ground almonds |
| 1 cup evaporated milk | ½ teaspoon almond extract |
| ¾ cup packed brown sugar | ½ teaspoon vanilla extract |

1. Melt 1 cup of the granulated sugar in a large cast-iron skillet over low heat, stirring constantly. Do not brown. Sugar should be in syrup stage.

2. Stir in 1 cup evaporated milk, stirring for 1 minute.

3. Stir in remaining cup of granulated sugar and brown sugar. Simmer, stirring constantly until mixture forms a soft ball when dropped in cold water, 235°F.

4. Remove from heat and stir in nuts, vanilla and almond extract.

5. Pour into buttered glass baking dish. Slice into 1-inch cubes when cooled. Wrap each caramel in wax paper.

**Yield: approximately 72 squares**

# LOW-CARB Almond Cookies

These are my absolute favorite cookies. I don't always follow a low-carb diet, but I don't care for cookies that are too sweet either. Good thing. I couldn't stop nibbling on these. Wonderful dunked in hot coffee, milk or tea.

**1 ½ cups almond flour**

**1 ¼ cups vanilla whey protein powder**

**1 ¼ teaspoons baking powder**

**½ teaspoon baking soda**

**1 teaspoon salt**

**¼ teaspoon ground cardamom**

**2 teaspoons almond extract**

**¼ teaspoon nutmeg**

**½ cup butter at room temperature**

**1 tablespoon canola oil**

**¾ cup, plus 1 tablespoon Splenda™**

**4 medium eggs**

1. Preheat oven to 350°F. Set aside a non-stick baking sheet.

2. Whisk together almond flour, protein powder, baking soda, salt, cardamom and nutmeg in a medium bowl.

3. Beat butter, oil, Splenda™, eggs and almond extract in a large bowl using an electric mixer set at high for 4 minutes.

4. Lower speed and slowly add flour mixture.

5. Divide dough in half and form two logs, 1 ½ inches in diameter. Slice in 1-inch wheels.

6. Bake for 15 minutes or until golden. Remove pan from oven and cool on wire rack. When fully cool, slide cookies off baking sheet. Store in an airtight container for up to 1 week.

**Yield: 36 cookies**

EACH SERVING PROVIDES APPROXIMATELY:
88 calories; **3 grams carbohydrates**, 3.5 grams of protein, 7 grams of fat

# LOW-CARB Chocolate Mocha Rum Cookies

I couldn't stop eating these either. Make a batch of the LOW-CARB Almond Cookies and serve alongside this divine recipe.

½ cup almond flour

¼ cup vanilla whey protein powder

¼ cup high-gluten flour

4 tablespoons cocoa powder (baking kind)

½ teaspoon salt

¼ teaspoon baking powder

1 teaspoon powdered instant coffee

¼ teaspoon baking soda

1/2 cup butter, room temperature

1 ½ teaspoons rum extract

2/3 cup Splenda™

1 large egg

1. Preheat oven to 350°F. Set aside a non-stick baking sheet.

2. Combine almond flour, protein powder, flour, cocoa powder, salt, baking powder and baking soda in a medium bowl.

3. Beat butter in a large bowl using an electric mixture set on medium until light and fluffy, about 3 minutes. Add rum extract, Splenda™, egg and instant coffee for 1 minute.

4. Beat in dry ingredients gradually. Dough will be sticky and stiff. Finish mixing dough with your hands.

5. Drop dough by tablespoonfuls on cookie sheet. Bake for 12 minutes.

6. Remove pan from oven and cool on wire rack. When completely cool, place in airtight container for up to 1 week.

**Yield: 22 to 24 cookies**

EACH SERVING PROVIDES APPROXIMATELY:
90 calories, **3 grams carbohydrates**, 3 grams protein, 8 grams of fat

# Ice Cream, Sherbert and Sorbet

You're probably wondering how all these ice cream and sorbet recipes ended up in a Puerto Rican cookbook. I wondered that myself. It's quite simple. As Anna, Doritza and I interviewed friends and relatives, begged recipes from local restaurant owners, chefs and hostesses, we turned up a surprising amount of frozen desert recipes.

It makes sense actually. Puerto Rico produces a rich supply of mango, passionfruit, guava, soursop and the ubiquitous coconut and pineapple. Moreover, the island can become quite hot, especially in the summer months.

Making homemade ice creams, sorbets and sherbert uses up this over abundance of fruit and providing a cooling and welcome refreshment from the torrid heat.

## Vanilla Ice Cream

*Mantecado de Vainilla*
Rich, smooth and golden.

| | |
|---|---|
| 4 cups half and half | 3 tablespoons cornstarch, sifted |
| 1 cup evaporated milk | 6 egg yolks, lightly beaten |
| 1 ½ cups sugar | 2 teaspoons vanilla |
| ½ teaspoon salt | |

1. Whisk the cornstarch in ¼ cup of the evaporated milk until smooth and no lumps remain.

2. Combine half and half, remaining evaporated milk, sugar and cornstarch mixture in a medium saucepan. Whisk until smooth. Stir in eggs, vanilla and salt.

3. Cook over medium heat, stirring constantly for 7 to 8 minutes. Do not allow mixture to boil.

4. Allow mixture to cool to room temperature, stirring occasionally.

5. Pour mixture into ice cream maker and follow manufacturer's directions.

6. Pour into freezer-proof container and freeze for 4 hours before serving.

**Yield: about 2 quarts**

# Vanilla Rum Ice Cream

*Mantecado de Vainilla y Ron*

This makes an impressive after dinner treat.

**3 cups half and half**

**¾ cup evaporated milk**

**1 ½ cups sugar**

**3 tablespoons cornstarch, sifted**

**8 egg yolks, lightly beaten**

**2 teaspoons vanilla**

**1 teaspoon rum extract**

**½ teaspoon salt**

1. Whisk the cornstarch in ¼ cup of the evaporated milk until smooth and no lumps remain.

2. Combine half and half, remaining evaporated milk, sugar and cornstarch mixture in a medium saucepan. Whisk until smooth. Stir in eggs, vanilla, rum extract and salt.

3. Cook over medium heat, stirring constantly for 7 to 8 minutes. Do not allow mixture to boil.

4. Allow mixture to cool to room temperature, stirring occasionally. Stir in rum when cool.

5. Pour mixture into ice cream maker and follow manufacturer's directions.

6. Pour into freezer-proof container and freeze for 4 hours before serving.

**Yield: about 2 quarts**

# Rich Vanilla Ice Cream

*Limber de Leche*

The cinnamon and lemon zest punch up the taste of this traditional favorite.

**1 large can evaporated milk**

**½ cup sugar**

**1 teaspoon vanilla**

**½ teaspoon grated rind of lemon**

**¼ teaspoon cinnamon**

**3 egg yolks**

**1 tablespoon sugar**

1. Whisk the evaporated milk and the ½ cup sugar together in a large bowl. Stir in vanilla and cinnamon.

2. Separately, beat the egg yolks, 1 teaspoon sugar and lemon rind in a small bowl.

3. Stir in the egg yolk mixture to the milk mixture.

4. Cook over medium heat, stirring constantly for 7 to 8 minutes. Do not allow mixture to boil.

5. Allow mixture to cool to room temperature, stirring occasionally.

6. Pour mixture into ice cream maker and follow manufacturer's directions.

7. Pour into freezer-proof container and freeze for 4 hours before serving.

**Yield: 4 servings**

# Mango Ice Cream
*Mantecado de Mango*

This remind me of childhood vacations in New Hampshire and peach vanilla ice cream bought at the country store.

| | |
|---|---|
| **4 large ripe mangoes, peeled, and diced** | **1 cup whipping cream** |
| **3 eggs, lightly beaten** | **½ teaspoon salt** |
| **1 ½ cups sugar** | **1 tablespoon fresh lime juice** |
| **2 cups half and half** | **2 tablespoons vanilla** |

1. Puree mango in food processor. Refrigerate.

2. Combine eggs, sugar, half and half, whipping cream and salt in a heavy saucepan over moderate heat, stirring constantly until mixture nearly boils. Keep from boiling.

3. Remove from heat and stir in lime juice and vanilla. Allow to cool to room temperature, about 45 minutes, stirring occasionally.

4. Fold in chilled mango puree. Pour into ice cream freezer and follow manufacturer's instructions.

**Yield: nearly 2 quarts**

# Guava Ice Cream

*Mantecado de Guayaba*

Serve scoops of chocolate, mango and guava ice cream at your next dinner party.

**3 pounds ripe and unripe guavas**

**2 ½ cups half and half**

**1 ½ cups heavy whipping cream**

**1 ½ cups sugar**

**½ teaspoon salt**

**3 eggs, beaten**

1. Peel the guavas, halve and puree in a food processor. Refrigerate.
2. Combine half and half, heavy whipping cream, sugar, salt and eggs in a heavy saucepan over medium heat. Cook until mixture nearly boils, stirring constantly, about 7 or 8 minutes. Do not allow to boil.
3. Remove from heat and allow to cool to room temperature, stirring occasionally, about 45 minutes.
4. Fold in chilled guava and pour into ice cream freezer. Follow manufacturer's instructions.

**Yield: about 2 quarts**

# Banana Ice Cream

*Mantecado de Plátano*

This is my favorite ice cream in the world. Well, next to Chocolate Rum Ice Cream…

**¾ cup sugar**

**3 large eggs, beaten**

**2 teaspoons cornstarch, sifted**

**1 teaspoon vanilla extract**

**¼ cup banana liqueur**

**¼ teaspoon salt**

**1 cup half and half**

**1 cup heavy whipping cream**

**4 large ripe bananas**

1. Combine sugar and eggs in a small bowl until creamy. Slowly add cornstarch, vanilla extract and salt, combining well. Set aside.
2. Heat half and half and heavy cream in a medium saucepan over moderate heat, bringing to a boil while stirring constantly.

3. Reduce heat and whisk in egg mixture. Stir constantly until mixture thickens. Remove from heat.

4. Pour through a strainer into a bowl.

5. Mash bananas in separate bowl and fold into custard mixture. Allow to cool to room temperature.

6. Stir in banana liqueur and pour into ice cream freezer. Follow manufacturer's instructions.

**Yield: almost 2 quarts**

## Soursop Ice Cream
*Mantecado de Guanábana*

If you haven't tried soursop fruit before, this is a good way to experience it.

3 pounds ripe soursop

2 cups half and half

1 cup evaporated milk

1 cup whole milk

1 ½ cups sugar

2 teaspoons cornstarch, sifted

3 large egg yolks, lightly beaten

½ teaspoon salt

½ teaspoon almond extract

½ teaspoon rose extract

1. Follow instructions for extracting soursop pulp by following steps 1 through 4 of *Soursop Sherbert*. Chill.

2. Combine half and half, sugar, cornstarch, egg yolks and salt in a large saucepan, stirring well. Whisk in milks.

3. Cook over medium heat, stirring constantly for 7 to 8 minutes until mixture thickens. Do not boil.

4. Remove from heat and allow to cool to room temperature, stirring occasionally.

5. Fold in soursop, almond and rose extracts; pour into ice cream freezer. Follow manufacturer's instructions.

**Yield: about 2 quarts**

## Vanilla Bean

Amazing as it seems, vanilla beans come from climbing orchids. The Spanish discovered vanilla from the Aztecs. Fresh vanilla pods have no scent. The pleasing aroma comes from the drying and fermentation process.

**Purchasing:** Buy pure vanilla, not the synthetic kind. Available as a bean, liquid or powder.

**Storing:** Keep at room temperature in a dry spot. Store beans in an airtight, glass, not plastic container.

**Nutrition:** Reported to aid digestion.

# Chocolate Rum Ice Cream
*Mantecado de Chocolate y Ron*

Chocolate and rum-a heady combination.

1 ¼ cups sugar

¼ teaspoon salt

2 teaspoons cornstarch, sifted

4 large egg yolks, lightly beaten

3 cups half and half

1 teaspoon vanilla extract

1 cup heavy whipping cream

3 ounces good quality baking chocolate, melted in top of double boiler

½ teaspoon almond extract

¼ cup Puerto Rican rum

1. Sift together the sugar, salt and cornstarch in a small bowl. Stir in beaten eggs until creamy. Set aside.

2. Heat half and half and cream in a large saucepan over medium heat, stirring constantly until very hot, 7 to 8 minutes, but not boiling.

3. Gradually stir in sugar mixture, stirring constantly until mixture thickens.

4. Remove from heat and stir in melted chocolate. Allow to cool for 15 minutes then stir in almond and vanilla extract.

5. Cool to room temperature, stirring occasionally. Stir in rum.

6. Pour into ice cream freezer and follow manufacturer's instructions.

**Yield: over 1 quart**

# Coconut Ice Cream

*Mantecado de Coco*

I enjoy the island's coconut candies, cookies and pies. But, I enjoy this smooth ice cream made from fresh coconut even more.

| | |
|---|---|
| **2 cups fresh coconut milk (see index)** | **½ teaspoon salt** |
| **2 cups heavy whipping cream** | **3 eggs, beaten** |
| **1 ½ cups sugar** | **½ cup fresh grated coconut** |

1. Combine coconut milk, cream, sugar, salt and eggs in a heavy saucepan.
2. Cook over moderate heat, stirring constantly until mixture nearly boils, 7 to 8 minutes. Do not allow to boil.
3. Remove from heat and allow to cool to room temperature. Fold in grated coconut and pour into ice cream freezer. Follow manufacturer's instructions.

**Yield: about 1 quart**

# Coconut Sherbert

*Helado de Coco*

Lovely, for those who wish to avoid dairy.

| | |
|---|---|
| **½ teaspoon almond extract** | **2 cups fresh coconut milk (see index)** |
| **½ teaspoon salt** | **1 teaspoon grated lemon rind** |
| **2 ½ cups sugar** | |

1. Combine coconut milk, lemon rind, almond extract and salt in medium saucepan over moderate heat.
2. Stir in sugar until dissolved. Remove from heat and allow to cool.
3. Pour mixture into ice cream maker and follow manufacturer's directions.
4. Pour into freezer-proof container and freeze for 4 hours before serving.

**Yield: 4 servings**

# Guava Sherbert
*Helado de Guayaba*

Omit raw egg whites for the immune compromised as they may contain deadly bacteria.

**guava, enough to make 4 cups puree, selecting both sour and ripe**

**1 ¾ cups sugar**
**1 large egg white, slightly beaten**

1. Wash guavas thoroughly, remove stems and dice. Do not peel.
2. Place diced fruit it deep skillet with ¼ cup water. Cook over moderate heat for 5 minutes.
3. Remove from heat and mash guavas with potato masher.
4. Press through a sieve. You should have 4 cups puree.
5. Add sugar and blend.
6. Pour into ice cream freezer and follow manufacturer's instructions. When puree begins to freeze, add egg white and resume freezing.

**Yield: about 5 cups**

# Mango Sherbert
*Helado de Mango*

Omit raw egg whites for the immune compromised as they may contain deadly bacteria.

**4 large ripe mangoes**
**2/3 cup sugar**
**¼ teaspoon cinnamon**

**3 tablespoons fresh lemon juice**
**1 large egg white, slightly beaten**

1. Remove skin from mangoes. Slice off meat, discarding pit. Puree in a food processor.
2. Stir in sugar and lemon juice.
3. Pour into ice-cream freezer and follow manufacturer's instructions.

4. When puree begins to freezer, fold in egg white and resume freezing.

5. Garnish lightly with ground cinnamon.

**Yield: about 4 ½ cups**

---

### Did You Know?

Puerto Rico has more than 547 **species of trees** indigenous to the island, and another 200+ naturalized species. Remarkable for a very small area.

---

## Soursop Sherbert
*Helado de Guanábana*

Omit raw egg whites for the immune compromised as they may contain deadly bacteria.

| | |
|---|---|
| **2 pounds ripe soursop** | **2 tablespoons fresh lemon juice** |
| **1 ¼ cups sugar** | **1 large egg white, lightly beaten** |

1. Slice soursop in two, lengthwise. Core, removing pulp and seeds together with large spoon.

2. Place pulp and seeds in large bowl. Mash with potato masher along with 1 cup water. Strain through a sieve, reserving pulp.

3. Place remaining pulp and seed back into saucepan, stirring in another cup of water. Strain pulp through sieve, reserving pulp.

4. Repeat steps 2 and 3 until all pulp has been extracted from seeds.

5. Stir in sugar and lemon juice. Pour puree into ice-cream freezer and follow manufacturer's instructions.

6. When puree begins to freeze, fold in beaten egg white. Resume freezing.

**Yield: about 5 cups**

## Pineapple Sorbet
*Helado de Piña*

Omit raw egg whites for the immune compromised as they may contain deadly bacteria.

I like to serve this fresh pineapple ice cream with fresh or frozen whipped topping.

| | |
|---|---|
| **1 large pineapple** | **3 tablespoons fresh lemon juice** |
| **¾ cup sugar** | **1 large egg white, slightly beaten** |

1. Trim top and bottom of pineapple. Slice down sides with long knife to remove skin. Discard any brown eyes. Slice in circles and dig out woody core, discarding it.
2. Puree in food processor. Add sugar and lemon juice.
3. Pour into ice cream freezer and follow manufacturer's instructions.
4. When puree begins to freeze, fold in beaten egg white and continue to freeze.

**Yield: about 5 cups**

## Piña Colada Sherbert

*Helado de Piña Colada*

The adventurous may drizzle Puerto Rican rum over the top of this frozen delight. Omit raw egg whites for the immune compromised as they may contain deadly bacteria.

| | |
|---|---|
| **2 cups fresh coconut milk (see index)** | **4 tablespoons fresh lemon juice** |
| **1 cup fresh pureed pineapple** | **1 egg white lightly beaten** |
| **1 cup sugar** | **½ cup fresh grated coconut (see index)** |

1. Combine coconut milk, pineapple, sugar and lemon in a large bowl.
2. Pour into ice cream freezer and follow manufacturer's instructions.
3. When puree is nearly frozen, fold in egg white and grated coconut. Resume freezing.

**Yield: about 4 cups**

## Bitter Chocolate and Orange Sorbet

Elegant and rich, dark creamy chocolate frozen treat. Compares well to Hagen-Daas.

½ pound good quality baking chocolate, melted in double boiler

3 ounces good quality milk chocolate, grated

¾ cup sugar

2 ½ cups warm water

½ cup Grand Marnier (orange liqueur)

1. Remove double boiler from heat. Blend warm water with melted chocolate in top of double boiler. Stir in sugar until melted.

2. Stir in Grand Marnier. Pour into ice cream freezer and follow manufacturer's instructions.

3. When semi-frozen, fold in grated chocolate. Resume freezing.

**Yield: 6 to 8 servings**

# Rum and Other Tropical Drinks

All of the drinks in this chapter naturally feature Puerto Rican rum. Other rums may be substituted, with almost as pleasing a result. As always, do not drink and drive or operate heavy equipment while under the influence of alcohol. Caution applies to pregnant women, those with heart conditions or other health issues.

For a comprehensive source for tropical and Caribbean drink recipes, using vodka, gin, rum, tequila, as well as rum and exotic liqueurs, please see *Don't Drink* The Water! A nearly 300-page book filled with drinks. Includes an appetizer chapter.

## Bacardi Cocktail

**2 ounces light Bacardi Rum**

**splash of Grenadine syrup**

**1 ounce sour mix**

Fill a shaker with ice, rum, sour mix and Grenadine. Strain into a chilled rocks glass

**Yield: 1 drink**

## Bacardi Mama

**1 ½ ounces light rum**

**½ ounce Triple Sec**

**1 ounce orange juice**

**1 ounce pineapple juice**

**splash of Grenadine syrup**

Fill a tall glass with ice. Add rum, Triple Sec, orange and pineapple juice and Grenadine. Stir.

**Yield: 1 drink**

# Bacardi Rapture

1 ounce gold rum
½ ounce coconut rum

½ ounce Banana liqueur
1 ounce light cream

Shake all ingredients in a cocktail shaker filled with ice. Strain into a rocks glass.

**Yield: 1 drink**

# Banana Daiquiri

No good drink book is complete without a recipe for Banana Daiquiri.

2 ounces light or gold rum
½ ounce Banana liqueur
2 ounces light cream

1 small ripe banana
½ cup crushed ice

Whirl all ingredients in blender until frothy. Pour into a tall glass.

**Yield: 1 drink**

# Black Puerto Rican

You've heard of a Black Russian drink? Well, here's the island version.

2 ounces dark Puerto Rican rum      ½ ounce Kahlua or other coffee liqueur

Fill a rocks glass with ice. Add rum and coffee liqueur. Stir.

**Yield: 1 drink**

# Banana Rama

1 ounce light rum
1 ounce Banana liqueur
1 ounce White Crème de Cacao

1 ounce light cream
½ cup crushed ice

Whirl all ingredients in blender until frothy. Pour into a tall glass.

**Yield: 1 drink**

# Captain Bligh

1 ½ ounces light rum

½ ounce Grand Marnier or orange liqueur

1 ounce pineapple juice

Fill a rocks glass with ice. Pour all ingredients over ice and stir.

**Yield: 1 drink**

# Caribbean Breeze

2 ounce light rum

1 ounce cranberry juice

1 ounce orange juice

Fill a tall glass with ice. Add rum and juice. Stir.

**Yield: 1 drink**

---

## Did You Know?

The **Bacardi Distillery** in Cataño is the largest of its sort in the world. Called the "Cathedral of Rum" visitors are treated to museum full of rum artifacts and history. Bacardi rum, some not available elsewhere, can be purchased here. Located at the distillery is a wonderful gift shop, featuring polo and tee shirts, knit skull caps with the Bacardi logo, sweat pants, keychains, etc.

---

# Christmas Rum and Coconut Punch

*Coquito*

Coconut eggnog, a traditional Puerto Rican holiday drink, is the quintessential tropical eggnog.

Commercially canned coconut may be substituted successfully.

2 cups fresh coconut milk (see index)

¼ cup sugar

¼ teaspoon salt

¼ cup fresh grated coconut
   ground nutmeg

1 egg yolk

2 cups white Puerto Rican
   rum, or to taste

¼ teaspoon cinnamon

1. Put ½ cup of coconut milk, sugar, salt and cinnamon in a blender. Whirl until sugar is dissolved.

2. Add remaining coconut milk, egg yolk and cinnamon and process until smooth.

3. Add rum gradually and puree 2 minutes until frothy.

4. Pour into clean bottles and refrigerate. Serve in liqueur glasses, dust with nutmeg.

**Yield: a little over 4 cups**

## Health Tip–Raw Eggs

To avoid salmonella contamination, use an egg substitute. These can be found in the refrigerator and frozen area of your grocery store. Usually they contain pasteurized eggs whites, vegetable oil, food coloring and vitamins. As a bonus, many substitutes contain no cholesterol and are low in fat.

# Christmas Egg Nog II
*Coquito II*

**3 ½ cups fresh coconut milk or tinned, unsweetened**

**2 cups light Barcardi rum, or to taste**

**1 cup evaporated milk**

**¾ cup sweetened condensed milk**

**4 egg yolks**

**½ teaspoon cinnamon**

**ground nutmeg**

1. Combine coconut milk and Barcardi rum in blender. Puree on medium speed for 20 seconds.

2. Add evaporated and condensed milk. Process on high for 1 minute.

3. Drop in egg yolks, one at a time, with blender running. Add cinnamon. Process for 1 minute until frothy.

4. Pour into clean bottles and refrigerate until chilled.

5. Serve in liqueur glasses, garnished with ground nutmeg

**Yield: about 7 cups**

# Christmas Eggnog III

*Coquito III*

**4 cups fresh or canned, unsweetened coconut milk**

**¼ cup sugar**

**8 egg yolks**

**2 teaspoons vanilla extract**

**½ teaspoon almond extract**

**½ teaspoon ground cinnamon**

**2 cups Puerto Rican rum, or to taste**

**ground nutmeg**

1. Combine coconut milk and sugar in a medium saucepan and scald.
2. Whisk egg yolks with vanilla and almond extract in small bowl. Add ground cinnamon.
3. Beat in ¼ cup of the scalded coconut milk into the egg yolks. Whisk another ¼ cup coconut milk into egg yolks.
4. Whisk all of egg yolk mixture into coconut milk. Simmer over low heat until mixture reaches 160°F. Do not boil.
5. Strain into bowl. Pour into bowl and allow to cool for 15 minutes.
6. Stir in rum. Pour into clean bottles and refrigerate.
7. Serve in cordial glasses and sprinkle with nutmeg.

**Yield: about 7 cups**

# Christmas Eggnog IV

*Coquito IV*

**2 cans cream of coconut (the kind you make piña coladas with)**

**2 cans evaporated milk (not the sweetened kind)**

**2 teaspoons good quality vanilla extract**

**¼ teaspoon cinnamon**

**1/8 teaspoon cloves**

**ground nutmeg**

**2 cups white Puerto Rican rum**

1. Combine cream of coconut with evaporated milk in blender. Process on medium speed for 1 minute.
2. Pour in rum and vanilla with blender running. Add cinnamon and cloves, processing 2 minutes until frothy.

3. Pour into clean bottles and refrigerate.
4. Serve in cordial glasses, dusted with nutmeg.

**Yield: about 6 cups**

# Christmas Eggnog V

*Coquito V*

This recipe makes a lot—over 4 quarts, party-size.

2 cups water

3 cinnamon sticks

8 large egg yolks

3 12-ounce cans evaporated milk

2 15-ounce cans unsweetened
   coconut milk

3 14-ounce cans sweetened
   condensed milk

¼ teaspoon ground cloves

2 cups Puerto Rican rum, or to taste

ground nutmeg

1. Bring to a boil the cinnamon sticks and water in a small saucepan. Reduce heat and simmer until liquid is reduced to 1 cup. Remove and discards cinnamon sticks. Set water aside to cool.

2. Beat egg yolks and evaporated milk until frothy in a large saucepan. Simmer for 10 minutes over low heat until mixture coats the back of a spoon. Do not boil. Remove from heat and cool for 10 minutes.

3. Stir in coconut milk into cooled cinnamon water.

4. Pour egg yolk mixture into large bowl. Stir in coconut/cinnamon mixture.

5. Whisk in condensed milk and ground cloves. Stir in rum.

6. Chill in clean bottles until ready to serve. Dust with ground nutmeg.

**Yield: over 4 quarts**

# Conquistador

1 ounce light rum

1 ounce Bailey's Irish Cream Liqueur

½ ounce Grand Marnier

½ ounce Kahlua or coffee
   liqueur

Fill a rocks glass with ice. First pour rum, then Bailey's, being careful not to disturb rum layer. Follow with Grand Marnier, then coffee liqueur for a layered effect.

**Yield: 1 drink**

# Frozen Lime Daiquri

**4 tablespoons fresh lime juice**
**3 tablespoons simple syrup (see index)**
**4 ounces white Puerto Rican rum**

**3 cups crushed ice**
**maraschino cherries**

1. Place lime juice, simple syrup, and white Puerto Rican rum in blender.
2. Add ice and blend until frothy.
3. Pour into tulip-shaped chilled glasses. Garnish with maraschino cherry.

**Yield: 2 drinks**

# Hangover Cure

Anna and I made up a huge pitcher of this remedy after sampling and writing this chapter.

**6 ounces light rum or more as needed**
**1 large can tomato or vegetable juice**
**2 tablespoons apple cider vinegar**
**1 tablespoon Tabasco™**

**1 tablespoon chopped onion**
**1 tablespoon horseradish**
**1 whole lemon, thinly sliced**

Combine all ingredients except lemon slices in a blender. Pour into a non-reactive container (preferably glass). Add lemon slices, cover and refrigerate overnight. Serve chilled over ice.

**Yield: about 1 quart**

# Hurricane

**½ ounce light rum**
**½ ounce dark rum**
**½ ounce Apricot brandy**

**1 tablespoon lime juice**
**½ ounce orange juice**
**½ ounce pineapple juice**

Shake all ingredients in a cocktail shaker filled with ice. Strain into a highball glass over crushed ice. Garnish with a lime wedge.

**Yield: 1 drink**

## Mariposa

| | |
|---|---|
| 1 ½ ounce dark rum | ½ ounce lemon juice |
| ½ ounce brandy | splash of Grenadine syrup |
| 2 ounces orange juice | |

Mix all ingredients in a cocktail shaker filled with ice. Strain into a chilled cocktail glass.

**Yield: 1 drink**

## Mojito

| | |
|---|---|
| 1 ½ ounces lime juice | 2 ounces light rum |
| 1 teaspoon powdered sugar | crushed ice |
| 3 mint leaves | club soda |

Combine sugar and lime juice in a highball glass. Add mint leaves and crush against sides of glass with a spoon. Add crushed ice and rum. Stir. Float club soda to top of glass.

**Yield: 1 drink**

## Orange Wine
*Vino de Chinas*

I'd add a lot of ice to this drink to water it down some. Smooth, but powerful.

| | |
|---|---|
| 4 cups Puerto Rican white rum | 1 whole nutmeg, crushed |
| 4 whole allspice | 3 tablespoons grated orange zest |
| 2 three-inch cinnamon sticks | ½ cup simple syrup XXX(see index) |
| 1 star anise | 8 cups fresh or store-bought |
| 1 vanilla bean pod | orange juice |

1. Carefully heat 1 cup of the rum in the top of a double boiler until hot, but not boiling. Remember, alcohol is flammable.

2. Place allspice, anise, vanilla and nutmeg in a clean glass jar or empty rum bottle. Pour hot rum over spices. Cover and allow to sit 2 days in a dark, cool place. Closets are good.

3. Add remaining rum, orange zest and simple syrup. Allow to sit for 2 weeks. Four weeks are better.

4. Add orange juice and refrigerate for 2 days.

**Yield: 1 ½ quarts**

# Piña Colada

When actress Joan Collins sipped her first piña colada at the former Beachcomber's Bar in the Caribe Hilton, she asserted it was better than slapping Betty Davis in the face. The creator of this famous drink was Ramon "Monchito" Marrerro in 1954. This recipe can easily be doubled.

**2 ounces light rum**

**splash of 151 proof rum (optional)**

**1 ounce light cream**

**1 ounce coconut cream**

**4 ounces pineapple juice**

**½ cup crushed ice**

Whirl all ingredients in blender until frothy.

**Yield: 1 drink**

# Planter's Punch

Another recipe no self-respecting drink guide would be without.

**2 ounces dark rum**

**1 ounce fresh lime juice**

**1 teaspoon Grenadine syrup**

**dash of angostura bitters**

Shake all ingredients in a cocktail shaker filled with ice. Strain into a tall glass, Garnish with a sprig of mint, cherry and an orange.

**Yield: 1 drink**

## Ponce Blast

**2 ounces light rum**

**1 ½ ounce anise-flavored liqueur**

**1 tablespoon fresh lemon juice**

Combine all ingredients in an ice shaker filled with ice. Strain into a chilled cocktail glass.

**Yield: 1 drink**

## Puerto Rican Sangria

*Sangria Criolla*

Watch out for this sangria. The rum sneaks up on you.

**1 cup fresh pineapple, cut in 1-inch cubes**

**3/4 cup white rum**

**2 cups red wine**

**2 cups lemon-lime soda**

**¼ cup frozen orange juice concentrate, thawed**

**1 cup pineapple juice**

**½ cup fresh lime juice**

**1 cup frozen passionfruit pulp, thawed**

1. Soak the pineapple cubes in the rum overnight. Two days is better. The rum will smell heavenly.
2. Pour the rum and pineapple bits into a large glass or ceramic pitcher. Do not use plastic as it will add an unappealing off taste.
3. Add wine, soda, pineapple, lime, passionfruit and orange juice to pitcher. Stir.
4. Chill at least 3 hours.

**Yield: over 2 quarts**

## Rum Bloody Mary

**2 ounces light rum**

**4 ounces tomato juice**

**splash of Worcestershire™ sauce**

**½ ounce lemon juice**

**½ teaspoon fresh horseradish**

**¼ teaspoon ground black pepper**

Fill a tall glass with ice. Add all ingredients and stir. Garnish with a celery stalk.

**Yield: 1 drink**

# Rum Collins

**2 ounces light rum**
**1 ounce lime juice**

**1 teaspoon powdered sugar**

Mix all ingredients in a cocktail shaker filled with ice. Strain into a rocks glass. Garnish with an orange slice and cherry.

# Rum Cooler

**2 ounces light rum**
**4 ounce pineapple juice**

**2 ounces club soda**

Fill a tall glass with ice. Add other ingredients and stir carefully. Garnish with a pineapple wedge.

**Yield: 1 drink**

# Rum Punch

**2 ounces light rum**
**1 ounce orange juice**
**1 ounce pineapple juice**
**1 ounce cranberry juice**

**½ ounce lemon or lime juice**
**splash of Grenadine syrup**
**club soda**

Fill a tall glass with ice. Add all other ingredients, except club soda. Fill remainder of glass with club soda. Stir. Garnish with thin lemon slices.

**Yield: 1 drink**

# Spiced Rum

*Ron Con Especias*

Delicious on the rocks or with fruit juice or cola. Use in baking as well.

**1 vanilla bean pod**

**4 whole allspice**

**2 three-inch cinnamon sticks**

**2 whole star anise**

**¼ teaspoon ground anise**

**4 whole cloves**

**½ teaspoon freshly grated nutmeg**

**1 liter gold rum**

1. Pour off about ½ cup of the rum to make room for the spices.
2. Place vanilla bean, allspice, cinnamon sticks, anise, and cloves in rum bottle with rum.
3. Store in a dark closet for at least 1 month. Two months or more are better. Shake gently once a week.

**Yield: just under 1 liter**

# Zombie

For those of you who have read my other cookbooks, you'll know I put a version of this recipe in nearly all my books. This was probably the first alcoholic drink I ever had. I was 18 years old, at the Mad Hatter on the island of Nantucket. It literally put me under the table.

**1 ounce light rum**

**1 ounce dark rum**

**1 ounce cherry brandy**

**1 ounce orange juice**

**1 ounce pineapple juice**

**1 ounce lime juice**

**1 cup crushed ice**

Whirl all ingredients in blender until smooth. Divide equally between two tall glasses.

**Yield: 2 drinks**

# BIBLIOGRAPHY

David Joachim with Andrew Schloss, Jan Newberry, Maryellen Driscoll, Paul E. Piccuito, *Brilliant Food Tips and Cooking Tricks*, United States, Rodale Publishing 2001, 604 pages.

Harry S. Pariser, *Adventure Guide to Puerto Rico, 3rd Edition*, New Jersey, Hunter Publishing, 1996, 329 pages.

Québec/Amérique International. *The Visual Food Encylopedia*, Montreal, Québec, Les Éditions Québec/Amérique Inc. 1996, 695 pages.

Wiley Publishing, *Frommer's Puerto Rico, 6th Edition*, New York, NY, Wiley Publishing Inc. 2002, 278 pages

# INDEX

## C

## S